The Art and Science of

RAJA YOGA

The Art and Science of

RAJA YOGA

FOURTEEN STEPS TO HIGHER AWARENESS

BASED ON THE TEACHINGS OF PARAMHANSA YOGANANDA

SWAMI KRIYANANDA (J. DONALD WALTERS)

ISBN 978-81-89430-29-0

Cover photo by J. Donald Walters
Cover design by Roberto Barigozzi
Book design by Tera Antaree and C. A. Starner Schuppe

Printed in India by Aegean Offset, New Delhi

Ananda Sangha Publications
B-10/8 DLF City Phase I
Gurgaon, Haryana 122 002

Mobile: +91 98992 67698
Phone: (0124) 405-9550
Fax: (0124) 410-3386

Mail Order Department
Website: www.anandamailorder.com
E-mail: mailorder@anandaindia.org

For the Trade:
Website: www.anandapublications.com
E-mail: publications@anandaindia.org

Ananda Sangha
Website: www.anandaindia.org
E-mail: ananda@anandaindia.org

Not all exercises are suitable for everyone, and this or any other exercise program may result in injury. Any user of this exercise program assumes the risk of injury resulting from practicing the exercises presented in this book. To reduce the risk of injury, consult your doctor before beginning this exercise program. The instructions and advice presented in this book are in no way intended as a substitute for competent medical counseling.

Dedicated with love and humility
to truth seekers everywhere

ANANDA COURSE IN SELF-REALIZATION

This book is Part II of the Ananda Course in Self-Realization. It stands alone as a comprehensive study of yoga and meditation, or can be used as a part of the complete Ananda home-study course. Information on Parts I and III is listed below.

Part I – Lessons in Meditation

Learn the basic techniques of meditation through clear, step-by-step instructions. Experience the importance of the breath/mind connection and the power of the focused mind. Learn also Paramhansa Yogananda's energization exercises, which teach a little-understood secret of success: gaining conscious awareness of and control over your energy.

This course offers techniques of the path of *Kriya Yoga*, including the *Hong-Sau* technique of concentration. There are also many simple, "do-able" suggestions, such as how to sit comfortably for meditation, how to still the restless mind, and how to take your experiences of peace and joy into daily life. Included with the illustrated, lay-flat book are two cassette tapes, with guided meditations, visualizations, and guided energization exercises.

Parts IIIA and IIIB
The Path of Kriya Yoga: Discipleship and Kriya Preparation

Part IIIA – Swami Kriyananda (J. Donald Walters) shares insights into the meaning and practice of discipleship. Stories of his personal experiences with Paramhansa Yogananda help to prepare the student for either an at-home or in-person initiation into discipleship to Yogananda and to the line of Masters of Self-realization, if he or she feels ready for this level of commitment.

Part IIIB – The Kriya Preparation section includes instructions in the AUM technique of meditation and further prepares the student for *Kriya Yoga* initiation. This part is available with permission from the Ananda Kriya Ministry after completion of Parts I, II, and IIIA.

STUDENT SUPPORT

It is our sincere hope that the teachings in this Raja Yoga book will fill your life with a deeper sense of peace, expansive love, and inner freedom.

In addition we offer all students support via our e-mail. One of the greatest benefits you receive by enrolling in the Ananda Course is being able to communicate with our staff of long-time meditators, meditation teachers, and experienced yoga instructors. We are happy to answer any questions you may have and discuss your progress.

Our email address is:
ananda@anandaindia.org

Joy to you!

TABLE OF CONTENTS

FOREWORD

by Sheila Rush

In *The Art and Science of Raja Yoga,* the original yoga science emerges in all of its glory—a proven system for realizing our spiritual destiny. The practice of *raja yoga* awakens us to our deepest reality of oneness with the Infinite. The key word here is *practice.* As a spiritual science, yoga is unique in that it encourages us to *test* the truth of its principles, not simply to believe. Using the many tools yoga gives us, we can determine first-hand whether it does in fact live up to its glorious promise. The "proof" comes in our growing experience of the love, joy, calmness, and courage of our soul nature. Yoga is thus empowering. It gives us the teachings, the tools, and the validation of our own deepening experience of the Divine to speed us on our inner journey to God.

The Art and Science of Raja Yoga was my first systematic introduction to yoga. Twenty-one years later, I am *deeply* grateful for this course and the opportunity to recommend it to others. Swami Kriyananda is a direct disciple of Paramhansa Yogananda, author of the spiritual classic, *Autobiography of a Yogi.* Yogananda, the first yoga master to live and teach in the West, brought with him the authentic, original yoga science of ancient India. For more than 50 years, Kriyananda has devoted his life to sharing these same teachings. The joyful enthusiasm with which he does so is a compelling invitation to yoga's inner journey.

The Art and Science of Raja Yoga gives us the balanced, comprehensive approach of *raja yoga,* which is also known as the "royal" yoga. The course is organized around seven topics—Philosophy, Meditation, Postures, Breathing, Routines, Healing Principles and Techniques, and Diet. It also includes in-depth discussions of the paths of *karma, bhakti,* and *gyana yoga.* Kriyananda excels in showing the interdependence of these seemingly separate areas and how all of them, when correctly approached, further our spiritual progress.

The main purpose of yoga postures, for example, sometimes thought to bestow only physical benefits, is to prepare the body and mind for meditation. Affirmations, visualizations, breathing exercises, healing techniques, the different paths of yoga, and, to a certain extent, diet are similarly helpful. What unites these various areas is *raja yoga*'s inward, spiritual focus, which achieves its fullest expression in the practice of meditation. Meditation, as taught in *The Art and Science of Raja Yoga*, gives us direct access to the inner world of Spirit. In the truest possible sense, meditation is yoga's laboratory and the primary means by which we test the truth of its teachings.

To prepare for the practice of meditation, the course offers numerous preliminary exercises that help us make the transition from the outer world of activity to the inner world of stillness. We learn how to let go of worries, physical and mental tension, and to focus the mind—skills that are helpful not only for meditation but equally in our daily lives. The meditation techniques of ancient India, presented by Kriyananda in step-by-step detail, turn out to be indispensable for quieting the mind, drawing it inward, and redirecting our awareness to the centers of spiritual awakening in the brain. Proper meditation, one soon discovers, is neither mechanical nor passive, but requires deep concentration and sustained, dynamic energy.

Meditation requires also what Kriyananda calls a "complete revolution" in "what are commonly looked upon as normal human attitudes." He explains:

"The competitive drive, for instance, implies an assumption that success must always be exclusive, even to the extent of being determined by other people's failures. . . . Such an attitude will thwart the most earnest of efforts to progress in meditation, for it will pit one against the universe instead of harmonizing him with it. Right attitude is essential to right meditation."

The "right attitudes" referred to by Kriyananda are the universal moral principles of yoga, the *yamas* (the don'ts) and *niyamas* (the do's). One of the best known of these is *ahimsa,* or non-injury, popularized by the protest movements of Gandhi and Martin Luther King, Jr. Ahimsa's proscriptions are directed not only against harmful actions, but also the harm caused by negative thoughts. The reasons go the heart of yoga. Kriyananda writes:

"The first step in the development of right attitude is to learn to see others not as rivals, but as friends. . . . The goal of yoga is to realize the oneness of all life. If I am willing to hurt the life in me as it is expressed in another human being, then I am affirming an error that is diametrically opposed to the realization I am seeking to attain. It is necessary if I would truly realize the oneness of all things, for me to live also in a way as constantly to affirm this oneness—by my kindness toward all beings, by compassion, by universal love."

To experience the deeper states of

meditation where Spirit resides, we must first put ourselves on its wavelength. Kriyananda advises that at the start of each meditation, we send out waves of forgiveness from the heart to those we may need to forgive. This helps us to resolve conscious and subconscious feelings of anger that draw the mind outward, and to relate to the people involved with more kindness and understanding. By affirming love for all beings, we open ourselves to the gentle vibrations of divine love. Increasingly, as we practice the *yama*s and *niyama*s, in our daily lives and as part of our meditation, our journey to the Divine becomes not only a search for love but also its expression.

We are encouraged, also, to view yoga's moral principles as directional, their perfection as the end not the beginning of the journey. We can gain considerably in peace of mind and inner strength long before we actually perfect our attitudes. India's great scripture, the *Bhagavad Gita,* offers the comforting reassurance that "even a little practice of this inward religion will save you from dire fears and colossal suffering."

Another subject thoroughly covered in this comprehensive course and equally basic to an understanding of yoga is *energy.* Matter in its essence *is* energy. Even the human body is not what it seems. Though superficially composed of flesh and bones, on a deeper level of reality it is composed of energy. Western scientists uncovered this truth only in the last century, but it has been known to the yoga tradition for thousands of years. According to Indian scriptures, the Earth repeatedly goes through cycles of higher and lower levels of spiritual understanding. Yoga originated in a higher age when ordinary people could grasp truths that modern science is only now discovering.

Countless vortices of energy make up our deeper reality. When these vortices work together in harmony we are healthy, happy, and life affirming. If we are unwell, depressed, or life negating, it is primarily because our energy is low, or because these vortices are out of sync with one another. *The Art and Science of Raja Yoga* gives us many ways to strengthen this energy and bring it into harmony—breathing exercises, healing techniques, yoga postures, affirmations, visualizations. Meditation, however, is the most powerful. Through meditation we become more sensitively aware of the body's subtle energies and increasingly able to harmonize and redirect this energy.

Until we are well along on yoga's inner journey, Kriyananda advises that we be careful about our "energy environment." As Paramhansa Yogananda said, "Environment is stronger than will power." Everything we do influences our energy. An environment of positive people, uplifting music, inspiring books and wholesome movies can greatly aid our spiritual efforts. Unfortunately, the reverse is also true.

Yoga's more esoteric subjects, such as the *chakras*, the role of a guru, and astrology (which evolved as an extension of yoga) are also clarified in *The Art and Science of Raja Yoga*. The *chakras* are simply the body's energy centers, whirling spheres that distribute energy to various bodily areas. When our energy is uplifted, we tap into the spiritualizing influence of the higher *chakras*. Contrary to popular opinion, the influence of a guru is inward, not outward. The guru's energy (and that of any highly advanced spiritual teacher) is concentrated in the higher *chakras*. Just as a strong magnet can strengthen a weak one, so also does the guru *magnetically* strengthen and uplift the energy of those who are receptive. Astrology's stars and planets are best understood as outer symbols of the shifting patterns of our inner energy. Through the practice of yoga, we can lessen the impact of the heavenly bodies by redirecting the inner energy that relates to their movements. We can, that is, outwit the stars!

Yoga means "union." Through diligent practice, *raja yoga* helps us to achieve unity within ourselves on ever-deeper levels, first by bringing body, mind and soul into harmony, and then by expanding our sense of self to include all life and creation. "No man is an island," wrote John Donne; life is an interconnected reality. But inner harmony and universal kinship are not the end of our journey. Life has given us one destiny only—union with God. Through yoga we gradually learn to see beyond our bodies and personalities to the underlying energy, and beyond that energy to the divine consciousness that produced us all. The faithful practice of *raja yoga* brings a deepening attunement with that consciousness and ultimately, the realization that we are, and always have been, one with the Infinite.

Nevada City, California
July, 2000

SUGGESTIONS FOR STUDY

We'd like to offer you a few helpful suggestions as you begin your study of these materials:

1) Study the lessons at your own pace. Originally these fourteen lessons were mailed out one at a time, every two weeks for twenty-eight weeks. You may find that two weeks is just about the right amount of time to spend on each lesson. Perhaps you'll want to go faster! But slower might be better, in order to have time to really savor the depths of these teachings, and, more importantly, to start actually doing them. In a way, *The Art and Science of Raja Yoga* is a lifetime study. You can re-read the book, or parts of it, repeatedly, whenever you want to re-inspire yourself to go more deeply into your yoga and meditation practices. The course can also be used as a reference book; you'll find a comprehensive index at the end.

2) Unlike intellectual study, this course can offer you a whole new approach to living, if you give it focused attention, and then put it into actual practice. Getting a real experience of yoga and meditation will teach you much more than just reading about it.

3) Practice some of the exercises and meditation techniques daily. There are several audiotapes we can send you to help guide you. You may need to begin your day a little earlier and end your evening activities sooner to be able to integrate these practices into your daily life. But don't set unrealistic goals for yourself or discourage yourself by trying to do too much, too fast. Even 5 or 10 minutes a day of meditation will help you very much. You can build up the length of your practice as you begin to enjoy it more and more.

4) Use caution with the yoga postures, especially the more advanced ones; there are some you may want to avoid if they cause you unusual pain or discomfort, or if you are pregnant or have severe health challenges of some sort. Listen to your body and be sure to check with a qualified yoga teacher if you have any concerns about body safety—we can help you with this by phone, letter, or e-mail.

5) If you can set aside more time, once each week, to do more yoga and meditation—perhaps on weekends—it will help your daily practices very much!

6) Try keeping a spiritual journal of your thoughts about particular parts of the lessons that are meaningful to you, or ways in which you are experiencing spiritual growth.

7) Let us know where you live, and we'll try to find an Ananda group near you, or at least, perhaps, another person who is also taking the Ananda Course. A "study partner" can be most helpful. Meditating or practicing yoga regularly with others, particularly people who have been at it for longer than you have, is a very valuable thing to do!

AUTHOR'S PREFATORY NOTE

In response to a previous book of mine, a well-known New Age musician and composer wrote me to say that while he liked my concepts, he took exception to my consistent use of the masculine pronoun. On principle I agreed with him and tried to follow his suggestion in the writing of my next book.

But every time I tried to adhere to the modern convention of writing "he or she" and "his or her" in reference to the individual, I found it cumbersome. And I realized anew why, in many languages, including English, the masculine pronoun does double duty, serving also as the impersonal pronoun. The word, "it," obviously won't do in reference to men and women. "They" is sometimes used, but this practice is clumsy and ungrammatical even when penned (as it was) by such a fine writer as Jane Austen. What would settle the debate would be, of course, some humanized version of the word, "it." "Ini," for example, accomplishes this purpose well in Bengali.

Until the arrival of some such solution in the English language, however, I simply refuse to think "pants" and "skirts." Expressions like "his or her" impose a consciousness of the sex of the person referred to, when what I'm talking about is the human being, stripped of sexual considerations.

Please, then, dear Reader, understand from the outset that my use of the masculine pronoun embraces *both* men and women. The question, for me, is simply one of style. If and when our English language produces an impersonal human pronoun, I'll be happy to use it. Meanwhile, my use of "he," "him," and "his" refers not specifically to the male of our species, but simply and sincerely to the individual.

Step One
The History of Yoga

I. PHILOSOPHY

The History of Yoga

Yoga is quite possibly the most ancient science known to man. Seals depicting human figures in various yoga postures have been unearthed in the Indus Valley, where the findings date back more than 5,000 years. Who knows how old yoga was at that time?

It is curious that information of this type should have come down from such ancient times. Primitive peoples, as all men are believed to have been then, see the world with a very different vision from that which is developed by yoga practice. For one thing, they see it clannishly. Usually they are so busy defending their territorial claims from marauding (and therefore, of course, vile) enemies that any question of the essential oneness of man would be less than academic: It wouldn't even arise. Their whole view of creation is based on a sense of differences: the Rain God at war with the mighty Sun; the River God in flood, seeking vengeance on ungrateful villagers who had disdained to address their prayers to it. Primitive man is consumed by no burning passion to learn the deeper mysteries of his identity, let alone to "realize the Self." If anyone were to ask him about his true identity, he would no doubt answer much as most people would in our own society, by simply introducing himself by name. It is only the more perceptive people even in our sophisticated age who recognize that all things, no matter how diverse, reflect an underlying unity. Science tells us that a loaf of bread is not essentially different from a stone, both being manifestations of energy. Even the scientist commonly finds this a hard crust to swallow. To primitive man, the thought would appear absurd.

Yet it is this thought which forms the very basis of yoga, the actual meaning of which is "union." It is the stated aim of this science to take the practitioner (or yogi) to an awareness, not only of the underlying unity of all things, but also of his own essential identity with this deeper reality.

Unlike the usual primitive observance of totems and taboos—unlike even the devotion to unproved, if beautiful, abstractions on the part of Western philosophers—yoga has always insisted on positive proof of its premises. Like modern science, its approach has always been pragmatic, even if in its pragmatism it has penetrated to regions far subtler than any yet contemplated by the physical sciences.

Perhaps the most striking contrast between the science of yoga and the musings of primitive peoples is yoga's specific emphasis on energy (*prana*) as the fundamental reality of physical matter. A simple person might, conceivably, imagine a sort of poetic kinship between himself and the rocks and trees. But that all the forms of nature are merely energy in different illusory manifestations would be, for him, unthinkable. Science itself has only recently attained this understanding. The ancient traditions of yoga are every bit as specific.

It would be well for the beginning yoga student to bear these facts in mind. A common tendency in our age is for people to esteem a thing in proportion to its newness. Unless a proposition can be represented as a "new scientific breakthrough," it is unlikely to be considered worthy of adult attention. Thus it is that while ancient traditions are sometimes viewed with a certain condescending amazement ("Don't tell me they knew that much *even then!*"), no effort is spared to "update" them. In this matter, the teachings of yoga have been blessed with no exemption. It seems as if most of the people teaching it in the West, and a number also in India, have felt called upon to "improve" it in some way—not merely in the manner of presentation (which would be admissible), but actually in some of its fundamental tenets.

A perfected yogi alone has the hard-won right to prune the tree of tradition, or to make such additions to it as he sees fit. For mere tyros to do likewise is like turning a horse loose in the living room. Yet, interestingly enough, perfected yogis have shown a deeper concern than anyone else to preserve yoga's central traditions.

What point is served by looking back to the origins of this science in what was, we have been told, the merest dawn of civilization? Until the student understands this point, he may feel tempted to "adjust" the yoga teachings at every turn to suit his own fancy. Basically, there are two reasons. The first offers at least an explanation for the fact that so ancient a culture asked questions of life that were far beyond the scope of a supposedly primitive society. The second reason underscores a truth that is basic to a right understanding of yoga.

The first reason is controversial, though more facts can be marshaled to support it than would commonly be supposed. It is a firm tradition, expounded in many ancient documents, and defended in all seriousness right to the present day by every one of India's great teachers, that high civilizations have existed at various times in the past, and that mankind has repeatedly attained, and fallen from, far greater heights of knowledge than we have reached so far in our civilization. The science of yoga is believed to have been handed down from such a high age. Indeed, it seems as if so advanced a teaching, as at home as it is among realities to which even our scientists are still struggling to adjust themselves, must surely have been born in an age of relative enlightenment.

Fascinating evidence keeps appearing in support of the hypothesis that man has possessed advanced knowledge in times past. There is the recently discovered, and apparently indisputable, proof that Stonehenge was a sort of fixed computer, giving the exact positions for various astronomical events, some of them occurring at intervals of fifty years or more—far too long a time for any but an advanced society, with carefully preserved records, to keep track of. On the west coast of North and South America there are numbers of huge, round boulders, arranged in geometrical patterns that can be discerned only from high-flying airplanes. One wonders: Were they put there in ancient times as signals for some sort of aircraft? There is the evidence of expert planning, including a sophisticated sewage system and radiant heating in the homes, in cities in the Punjab that were abandoned 5,000 years ago. There are the huge steps, apparently carved by man into solid rock, and leading down to great depths in the Atlantic Ocean off the northern coast of Puerto Rico. There are the domesticated grains, developed in ancient times, evidence of an agricultural skill quite possibly more advanced than our own. There are ancient, supposedly mythological, accounts of flying vehicles, even of interplanetary travel. Is it possible that some of these tales are not mythological? There is an ancient manuscript in India that has survived to this day, in which the lives of many thousands, perhaps millions, of people were recorded in detail—a fact that assumes astounding proportions when one learns that most of these people had not yet been born. Many of them, in fact, would live on earth only after thousands of years. I found my own life accurately described—even to my correct name and birthplace—in this work, including predictions of future events that have since come to pass. It is entirely possible that your life, too, is recorded there, as are those of countless people living today. (I have described this discovery in a booklet of mine, *India's Ancient Book of Prophecy,* which includes a detailed discussion of further points that I have only touched on here.) The question naturally arises: What knowledge did those ancients possess that made possible such amazing prophecies? Obviously, we are not even close to possessing any comparable science.

The great yogis of India long ago claimed that human enlightenment depends only partly on the mechanical make-up of the brain and the quality of information that is introduced into it. Most important, they said, is the energy itself flowing through the complex circuit of cerebral nerves. If this energy-flow is weak, no amount of crammed information can result in great and original ideas.

This energy-flow can be strengthened by self-effort in two ways: Blockages in the nerves can be eliminated, and the flow of energy itself can be increased. Both of these ends may be accomplished by the diligent practice of yoga. It is perhaps for this reason above all that yoga is termed a science, not merely an art.

But the wise men taught that the strength of this energy-flow depends also on certain external factors. Our environment, the company we keep—these aids will be readily recognizable; it is for these reasons that great saints have always stressed the importance of *satsanga* (good company) and of living in spiritual environments. The ancients also said, however, that our planet receives vast amounts of energy from the surrounding universe, and that a fine attunement with this energy can bring one speedy inner enlightenment.

They taught that the rays of energy are strongest at the center of our galaxy. Our sun, they claimed, moves not only in a fixed orbit around the galaxy, but also revolves inwardly around its dual, with the result that it is alternately closer to and farther from our galactic center. As it moves closer, mankind as a whole becomes more enlightened. As it moves farther away, only those persons who conscientiously develop their own inner energy, and who, by sensitizing themselves, make full use of whatever energy comes to them from without, are able to transcend humanity's general plunge into darkness.

Swami Sri Yukteswar, my own guru's guru, and a profound astrologer as well as one of the great masters of yoga of modern India, explained that our sun completes one complete revolution around its dual every 24,000 years. He said we reached the farthest point from our galactic center in the year 499 A.D. We are now once again on an upward cycle, and have entered the second of four ages—*Dwapara Yuga,* the age of atomic discovery, lasting a total of 2,400 years—which he said began in 1699 A.D. (Astrologically speaking, then, 2000 ought to be called the year 300, *Dwapara.*)

The science of yoga was born in an age when mankind as a whole was more enlightened, and could easily grasp truths for which our most advanced thinkers are still only groping. (I refer here to ordinary, worldly, men, whose sole means of achieving understanding are the clumsy tools of logic, and not to those great saints and yogis who in any age are fully enlightened from within.) It is because the groping for these truths has begun again that great yogis have reintroduced this ancient science to humanity at large, and that people in growing numbers are becoming so receptive to it.

The other reason for looking back to ancient traditions for a true insight into the yoga science is that the perception of truth is not something to be built up from generation to generation, like money in a bank. It is not dependent on an acquisition of outward knowledge.

Truth is eternal. Man can perceive it; he cannot create it. Once his perception is keen enough to behold Absolute Truth, he will partake of a reality that all share who attain the same vision. The great religions have come to man from those regions. The greatest spiritual teachers in all times have spoken from that vision. It is worldly people who, because they see the world through a filter of their own ideas and emotions, distort everything, including religion, with their personal prejudices. The endeavor of great teachers always is to bring man back to central, eternal realities. If man strays too far south, they tell him to go north. If then he makes a dogma of moving northward, straying too far in that direction, they tell him he must go south. Those who were told to go south will quarrel with the others who were told to go north, but only because both groups are blind to the fact that all their teachers wanted them to do was find the spiritual "equator," the center of their own being. It is this teaching which constitutes the true tradition of religion; it is for this reason alone that great teachers uphold the old traditions.

The history of yoga, then, must begin with its origins in the vision of great masters in ancient times. Later masters of this science are important to us now, not for what they did to improve on the ancient teachings, but for what they did to preserve them. As divine truths, the teachings of every true master are eternal, and as worthy to be considered scripture as the writings of the most ancient sage. As history, however, their special interest lies in how they clarified what now have become archaic distortions of tradition, or in how they emphasized aspects of tradition which the people of their times were prepared to understand.

Truly, the most meaningful second step in the history of yoga is, in every age, the very long one from its ancient origins to the present day. More important than this medieval saint or that are the lives of present-day masters of yoga, whose concern is to correct mankind's contemporary distortions of reality, or to reveal to man new aspects of reality for which his development has now prepared him.

In our age a number of such great masters have appeared. They have come with different missions, each one to stress a different aspect of the Truth, each aspect sorely needed by modern man in general, or by the groups of disciples to whom they spoke in particular. As part of this present-day renaissance of ancient teachings, one particular line of great masters have devoted their lives to reestablishing the original, central teachings and practices of yoga.

The lives of these great masters are eloquently described in *Autobiography of a Yogi,* by Paramhansa Yogananda, my own great guru. Yoganandaji, himself a perfected master, was sent to the West in 1920 by his line of gurus (Babaji, Lahiri Mahasaya, and Swami Sri Yukteswar). Here he established thriving centers for the practice and spread of the authentic, original yoga science of ancient times. Since his passing in 1952 his work continues to flourish and to grow.

Most important to the mission of this great line of *avatar*s (perfected beings whose sole purpose in returning to this level of existence is to uplift others) was the revival of the highest of ancient yoga techniques, to which they have given the somewhat unassuming name, *Kriya Yoga. Kriya* means, simply, action. Any number of yoga practices may be, and are, called *kriya yoga.* In the present case, the action referred to is of a particular sort; its special purpose is to awaken energy in the spine and brain, by means of which the Kriya Yogi can attain enlightenment by the shortest possible route. This technique may be learned from Ananda by contacting the Ananda Kriya Ministry at the Church address given above, or at 530-478-7560 or kriyayoga@ananda.org. The technique can also be learned from the organization which my guru founded: Self-Realization Fellowship, 3880 San Rafael Avenue, Los Angeles, California 90065. (Ananda is not affiliated with this organization.) Preparation for it is essential if the technique is to be practiced correctly and effectively. As a preparation, this present course of study will, I believe, prove invaluable.

The history of yoga suggests two principles that are basic to the successful practice of even the simplest *asana* (posture) of *hatha yoga:*

1. The widespread enlightenment that was said to have existed at the time of yoga's beginnings has been attributed to the proximity of our solar system to the mighty radiations of energy pouring from the center of our galaxy. In even the darkest age, however, some souls are fully enlightened. And in even the most enlightened age, some men live in

a self-created darkness. The most important thing for man to remember is that he must *receive* enlightenment; he cannot manufacture it. A room that is painted white seems brighter because it reflects more light than will any other color. The purpose of yoga, similarly, is to open the windows of the mind, and to awaken every cell of the body and brain to reflect and magnify the energy that comes to it from the surrounding universe. (A comparison might be drawn to modern transistor radios which, because of their efficiency, can pick up programs where, a few years ago, nothing so small would have been able to get a sound.)

As you pursue your yoga practices, remember that your aim must be to become spiritually completely open, to *receive.* Never hurry. Never strain. Feel that what you do is, in a sense, being done *through you,* by your willing cooperation with divine forces.

2. As the history of yoga is a long record of great yogis who brought this science back again and again to its central focus, so the practice of each individual must be directed, not toward outward appearances and display, but inward to the center of his own being. Every outward movement must proceed from this inner center. Every posture must be an affirmation of, and must be followed by a return to, the divine Self within.

II. YOGA POSTURES

Special Guidelines

The student is urged to study these lessons, and to practice at least a little bit from them, every day. He should not, however, "bolt his food." My great guru cautioned me on this point: "Do not get excited or impatient. Proceed with slow speed." Read the first section on philosophy first. It is important for a right understanding even of the yoga postures, lest one fall into the common mistake of seeking only the shallowest benefits from this great science—slim hips, or a glowing complexion. In a forest strewn with rubies, why fill one's sack with pine needles?

Don't overdo. A half an hour to an hour at a time is quite enough for most people. The beginner, especially, should start slowly and work up gradually. (*How* slowly and *how* gradually will depend upon his health, and upon the limberness and vitality of his body.) If you want to do two or three hours of yoga postures a day, get yourself a qualified personal teacher. All the yoga books are firm on this point. But don't imagine in any case that long hours of postures are necessary for glowing health or even rapid spiritual progress. "Keep exercised and body fit for God realization," my guru once wrote to me; yet he stressed the greater importance of mental and spiritual development even for lasting physical well-being.

Age is not in itself an obstacle to practicing these postures, except for the stiffness and other ailments that often accompany old age. Some of the stiffest people I have seen, however, have been young men in their twenties, and I have known old people who were remarkably supple. Interestingly, it has been my observation that physical stiffness often accompanies a certain mental inflexibility, a tendency toward dogmatism that is not necessarily limited to any age bracket.

A general precaution for everyone is simply to take stock of one's own physical condition, and to proceed with common sense. When unwell, be extra cautious; it may be safest for the time being not to do the postures at all. There are people with extreme physical problems who ought never to do any but the simplest poses. If you have very high blood pressure, for example, or a weak heart, exercise great caution; *Savasana* (the restful "corpse" pose) may be all that you should attempt.

Women in menstruation should avoid the stomach poses (*Uddiyana Bandha* and *Nauli*), and the other poses, too, unless they are in sound health. Pregnant women, and women who have recently (within the past twelve weeks) given birth, would do best to avoid especially the forward-bending exercises (*Janushirasana,* the Jackknife Pose, etc.), and the stomach exercises. Many of the other yoga positions, however, may be practiced with benefit during pregnancy, and have been found to ease the difficulties of childbirth.

If you experience pain (other than muscular) in the chest, abdomen, or brain while doing any posture, discontinue that pose until the cause of the pain has been ascertained. If you have any serious doubts about your fitness to do the yoga postures, please consult your physician (or, in the case of spinal problems, your osteopath or chiropractor) before attempting them.

Bear in mind, however, that *hatha yoga* is one of the best systems known to man for the relief of physical distress. Cautions must be borne in mind, but they ought certainly not to be viewed with alarm. The yoga science is safe for anyone who uses it with common sense. It is not a system of vigorous calisthenics, but of gentle, *natural* movements that place a minimum of strain on the bodily system, with a maximum of benefit to it.

Remember, it is important never to force oneself into a pose. The postures are a process of gradual discovery of the body's potentials. Think of them as an adventure in awareness. Through growing *awareness* of tension, for example, one will be able to release that tension and thereby to perfect a pose. By perfect relaxation the whole yoga science can be mastered. This is as true for *raja yoga* as it is for *hatha yoga,* for relaxation must be taken into progressively subtle realms, through mental and emotional calmness to spiritual expansion and receptivity.

Stretch into a pose only a little bit, if at all, beyond the point of comfort. Be aware of the tensions that prevent you from stretching further. Relax them. (To relax, think space at the points of strain.)

Don't worry if it takes a long time to do a pose well. There is no such thing as *failure* in a pose, short of simply not doing it at all. Any stretch in the general direction indicated will be important for you. The stiffer you are, indeed, the more important it will be for you to make an effort—even if you can only reach your fingers as far down as your knees when the instructions clearly state that you should be holding your toes. There will always be someone better than you are. So also will there always be someone worse. Compare yourself only with yourself. Are you a littler freer in your body now than you were a few days or weeks ago? So long as you are progressing in the right direction, you have cause for nothing but self-congratulation.

One of the gratifying aspects of the yoga postures, however, is that the most beneficial of them are not always the most difficult. Some of the best of them, indeed, are among the easiest.

Here are three easy ones to begin with. Try them.

Sasamgasana

(The Hare Pose—First Phase, also known as *Balasana*, The Child Pose)

"I relax from outer involvement into my inner haven of peace."

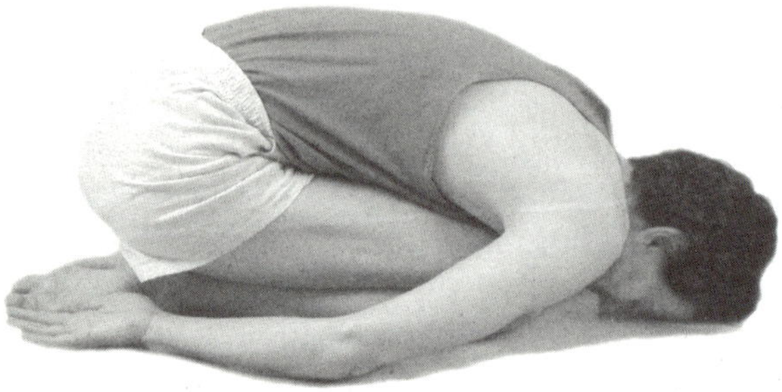

Sit on your calves with your feet outstretched behind you, your right big toe over the left big toe. If you cannot sit down all the way, never mind for the purposes of this particular pose.

Lean forward gently, exhaling, until your head touches the floor in front of you, close to your knees. Put your hands backward and down by your side. Rest in that position, breathing normally, thirty seconds to one minute.

Benefits: The gentle inversion of your body will bring blood to your brain. It will benefit your sinuses. This position is refreshing to the brain; it helps to banish mental fatigue. If you can squat down completely on your calves, the gentle pressure of your weight on your legs, feet, and abdomen will help to relieve fatigue in the lower body.

In a later lesson a variant of this pose will be taught to relieve headaches and a feeling of pressure in the brain.

Bhujangasana

(The Cobra Pose)

"I rise determinedly to meet all obstacles."
Or: *"I rise joyfully to meet each new opportunity."*

The reader who has any knowledge of the yoga postures will probably be familiar with this pose. The Cobra Pose is easy to assume; its benefits are great.

Lie face downward, with the palms flat against the ground at about the level of the shoulders. Keep the elbows close to the body. The forehead should rest against the ground.

First Phase: Slowly raise the forehead, feeling the tension at the back of the head. Concentrate not on the tension itself, but on the causal gathering of energy in the spine.

Second Phase: Draw the head slowly farther and farther back, until the shoulders become lifted off the ground. Now draw the back slowly upward, until you can raise it no farther by its own strength.

Third Phase: Then, with the arms, push yourself upward as far as your body will bend, *without raising your navel from the ground.* As you raise your back slowly, feel the gradual course of energy downward from the head through the spine with the tensing of each successive portion of the neck and back.

After attaining the final position, relax: You will find that you can bend farther still. Visualize yourself as rising bravely to meet the challenge of all obstacles in your life. Affirm mentally: *"I rise determinedly to meet all obstacles,"* or, *"I rise joyfully to meet each new opportunity."*

After 5 or 10 seconds in this final phase (more, of course—up to 3 minutes—for adepts), return slowly to the prone position, reversing the sequence of tension and feeling the energy flow back up the spine gradually to the brain. Repeat this posture, if you like, 3 to 7 times, resting briefly after each practice.

Beginners may breathe naturally, but after proficiency is attained one should inhale slowly while bending upward, and exhale slowly while returning to the first position.

Benefits: The Cobra Pose is wonderfully relaxing to the spine. It refreshes the brain. It strengthens the back muscles, and exerts a gentle, beneficial pressure on the visceral organs. It helps one particularly to overcome flatulence after meals. The psychological and spiritual benefits are more important. Psychologically, the Cobra Pose increases one's strength to overcome obstacles. Spiritually, it increases awareness of, and hence control over, the subtle energy in the spine.

Utkatasana

(The Chair Pose)

"My body is no burden; it is light as air."

First Phase

Second Phase

First Phase: Stand up. Inhale, raising your arms straight out in front of you, palms upward, and rise up simultaneously on your toes as you raise your arms. Crouch down part way, as if you were sitting down, but were so light that you needed nothing but air to rest upon. Affirm mentally: "*My body is no burden; it is light as air.*"

Second Phase: For the second phase of this posture, squat down all the way, remaining on your toes. In this position, place your hands on your hips.

When you are ready to come up again, sweep your arms forward and upward, with the palms turned up; inhale as you come up, and raise your arms in a graceful sweeping motion over your head, backward, and down as you settle back onto your heels, exhaling.

Benefits: Some of the yoga postures are beneficial primarily for their psychological and spiritual effects. This pose is one such exercise. Its physical benefits are simply that it tones up the leg muscles and helps (in the second phase) to relieve tired feet. Psychologically, the Chair Pose is far more valuable. It suggests to the mind a sense of lightness and vitality, a freedom from bondage to the heavy, downward pull of earth.

III. BREATHING

"And the Lord God formed man of the dust of the ground, and breathed into his nostrils the breath of life. . . ." (Genesis 2:7) Probably for as long as man has been polluting this fair planet, the breath has been associated with life. At first glance, this association seems based merely on an obvious consideration; ordinarily, the quickest way to tell whether a person is alive (assuming the absence of voluntary movement) is simply to see whether he is breathing. Yet the relation of breath to life has often been treated by wise men, including great yogis, as a deep mystery. Why? Life, of course, *is* a mystery, but it would seem to be reducing its magical aura almost to nonexistence to say that life is nothing but breath.

What is life? What do we mean, for example, when we say, "I feel so *alive* today"? Obviously, not, "My existence is more actual today than it was yesterday." A fact is a fact; it cannot be more so or less so; it can only cease—apparently at least—to be a fact altogether. Essentially, what we mean is that we have more *energy.* We instinctively identify life with energy, not with mere existence.

Then what is the breath? The body depends for its functioning on the intake of oxygen, and on the exhalation of waste matter in the form of carbon dioxide. But is the breath only a chemical? Not so, say the great yogis. They equate it with life, because they equate it with energy. In India, in fact, one word, *prana,* is used for all three. For one thing, the breath is a valuable *source* of energy. Also, it acts as a strong stimulus to the natural energy-flow (or life-flow) in the body. Life, or energy, is more than the breath; nor is our understanding of life particularly enhanced by equating the two. But our understanding of the breath is greatly expanded by the association.

Proper breathing can help immensely to make you more "alive" and energetic. Begin from today to pay careful attention to your natural rhythms of breathing. You will soon discover in this seemingly simple life-function hidden spiritual treasures.

A Simple Exercise: Try lying flat on your back in *Savasana,* the Corpse Pose. (I shall discuss this important position at length in Step Three.) Let your arms rest at your sides, keeping the palms turned upward.

Inhale very slowly and deeply, and imagine that the breath is filling your feet. Feel the muscles, bones, and skin becoming permeated with the breath's energy until they fairly tingle with vitality. Hold the breath only as long as you can do so comfortably, repeating the process, if you like, rather than overextending the breath.

Do the same thing for the calves, the thighs, the hips, abdomen and stomach, hands, forearms, upper arms, chest, shoulders, back, neck, throat, jaw, tongue, facial muscles, eyes, brain—always slowly and gently, always with the deepest attention.

You will find that this simple exercise has power not only to energize your body, but also to heal it of many ailments.

Savasana

(The Corpse Pose)

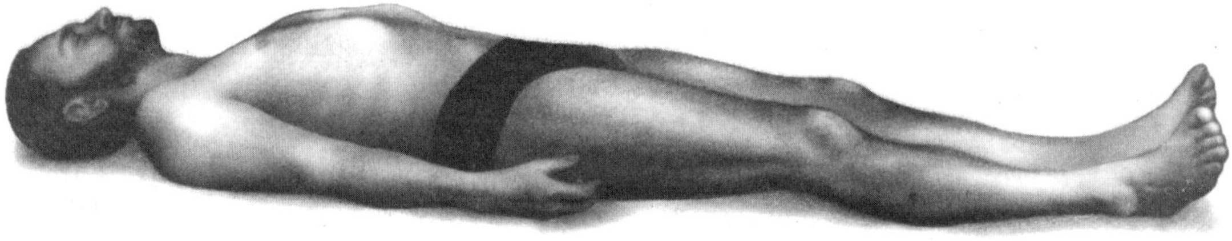

IV. ROUTINE

The postures you have learned so far are so few, and so simple, that you might as well do them twice a day. As you learn more postures, you may prefer to divide them into two sets, or to set aside more time once each day for their practice.

Normally, the body is more limber in the evening than in the morning. Morning practice of the postures can help you to wake up and face the day fully relaxed and at peace in yourself. Evening practice will help you to free yourself, physically and mentally, of the cares and tensions of the day. If you need a boost to your self-confidence, especially in the more difficult poses, do them in the evening when your body is more responsive. As a rule, the best time for doing the postures depends on personal choice. Most of them, however, should be done before meals, or on an empty stomach.

V. HEALING

Insomnia, Part One

One of the most gratifying aspects of teaching this science is the immediacy of some of its results.

A student of one of my beginning classes in San Francisco, some time ago, drove with me to our meditation retreat in the Sierra Nevada foothills. Halfway through the journey her purse fell open. Out fell an assortment of green pills, yellow pills, blue pills.

"What on earth are you doing with all those pills?" I asked.

"Why, I couldn't get along without them!" she exclaimed. "I need the green pills to put me to sleep at night. They leave me groggy in the morning, so I take the yellow pills to help me wake up. The yellow pills make me edgy, so I take the blue pills later in the day, as tranquilizers."

"Well," I said, "you've been practicing yoga for two weeks now. Why don't you try doing a few postures before going to bed, and see if you can't get along without all those crutches?"

"Impossible!" she cried in alarm. "You don't know me. I've *never* been able to sleep without them. I'm a complete pill addict!"

After a week, however, she worked up enough courage to try my suggestion. The next day she telephoned me to say that she had never slept so well in her life. A year and a half later we spoke again on the phone. She was still practicing yoga postures. Her dependence on pills had been overcome completely.

Insomnia is one of the miseries of the modern age. This might, indeed, be called the Age of Anxiety. People who fail to get the rest they need at night often resort to heavy doses of coffee and other stimulants to remain awake during the day. They sleep badly the following night as a result of these stimulants, and so by degrees enter a life-cycle that leaves them chronically out of tune with life (or energy)—like an eight-cylinder motor functioning on only one cylinder.

If you are troubled with insomnia, try doing a few yoga postures before going to bed. Get the energy in your body flowing smoothly, instead of leaving it gathered and blocked in local knots of tension. (Physical tension activates related areas in the brain, making sleep difficult.)

Then lie in bed flat on your back. Inhale deeply; tense the whole body, equalizing the flow of energy throughout the body; throw the breath out and relax. Repeat this alternate tension and relaxation two or three times if you so desire.

Then watch the breath mentally for awhile, allowing its steady rhythm to soothe you, like the waves of an ocean stroking the shore on a calm day.

After some time, inhale deeply; then exhale slowly and completely, as if with a sigh, and feel that you are surrendering yourself to an infinity of peace. Hold the breath out as long as you can comfortably, and repeat mentally, "AUM, peace, peace, amen," or, "AUM, *shanti, shanti, shanti.*" (*Shanti* is the Sanskrit word for peace.) Visualize an ocean of peace spreading out in all directions around you—or think of peace as gathering protectingly around you in great, soft clouds. Repeat this breathing process six to twelve times. If after that you are still awake, continue watching the breath, calmly, passively.

Yogis say that one's bed should be arranged so that its head is not pointed towards the west. A westward position is said to induce fitful sleep and restless dreams; eastward, to aid the development of wisdom; and southward, to promote longevity.

Never go to sleep with the thought that you are utterly exhausted. Not only will the desperate desire for rest often drive sleep away (simply because desperation is the antithesis of repose), but the mental affirmation of exhaustion will be carried into the subconscious mind, and will affect even your wakefulness the next day. No matter how long you sleep, if you go to sleep exhausted, you will probably wake up exhausted.

Any strong thought that you carry into your subconsciousness as you fall asleep will affect your waking state the next day. This principle is said to hold true also for death—the "Big Sleep"—and subsequent rebirth. Above all, therefore, try meditating before you go to sleep. Sow in the fertile soil of your sleepland the nourishing seeds of God's peace.

VI. DIET

Insomnia, Part Two

Before sleep, and also before meditation, it is better not to eat anything. Especially to be avoided are starchy or other high-carbon foods. The heart and lungs clear the body of waste products, expelling them in the form of carbon dioxide. Starches and sugars give the heart more carbon to pump out of the body. A hard-working heart, with resultant heavy breathing, makes perfect rest perfectly impossible.

If you must eat anything just before going to sleep, try taking your food warm (warmth is relaxing) and if possible in liquid form. Yogis recommend warm milk in such cases.

Sleep "Potion": Although garlic, for culinary purposes, is not generally recommended by yogis (for reasons that will be gone into in a later lesson), garlic has certain medicinal properties that recommend it in specific cases. If, for example, you cook a little chopped garlic in milk, simmering it for ten minutes, the resulting beverage has been found to induce sleep.

VII. MEDITATION

Meditation is to religion what the laboratory is to physics or chemistry. Whether one follows the outward forms of religion depends more or less on personal taste, but whether one seeks in his life some of religion's practical, inner benefits is a matter of life or living death. The reason religion persists in spite of the general worldliness of man is not that a few otherworldly types keep fanning the dying embers, but rather that all human life would be insufferable without at least *some* of the inner peace that religion offers. The essence of religion is not its ceremonies, nor even its talk of a life hereafter, but its emphasis on an inner life here and now, and on the lasting peace that accompanies this inner life once it is discovered. The true purpose of religion is to point out that human existence *on every level* is empty when only emptiness is affirmed, and when inner awareness is allowed to become nothing more than an echo of the world, offering nothing creatively to the world in return.

Some people confine their understanding of religion to a reproving frown, or to some pious (and usually fleeting) emotion. They see not that religion is one of the very sinews of a healthy, normal existence. Without ever going to church or reciting a single creed, one can be religious in the true sense of the word. Simple, genuine good will for one's neighbors is a religious phenomenon. So also is an experience of wonder at the mystery of the vast universe. The central teachings of religion are universal truths of life itself. To reject those teachings is to reject life.

Outward religious practices, of course, without the development of an inner life, are of secondary value. In their practical effects they are rather like trying to fly an airplane with an insufficient wingspread: No matter how much of a "racing start" one gets with them, he can't quite get up off the ground. Essential to the religious life is an inner unfoldment. Vital to this unfoldment is the daily practice of meditation.

What is meditation?

It is not, as so many people assume it to be, a process of "thinking things over." Rather, it is making the mind completely receptive to reality. It is stilling the thought-processes—those restless ripples that bob on the surface of the mind—so that truth, like the moon, may be clearly reflected there. It is *listening* to God, to Universal Reality, for a change, instead of doing all the talking and "computing" oneself.

This is how all the great discoveries have been made—not by human creation, but by receptivity to rays of inspiration from higher sources than those with which the conscious mind is familiar.

Try meditating every day for at least fifteen minutes (half an hour would be even better). Usually, the best time for meditation will be directly after your practice of yoga postures.

A Meditation Exercise: Sit very straight and still. Think of your mind as a lake. At first, the ripples of thought may seem very important to you. That is because your awareness is centered in such a small section of your mental lake that even little ripples create a tumult. Gaze mentally outward in all directions; see how vast the lake really is. Mentally expand its shores farther and farther, until you realize how insignificant, in relation to its vastness, are the little thoughts that bob up and down here at the center.

Tell these thoughts to be still, to allow you to listen to the waves lapping on the distant shores of your mind. Then listen intently.

When everything is perfectly calm, feel on the still surface of your mind the soothing breath of Spirit. Do not be impatient. Allow the breezes of divine inspiration gently to caress you, to play over you as they will. Seek not to control them; remember, in nothing in life are you really the doer. Your ego is only an instrument. Offer yourself wholly, ever more deeply and calmly, to the Divine.

AUM, *Shanti, Shanti, Shanti!*

Step Two

The Paths of Yoga

I. PHILOSOPHY

The Paths of Yoga

Yoga, literally, means "union." This union can be understood on different levels: philosophically, as that of the relative, limited self with the absolute Self; religiously, as that of the individual soul with the Infinite Spirit; psychologically, as the integration of the personality—a state wherein a person no longer lives at cross-purposes with himself; emotionally, as the stilling of the waves of likes and dislikes, permitting one to remain in all circumstances complete in himself.

It is this last level that serves as the classical definition of yoga by the ancient sage Patanjali. Patanjali's profound *Yoga Sutras,* or aphorisms, have been looked upon for millennia as yoga's definitive scripture. He wrote: "*Yogas chitta vritti nirodh*"—"Yoga is the neutralization of the waves of feeling." *Chitta* (feeling) has been variously translated as "mind-stuff," "consciousness," "subconsciousness," "the lower mind." In a series of classes on Patanjali's *Yoga Aphorisms* many years ago, Paramhansa Yogananda pointed out that those waves in the mind which produce delusion and bondage are primarily the likes and dislikes, the biased feelings of the heart. *Vritti* (vortices) literally means, "whirlpools"—the whirling eddies that interfere with life's smoothly flowing stream, sucking into a purely private orbit whatever one likes, making one so preoccupied with egoistic selections and rejections that he is no longer consciously a part of the stream. Thoughts pass through the minds even of enlightened sages whenever they wish them to, though they subside easily because of the sages' nonattachment to them. Other functions of the mind, too, such as memory, idea-association, and analysis, the sage can perform far better than the average person. It is not as if he ceased completely to function as a human being after achieving enlightenment. What cease for him are the waves, or eddies, of selfish likes and dislikes of attachment. Entering thereby into the sacred life-stream of *Pranava,* or AUM, he merges consciously into the silent, infinite ocean of Spirit.

Yoga *is* the neutralization of ego-directed feelings, because once these become stilled, the yogi realizes that he is, and that he has always been, one with the Infinite—that his awareness of this reality was limited only by his infatuation with limitation.

The different paths of yoga, then, must be understood in the light of how they help to bring about this neutralization of the waves of feeling. Merely to whip oneself into a lather of devotional excitement does not constitute *bhakti yoga* (the attainment of yoga by the path of devotion). Merely to work hard, even in a good cause, is not truly *karma yoga* (yoga attainment by the path of action). Merely to study and philosophize intellectually is not the path of *gyana yoga* (the path of wisdom). All these paths must be followed with a firm awareness of the goal of all yoga practices: *Yogas chitta vritti nirodh.*

This is, moreover, the true goal of all seeking. The reason Patanjali's aphorisms are accepted as a universal scripture is that he was dealing with universal spiritual truths, not with sectarian practices. *Every* truth seeker, regardless of his religion, eventually reaches the same state of divine calmness that is yoga.

Consider the path of *bhakti yoga,* the yoga of devotion. Those true saints in all religions, no matter how eagerly they prayed, sang, or danced in their devotion, reached a point in their development where deep inner calmness took over. All movement ceased. Saint Teresa of Avila reported that in this state she could not even pray, so deep was her inner stillness. Truly, she was a yogi though she had never heard of yoga. But because she was not aware that such perfect stillness is the goal of the spiritual search, she wasted many years (as she later stated) in trying to force her mind to return to superficial devotional practices which the soul was endeavoring to transcend.

Bhakti yoga, then, must lead from personal fervor to impersonal calmness. The important thing is not how one defines God, but how one approaches Him. The *bhakti yogi* thinks of God first in personal, human terms: as Father, Mother, Friend, or Beloved. Such a personal view helps him to awaken and direct love towards God. Ignorant followers of this path waste much energy in arguing over the respective merits of their chosen deities. They see not that Spirit is *all* forms, and *no* form (because essentially beyond all forms). It is not *what* we love, but *how* we love, that is important if our devotion is to lead us to enlightenment. Sectarian differences only create more waves of likes and dislikes; they do not result in *yoga.*

Bhakti yoga, or pure devotion, is essential to some extent for every seeker. Selfless love is one of the quickest ways of smoothing the selfish eddies of desire, and of drawing one's feelings out of an egoic orbit to merge in the Divine Stream. *Bhakti yoga* must be above all a self-offering: not noise and loud chanting only, but also silence—a *listening* for the divine reply. Devotion is a way of creating such a strong current of pure energy that all impure desires are simply carried along in its wake.

The path of *karma yoga* (yoga through action), similarly, leads not to ever-more-frenzied activity, but to deep inner calmness and freedom. Fulfillment in *karma yoga* lies not so much in doing many things as in acting more and more, even in little things, with the consciousness that it is God who, truly, is the Doer. Everyone engages in mere activity, yet few people are *karma yogi*s. The true *karma yogi* tries, by God-reminding activities, to redirect all the wrong impulses of his heart into wholesome channels. More than that, he tries to become aware of the divine energy flowing through him as he acts. As the *bhakti yogi* is taught to be more concerned with loving purely than with defining exactly what it is that he loves, so also the *karma yogi* is taught that the spirit in which he serves is more important than the service itself. *Nishkam karma,* desireless action, or action without desire for the fruits of action, is *karma yoga.* All other activity leads, not to yoga (union), but only to further bondage, for it stirs up more waves of likes and dislikes in the heart. ("I'll just die if I don't succeed!" "Look everyone—John, Mary, Bill—Isn't it wonderful what I've done? What else could possibly matter any more?" "What happened? John liked what I did, but Mary didn't. I'll have to work harder now, until *everyone* is impressed with my achievements." Or: "I failed! Nothing in life now is worth living for!") With all this personal excitement, the mainstream of life flows by, and all we ever notice of it are the few little sticks that we struggle so desperately to draw into our private orbits, thinking in the acquisition of them to find peace, not realizing that in the very act of whirling with desire we only destroy whatever peace we may presently have.

Activity is a part of being human. We could never find inner freedom if we starved every impulse by inaction. Attunement with the Infinite Creator comes in part by wholesome, creative work, not by denying every manifestation of His power in us. The neutralization of the waves of feeling comes partly by the satisfaction of our wholesome desires. But this satisfaction must result in just that: the neutralization of the feeling-waves. Personal satisfaction must be offered up to the Divine; it must be perceived as a mere ripple on the ocean of cosmic bliss. In this way right activity leads to inner freedom, which is the true, spiritual goal of all action.

Karma yoga does not necessarily consist of building hospitals or doing works that people commonly label religious. Since freedom is the goal, it is also the criterion of right action. If, for example, one's own nature (which is determined by past *karma*) impels him to work in the soil, gardening may be a more important—because liberating—activity for him than preaching to multitudes. In every man's life, the criterion of right activity is that which will bring him, in the highest sense, to a divine state of inner freedom.

It will be seen, then, that *karma yoga* is not only a distinct and separate path. Even *bhakti yoga* involves a kind of activity: the expression of devotion. So also does the exercise of discrimination. So also does meditation, and the practice of the yoga postures. The teaching of *karma yoga* is not, "Do this or that, specifically," but, "Whatever you do, do it with a sense of freedom. Realize that you are only an instrument of the Divine. Do nothing for selfish ends. Instead, act so as to neutralize, not to agitate, the waves of your likes and dislikes."

By acting without desire for the fruits of action, the yogi learns to live, not in the past or future, but in the timeless NOW.

By acting consciously as a channel for the Divine, finally, he realizes that actions are effective even objectively, not according to how zealously he works, but according to how much of God he expresses in his work. Because energy is an aspect of God, hard work will bring greater divine attunement than half-hearted, slovenly work. But a simple, divine smile may change more hearts than a thousand windy sermons or learned treatises. A single walking stick made with divine joy will be, to one sensitive enough to see deeply, a greater work of art than a gigantic sculpture carved with consummate skill, but without profound understanding. The more the yogi, by his selfless actions, develops an awareness of the divine power flowing through him, the more he realizes that he can accomplish more, even for humanity, by becoming still and serving as a transmitting station for the Infinite Power, whose sermons are Silence.

Thus, outward work falls away, and the yogi's true work becomes the upliftment of others by the silent emanations of his peace. (A word is in order here, however, to those self-proclaimed "free" souls who, in the name of high Vedanta philosophy [usually with a generous admixture of drugs], imagine that they are serving in the highest way by sitting and doing nothing, claiming to be divine instruments when all the inspiration they feel is the vague prompting of their subconscious minds. Hard work is purifying. The great yogi, though not necessarily outwardly active, is conscious of directing a great deal more energy than any thousand ordinary men. His activity is enormous. It is merely so sensitive as no longer to require muscular application. Neophytes, however, should devote themselves to the generous exercise of their muscles.)

Gyana yoga is the yoga of wisdom. Wisdom first comes through the practice of *viveka* (discrimination). The temptation of the ego, once it takes up this practice, is to flatter itself with its own profundity by stepping further and further afield in its analyses of different aspects of reality. *Yogas chitta vritti nirodh*. The important thing is not how many different deep truths one can grasp, but rather how deeply one grasps the central truth: the need to rise above personal likes and dislikes. Many *gyana yogi*s, in their exercise of incisive discrimination, actually feed their likes and dislikes—in the form of an inordinate fondness for profound ideas.

Discrimination means in all things to look for the kernel of reality. It means penetrating to ever-deeper levels of insight. One person's gift to another, for example, may really be intended only to buy the recipient's friendship. Yet his apparently cynical wish to buy friendship may actually spring from a pathetic fear that he couldn't win it in any other way. This fear, in turn, may be due to an awareness, on a still deeper level, that friends can never be won, nor owned—that nothing, in fact, can be owned. Such an awareness, again, though sad at first glance, springs from the soul's even deeper knowledge that it is complete in itself, and need look nowhere outside for its fulfillment. Its sense of self-completeness, finally, is rooted in the deepest fact that, essentially, it is the Infinite Itself. The gift given for selfish gain, then, was due in the last analysis to the soul's inner, divine urge to claim the very universe as its own.

"Neti, neti"—"Not this, not that." By looking behind veil after veil that obscures the door to Truth, the *gyana yogi* comes at length to the Truth Itself, stripped of every superficial appearance.

But he will never come to this reality so long as he seeks it only on a level of ideas, some of which will attract him, others of which he will find repulsive. His search must take him within himself, to ever deeper levels of realization of who and what *he* is. It is his own heart's false identifications that he must dispel. As in *bhakti* and *karma yoga,* it is not *what* he sees, but *how* he sees, that really matters.

And that is why this path is called *gyana yoga* (the yoga of wisdom), not *viveka yoga* (the yoga of discrimination). Wisdom is not only the goal; it is also the path. The *gyana yogi* must view all things with the impartial consciousness of a sage. It is less important that he see through human follies than that he not be affected by man's supreme folly: delusion itself.

The *Bhagavad Gita,* India's favorite scripture, states, "He finds contentment who, like the calm ocean, absorbs within himself all the rivers of desires." (II:70) Man seldom realizes that even his outward, worldly enjoyments spring in fact from within himself—from his reactions to things rather than from the things themselves. The *gyana yogi* tries, even at the time of outward enjoyment, to interiorize his consciousness, feeding the inner flame of soul-consciousness. He knows that if, like worldly people, he borrowed its embers to give light to things, the true source of joy within himself would burn itself down at last to gray ashes.

He deals similarly with his desires. He realizes that their fulfillment depends entirely on his own mental pictures that he has formed of fulfillment, and not on any outer circumstance. He therefore sets mirrors, as it were, around himself. He refers his mental images back to the light of joy within himself, and sees those images as reflections, only, of that inner joy. In this way his soul's light becomes intensified, not diffused.

A comparison might also be drawn here to the extra comfort one derives from a blazing fireplace in a warm home, when one is aware at the same time of a raging blizzard out-of-doors. The more deeply aware one becomes that all joy is centered in the Self, the more the lures of the world serve only to strengthen one's affirmations of soul freedom.

Gyana yoga is not only a particular path to God. It also points out the direction all our thinking should take, even in *bhakti yoga* and *karma yoga,* if we want it to lead to liberation.

The different paths so far outlined are designed to fit the basic temperamental differences of men: those who live more by feeling, by action, or by thought. Because every man is a composite of all three of these attributes, regardless of which is uppermost in his particular nature, all three of these paths of yoga should be followed to some extent by everyone.

But temperament is a superficial consideration. It is not a quality of the soul—only of the ego. The perfection of each of these paths transcends temperament, leading from outward practices to deep inner stillness. Again, unless there is a degree of "inwardness" even from the beginning of one's journey, outward practices will remain outward; they will not lead to the neutralization of the eddies of feeling which alone constitutes yoga.

In addition to these outward practices, therefore, one should also practice daily meditation. Meditation will give force to one's devotion, to his activities, and to his divine understanding; the special practice of these yogas will in their turn give force to, and will help to determine the course of, his meditations. Not meditation only, but the harmonious combination—with meditation as the supreme guide—of all these yogas, constitutes the path of *raja yoga,* the "royal" yoga.

Raja yoga views human nature as a kingdom composed of many psychological tendencies and physical attributes, all of which require considerate attention. A king cannot afford to favor one class of his subjects at the expense of all others, lest dissatisfaction among the rest sow seeds of rebellion. Man, similarly, progresses most smoothly when all aspects of his nature are developed harmoniously. The *raja yogi,* or kingly yogi, therefore, is enjoined to rule his inner kingdom wisely and with moderation, developing all aspects of his nature in a balanced, integrated way. Since it is the soul which is the true ruler of man's inner kingdom, the development of soul-consciousness, by daily meditation, forms the principal activity of *raja yoga.* But even meditation, if one-sided, can result in imbalances. The *raja yogi* is therefore encouraged to develop all sides of his nature—always, however, with a view to neutralizing the waves of his likes and dislikes, and not, by egoistic self-expression, to creating ever-new eddies of selfish involvement.

II. YOGA POSTURES

Basic Principles and Practices

Hatha yoga, the yoga of physical postures, is not a separate yoga science in its own right; rather it is the physical discipline of the integral teaching known as *raja yoga.*

Yoga means "union." On a physical level of application, this signifies the complete harmony of all parts of the body—a balanced support of all the members for one another in such a way that disease, or disharmony, is faced with a united defense and can hardly make any inroad into the body.

Yoga—the neutralization of the waves of feeling—returns man to his natural state. Delusion is an unnatural condition; divine vision, the only true, or natural one. Applying this teaching to the body, we may understand that disease and other symptoms of bodily inharmony are not natural to man. If one can return to his natural state, disease will vanish as a matter of course.

Western medicine, lacking this philosophical foundation, treats disease as a natural phenomenon, one to be conquered, to be driven out of the body with new, man-made nostrums, as if the conquest of disease were possible only by battling the natural processes, by going against nature.

What are the results of the approach of Western medicine? Inevitably, doctors have discovered many natural truths and have applied them. But the philosophical orientation underlying their science is such that nature is brought into play only because man cannot possibly get away from her, being himself a product of nature. No effort is spared in Western medicine to substitute the man-made for the natural wherever possible. There is the constant expectation of some new "breakthrough" in the field of drugs that will banish this or that disease from the face of the earth. Pathetic it is to hear how many people, embracing this unnatural outlook, become virtual slaves to the doctor's office. Embracing the unnatural, they must also accept those basic symptoms of man's unnaturalness: physical inharmony and disease. Doctors have been said to kill as many patients as they cure. Whether or not this is an exaggeration, certain it is that the patient who relies excessively on medical care, rather than on his own inner strength, never seems to get well, and finds ample justification in his chronic ill-health for continued (and costly) visits to the doctors.

The yoga postures help to harmonize the body with natural law. The yogi is shown how to develop his own latent powers rather than lean weakly on some outer agent for his physical well-being. Inasmuch as ill health is the unnatural, not the natural, condition of the body, primary emphasis in *hatha yoga* is placed on freeing the body of any impurity that may prevent it from functioning as it should, rather than on introducing outside forces strong enough to destroy all disease. A piano placed without rollers on sandpaper would be difficult even for the strongest man to move. But if the piano were placed on well-oiled rollers and on a slick floor, even a child might be able to push it with ease. Even a little physical vitality can become dynamic, if the unnatural obstructions to its flow are removed.

Yogis and Western medical doctors both say that the toxins in the body soon leave the bloodstream and settle in the joints. Yogis go on to say that old age, too, settles first in the joints. Western medical doctors have actually stated that the spinal discs of many people even in their twenties already show signs of deterioration, owing to want of proper irrigation. Western systems of physical exercise—sports, calisthenics, and the like—do not develop the limberness necessary to keep the joints free of toxins and the spinal column well irrigated with life force. In both of these matters, the science of *hatha yoga* stands supreme.

Hatha yoga also exercises a gentle massage on the internal organs and glands, gradually strengthening them to the point where providing outside aid for them would only be "carrying coals to Newcastle."

Much emphasis is given in yoga to the elimination of waste from the body. One form of waste, not commonly thought of as such, is tension. Tension blocks the natural flow of energy in the body. It paralyzes one's normal sense of physical and mental harmony. Human ills all derive more or less directly from impairments in the body's energy-flow. The main reason for eliminating waste from the body is to permit the free flow of energy. Tension, the chief obstruction to this flow, is the first obstacle to be overcome if the body is to return to its divinely natural state.

It will be evident from the foregoing that the secret of success in yoga is relaxation, not strain. One should not force himself into a new condition, but seek only to free himself of tensions and inharmonies that have prevented him thus far from being fully himself. As I said in the first lesson, *relax* into the poses, don't force yourself into them. This is particularly true for the stretching poses.

Always do the postures when you are calm, physically and emotionally. They should be done if possible in the open air, or near to an open window. It's best not to practice them in a closed room, or where the air is stale. Don't be in a hurry to go through the poses. Hold each pose after you get into it; remember that the benefits often begin only after you have remained in a pose for awhile.

Rest after each position for about as long as you held it, or for as long as it takes for your heart to return to its normal beat.

A little judicious "cheating" is quite permissible. If you cannot keep your balance in the Tree Pose, for example, don't be afraid to take the support of a wall. In time you will find that you can do the pose properly, but the road to perfection may be uphill.

Try to do the postures at the same time every day. Regularity is an important feature of yogic discipline. As my great guru said: "Routinize your life. God created routine. The sun shines until dusk, and the stars shine until dawn."

Approach the postures with an attitude of peace.

Vrikasana

(The Tree Pose)

"I am calm, I am poised."

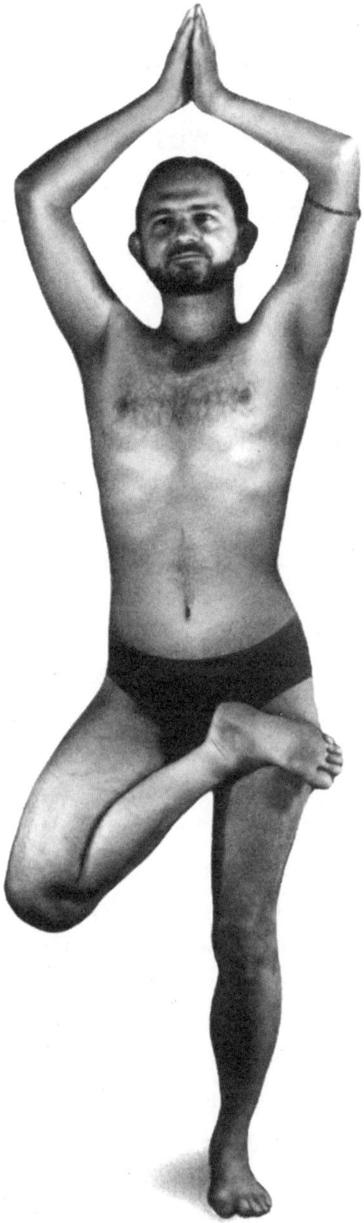

Stand upright. Bring your right foot up and place it on the opposite thigh at the junction of the abdomen, pointing the knee downward. Raise your arms slowly sideways, keeping them straight, palms upward, until you can join the palms together above the head. Inhale as you come up. Mentally feel that there is a straight line extending upward through your spine between your palms to your fingers. Feel that you are mentally centered in this straight line. Relax your body as much as possible. Mentally affirm, *"I am calm, I am poised."* Hold the pose for about 30 seconds, breathing naturally when you need to. Then exhale slowly, bringing your arms down sideways, and lowering your foot to the floor.

Repeat with the opposite leg.

If you find it difficult to bring your foot up as high as the junction of the thigh and abdomen, you may rest the instep against the inside of the opposite knee.

Benefits: The Tree Pose is excellent for helping one to become more centered in himself (in a spiritual, not in an egoic, sense) and to develop right posture.

Chandrasana

(The Moon Pose)

"Strength and courage fill my body cells."

Stand with your feet together. Inhale slowly; bring your arms out sideways, palms upward, and straight up above your head, joining your hands and rising up on your toes. Stretch upward. Then extend that stretch slowly down to the left, bending at the waist and remaining slightly up on your toes. Affirm mentally, *"Strength and courage fill my body cells."* Try to be aware of this upward movement of energy in your body as if it were the energy itself that is stretching your body and extending your stretch to the left. Breathe naturally when you need to, and hold this pose for approximately 30 seconds. Then inhale, returning to an upright position. Stretch, then exhale and bring your arms slowly down to your sides, settling back onto your heels.

Repeat this pose in the opposite direction.

Benefits: This exercise will help to make you more conscious of the spine, a vital necessity in future poses.

Trikonasana

(The Triangle Pose)

"Energy and joy flood my body cells! Joy descends to me!"

Spread your feet wide apart. Inhale, lifting your arms outward to the side, palms upward. Stretch the arms outward. Then exhale slowly, bending over and slightly forward to the left till your left hand touches your left foot. Extend your right arm upward above your head, turning your head to look up at the outstretched fingers. Affirm mentally, *"Energy and joy flood my body cells! Joy descends to me!"* Hold the pose as long as you find it comfortable—approximately 30 seconds for most people—then return slowly to a standing position, inhaling. Stretch your arms out sideways, palms upward, then slowly exhale as you allow your arms to come down to your sides again.

Repeat the same movement to the right.

Benefits: In the Moon Pose the stretch is completely to the side. In the Triangle Pose there is a slight forward angle to the stoop, which provides a different kind of stretch to the back.

Paschimotanasana

(The Posterior Stretching Pose)

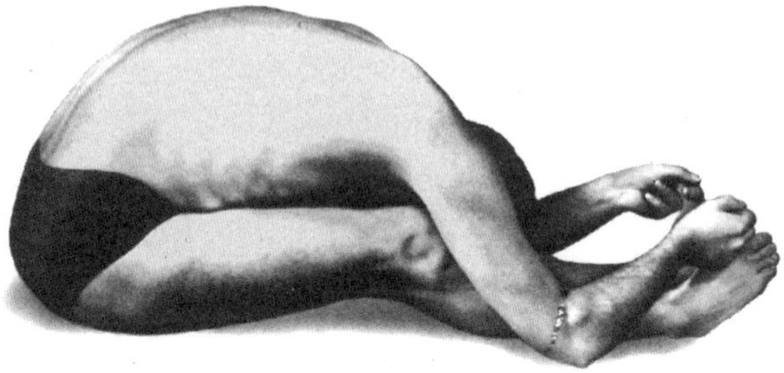

To practice *Paschimotanasana,* sit on the floor with your legs stretched out in front of you. Inhale, then exhale slowly, and slowly stretch, but don't pull, your body forward, offering yourself into the posture. Continue to relax forward, keeping your legs flat on the floor, until your fingers can grasp the big toe of each foot, your elbows can touch the floor, and your whole upper body can rest on your thighs, with your head on your knees or a little below them. The proper way, if you can do it, is to grasp the big toe with the thumb, forefinger, and middle finger of each hand, just as if you were grasping an upright post with them.

This is not an easy posture to assume, particularly for older persons. If you find that you cannot reach your feet, then grasp your ankles, or your knees, or whatever you can to steady your upper body. Be aware of the tension under the knees and at the base of the spine that is preventing you from going farther forward. Think space at those points of tension, and you will notice, surprisingly, that after a few moments you will be able to bend farther forward without any straining. Repeat this process, and over a period of a minute or two you will see that you have bent forward much farther than you may have thought possible. (The more difficult you find this position to practice, by the way, the more vital your need for it!)

Beginners should not hold the pose more than 15 or 30 seconds, but do not fear to do it longer—up to 3 minutes—if you feel that you can comfortably. Then, gradually lie back and rest in a supine position for a minute or two.

Benefits: Paschimotanasana helps to tone up the nervous system. It improves the functioning of the abdominal pelvic organs, and is excellent generally for digestion. Because of its stretching action on the tendons in the legs, it is also an excellent limbering exercise to practice before attempting the more difficult of the sitting postures. (Psychological and spiritual benefits of the pose will be discussed in Step Three.)

Halasana

(The Plow Pose)

"New life, new consciousness now flood my brain!"

This pose is one of the most important in *hatha yoga.* Many parts of the body are benefited by it. Gratifyingly, it is also one of the easier poses to assume, but proceed gently just the same. In all of the yoga postures one should be deeply aware of every body movement, of every muscle that is brought into play. In *Halasana,* because so many parts of the body are involved, this principle of awareness is especially important to keep in mind. Breathe normally in all phases of the Plow Pose.

To assume *Halasana,* first lie flat on your back with your arms down at your sides, palms down. Relax. Then raise both legs simultaneously, keeping them straight, to an angle of approximately 45 degrees from the floor. Be aware of the various muscles involved in the action. Hold this position briefly, feeling the tension in the thighs and abdomen.

Now raise the legs slowly until they are perpendicular to the floor. Hold them there momentarily, feeling the pressure of the entire back against the floor.

Then, starting with the lower spine, release this pressure bit by bit as you continue to bring your legs up over your head, until they are in a position parallel to the floor. Hold this position a few moments, deeply relaxing your spine to prevent any strain when you assume *Halasana* itself. Then come down into the first phase of the Plow Pose:

First Phase: Bring the feet down to the floor as close to your head as is comfortable. Feel the stretch in the lower and middle back. The knees should eventually be right above the eyes, with the legs kept straight.

Second Phase: When you feel relaxed in the First Phase, move the feet back somewhat farther, and feel the stretch extending up into the middle and upper back. Hold this position, too, until you feel relaxed in it.

Third Phase: Then go back as far as you can, and feel the stretch extending up into the upper back and lower neck.

Fourth Phase: Finally, bring your arms up above your head and you will find that you can extend even farther back, stretching the upper vertebrae in the neck. While in the fourth phase, affirm mentally, *"New life, new consciousness now flood my brain!"*

Hold the pose for 30 seconds to begin with—up to 2 minutes with practice—then return slowly back through the different phases to the supine position, lying flat on the floor, and rest awhile.

Benefits: Holding the legs at 45 degrees helps to tone the muscles of the thighs and abdomen. *Halasana* itself is good for the abdominal muscles and for the posture, besides its prime purpose of releasing the energy to flow freely in the upper spine. The third and fourth phases of this pose are beneficial not only for stretching the upper spine and the neck, but also for the gentle stimulation they give the thyroid gland when the chest is pressed hard against the chin. This pose also brings blood into the brain.

III. BREATHING

As I mentioned in the first lesson, the Hindu word for "breath," "life," and "energy" is the same: *prana*. *Prana* surrounds us in the air we breathe. We shall learn in a later lesson how to draw on this *prana* by other means than the breath. The breath is, however, one very important means. We draw not only air into our body when we breathe, but also vitality, strength, courage. When we exhale, we throw out of our system not only carbon dioxide, but also mental and emotional impurities: discouragement, weakness, despair. But inasmuch as these are mental and emotional tendencies, we must use mental "lungs" to draw them into us or to expel them, even as we must use our physical lungs to inhale and exhale air. When a deliberate mental effort is made to absorb *prana* from the air that we breathe, then breathing can give us psycho-spiritual benefits as well.

The movements of *prana* are not only those by which it enters the body through the breath. There are movements of *prana* also within one's own body. These, too, reflect themselves in the breath. When we are emotionally disturbed, the flow of energy in the body is similarly disturbed, and the effect on the breath is instantaneous: The breathing becomes erratic, jerky, rapid. An intimate connection exists between the mind and the breath. This interesting truth can be turned to good advantage, for as the mind influences the breath, so also the breath influences the mind. Harmful emotional states can be overcome to a large extent by deliberate, deep, harmonious breathing.

Books have been written sounding an alarm on the dangers of yogic breathing exercises. A blanket condemnation of breathing exercises is absurd. As Paramhansa Yogananda pointed out, nature obliges man to do one "breathing exercise" all his life if he wishes to remain in this body. There are some exercises, and also some ways of going at these exercises, that can be harmful. We shall discuss this aspect of the subject in a later lesson. For now, let us say only that reasonable caution and common sense are all that are required.

While doing the yoga postures, it is a general principle to breathe in when the body comes up—whether into or out of any position, and to breathe out when the body goes down—either into or out of a position. For example, when coming up into the Moon Pose one should inhale; when coming down out of it, one should exhale. One may breathe normally while holding the position. On the other hand, when going into the Triangle Pose, which involves stooping, one exhales as one goes down into the pose, and inhales as he comes up out of it. There are exceptions to this principle. In the Chair Pose (*Utkatasana*), for example, one inhales as he comes up, but holds the breath all the way down into the crouching position.

As a general principle (there are exceptions in some of the yogic breathing exercises), one should always inhale through the nostrils. The reasons for this principle are subtle as well as obvious. The obvious ones are that breathing through the nostrils filters out dust and impurities that otherwise would enter the lungs, and warms the air before it reaches the delicate inner membranes. The subtle reasons are many, and will be gone into in the course of these lessons. One is that the air coming up through the nostrils cools the brain and clarifies one's thinking. People who breathe habitually through the mouth tend to be somewhat dull-minded. Try sometimes, when you inhale, to feel the air coming up into your brain, refreshing and cooling it.

A Breathing Exercise: The next time you feel moody, depressed, worried, or simply scattered, instead of brooding over why you feel so moody, or worrying over the fact that you worry too much, try breathing your way to better spirits. Inhale very slowly and deeply. Feel that you are inhaling, not merely air, but joy, peace, strength, or courage—whatever positive quality you want especially to affirm. Sit very straight as you practice this exercise. Imagine the breath to be filling not only your lungs, but your whole body, starting at the feet, and culminating at a point midway between the eyebrows. Focus the breath at that point, and hold it there as long as you can do so comfortably; feel that you are burning up all negative thoughts in the blaze of divine light. As you exhale, do so forcibly, expelling forever from your body and mind the last vestiges of weakness and negativity.

Repeat this exercise six or twelve times, or as often as you need to to put the forces of darkness to full flight.

IV. ROUTINE

If you can do the postures with a calm mind and with interiorized awareness, the benefit you derive from them will be vastly greater. Before practicing the postures, sit upright for awhile; do a few breathing exercises, then meditate at least a few moments.

For the next two weeks, try the breathing exercise I have just given you. There is no reason to practice it only when you are in a mental slump. If you start it already in a mood of peace and courage, you will end up only feeling all the more calm and divinely confident. Above all, in your daily postures routine cast out of your body with every exhalation all laziness, hesitation, restlessness, and indifference.

Practice

Vrikasana (the Tree Pose)—30 seconds on each leg. Rest 30 seconds after each practice.

Chandrasana (the Moon Pose)—30 seconds each side. Rest.

Trikonasana (the Triangle Pose)—30 seconds each side.

Utkatasana (the Chair Pose)—30 seconds. Lie down on your back for one or two minutes.

Paschimotanasana (the Posterior Stretching Pose)—30 seconds, followed by another 30 seconds in the supine pose.

Halasana (the Plow Pose)—30 seconds in the final position.

Bhujangasana (the Cobra Pose)—30 seconds.

Sasamgasana (the Hare Pose)—30 seconds to one minute. Lie flat on your back and rest for 2 to 5 minutes.

Approximate total time: 30 minutes

V. HEALING

Integration vs. Disintegration

Integration has become an important issue nowadays in our country. There is a dawning awareness in many people's minds that racial exclusiveness may lead to the disintegration of our society. That such disintegration is an actual possibility is also awakening people to the realization that integration must now be worked towards actively and consciously. It can no longer be awaited passively, in the pleasing expectation that, someday, it will come to pass "naturally."

The issue in which so many people have joined is only one instance of a struggle that is cosmic, and eternal. The whole universe is a battleground, where the forces of integration and of disintegration clash swords in a ceaseless conflict. According to the Second Law of Thermodynamics, everything is moving inexorably toward randomness, losing heat, losing speed, losing definition: in a word, disintegrating. Yet, obviously, some other force is just as actively pulling loose strands together again. Without such a force, there would have been nothing integrated to disintegrate in the first place.

These forces of integration and disintegration battle each other for supremacy in our own lives as well. A simple example is the struggle between health and disease. If we wait passively for nature to take its own course with us, we are already giving strength to the forces of disintegration, which thrive on passivity. To expect things "naturally" to come out all right in the end is not positive thinking, for it is not thinking at all. Integration follows only from actively pulling things together. Disintegration is implied in the very process of "just letting things go."

Health is one product of the integrative process. To achieve glowing health, one must deliberately cooperate with this process. He must develop the body as a whole, not as a bundle of separate parts related together only by the accident of existing together in a more or less common enterprise. He must bring the body and the mind into active harmony with each other. He must, moreover, recognize his kinship with the surrounding universe.

Analysis is the special genius of Western man. He has a natural gift for seeing things in terms of their separate parts. But the human body is far more intricate and subtle than the motor of an automobile. There is a kind of intelligence working in it that is quite independent of the mechanical efficiency of its several parts. There is a vitality in the body which, if high, can bring the whole body into united action to protect any threatened part, even to repair a damaged one. Medical science is obliged to recognize these imponderables, simply because they exist, but the natural bias of Western thinking leads doctors to prefer to think of the body as a machine. What one wants to see is, other things being equal, what one will see. Western medical science still concentrates on—and is extremely skilled in—repairing or replacing defective parts. It does little, however, to strengthen the entire bodily system, and thereby to give defective parts a chance to repair themselves.

In this almost exclusive attention to the individual parts of the body, as if they were separate bits of machinery, and not parts of a living whole, one is tempted to see the forces of disintegration, not of integration, at work. Perhaps it is unfair to say so, considering the miracles medical science has performed. Yet I remember listening to a recent advertisement on the radio: "Medical research over recent decades has made tremendous advances. Now, the problems are greater than ever. So—give to the United Crusade." I couldn't help thinking, if after all these years the problems are greater than ever, maybe we ought to try taking a new tack!

Yoga says, learn more and more to think of your body and mind as an integral whole. Live in your body, instead of merely existing in it. True health implies a buoyant sense of vitality. It is not merely an absence of fever.

It has been found that people who maintain a cheerful outlook, who forget themselves serving others, and who are always constructively busy, rarely become ill. They simply haven't time to be ill! If you concentrate on illness, you will tend to become ill more frequently. If you concentrate on health, you will usually be healthy.

People, again, who feel a deep sense of kinship with life and with objective Nature seem actually to draw strength from them. People, on the other hand, who selfishly isolate themselves from the surrounding universe seem to grow old prematurely; even in their youth they never seem to be vital, complete human beings.

Remember, integration must be consciously worked for. It takes energy to generate more energy, a sense of harmony to develop greater harmony, a unifying zeal to achieve perfect unity, which is yoga. Left to itself, the natural trend is that of the Second Law of Thermodynamics, a trend toward gradual disintegration. It is up to you to live in the divine trend of self-integration.

VI. DIET

To return one's body to a natural state, it is necessary to eat natural foods. In our modern age, emphasis in diet, as in medicine, is on the unnatural, on the man-made. The result of wrong diet, as of other forms of wrong living, is disease.

We shall talk more in the next lesson about unnatural foods. In this lesson, let us consider an interesting emphasis of the yoga teachings, one that is related not only to natural diet, but also to the principle of relaxation—so vital to self-integration that we have just considered in the foregoing section.

Yogis emphasize the importance of food that is cooling to the system. Harmful food, they say, heats the system by introducing impurities into it that block the normal flow of *prana* in the body. Resistance to an electrical current will heat the wire through which the electricity passes. The same thing happens with resistance to the flow of *prana* through the nervous system. Heat is only a symptom of a system that is not working as freely and harmoniously as it should. The principle is similar to that of heat that is produced by friction. It is no accident that when we tell someone to relax, we may say, "Keep cool." When a person is upset, on the other hand, we may describe him as "hot and bothered." Emotions have a heating or a cooling effect on the entire nervous system; so also do foods.

Excessively spiced foods, alcoholic beverages, too many carbohydrates, artificial stimulants, and stale or devitalized foods are unnatural to the body and are said to have a heating effect on it. Overcooked foods have a similar effect. Fresh fruits, nuts, raw or lightly cooked vegetables, milk or fresh milk products, and also whole grains are said to be cooling to the nervous system. Anything that excites the body is heating to it; anything that relaxes it is cooling.

Try this cooling beverage: Combine two parts plain yogurt to one part water. Add sugar (preferably raw or brown) or honey to taste. The taste of the finished drink should be neither sweet nor sour. Stir well and drink. A quarter of a lime may be added to this drink, if desired.

Or try this drink: A quarter of a fresh lime in a glass of water, sweetened with brown sugar or honey in such a way that the sweet and sour tastes balance each other. Both of these drinks are said to be cooling to the entire system.

Yogis believe in mixing yogurt liberally with their cooked vegetables, either in the cooking process or towards the end of a meal. You can make your own yogurt (or *dahi,* as it is called in India) by mixing a tablespoonful of yogurt with one pint of boiled lukewarm milk. Keep this mixture in a warm place for twelve to eighteen hours. When the culture is set, the *dahi* is ready. You may use a tablespoonful of this new culture to make successive batches.

Another way to make *dahi* is to put one or two tablespoonsful of lime juice or lemon juice in a pint of boiled lukewarm milk. Let it set as above. This first setting will be thin, but if you use a tablespoonful or two of this mixture again in a pint of milk, as above, it will make still better *dahi.* The *dahi* will improve with every successive batch.

Yogurt is good even for those people who are allergic to milk. Incidentally, for milk allergy (excessive mucous, for example) goat's milk will be an excellent substitute. An excellent fresh cheese can be made by boiling a little more lemon juice in a potful of milk. The curds will separate from the whey. The mixture may be poured into a cheesecloth or muslin bag and allowed to drip overnight.

VII. MEDITATION

Don't put meditation in the "someday-when-I-find-the-time-for-it" category of your life. If you make it a point to meditate daily, you will soon see that the mental efficiency you derive from this practice will actually give you the time to get all those other things done which now seem so difficult to squeeze into your busy schedule. Your problems will be solved much more easily. Your work will be done much more quickly, because your energies will now be focused, not diffused. Success in everything demands that you act from your inner center, and not merely as the breezes of circumstance happen to blow you. Meditation, because it brings you to this inner center and thereby facilitates every other activity, should be your first duty in life.

If you can set aside a room in your home as a little chapel, and use it only for meditation, you will find in the course of only a few months that it will develop an "atmosphere" of peace which will help you to go deep when you sit to meditate. Places develop vibrations of their own according to the activities that take place in them. If you cannot set aside a special room, try at least to screen off a portion of your bedroom for meditation.

Part of the process of neutralizing the eddies of feeling, or chitta, in the mind (Patanjali's definition of yoga, which was treated earlier in this lesson), is an effort to align oneself with the forces of nature. In this way the mainstream of life may be used as an aid in drawing us out of our own egoistic eddies.

Yogis say that there are certain magnetic currents which flow from east to west. (Certain Western thinkers have made the observation that the development of civilization itself seems to flow in a westward direction.) If you will face east when you meditate, you will receive these currents; they will help you to attain inner enlightenment. North, too, is said to be a good direction; facing in this direction in meditation helps one to become mentally free of physical limitations. (It is curious to notice how often, in worldly conflicts, the north seems to represent the consciousness of liberation—as in the Civil War in America. Sometimes liberation can represent only chaos, and a disintegration of true values. Thus we see the wild hordes that, many centuries ago, repeatedly invaded England from the north, or the vandals that sacked Rome, or the socially destructive forces of communism in North Korea and North Vietnam.) It is better to face east, because one must attain enlightenment before he can be liberated from all karma.

Yogis say also that certain hours of the day are especially good for meditation: sunrise and sunset (when the sun is at right angles to the pull of the earth on our bodies), noon (when the sun's pull opposes that of the earth), and midnight (when the two bodies pull together). These are said to be "rest points" in Nature, when the energy-flow in our bodies is brought into temporary (if relative) balance. If you cannot meditate these hours, then at least try to meditate at the same times every day—for the same reason, essentially, that a separate meditation room is helpful: You will come gradually to associate those hours strictly with meditation, and will find it much easier to dismiss for that time all worldly thoughts from your mind.

If one would flow with the beneficial currents of Nature, he must also protect himself against those which are detrimental to his meditative efforts. Yogis say that there are subtle currents in the earth (other than the force of gravity) which pull the energy-currents in the body downward. The goal of yoga practice is to direct this energy-flow toward the brain. Yogis advise, as an insulation against this downward pull of earth currents, that one sit on what they call an *asan* when he meditates: a deerskin, or a woolen blanket. For still better insulation, cover the woolen blanket or other fur with a silk cloth.

Any comfortable sitting position will do, provided that the spine is kept straight, and the body relaxed. There are several sitting poses that *hatha* yogis recommend, which will be taught later in these lessons. For now, you may simply sit cross-legged on your *asan*. Even a chair would be quite all right; in this case, your *asan* should extend under your feet, and up over the back of the chair.

Place your hands palms upward on the thighs at the junction of the abdomen. Keep your chest up (but relaxed), and your shoulder blades drawn slightly together. Thus your body will resemble a bow, drawn into a position of spiritual readiness by the straight "string" of the spine.

Calm yourself in this position by practicing the breathing exercise in this or in the last lesson. Then practice the meditation exercise that was given in the last lesson.

Relax when you meditate. Don't strain. Everything in this world is done by straining—or so it seems to the worldly mind. But meditation comes only by deeper and deeper relaxation: physical, emotional, mental, and spiritual.

AUM, *Shanti, Shanti, Shanti!*

Step Three
Patanjali's Ashtanga Yoga

I. PHILOSOPHY

Patanjali's Ashtanga Yoga: *The Eightfold Path*

Hatha yoga is the physical branch of the meditative science of *raja yoga.* Patanjali, the great ancient exponent of *raja yoga,* wrote that the path to enlightenment embraces eight stages. (His teaching is also known as *ashtanga,* or "eight-limbed," *yoga.*) An explanation of these eight "limbs" will help to give an understanding of the deeper purposes and directions of yoga. It will help also in the study of the yoga postures.

The first two stages of Patanjali's eightfold path are known as *yama* and *niyama. Yama* means control; *niyama,* non-control. Literally, these two stages mean the don'ts and the do's on the spiritual path. They are, one might say, the Ten Commandments of yoga. Interestingly, there are ten of them, too. We shall discuss them in detail later. Their essential purpose is to permit the milk of inner peace to be gathered in the pail of the mind by plugging holes that have been caused by restlessness, wrong attachments, desires, and various forms of inharmonious living.

The rules of *yama* (the don'ts) are five:

Non-Violence or *Ahimsa*
Non-Lying
Non-Stealing
Non-Sensuality or *Brahmacharya*
Non-Greed or Non-Attachment

It is interesting to note that all of these virtues are listed in negative terms. The implication is that when we remove our delusions, we cannot but be benevolent, truthful, respectful of others' property, etc., because it is our nature to be good. We act otherwise not because it is natural for us to do so, but because we have embraced an unnatural state of egoistical inharmony.

The rules of *niyama* (the do's) are:

Cleanliness
Contentment
Austerity
Self-Study or Introspection
Devotion to the Supreme Lord

Each of these principles, when practiced perfectly, bestows definite spiritual rewards, as we shall see in Step Four.

The third stage on the eightfold path is known as *asana,* which means, simply, posture. Some writers have tried to make the point that Patanjali refers here to the need for practicing the yoga postures as a preparation for meditation. But Patanjali was talking, not of practices, but of the different stages of spiritual development. Here, then, posture means no particular set of postures, but only the ability to hold the body still as a prerequisite for deep meditation. Any comfortable posture will do, as long as the spine is kept erect and the body relaxed. A sign of perfection in *asana* is said to be the ability to sit still, without moving a muscle, for three hours. Many people meditate for years without achieving any notable results, simply because they have never trained their bodies to sit still. Until the body can be mastered, higher perceptions, so subtle that they blossom only in perfect quiet, can never be achieved.

It is good, of course, to practice some of the yoga postures before meditation. These postures help one to attain *asana,* or firm posture. Many beginning students, however, make the mistake of assuming that they must perfect their practice of the yoga postures before even attempting to meditate. This is quite untrue. It is not even necessary to practice the postures at all in order to learn meditation. The postures are only an aid, though a very great one, to meditation.

The fourth stage of Patanjali's path is *pranayama.* Many writers, again making the mistake of thinking that Patanjali was speaking of practices rather than of the different stages of spiritual development, have claimed that here he was referring to breathing exercises. *Pranayama,* even as a spiritual practice, is connected only secondarily with the breath. It is a mistake (though one often made) to identify this word solely with breath control. *Prana* does mean breath, but only because of the close connection that exists between the breath and the causative flow of energy in the body. The word *prana* refers primarily to the energy itself. *Pranayama,* then, means energy control. This energy control is often effected with the aid of breathing exercises. Hence, breathing exercises have also come to be known as *pranayama*s.

Patanjali's reference is to the energy control that is achieved *as a result* of various techniques, and not to the techniques themselves. His word signifies a state in which the energy in the body is harmonized to the point where its flow is reversed—no longer outward toward the senses, but inward toward the Divine Self that lies in the hearts of all beings. Only when all the energy in the body can be directed toward this Self can one's awareness be intense enough to penetrate the veils of delusion and enter superconsciousness.

The very energy with which we think is the same energy that we use to digest our food. To test this claim, consider how difficult it is, after a heavy meal, to think about weighty problems, and how clear the mind becomes after a fast. To divert all the energy from the body to the brain cannot but intensify one's awareness, and the keenness of one's understanding. To direct this energy inwardly is the first step in divine contemplation.

The fifth stage on Patanjali's journey is known as *pratyahara,* the interiorization of the mind. Once the energy has been redirected towards its source in the brain, one must then interiorize one's consciousness, so that his thoughts, too, will not wander in endless by-paths of restlessness and delusion, but will be focused one-pointedly on the deeper mysteries of the indwelling soul. A thread must be gathered to one point before it can be put through the eye of a needle. Similarly with the mind: It is necessary to concentrate one's thoughts as well as one's energies, if he would hope to penetrate the narrow tunnel that leads to divine awakening.

Patanjali's sixth stage is known as *dharana,* contemplation, or fixed inner awareness. One may have been aware of inner spiritual realities—the inner light, for instance, or the inner sound, or deep mystical feelings—before reaching this stage, but it is only after reaching it that one can give himself completely to deep concentration on those realities.

The seventh stage is known as *dhyana,* meditation, absorption. By prolonged concentration on any stage of consciousness, one begins to assume to himself its qualities. By meditating on sense pleasures, the Inner Self comes to identify its happiness with the gratification of those pleasures; the individual loses sight of the indwelling Self as the real *source* of his pleasures. (If anything material were really a cause of happiness, it would cause happiness to all men. The fact that it does not proves that it is our reactions to those things, rather than the things themselves, that give us our enjoyment.) Again, by concentration on our personal faults, we only give strength to those faults. (It is a serious mistake continually to call oneself a sinner, as many orthodox religionists would have one do. One should concentrate on virtue if he would become virtuous.) By concentrating on the inner light, then, or upon any other divine reality that one actually perceives when the mind is calm, one gradually takes on the qualities of that inner reality. The mind loses its ego identification, and begins to merge in the great ocean of consciousness of which it is a part.

The eighth step on Patanjali's eightfold journey is known as *samadhi,* oneness. *Samadhi* comes after one learns to dissolve his ego consciousness in the calm inner light. Once the grip of ego has really been broken, and one discovers that he *is* that light, there is nothing to prevent him from expanding his consciousness to infinity. The devotee in deep *samadhi* realizes the truth of Christ's words, "I and my Father are one." The little wave of light, losing its delusion of separate existence from the ocean of light, becomes itself the vast ocean.

In the higher stages of *samadhi,* the devotee is able not only to retain his sense of identity with the Infinite Ocean, but also to be aware of and work through the little wave of his ego. He can talk, work, smile, and live in all ways as a normal human being, yet never lose his inward realization of Divinity.

It must not be imagined that these states are delusive. They are Reality; our present limitation is the delusion. Great yogis have demonstrated their omnipresence in many ways. Interested students would do well to read Paramhansa Yogananda's *Autobiography of a Yogi,* which describes many such great souls and their experience with God.

These subtle stages of spiritual unfoldment may be achieved, on a lower level, in normal human existence. For just as a high mountain has in common with a little mound the fact that both slope upwards to a peak, so the highest truths relate also in practical ways to everyday life. This, in fact, is the immediate reason why every intelligent person can benefit from studying philosophy.

The need for applying the basic moral commandments of yoga to daily life will be obvious, and requires no special comment here. But *asana* (physical calmness), too, is necessary, lest we scatter our forces, and even undermine our health. We need also to channel our energies (the principle of *pranayama*) if we would really accomplish anything worthwhile. Self-sufficiency, and the ability to remain at peace in oneself (the spirit, in other words, of *pratyahara*), is the mark of a poised and gracious human being, whether or not he ever thinks of spiritual realities. And to be sensitively aware of life, finally, to enter into it, to become in a sense one with it (reminiscent of the final stages of yoga: *dharana, dhyana,* and *samadhi*) is the genius of what is normally considered a fully alive, but not necessarily supernormal, human being.

These subtle stages of yoga should be expressed also in one's daily practice of the yoga postures.

The first two stages, *yama* and *niyama,* are necessary for any real progress in the postures. Without them the postures become simply a system of calisthenics—good for a few muscles and bones, but not much more.

The next stage, *asana* or physical stability, is necessary also. If one practices the postures hastily and restlessly, the benefits that he receives from them will be minimal. One must practice slowly, hold each posture for a time, and above all maintain an *attitude* of physical relaxation and control.

An understanding of *pranayama,* also, is essential to *hatha yoga,* not only because of the breathing exercises involved, but also because, until one is aware of the movements of energy in the body, and of the effect of the postures upon those movements, one cannot attain the deeper benefits of *hatha yoga.*

Pratyahara (interiorization), too, is necessary. Unless one interiorizes his consciousness while performing the postures, the benefits he derives from them will be superficial. It is a good practice, therefore, before beginning the postures, to calm oneself within and without, so that when he begins his "daily dozen" his mind will be in a state of quasi-meditation.

The foregoing paragraph explains the need for *dharana* (calm inner awareness) in the practice of yoga postures. Concentration on what one is attempting to accomplish can increase the value of the postures up to a hundred times.

What one is striving to accomplish with the postures is to make himself over anew. Here, then, we see the value of *dhyana* in the practice of the yoga postures. Every posture is associated with certain mental and spiritual states which, if one meditates on them while doing the posture, will come to him more easily than if he goes through the postures absent-mindedly, or thinking only of their physical benefits. From the standpoint of physical health, too, if one meditates on health, affirming it with every fiber of his being while he practices the postures, they will speed him on the road to perfect health more quickly than if he merely goes through the postures automatically, with his mind roaming in foreign lands.

Samadhi, finally, applied to the postures, signifies a state where one has so established himself in physical and mental harmony that all of his daily movements become, in a sense, yoga postures, proceeding from the creative source within himself. He is practicing *hatha yoga* not only when he moves into some anciently prescribed position, but even when he gets up out of bed, greets a neighbor on the street, or lifts a cup of tea to his lips. His every smile will be a yogic mudra, awakening energy that conveys itself as joy to all who behold him.

II. YOGA POSTURES

I have already pointed out the importance of being aware enough of one's body to relax it, and of *relaxing* into every pose instead of forcing oneself into it. It is time now to learn the supreme relaxation pose, *Savasana* (the Corpse Pose).

On the surface, this would seem to be the simplest of all the poses to assume. In fact, however, because relaxation itself is so difficult, perfection in *Savasana* is rarely attained.

To practice *Savasana,* lie on the floor. Turn the palms of your hands upward (this position will help to induce a feeling of relaxation and of mental receptivity). The head, neck, trunk, and legs should be in a straight line. One should not use a pillow in this position; the flow of blood should be equal to all parts of the body.

I have said that awareness is the necessary precursor of relaxation. There are many parts of the body that are tense without our conscious knowledge. How are we to become enough aware of them to relax them? The answer is, by increasing the tension throughout the body. Often it happens on a psychological level that we only overcome our faults when they have become so exaggerated as to be obvious to us. The same is true with physical tension. The best way to induce preliminary relaxation in the body is first to inhale, tense the whole body (equalizing the flow of tension throughout the body), then throw the breath out and relax the entire body at once.

After this preliminary relaxation (which you may repeat two or three times), lie very still. Be aware of your breath, if you like. You may watch it in the nostrils, or simply be mentally aware of the rhythmic rise and fall of your navel. As your calmness deepens, feel your consciousness becoming centered increasingly at the point between the eyebrows.

Now, strive for *deep* relaxation. Think of your body as surrounded by space—space in all directions spreading out to infinity.

Now think of your feet, and visualize this space gradually seeping through the pores of the skin into your feet, until your feet become space. Visualize this space as gradually coming up into the calves, thighs, hips, the abdomen and stomach, the hands, forearms, upper arms, shoulders, chest, the back of the neck, sides of the neck, the throat, jaw, tongue, lips, cheeks, eyes, and brain. In feeling space in your brain, release from your mind all regrets about the past, all worries about the future. Rest in the infinite ocean of the eternal Present. The objects of endless human concern no longer exist. There is nothing in all eternity but the Right Here, the Right Now.

Affirm mentally: *"Bones, muscles, movement I surrender now; anxiety, elation and depression, churning thoughts: All these I give into the hands of peace."*

Savasana may be practiced more briefly between the other postures, until the heartbeat and the breathing have returned to normal. At the end of one's posture session, however, one should go into deep relaxation in *Savasana* for at least five or ten minutes, or until you have felt the deeper rejuvenating effects of total relaxation.

Relaxation may be particularized after each posture. If you have been stretching a particular part of the body (as, for example, the lower back in the Posterior Stretching Pose), while doing *Savasana* after it concentrate especially upon the relaxation of the lower back, rather than on the relaxation of the whole body.

Benefits: Savasana brings supreme relaxation; helps in the development of receptivity, so important to yogic practice; rejuvenates the body cells; and aids in mental and physical healing.

Savasana

(The Corpse Pose)

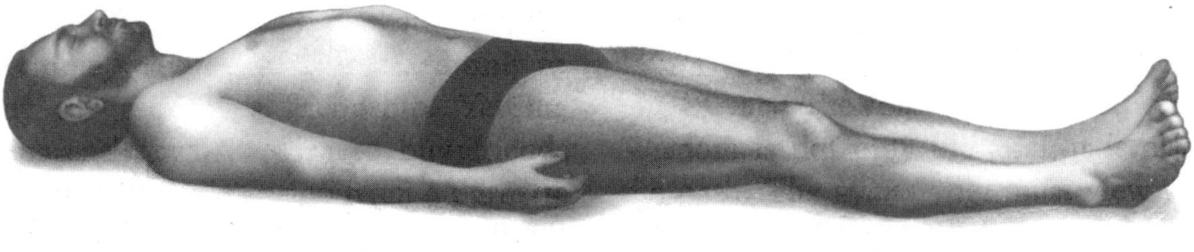

"Bones, muscles, movement I surrender now; anxiety, elation and depression, churning thoughts — all these I give into the hands of peace."

Paschimotanasana

(The Posterior Stretching Pose)

"I am safe, I am sound. All good things come to me; they give me peace!"

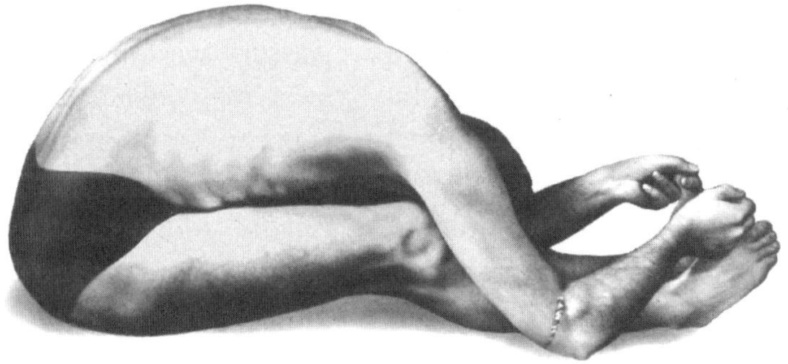

Since I have just mentioned *Paschimotanasana,* it would be well, now that you have been practicing it for two weeks, to include in your practice an awareness of its mental and spiritual benefits.

In *Paschimotanasana* the main stretch is, as the name of the posture implies, in the lower part of the back. There is also a stretch in the tendons behind the knees—a secondary, but very real, purpose of the exercise. The stretch in the lower back releases the energy to flow freely to and from that area of the spine. The stretch behind the knees, too, is useful in more ways than physical: It helps to release certain deep-seated psychological tensions.

Modern-day insecurity creates in man many tensions. Among these is a chronic tightness behind the knees—the result of a mental shrinking away from expected dangers and difficulties. Releasing the tension behind the knees can help, indirectly, to overcome this sense of insecurity. Coupled with mental affirmation, especially while resting in *Savasana* after the practice, the effect can be considerable.

It might be well, therefore, to practice this posture twice, first giving special attention to the knees; second, to the lower spine. During the rest period following the first practice, concentrate on the feeling of release in the legs behind the knees and affirm: *"I am safe. I am sound. All good things come to me; they give me peace!"* After the second practice, feel the surge of joy and vitality rising from your lower spine toward the brain.

III. BREATHING

It is time we learned the Full Yogic Breath. Most people do not breathe as they should, owing to faulty posture, to wrong mental habits, and possibly even to the reluctance one feels in our modern environment to breathe air that is so generally impure. (Notice how you often may tend to curb your natural breathing process when driving on the freeways, or through a tunnel thick with exhaust fumes.)

To breathe properly, one should begin with the diaphragm—that membrane which separates the lungs from the visceral cavity. The diaphragm works by a downward movement that causes the lungs to expand, creating a lower air pressure within the lungs than outside the body. Thus, air is drawn into the lungs. The downward movement of the diaphragm forces the stomach a little outward. If your stomach does not expand as you inhale, you are not breathing diaphragmatically.

Considering how important the diaphragm is to the breathing mechanism, it is alarming how small a percentage of people breathe with it at all. Women are the worst offenders, owing no doubt to their wish to appear slender. (Can a "wasp-waisted" semi-invalid be compared in beauty to one who is in the full bloom of health? Without proper breathing, true health is impossible.) There are of course many causes of faulty diaphragmatic action. Poor posture is one. When a person stoops forward habitually, he cannot breathe diaphragmatically. Another cause is mental tension. Ulcers are but a symptom of stomach tension—the result of intense mental anxiety. When the stomach is kept always tensed, diaphragmatic breathing is impossible. With diaphragmatic breathing, however, this tension may be gradually overcome. Proper breathing is, indeed, one of the most effective forms of psychotherapy.

One of the best ways to learn to breathe diaphragmatically is to lie flat on your back in *Savasana*. Practice the whole technique of *Savasana* as explained in the foregoing section, finally watching the navel rise and fall with the respiration. When the body is perfectly relaxed, as it is in sleep, diaphragmatic breathing becomes natural and effortless.

The diaphragmatic expansion is only the first part of the full natural breathing process that has come to be called the Full Yogic Breath. The next stage is the outward movement of the floating ribs. People who hold themselves mentally too much inward from the threat of the world around them tend to become tensed physically around the sides of the ribs. People who breathe freely sidewise tend to be courageous, expansive in their outlook. A deliberate effort to breathe outward sidewise can help one to develop these wholesome attitudes.

The third stage in a Full Yogic Breath is the one to which many people, women especially, limit themselves, though too few people breathe properly even here: the upper part of the chest. Development of the upper chest is associated with the capacity for feeling, for emotional expression. People whose chests are flat in the region above the breasts tend to be over-intellectual, emotionally repressed. Men are particularly at fault here. In the Full Yogic Breath, the lungs are finally expanded to include this upper portion. By learning to breathe deeply here, one can help to enrich his capacity for emotional feeling.

Apart from *Savasana,* a good technique for learning the Full Yogic Breath is to stand up and inhale as deeply as you can in a smooth, flowing motion. Again, begin with the diaphragm; continue to the sides of the rib cage; lastly, fill the upper part of the lungs. Hold the breath several moments, and then exhale slowly in reverse order.

It may help you to breathe more deeply if you begin by stooping forward, your arms hanging limply before you. Exhale. Inhale first with the diaphragm, and feel that the downward movement of this membrane, in pushing the stomach outward, is forcing your body gradually into an upright position. Feel also, as you inhale, that you are filling your lungs from the diaphragm, and not only your lungs, but your whole body with air. Straighten up slowly, and bring your arms upward, your elbows out to the sides, your hands close to the body. Feel that you are stretching your rib cage outward, filling the middle part of your lungs. Then, with a graceful movement, extend the arms upward and outward above your head, filling the upper part of your lungs, and imagine that the air is filling your arms all the way to the fingertips.

Hold this position momentarily, then exhale slowly, lowering your arms and stooping forward again.

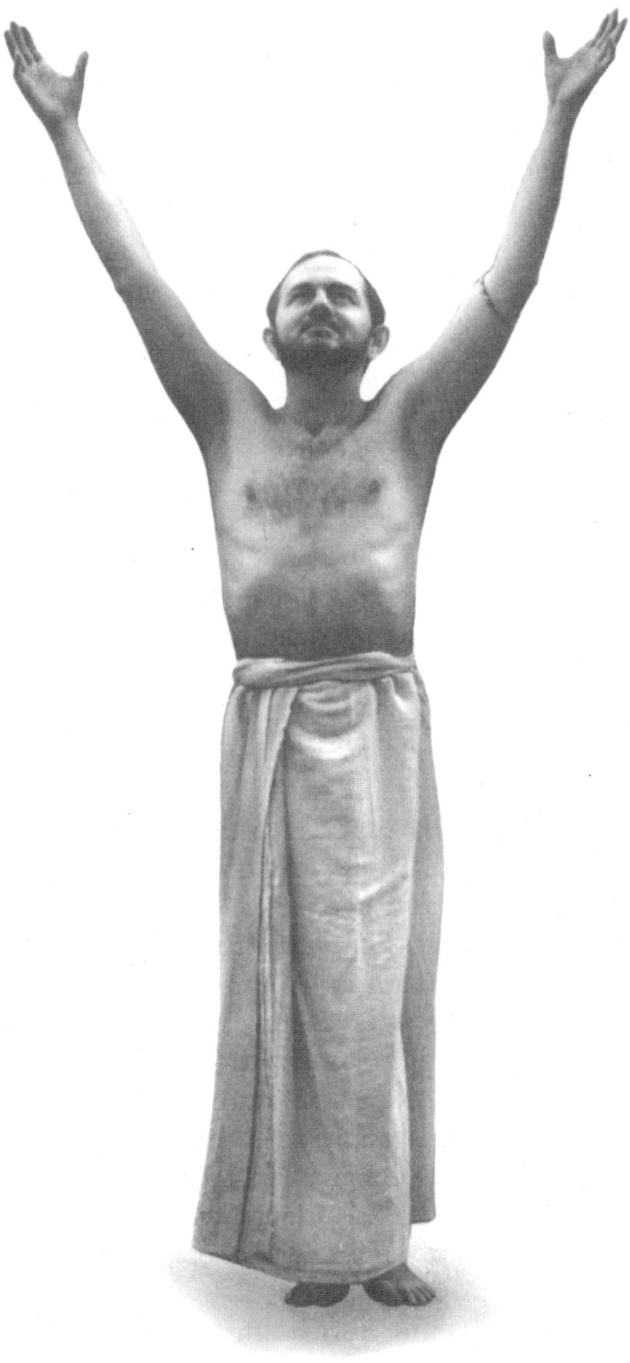

Full Yogic Breath

With every inhalation, feel that you are drawing, not air only, but strength, vitality, and joy into every body cell, from the toes all the way up to the crown of your head.

With every exhalation, feel that you are expelling from your mental world all weakness and negativity.

With the last exhalation, lower your arms, but remain standing upright.

With or without the foregoing movement of body and arms, the Full Yogic Breath is a good exercise for filling the body with energy, particularly when you are fasting. Also, the practice of deliberate, slow, deep breathing several times a day will gradually accustom your lungs to proper breathing habits. This does not mean that correct breathing must always be slow and deep. But this deep breathing practice will in time relax whatever muscular restriction there is around the diaphragm, the sides, and the upper part of the chest, permitting the breath to flow freely and naturally at all times.

IV. ROUTINE

Begin with deep, slow breathing, filling your whole body with air and with energy. Sit in meditation awhile. Then stand up and do the Full Yogic Breath, raising the hands high above the head as you inhale.

Follow with the same routine of postures as was given in the last lesson, except that where the instructions say to lie down, lie down in *Savasana* (the Corpse Pose).

Practice

Vrikasana (the Tree Pose)—30 seconds on each leg. Rest 30 seconds after each practice.

Chandrasana (the Moon Pose)—30 seconds each side. Rest.

Trikonasana (the Triangle Pose)—30 seconds each side.

Utkatasana (the Chair Pose)—30 seconds. Lie down on your back for one or two minutes.

Paschimotanasana (the Posterior Stretching Pose)—30 seconds, followed by another 30 seconds in the supine pose.

Halasana (the Plow Pose)—30 seconds in the final position.

Bhujangasana (the Cobra Pose)—30 seconds.

Sasamgasana (the Hare Pose)—30 seconds to one minute.

Savasana (the Corpse Pose)—2 to 5 minutes.

Approximate total time: 30 minutes

V. HEALING

Hypertension and Nervousness

The twin chief curses of modern times have been said to be hypertension and nervousness. Both are essentially mental disorders, but the physical results of these disorders are far from pleasant: sleeplessness, exhaustion, an inability to digest food properly—such a host of ailments, indeed, that one would find it difficult to name them all.

The deep breathing that we have described in Section III is a *must* for people suffering from these ailments. However, the energy that one brings into his body by breathing and by other practices must be introduced with a consideration for the present state of one's nerves. Too much energy could overwhelm an already weakened nervous system. Proceed gradually, therefore, and remember above all to be calm and relaxed in *all* your yoga practices.

Postures that incorporate deep, slow breathing—*Savasana* in particular—will be invaluable. The first phase of the Hare Pose, which was taught in Step One, will be extremely beneficial. So also will be the Cobra Pose and the Bow Pose. Among the postures that have not yet been considered, most helpful will be the Headstand, the Shoulder Stand, and the Lotus Pose. But all the poses in one way or another help to calm the nervous system.

Diet (particularly fruits, and the foods that were described in the last lesson) is also important.

Of supreme importance is environment, both natural and human. The subtle influences of the city act harmfully on the nervous system, deranging it. The impurities in the air, the speed of the traffic, the threat to one's privacy that is felt from the crowds, the heterogeneous vibrations of countless human beings with diverse and conflicting desires and interests—all of these conspire to produce tension, the supreme disease of our times. The countryside, by contrast, and the spiritual environment of harmonious people are a powerful influence for peace.

At The Expanding Light, our guest facility (near Grass Valley, California), we have seen the effect on newcomers of even a two-weeks' stay. Their eyes begin to shine, their faces to look relaxed; everything about them suggests a growing inner harmony and peace. It is necessary to reassure people who must in any case live in the city that they can find truth wherever they are, but there is no gainsaying that anyone who is free to come to a spiritual environment, even for brief visits, will find himself making spiritual progress a great deal more rapidly.

If one cannot live full-time in a wholesome environment, every effort should be made to surround oneself with spiritually magnetic influences: spiritual music, spiritual books, spiritual thoughts. Shun the company of people who would pull you down from your state of peace. Do not waste too much time on what my guru used to call "fillers": television, magazines, radio, etc.

There is no person, no matter how nervous or tense, who cannot overcome this condition to a large extent, even perfectly, with time and patience. The most restless person on earth can become a shining example of peace.

VI. DIET

Go into any supermarket and examine the labels on the countless attractive packages. Look to see what the ingredients are, and note the various chemicals that are added to preserve the food, to make it tastier, to add color, etc.

Still the whole story has not been told.

What about all the wholesome ingredients that they took *out* of the food? If you leave the wheat germ in the wheat when you grind it to flour, the wheat will in time turn rancid. For the preservation of the flour the wheat germ is usually removed. White flour, similarly, is not only less coarse to chew upon; it also keeps longer. In fact, if you place a barrel of white flour next to a barrel of whole wheat flour, and allow the bugs to get at both of the barrels, you will notice that they are not even interested in the white so long as they can get to the brown. The white is lifeless; it doesn't tempt them. In this sense, modern man shows less discrimination than a beetle!

Missionary ladies in the Philippines in 1898 took pity on the natives for their wretched diet. These "unhappy" people ate nothing but brown rice. Lovingly, the missionary ladies introduced the natives to a diet of white rice. Beriberi, an illness which soon assumed epidemic proportions, was finally traced to this change of diet.

White flour, white rice, white sugar, and other similarly refined products may taste better, look more "refined" (this they certainly are!), or pamper teeth that won't chew anything coarser than Cream of Wheat, but they are exceedingly harmful to the human body and nervous system. Many diseases have been traced to them. Indeed, one might almost say that there is a direct correlation between the devitalization of food and the devitalization of the human being who eats it.

To repeat what I have said before, try to eat only natural foods, as close to their natural condition as possible. It would be good to eat fruits in season. There is a natural rhythm in nature as it passes through the four seasons. Man's body, being a part of nature, enters into this rhythm. Man would do well to harmonize himself with the seasonal products. An added advantage in doing so would be, of course, that foods in season tend to be less expensive!

Because wheat germ has a tendency to turn rancid, it is generally removed even from whole wheat flour, if the flour is sold in a store. The best plan then, if one wants flour that is truly made from the whole kernel, is to grind one's own wheat as he needs it.

RECIPES

An excellent form of bread is the Indian *chappati:*

Chappati

2½ cups whole wheat flour
about 1 cup water
1 tablespoon *ghee* (see next page)
or other oil
1 teaspoon salt (optional)

The Indian recipe calls for 1 teaspoon of salt, but yogis have always said that mineral salt is not good for the human system. Salt is obtained in a natural form from the vegetables one eats.

Put 2 cups of flour through a sieve into a mixing bowl; add the salt, if desired, and gradually stir in the water. Pound and knead the mixture with the hands for several minutes. For best results, let the dough stand for at least an hour, then knead once again, if necessary sprinkling a little more water onto it. Shape each *chappati* by breaking off a small portion of the dough, molding it into a ball, and, with the help of a little dry flour, rolling the ball out very thin and round like a pancake. Fry it on a lightly greased iron frying pan, first on one side, quickly, then on the other, then back again.

The *chappati* has to be cooked quickly, otherwise it will become hard. It should rise like a balloon; it can be encouraged to do so by pressing the sides while on the frying pan, or by placing the already-fried *chappati* over direct heat for a few moments, turning it quickly.

Oil or *ghee* may be spread lightly on one side of the *chappati* after it has been fried.

Whole Wheat Bread

1 cup milk
3 tablespoons liquid honey
2 teaspoons sea salt
2 tablespoons oil
1 cake fresh yeast or 2½ teaspoons granular yeast (1 package)
½ cup cold water
½ cup warm water
4–5 cups (approx.) whole wheat flour

Scald milk. Add honey, salt, and oil. Stir until dissolved. Add ½ cup cold water (should make mixture lukewarm). Dissolve yeast in ½ cup of warm water; add to first mixture.

Gradually add 4 cups flour. Mix to smooth, stiff dough. Knead on lightly floured board until smooth and satiny, adding more flour if the dough is too moist. Put dough in mixing bowl, turning the dough over to oil the top. Keep in a warm place covered for about an hour, or until double in size. Knead again. Shape into a loaf, and place in a greased 9" x 5" bread pan. Let rise about 45 minutes to an hour, and bake in a moderate oven (350°) for about 40 minutes, or until a rich brown color and hollow sounding when the loaf is tapped on the bottom.

Ghee
(Clarified Butter)

In the last lesson I mentioned the "cooling" properties of certain foods. In this connection yogis often stress the benefits of *ghee*, or clarified butter. It may be used in cooking, or in place of butter. It has a very different taste from butter; it is quite sweet. Some people like it instantly; others must acquire a taste for it. It *is* good for you, and it will keep indefinitely. (There is a recipe for a certain religious ceremony in India that calls for the use of ghee a thousand years old!)

Place as much butter as you want to clarify in a saucepan, and simmer very slowly for one to one-and-a-half hours. You may also place the pan in the oven at a low temperature for the same length of time. Remove the pan from the heat and strain the melted butter through a fine cloth.

VII. MEDITATION

Every now and then one hears a farmer or a construction worker say of some member of his own sex that works in an office: "Why doesn't he do a *man's* work?" Businessmen sometimes scoff that artists, no matter how dedicated to their work, are "unproductive." A promoter of phonograph records was once asked by a friend of mine to listen to the first recording of my songs, *Say "YES" to Life!* These songs are presented in such a way as (hopefully) to attract people to my philosophy (which is to say, to the universal principles of yoga philosophy) without clobbering them with it. The promoter's thoughts, however, were not provoked. After making several phone calls while the record was being played, his comment was, "It needs a heavier beat."

Many people equate power with muscle, or money, or noise. Yet man's ascendance among the animals lies not in his physical prowess, but in the strength of his mind. The greatest periods of history have been times of spiritual or cultural awakening, not of bloodshed. A man's true glory depends not on outward factors, but on how deeply he can tap his *inner* resources. Meditation, far from representing an activity for timid, vague, or otherwise weak natures seeking an escape from reality, is an essential activity for everyone who would develop his full potential as a human being.

In your meditation room (or nook), you would find it helpful to have an altar. While your *real* altar is your own inner awareness, outer symbols can help to keep you mindful of those inner realities. You might place on your altar one or two of your favorite spiritual symbols, or pictures of great saints whom you particularly revere.

As focal points for your concentration,

these images may help you to awaken inner devotion. The photographs of great masters can help you, besides, to attune your consciousness with theirs. Just as a weak, sputtering flame on wet wood can be brought to a full blaze by joining it to a strong fire, so attunement with great souls can help us very greatly to "fire up" our own spiritual efforts. Indeed, this is considered perhaps the one most important point of yoga teaching. I myself always keep on my altar in my meditation room the pictures of the great gurus (teachers) of our line (Jesus Christ, Babaji-Krishna, Lahiri Mahasaya, Sri Yukteswarji, and Paramhansa Yogananda). More than that, I keep the presence of my own guru, especially, ever on the altar of my heart.

For it is within, finally, that our concentration should be directed. Yoga, as I said in the last lesson, is the neutralization of the waves in the lower mind, the eddies of feeling, so that the "moon" of reality may be reflected truly within us. The purpose of meditation is to assist this inner process of neutralization.

But even after we go within, certain mental images may be helpful to us for a time. As a child on a playground swing returns to a state of rest by pushing the ropes in a direction opposite to that of the swing's motion, so, similarly, certain ideas may help us to offset other ideational currents, with the result that the mind is, finally, not more agitated, but at peace.

If idolatry has been the bane of religion, it is only because people so often use devotional images, not to counteract their worldly tendencies, but to exaggerate them—seeking to enlist help from the gods only to gratify their own selfish desires. But if images are used as focal points for one's concentration, they can help one to draw the loose strands of desire to a single point of pure devotion. This is especially true if one sees images only as symbols for higher, divine states which are essentially formless. *Any* expression of selfless love—to other people as well as to images—can help to stem the tides of natural selfishness in the heart. It is infatuation, not love, which adds force to our delusion. Pure love in any form should never be confused with idol worship.

The right mental images can help us to attain yoga in three ways: by suggesting peace to a restless mind; by stirring up energy in a sluggish mind and directing it toward God; and by recalling to mind, on deeper than conscious levels, eternally true states of the soul. The goal of meditation is to pass beyond all mental images to the perception of spiritual reality as it is. One cannot *create* that reality. One can only attune oneself with it.

The meditation exercise that was taught in the first lesson is helpful in bringing peace to a restless mind. Other visualizations also may help. If you are agitated by a specific thought, for example, its opposite thought may help you to return to a state of inner balance. If, for instance, you become angry, try dwelling for a time on thoughts of forgiveness; mentally dissociate the person who offended you from the action that gave offense. (Remember what Jesus said: "If, while you are offering your gift at the altar, you should remember that your brother has something against you, you must leave your gift there before the altar and go away. Make your peace with your brother first, then come and offer your gift." (Matthew 5:23,24) If plans for the future disturb your meditation, you may generate a different, God-ward current of energy by singing devotional chants until your mind "comes back" to you.

If, temperamentally, you are more of a *karma yogi* than a *bhakti yogi,* chanting at those times when your mind is busy planning things may not penetrate deeply enough to the core of your thought processes to redirect them. In this case you may simply feel God's energy working in your plannings, and gradually identify your consciousness more with the energy itself. Indeed, the more you feel identified with this causative energy, the more your problems will resolve themselves; excessive thinking on your part will only obstruct that divine flow. You can also offer your plans mentally to God, both in a spirit of service and in the understanding that this universe is, ultimately, His responsibility, not yours.

If your temperament leans more toward *gyana yoga,* dissociate yourself from your thoughts and plans by simply observing them. Reflect that they are not really *you;* they have nothing to do with what you are, essentially. "*Neti, neti*—not this, not that." This is a positive application of the negative principle in man, which so often focuses only on imperfections in the objective world, and tries by mere criticism to affirm an inner freedom from those outer inharmonies.

If the mind is dull, devotional chanting, or thoughts of self-offering to the Divine, accompanied by a deliberate stirring up of energy in the heart, will help to break the tentacle-hold of unresponsiveness. Dullness, remember, is not *calm* feeling; it is only trapped feeling.

Patanjali said that divine awakening comes by a process of *smriti* (memory). The soul already *is* divine. Self-realization is a matter of remembering who and what we really are. In delusion, man lives in a dream state. He imagines a world of appearances to be made up of solid substances. Mental images of reality, even though they, too, are a sort of dream, can help to stir deeper-than-conscious soul memories within us, and thereby to give us the power to reject the hypnosis of this false dream of delusion.

You will find it helpful in meditation to visualize an expanding light, or infinite space and freedom, or ineffable love and bliss. In later lessons, specific visualization exercises will be given to help you in this direction.

When you sit to meditate, begin by inhaling, counting mentally to 12; hold the breath, counting to 12; exhale, counting to 12. Gradually, *if you can do so comfortably,* increase this count to 20-20-20, but keep the count equal for all three phases of breathing. Repeat this breathing exercise six to twelve times.

Then inhale and tense the whole body; throw the breath out and relax. Repeat two or three times. Your body should now be completely relaxed, and your mind ready for meditation.

In meditation, concentrate with deep calmness at the point between the eyebrows, the *ajna chakra.* This is the seat of concentration, as well as of divine vision in the body. Affirm mentally: "*Thy light flows into me; I am filled with peace.*"

AUM, *Shanti, Shanti, Shanti!*

Step Four
Yama

I. PHILOSOPHY

Yama

The evolution of moral values is commonly explained in one of two ways. Religionists claim that God simply ordained how man should behave. Social thinkers, on the other hand, claim that because the laws of morality differ so radically from culture to culture, they must be seen as having grown out of the demands of social convenience. It is socially inconvenient, for example, for a tribe to allow its members to steal from or to kill one another. Laws therefore get passed against stealing or killing—at least within one's own tribal "family"! This is supposed to be the only valid argument against theft and murder.

That God should ordain, or *command,* certain human behavior suggests that man's own predilections would lead him in quite a different direction. That the basis of God's commandments should be *His* pleasure, not man's, suggests also the possibility that man is trapped in the coils of divine whimsy, and in servitude to a Lord who is indifferent to our feelings, quite possibly even antagonistic to them. (Why else would His commandments sit so heavily upon a large percentage of the human race?)

The teachings of yoga, however, make it clear that the scriptural "commandments" have a much more acceptable basis. They are founded on basic realities of human nature itself, and are intended simply to help man to fulfill that nature.

As for the explanations of the sociologists, the yoga teachings point out that certain moral principles are universally true, and have little to do with a communal consensus. Societies may agree to defy one or another of these principles, but whole societies have also been known to suffer because their standards were out of harmony with natural law.

The basic moral principles of yoga

are listed in the *Yoga Sutras* of Patanjali under two general headings: *yama* (the restraints), and *niyama* (the observances). Under each of these two headings are five rules, or guidelines, making a total of ten (reminiscent of the Biblical "ten commandments"). The reason for offering such guidelines is obvious: Man does not easily perceive, except after much painful trial and error (and then often too late), the laws governing his own nature. Many of his actions, seemingly natural to him simply because they come easily, are actually self-destructive: drunkenness, for example, or (on a mental level) a bad temper.

Man is not free so long as he merely indulges his inclinations indiscriminately. He may say, "I am free to get drunk as often as I choose, and no one has a right to stop me." From a sociological standpoint he will be right. This is not, however, the true exercise of freedom. At best it is only the abuse of freedom, as may be seen from the fact that continued drunkenness leads to mental bondage. It is by understanding the body's laws and abiding by them that one attains true freedom. The universal moral principles are in reality guideposts to true, lasting freedom.

The principles of *yama* and *niyama* are intended as guidelines for everyone, but they are meant especially for those who are seeking to advance spiritually.

The five rules of *yama,* or control, are proscriptive. When a man can remove physical and mental inharmony from his system, he will not have to *work* to become harmonious. He *is* Spirit; all that shows him to be otherwise is merely a veil of delusion that has been cast over the eternal perfection of his true nature. Gold may be buried under mud, but if we clear away the mud we shall not have to work on the gold to make it more golden. The rules of *yama,* then, are:

1) *Ahimsa*, Non-Violence or Non-Injury
2) Non-Lying, or Truthfulness
3) Non-Stealing
4) Non-Sensuality
5) Non-Greed

Each of these rules must be understood in a subtle as well as in an obvious sense.

1) *Ahimsa* is a term that was popularized in our times by Mahatma Gandhi. By non-violent resistance he led India to political emancipation from Britain. But alas, he was not able to teach the Indian people the deeper implications of this teaching. It is seen by most people even today as the last hope of the underdog. Yet *ahimsa,* rightly understood, is the Ultimate Weapon of a strong man; it turns one's enemy into a friend, thereby banishing the possibility of further conflict.

In the practice of yoga, it is important to understand that the life flowing in our veins is the same life which flows in the veins of all creatures. All of us are expressions of God, in the same way (to use a favorite illustration of my guru's) that the individual jets on a gas burner, though appearing separate from one another, are only manifestations of the unifying gas underneath. If I hurt you, I am in a real sense hurting myself. The saying of Jesus, "Love thy neighbor as thyself," means, in a deeper sense, "Love thy neighbor; he *is* thy Self."

The goal of yoga is to realize the oneness of all life. If I am willing to hurt the life in me as it is expressed in another human being, then I am affirming an error that is diametrically opposed to the realization which I am seeking to attain. It is necessary, if I would truly realize the oneness of all things, for me to live also in such a way as constantly to affirm this oneness—by my kindness towards all beings, by compassion, by universal love.

Some people carry this teaching so far as to try never to kill anything. When any rule becomes so paramount in our minds that we can see nothing beyond it, it may only obstruct our development instead of opening a pathway to liberation. There is a sect in India that insists on boiling water so as not to kill the germs in the water when they drink it. They overlook the obvious fact that they kill the germs also when they boil the water. Every time we inhale, we kill germs. Every time we walk out of doors, we may step on some harmless insect. Every time we go driving, the windshield of our car becomes coated with the bodies of flies and gnats. It is impossible to practice *ahimsa* to literal perfection without killing ourselves, which is the worst crime of all.

What Patanjali referred to, essentially, was the attitude of the mind, rather than the literal acts of the body. It is one's *attitude* that can either lead him toward liberation, or hold him in greater bondage. An *attitude* of harmlessness (and its corollary, a feeling of universal benevolence) is what is meant by *ahimsa*. We could not in any case kill anyone: His soul is immortal. What we *can* do, however, by wishing harm to another living being, is develop in ourselves a consciousness of death that keeps us enclosed in darkness. In killing another person, we would be hurting ourselves far more than we could possibly hurt him.

The principle of *ahimsa* must be understood in subtle ways, not only in gross. If you harm anyone in the slightest way—if, for example, you kill his enthusiasm (which is in a sense the life within him), or if you deride him, or if you treat him with disrespect—in all of these ways you will be harming him, and also, by reflection, yourself. The perfect practice of *ahimsa,* then, may be seen to be rare indeed. For though not many men would actually kill their fellows, it is common to find people slashing at one another with angry words, or with contemptuous glances. Patanjali gives us a test by which we can tell if we have developed our practice of *ahimsa* to perfection. He says that once this has been accomplished, even wild animals and ferocious criminals will become tame and harmless in our presence. Many were the instances in the life of my own guru, Paramhansa Yogananda, in which this promise was fulfilled.

In the jungles near Ranchi, where he had gone one time with a group of students and teachers from his school, he prevented a wild tiger from attacking their cows by standing between it and them, and looking at it with love. On several occasions in America he converted hardened criminals with a glance.

When you meditate, begin by sending out waves of blessing to all men. If there is anyone, especially, with whom you have had a difference, send him your love. Until you develop this attitude you will never be able to meditate deeply. Subconscious antagonism will keep you tensed physically, as well as egoistically aloof from the great stream of life into which meditation should help you to merge.

As far as the yoga postures are concerned, an attitude of non-injury signifies that one should not do violence to his own body, either. As I have said before, *relax* into each pose; don't force yourself into it. Make your practice of the postures a process of self-exploration rather than of grim self-punishment.

2) Non-lying must be understood in a subtle sense also. Some self-styled moralists are actually so shallow as to counsel truthfulness on the ground that it is so difficult to remember all one's lies that sooner or later one is bound to trip oneself up. Well, better this much justification than none at all! But the real value of truthfulness goes considerably deeper.

Truthfulness is the necessary attitude for us if we would overcome our own false notions about life. Our path to God is entirely a matter of ridding ourselves of our delusions. The scientist who probes deeply into the nature of things, refusing to permit any personal bias to influence his investigations, is, to a degree, practicing truthfulness. The person who examines without prejudice his own likes and dislikes is practicing truthfulness also, and in a more vital form because a deep probe into the nature of reality demands above all that man's own vision be made crystal clear.

The untruthful person is always wishing that the world, or the more intimate circumstances of his own life, were different from what they are. "If *only* it weren't raining! If *only* he'd stop talking! If *only* she weren't so stupid." Granting that circumstances might always be improved, the first step toward that improvement is a recognition, and acceptance, of the state of things as they actually are. We can only work with what *is*.

There are higher, as well as lower, truths. To call a man stupid is not a higher truth, though he may in fact be a moron. The soul within us is ever wise, ever perfect. To be truthful, then, does not necessarily mean to be literally factual. It might be well to tell a dull fellow that he is bright, if in the telling we try also to penetrate his mind with an affirmation of his inner potential for intelligence. Truth is always beneficial. To make harmful statements, even if they are based on obvious, but superficial and temporary, facts, is in the deepest spiritual sense untruthful.

An attitude of truthfulness means to try always to see things as they are, to accept the possibility that one may be mistaken in his most cherished opinions, to entertain no likes and dislikes that might prejudice his perception of reality as it is. Truthfulness means to look always for the Divine Light that shines in the midst of universal darkness, to see God in everything and everyone, to affirm goodness even in the face of evil, and yet always to do so from a center of absolute honesty, never of mere wishful thinking.

When one attunes himself with Nature, he attunes himself to the power of the universe. His strength then becomes limitless. When one attunes himself to the Divine behind all natural, universal phenomena, he makes himself a channel for the Divine to flow in pristine splendor into the dark alleys and buried chambers of this relative world.

Patanjali gave us a test by which we might tell whether we have achieved perfection in this virtue. He said that a person in whom this principle of truthfulness becomes firmly established will develop the power to attain the fruits of action without even acting. His mere thought, his mere word will be binding on the universe. Relative facts will have to accommodate themselves to his will, attuned as he is to a deeper reality. A saint can heal others by simply saying to them with deep concentration, "Be well!"

In meditation, an attitude of perfect truthfulness is essential as a safeguard against hallucinations, as well as against attachment to the more common delusions of mankind. To overcome your hypnosis of human limitations, observe them dispassionately in meditation. Ask yourself, "Is this really *I*? *Who* am I, really?!" The deeper you pursue this question of self-identity, the more clearly you will see yourself as the ever-free soul, stripped of all egoistic delusion.

In the practice of *hatha yoga,* one finds that he can master his body, also, in proportion to his awareness of it. I knew a yogi whose physical awareness was so keen that if, in a meal, he had swallowed one morsel that disagreed with him, he could regurgitate it, leaving all the other contents of his stomach undisturbed. In practicing the postures, be *inwardly* aware of your body. While practicing the stretching poses, for example, concentrate on the tension that prevents you from stretching further; be complete in your recognition of it. You will notice that once you have really "faced" this obstruction, accepting it for what it is, you will be able to release it as you could never do if you tried merely to ignore it. In all of the yoga postures, an attitude of strict truthfulness, which is to say, simply, awareness, is a necessary prerequisite to final mastery.

3) Non-stealing means more than simply not taking another person's property. It means also not *coveting* his property. It means not desiring anything that is not yours by right. It means actually not even to desire that which *is* yours by right, in the realization that whatever is rightfully yours will surely come to you anyway, but that your happiness is not conditioned by whether you get it or not. Desire only keeps one looking to the future for his fulfillment, instead of realizing that perfection is his already. You need only to realize more and more deeply your already-existing oneness with all life. Why feel that you *need* anything in the universe, when in truth you *are* the universe! Covetousness is like a rope that ties the balloon of consciousness to the ground, preventing it from soaring into the free skies of spiritual bliss.

In shuffling a deck of cards, although the sequence of the cards can be changed almost indefinitely, the number of cards remains the same. An increase of aces in one part of the deck will not mean an overall increase in the number of aces. To take from another person in order to gain for oneself is, similarly, to reshuffle the relationship of things. No overall gain is achieved thereby, and therefore no gain to our *true* self. To emphasize one's own ego at the expense of those of others is to give strength to a delusion. Ego is the supreme obstacle to the true vision of life's all-embracing unity.

Stealing, or coveting, need not be limited to material objects. There are many people who, in the words of Sri Yukteswar, "chop off other people's heads to appear taller themselves." To speak unkindly to another being, or even *of* another human being, is to claim an exclusive virtue for oneself. Virtue is the result of attunement with the natural order of things. We cannot claim special virtue for ourselves, or try to exclude others from it, without impairing that sensitive attunement with the totality of life, and thereby lessening our own virtue.

As a test of one's progress in the development of this virtue, Patanjali says that when non-stealing becomes firmly rooted in one's consciousness one will find wealth coming to him whenever he needs it. For when one truly recognizes that the very universe is his own, and no longer cuts himself off from the rest of life by egoistically demanding his own "share" of it, he finds himself supported, no longer ignored, by the universal law.

In meditation, the slightest yearning for things will take the mind out of itself. The outward flow of energy from the heart must be channeled inward, and up toward the brain and the point between the eyebrows, if meditation is to lead to enlightenment. Until one can still the desires of the heart, perfect meditation will not be possible. Try, therefore, as you begin your meditation, to affirm mentally that you are complete, and completely at rest, in yourself.

In the practice of the yoga postures, too, try entertaining the awareness that all the energy of the universe is yours already to command. Open yourself mentally to its inflow, and direct it through your body by the direct exercise of your will. Radiate it also outward, in harmony and blessing to all men, for it is not enough merely to cease taking from the ocean of life; if the proscriptive rules of *yama* are practiced perfectly, they will release energy in a positive way. It is the soul's own nature to expand outward to infinity. The greatest fallacy, finally, of an attitude of taking is that it causes one's consciousness to contract into itself.

4) *Brahmacharya,* or non-sensuality, is based on a little-known fact: Although man's inner peace is disrupted by physical and emotional tension, he cannot find inner harmony by merely releasing that tension outwardly in sense indulgence. The reason many people find this truth so difficult to grasp is that sense indulgence is accompanied, typically, by an apparent *increase* of inner peace, as well as a feeling of freedom. The libertine consequently looks down on people of self-control; he considers them simple-minded for rejecting a felicity so easily won.

But if one examines the lives of people who seek peace and freedom through sense indulgence, it soon becomes evident that, whatever their success in ridding themselves of inner tensions, they in no way become thereby shining examples of peace. In fact, if anything they are more nervous, moody, and irascible than their self-controlled and supposedly frustrated fellow men. Nor is their special sort of freedom particularly enviable. True freedom ought to convey a sense of power, of expanding awareness and well-being. The libertine's "freedom," by contrast, suggests little more than a sort of coming apart at the seams.

Why this loss, in the expectation of nothing but gain? The reason is that a true sense of peace and freedom is impossible if the release of one's tensions is accompanied by a dissipation of energy. Fulfillment cannot be attained in a state of unconsciousness. Peace is not a state of being merely dead to any further excitement. One of man's commonest errors is to imagine that he can achieve a state of inner balance and harmony by dulling his responses to the universe around him. When the pressure of desire builds up within him, he considers his only recourse to be to "let off steam." He enjoys the fleeting sense of power that comes to him at the time of release. His main aim, however, seems to be to revert to a state of relative numbness, wherein desire no longer importunes him. He sees the buildup of inner energy as something merely to be got rid of. He little dreams that this very energy is the key to his inner self-development, or that true peace and freedom require more, not less, of this energy.

For a person's degree of awareness depends entirely on the *amount and direction* of his inner flow of energy. A truly aware person is always one who possesses great energy. If the converse is not true (for, obviously, a man of great energy is not always exceptionally aware), it is because this energy must be directed toward the brain before it can result in a heightened awareness. To be continuously and *consciously* at peace, one must find a way of releasing his inner tensions without losing the energy with which his ensuing peace may be fully savored.

Observe how, when you feel happy, your energy and consciousness seem to soar upward. You tend to sit a little straighter, to stand more on the balls of your feet, to look upward more frequently, even to feel physically lighter. You describe yourself at such times as feeling "uplifted, light, on top of the world." Heaven itself is commonly thought of as situated somewhere up above us—as if it represented a sort of culmination of this upward movement in our own consciousness.

When, on the other hand, you feel unhappy, note how your energy and consciousness move downward, away from the brain. Your shoulders and back tend to slump forward, you walk more heavily on your heels, your natural impulse is to look downward. The very expressions you use to describe your condition at such times suggest the downward movement of your energy: "I feel depressed, downcast, heavy, in the dumps." Hell itself is commonly conceived of as being situated somewhere below us—as if it were a sort of terminal station on this downward journey of man's consciousness.

Two of the primary requirements for enjoying life to the fullest are the preservation of one's inner energy, and its upward direction toward the brain. These are among the most basic requirements also for spiritual advancement.

Every outward direction of energy constitutes, in a sense, an expenditure. As in business ventures, however, there are certain expenditures which are necessary if one would increase his inner wealth. Activities that are undertaken in a spirit of joyous service have the effect of putting one in tune with the infinite source of all power. The more consciously one acts as a channel for divine energy, the more he finds his inner powers actually *increasing*. If one expends his energy *after uplifting it,* his activities bring him *more,* not less, peace, freedom, and joy. It is the outward expenditure of *downward-directed* energy that results in mere dissipation, for it entails no corresponding inflow of cosmic energy.

An expenditure of downward-directed energy results from any sense indulgence where there is a wish merely for release of inner pressures; where the thought of self-indulgence, not of self-giving, predominates; or where the aim is not superconsciousness, but only a form of unconsciousness—if only a lessened consciousness of the inner discomfort produced by desire. All of these entail a downward movement of energy. It must be understood that not all sense pleasures entail sensuality, as defined by Patanjali. God never meant for this world to be shunned by His human children as a thing of evil. Any God-reminding activity, including pure sense enjoyments, can help to uplift the soul. But when we take from life without giving to it in return, we live like thieves and murderers. "No man is an island"; John Donne was right. To live rightly in this world we must maintain a sensitive awareness of our divine kinship with all life.

Any sense pleasure that does not heighten this sense of universal oneness, but that tends rather to emphasize our consciousness of egoic separateness from other beings, may be classified as sensuality. No physical experience in this relative universe can be absolutely either sensual or non-sensual. The important thing in any search for growing awareness and harmony is first to avoid as much as possible those experiences which are, by the criteria we have just considered, more sensual than spiritual. The more sense-oriented and selfish an experience, the more it deadens one's spiritual sensitivity. Sense experiences that are not strongly or grossly sense-oriented may even, with practice, be turned to good spiritual advantage.

That form of sensuality which is most obviously associated with a downward direction of human energy is sexual enjoyment. Sex pleasure dissipates one's energy in direct proportion to the consciousness of self-indulgence. Where there is self-giving love, there is to some extent an upward flow of energy in the spine, and thus also an inflow of divine energy in the form of love. There will still be a loss of energy, however, on other mental and physical levels. Prolonged indulgence in sex, therefore, even by people who love each other deeply, cannot but be debilitating in the long run; by dulling the awareness, it becomes harmful even to the feeling of love itself. It follows that, while human love may incline naturally, in its early stages, to physical expression, the more a couple can learn to express their love for one another non-physically, the more perfect their love will grow over the years.

Even where there is pure, self-giving love, moreover, the more physical its manifestations the more all-absorbing it will tend to be. If you hold a matchstick up close to your eyes, you will not be able to see much of the surrounding scenery. Similarly, when one becomes engrossed in sexual love one's personal feelings cannot but obscure one's awareness of life's broader realities. That is why the Hindu scriptures state that sexual indulgence, no matter how refined, increases the grip of egoism on the mind.

Much has been made during this past century of the harmfulness of repression. Little or no mention has been made of the uplifting effects of transmutation. If a person is fairly exploding with anger, it may sometimes be better for him to "get it off his chest" (though preferably without implicating the person with whom he is angry). The same is true with sexual expression, the desire for which is so inherent in human nature that to repress it can indeed lead to various physical and psychological problems. It is not repression, however, when a person seeks with understanding to redirect the flow of this energy upward toward the brain. Energy so directed can give one tremendous powers of accomplishment on all levels of life. Where there is the consent of the will there is not repression, but transmutation.

Water that is left to gather with no outlet in a pool may become stagnant, but if the water can be kept flowing it will remain sweet and pure. When one can learn how to direct his energy into wholesome channels instead of letting it stagnate in a pool of unfulfilled desire, or instead of wasting it on a field of clay, he finds that, far from there being any harmful effects in this deliberate effort at self-control, the effects are entirely positive: greater joy, a more dynamic power of concentration, greater physical strength. It is no accident that even in the West, where celibacy has been underrated and scorned as contrary to God's law, many creative geniuses have never married, or have remained celibate for long periods. Examples spring readily to mind: Brahms, Beethoven, Newton, Kant, Nietzsche, to mention but a few out of a veritable crowd.

Yoga teachings are never put forth as commandments. The yogi is taught not to feel guilty if he slips, nor to beat himself mentally if he cannot as yet live up to an ideal. He should, however, for his own sake—not for the sake of an indifferent society—strive gradually to redirect his energies upward from matter to Spirit. Growth must come naturally, not in violence to one's nature. Self-control in all things, however, is the direction of true growth. In a later lesson we shall give techniques that will help the student in this heroic effort.

The pleasure of sexual experience is fleeting, but the joy that comes from redirecting that energy upward toward the brain is unending. It fills the whole body. Even in sleep and in other nonmeditative activities, every cell of the body dances with joy.

Patanjali says that when nonsensuality becomes confirmed (mentally as well as physically), the yogi attains great vigor. Swami Vivekananda attributed his phenomenal mental powers to a lifelong observance of this principle. Someone once gave him the entire *Encyclopædia Britannica*. Two weeks later he had already read the first thirteen volumes. A disciple of his remarked, "But you can't have retained much of what you have read!"

"Question me on anything you can find in those thirteen volumes," challenged the swami. He answered every question correctly, even to dates and names of places.

Granting that he was a born genius, it is nevertheless possible for everyone, through perfect transmutation of the sex energy, to achieve extraordinary mental clarity and vigor.

This principle of non-sensuality must be applied also in meditation. It is more than a matter of not dwelling on sense pleasures instead of on the thought of God. As my paramguru (my guru's guru) Swami Sri Yukteswarji said, many people renounce sense pleasures only to seek them on a subtler plane in the form of visions and other spiritual phenomena. The goal of the spiritual path is union with God. Anything less than that constitutes only a type of self-indulgence. It can become a distraction from the true search unless it is offered back with devotion to the Supreme Lord.

In meditation, try to raise your energy and consciousness up through the spine to the point between the eyebrows. This principle should also be followed during the practice of yoga postures. Seek by means of these postures to direct the body's energy up toward the brain. Do not allow it to become wasted in physical or mental tension, or in restless movements.

5) Non-greed has often been translated to mean the non-receiving of gifts. I read Patanjali's meaning differently. He says, later on, that when a person becomes perfected in this virtue he can remember his former incarnations. What has the non-receiving of gifts to do with such a memory? Patanjali is not even talking of specific practices, but rather of states of consciousness. Non-greed is closer to the right translation. It differs from Patanjali's third rule of non-covetousness in the sense that non-covetousness means not to desire what is not rightfully one's own, while non-greed means not to be attached even to what already *is* one's own. Non-greed, perfectly practiced, leads one to become non-attached even to his own body. It is by such perfect non-attachment that the blindness of temporary identifications is overcome, with the result that one can remember his past identifications with other bodies, other places and events.

The yogi should realize that everything is God. Greed, or attachment, limits the mind to one body, and obscures the truth that the soul is, in essence, infinite and eternal.

Paramhansa Yogananda once said to a disciple: "You have a sour taste in your mouth, haven't you?"

"How could you know?" asked the surprised disciple.

"Because," replied the Master, "I am just as much in your body as I am in my own."

Freedom from physical limitations is no imaginary state, though even as such it would be preferable to imaginary bondage. But it can only be achieved if one is so perfectly non-attached to his limitations that they are no longer limiting to him.

In meditation, you will find it helpful to free yourself mentally from all worldly identifications. Cut the emotional strings that tie you to your possessions. Completely relax your body. Affirm mentally: *"I am not the body! I am Spirit—ever blissful—ever free!"*

In your practice of the yoga postures, too, it is important to conquer body attachment. Realize that the body is yours to use, not to pamper. You are the ever-perfect, eternal soul. Learn not to give in to the body's dictates, nor to assume to yourself its feelings of fatigue. One should never say, "I am tired." The body may be tired, but the body is not the Self. Say, if you must, "My body needs rest," but try gradually to discipline the body as one would a wayward child, until it obeys every command of your will.

Conclusion. It may be said, finally, that all five of the rules of *yama* unite in a single purpose: to prevent the yogi from misdirecting his energies, that he may channel them all toward constructive purposes, and thereby achieve the power necessary to the highest forms of success.

By an attitude of non-injury (*ahimsa*) he no longer wastes his energy in animosities, of which the sum of all gains and losses is always zero. By strict truthfulness he no longer wastes his strength in creating and sustaining a private dream world of his own, or in wishing out of existence realities over which he has no control; allying himself with reality as it is, he finds that he can actually draw on universal forces to improve his circumstances. By an attitude of non-stealing, or non-covetousness, he no longer scatters his forces in desiring what is not rightfully his, and what therefore could not help him in his own path to perfection. By non-sensuality he withdraws his energy from over-identification with outward enjoyments, that he may freely enjoy the much greater, if exceedingly subtle, bliss of the soul. By non-greed, or non-attachment even to what is rightfully his, he keeps his energy free to move ever forward on the highway to infinity.

A bucket that is riddled with holes cannot be filled with milk. The mind of man, similarly, cannot be filled with divine peace so long as its powers are continuously drained by attachments and desires. The rules of *yama* are intended to help the yogi to seal those "holes," that he may begin to store in his body and brain the "milk" of divine peace.

II. YOGA POSTURES

The spine is the river of life. Through the spine man's energy flows, sending impulses to the brain, transmitting commands from the brain to the muscles and internal organs. In meditation the yogi becomes deeply aware of these spinal currents.

The juice of an orange is inside; all that shows from without is the color. The subtle energies in the body, similarly, when experienced from within in meditation, are very different from their outward manifestations: physical tension and movement. Tremendous joy and awareness are experienced as one's consciousness becomes centered sensitively in the spine. The spine is, indeed, the holy river of baptism in which the Godward-moving soul becomes cleansed and regenerated in waters of divine joy.

The *hatha yogi* should train himself to be deeply aware of the spine. The majority of the yoga postures relate in some way or another to the development of this spinal awareness, either by stretching and irrigating the spine, or by inducing a more centered consciousness.

Centeredness in the spine is important not only for spiritual awakening, but even in sports and in other daily human activities. I have found when skiing, for example, that if I deliberately center my awareness in the spine, feeling all my movements to be radiating outward from that center, I can ski very much better. One who can remain consciously centered in his spine will always be poised, ready to meet any situation that arises—even as a man who is well-balanced while running can turn quickly, whereas one who is not will very likely fall if he turns too suddenly.

Right posture is vitally important to the yogi. A bent spine impairs the flow of energy. It also cramps the breath, making it almost impossible to breathe deeply. Right posture, however, from a standpoint of yoga, is by no means the rigid stance of a soldier on parade. One must be relaxed even while standing straight. Indeed, until one can learn to keep his spine straight he will never know how to relax perfectly. Stand in such a way that you feel yourself centered in the spine, with the rest of your body suspended from the spine in much the same way as branches are suspended from the trunk of a tree. The chest should be somewhat (but not too much) out, the shoulders a little bit back, the head neither hanging forward nor drawn back too rigidly. If you stand perfectly straight, you will find that it takes very little strength to remain standing—only enough strength to maintain your balance.

Paramhansa Yogananda once said to me, "Always remain in the Self. Come down every now and then to eat or talk a little bit as necessary, then withdraw into the Self again." To remain more in the Self means to live more in the spine, and at the point between the eyebrows. The yogi's awareness of the spinal energy must ever be directed *upward.* (We shall go more deeply into this aspect of the postures in the next lesson.)

Vrikasana (the Tree Pose) is excellent for developing right posture. When you practice it, feel that your consciousness is centered in the spine. Raise your hands high above your head, placing the palms together. Straighten up, and a little backward, and feel as if a straight line were

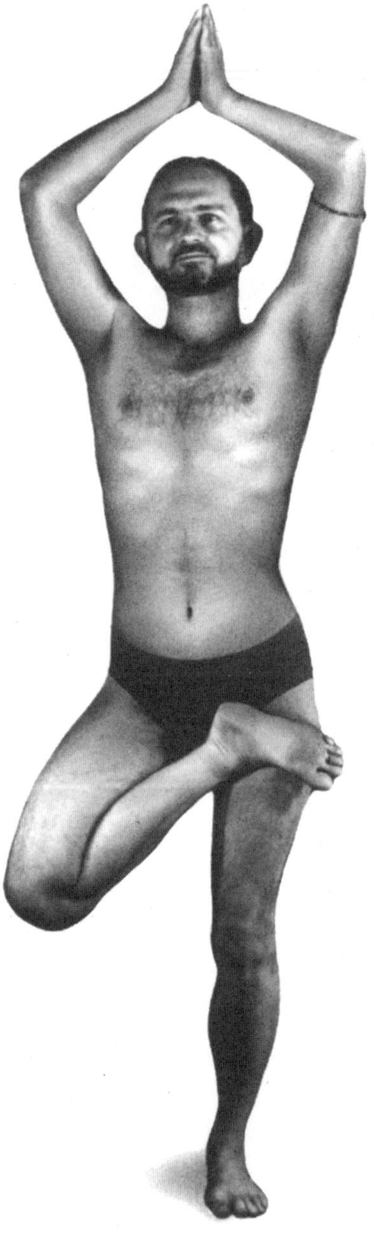

Vrikasana

(The Tree Pose)

"I am calm! I am poised!"

extending up through the spine and between the hands. (This posture was taught in detail in Step Two.)

The development of right posture is the prime benefit of this position. It is therefore important that the mind be centered mainly in the spine. This is to say that the raised leg should be relaxed, so as not to divert the attention from the spine by the sheer physical effort of holding the foot up. If, then, you cannot place the foot at the top of the opposite thigh, rather than hold the foot halfway up the thigh—a position that requires considerable tension—place the instep against the inside of the opposite knee.

Padahastasana

(The Jackknife Pose)

"What in this world can hold me?"

Stand up straight. Inhale deeply, then exhale, bending forward slowly at the waist until your hands can grasp your ankles. You may, if you prefer, grasp the toes in a more complete forward stretch. Breathe normally in this position. Hold the position for about 10 seconds to start with, with practice gradually increasing the time to about one minute; then inhale, and return slowly to an upright position.

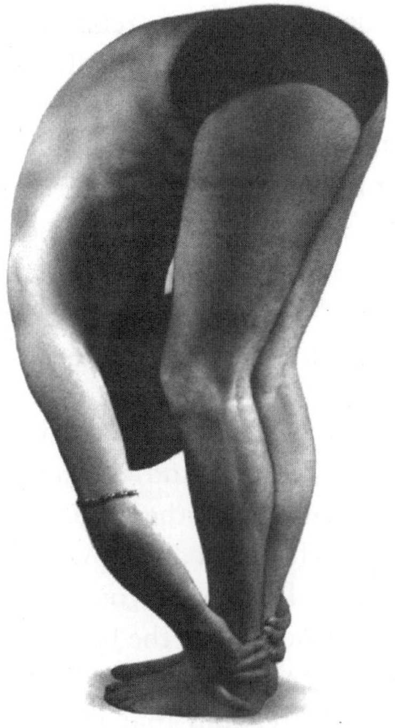

While in the posture, drop your head, and relax at the base of the spine. Try to keep the legs straight. You will find that the more you relax at the base of the spine, the more easily you will be able to bend forward.

Benefits: This posture exercises a beneficial pressure on the abdomen. It helps to stretch the spine in a slightly different manner from the sitting stretches, inasmuch as here the entire weight of the upper body is brought into play. It is somewhat more difficult to keep the legs straight in this position than in the sitting stretches, where the pressure of the floor may be used to good advantage. Here, there is no such pressure to suggest straightness to the legs. From a standpoint, then, of the stretch of the upper body, this pose is easier than the sitting stretches, but from a standpoint of keeping the legs straight, it is more difficult.

There is also a psychological benefit to this position. The yogi is taught, as an exercise in mental freedom, to meditate on vast space. Normally, such spatial awareness is obstructed by one's sense of physical heaviness. In *Padahastasana,* this natural sense of gravity is disoriented by the half-upward, half-downward, position of the body. If one can relax in this position, one finds that the conflicting directions help the mind to overcome its bondage to gravity. Affirm mentally, *"What in this world can hold me?"*

The Backward Bend

"I am free! I am free!"

Follow the Jackknife Pose with the Backward Bend. Stand up, and put one foot in front of the other. Inhale, and raise your hands forward and upward, with the palms turned up, until you can join your palms together above the head. Stretch the hands upwards and backwards. Feel the triumphant freedom that is suggested by this position. Feel your energy and consciousness being swept upward to the sky. Affirm mentally: *"I am free! I am free!"* Repeat, placing the other foot forward.

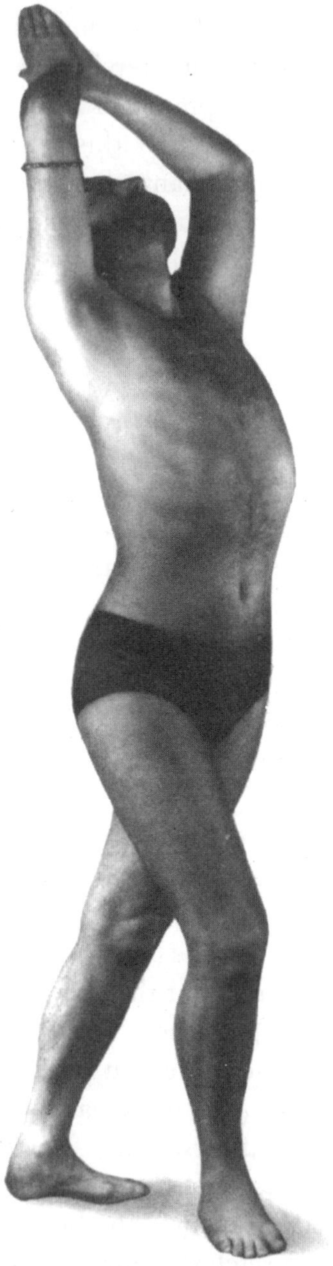

The Backward Bend
"I am free! I am free!"

Janushirasana

(The Head-to-the-Knee Pose)

"Left and right and all around—life's harmonies are mine."
Or: *"Waves of harmony surge up my spine."*

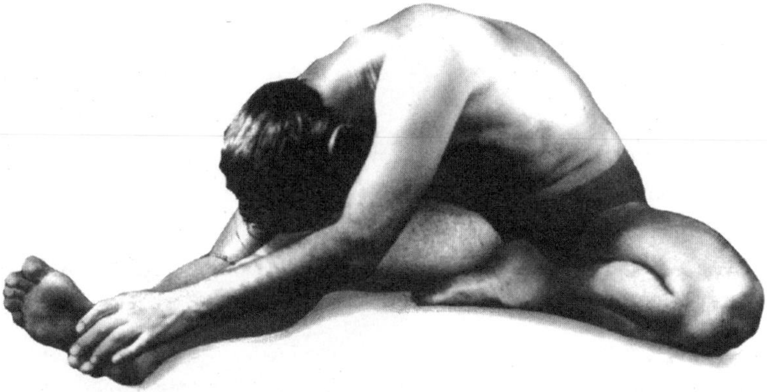

Sit on the floor. Extend your legs outward in front of you, separating them into as wide an angle as is comfortable for you. Bring one foot in, and place it in the crotch. Inhale, raising the hands gracefully up the sides of the chest as if to draw the awareness into and up the spine, then exhale slowly, bending forward and letting the hands offer the self toward the outstretched foot.

Grasp the foot with your hands, and bring the head slowly forward until the forehead rests upon the knee. If you cannot grasp your foot, then grasp your ankle or your calf, so as to give your upper body the support that it needs if it is to relax properly. If you cannot touch your head to your knee, do not bring your knee up to touch your head like Mohammed, who said that if the mountain would not come to him, he would go to the mountain! Keep the outstretched leg straight, and bring your head as far down to it as it will go *comfortably.* (This is a head-to-the-knee pose, not a knee-to-the-head pose!) Relax at the base of the spine and on the side of the back opposite to the outstretched leg. You will find by progressive relaxation that you can bend further and further forward, until you have mastered the pose.

Hold the pose only a few seconds to begin with, increasing the time gradually to one or two minutes as it becomes comfortable to you. Repeat, with the other leg outstretched. Affirm mentally: *"Left and right and all around—life's harmonies are mine,"* or, *"Waves of harmony surge up my spine."*

Dhanurasana

(The Bow Pose)

"I recall my scattered forces to recharge my spine."
Or: *"Each wave of trials can only raise me to new heights."*

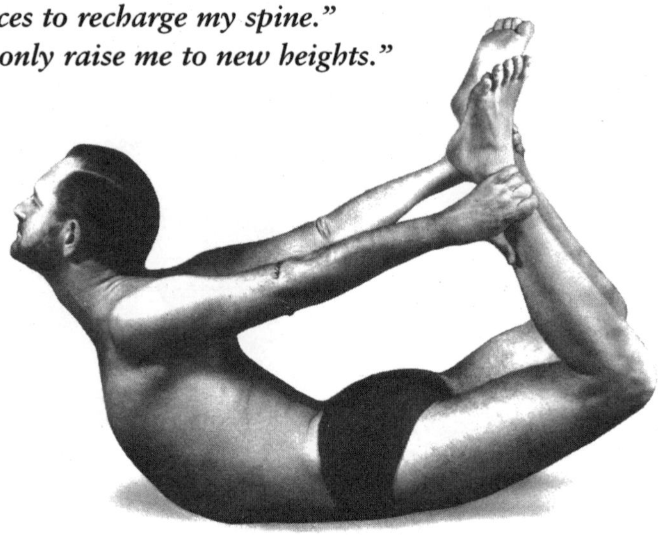

This pose completes what the Cobra Pose began. The Cobra Pose bends the upper spine backward. *Dhanurasana* bends the middle and lower spine.

Lie face downward. Bend your legs at the knees and, reaching back with your hands, firmly grasp the ankles or the feet. Lie in this position with your forehead on the floor. Inhale, and pull your feet away from the body, forcing your chest and your knees up off the ground until your weight rests solely on the abdomen. You may find it necessary to use the strength of the thighs also, to raise the knees. Breathe normally in this position. Be keenly aware of the bend in the *lower* spine. Feel the awakening energy there, and the drawing of energy to the lower spine from the legs. Affirm mentally: *"I recall my scattered forces to recharge my spine."* Or, visualize yourself floating cheerfully over the crests of all difficulties, and affirm mentally: *"Each wave of trials can only raise me to new heights."* You will find your awareness of energy increasing if you hold the pose slightly beyond the point of comfort, though never, of course, to the point of pain. Concentrate on your feeling in the spine, not on the tensed muscles, and you will discover you can hold this pose long past what you might consider to be your limit of "strength."

Benefits and Cautions: Persons with an enlarged liver or spleen ought not to practice this position, or *Bhujangasana.* The benefits of *Dhanurasana* are also much the same as those for *Bhujangasana.* Physically, the gentle pressure of this pose upon the abdomen helps to stimulate the internal organs and to reduce flatulence. Psychologically, the Bow Pose increases one's strength to overcome obstacles. More important still are the spiritual benefits. *Dhanurasana* is a wonderful pose for awakening and increasing your awareness of, and hence your control over, the subtle energy in the spine.

III. BREATHING

The breath is intimately connected with the strength of the body. Notice how, when you go to lift a heavy object, you always inhale first. Instinctively you understand that inhalation will help to bring you the strength you need for the work at hand. If you inhale energy consciously and deliberately while inhaling air, you will find that breathing is one of the prime means of drawing energy into the body. Try to breathe more often with full awareness.

A breathing technique that can help to increase the inflow of energy into the body is one that is known as the Double Breath. Inhale through the nostrils: a short breath, then a long; exhale through the mouth and nose, short and long.

An excellent breathing exercise for making one more aware of the air and energy as it enters one's lungs, and also for developing the diaphragm, is known as *Sitkari.* Put the tongue against the teeth, and inhale forcibly through the mouth with a hissing sound. Exhale through the nose, closing the lips, and feel the coolness of the breath penetrating up into the brain, and spreading out into the entire nervous system. Make the inhalation and exhalation equal. Hold the breath in the lungs as long as you can do so comfortably.

IV. ROUTINE

Sit cross-legged on the floor and inhale deeply, counting mentally to 6; hold the breath 6; exhale counting 6; hold the breath out 6. Repeat 3 times.

Practice *Sitkari Pranayama* 6 times, feeling the coolness of the exhalation permeating your entire nervous system.

Concentrate at the point between the eyebrows for 2 or 3 minutes. Then practice the postures:

Stand up, and do the Full Yogic Breath 3 times, extending your hands high above the head.

Vrikasana (the Tree Pose)—30 seconds on each leg, with 30-second rest after each position.

Chandrasana (the Moon Pose)—30 seconds each side, with 30-second rests.

Trikonasana (the Triangle Pose)—same as above.

Utkatasana (the Chair Pose)—30 seconds to 1 minute.

Padahastasana (the Jackknife Pose)—30 seconds total time, followed by the Backward Bend.

Lie down in *Savasana* (the Corpse Pose) for 2 minutes.

Sasamgasana (the Hare Pose—First Phase)—1 minute.

Janushirasana (the Head-to-the-Knee Pose)—10 to 15 seconds each side with rests in between.

Paschimotanasana (the Posterior Stretch)—30 seconds, followed by 30 seconds in *Savasana.*

Dhanurasana (the Bow Pose)—15 seconds.

Bhujangasana (the Cobra Pose)—30 seconds.

Lie on your back in *Savasana,* and go into deep relaxation for 5 minutes.

Approximate total time: 30 minutes

V. HEALING

Chronic Fatigue

Chronic fatigue is one of the most widespread ills of our age. It is not due to overwork (modern man does not work nearly so hard as his ancestors did), but rather to a scattering of our forces. Ours is not a "focused" age. Countless influences pull us in conflicting directions. We find ourselves trying to do a hundred things hastily, rather than one thing at a time carefully and well. We measure achievement by numbers rather than by excellence. A result is the exhaustion that one finds written on the faces of so many men and women in our bustling cities, where strangers pass one another with never a smile nor even a glance of greeting.

Chronic fatigue is due not only to a scattering of our energies, but also to over-stimulation. Where there is too much stimulation, one's capacity for response is weakened. One loses his natural enthusiasm. A Hollywood writer once showed a script to a movie producer. The producer, after reading it, said, "It's stupendous! Colossal!" The writer asked dejectedly, "You mean you don't like it?" It is difficult in a world in which superlatives form a constant crescendo to take anything seriously—to react with wonder even to a miracle. Our very superlatives become but expressions of ennui.

Fatigue is a direct result of a loss of interest. Our energy supply depends not primarily upon nutritious food and other external causes, but upon our capacity for smiles, for enthusiasm. People lead one-horsepower lives when they forget how to smile, when they overcomplicate their daily routine, and clutter their minds with the debris of useless desires and preoccupations. The man who can simplify his life and marshal his energies to do a few things well, instead of scattering his forces restlessly to the winds, will find that he has more than strength enough for whatever he has to do. Be *willing* in everything that you do. Willingness begets energy. "The greater the will," Yoganandaji used to say, "the greater the flow of energy." Will in this context means willingness—not physical or mental strain, but a pleasant, steadily increasing focus of the whole attention on a goal.

A technique for drawing energy into the body is to stand facing the sun. Raise your hands above your head. Feel the warmth of the sun striking your forehead at the point between the eyebrows, and the palms of your hands. Feel that you are drawing warmth and energy into your body through those "windows." After some time, turn your back to the sun, and feel its warmth upon the area of the medulla oblongata (at the base of the brain). Keep your hands raised above the head. Again, draw the sun's rays into your body.

The next time you feel fatigue, do some deep breathing. Then fill your mind with the sense of wonder that a child feels who sees this world with a fresh outlook. Have nothing to do with the jaded vision of people who live always, as it were, with their eyes to the ground.

Fatigue, finally, is a symptom of self-centeredness. One who can forget himself in helping others and in giving strength to them will find himself rarely exhausted.

Postures good for chronic fatigue: *Dhanurasana* (the Bow Pose) and *Janushirasana* (the Head-to-the-Knee Pose)—both taught in Step Four; *Chakrasana* (the Circle Pose)—to be taught in Step Five; and *Akarshana Dhanurasana* (the Pulling-the-Bow Pose)—to be taught in Step Nine.

VI. DIET

In the foregoing section we discussed the harmful effects of over-stimulation upon the nervous system. Foods, too, can be over-stimulating. Like many of their visual and auditory counterparts, the stimulation that one receives from such foods is due not to the energy they give us, but only to their irritating influence upon the bodily mechanism. Loud noise may seem to give one energy, but in fact it only lashes the nervous system into a kind of frenzy. The nervous movements of people whose senses have been over-stimulated express rather an unconscious effort to rid themselves of the stimulation than any deep drive toward constructive activity.

Similarly with stimulating foods. It is a physiological principle that, although a strong dose of poison may kill, a small dose may actually stimulate an organism. Any stimulation from without, however, unless it also builds up the inner organism, will exert its apparently wholesome influence primarily as an irritant.

Coffee is a well-known example. While its immediate effect is sometimes uplifting, its long-range effect is depressing. Caffeine has been said to kill Vitamin B in the body. People who drink too much coffee find that their own natural supply of energy is, if anything, lessened. They require more and more coffee to get the "lift" they seek. The same may be said of tea, tobacco, and other stimulants.

In yoga teachings, much emphasis is placed on a harmonious, rather than a stimulating, diet. If the inner Self is allowed to work through a relaxed and peaceful nervous system, it will be able to fill the body with energy and strength. External stimuli prevent this harmonious expression from within. Dietary stimulants are therefore self-defeating.

Stimulants, according to yoga teachings, fall into the category of *rajasic*, or activating, foods, as opposed to foods that completely enervate (*tamasic* foods), or to those which spiritualize man's consciousness (*sattwic* foods). *Rajasic* foods would include meat, eggs, garlic, and onions. Onions and garlic have some medicinal properties, but—from a standpoint of yoga practice—they tend to excite the nervous system and are usually excluded from the yogi's diet. I do not know what to say here in the West, where the demands of our environment are themselves so rajasic. Yoganandaji fed us onions and garlic in America, as well as eggs. I assume that his reason for doing so was that the Western world demands a certain adaptation of the Eastern teachings. Here, perhaps, some *rajasic* food is desirable, if only to help us to keep abreast of the currents of consciousness swirling around us.

Nonetheless, one should endeavor on the yogic path to introduce into his diet foods that are rather wholesome than stimulating. Coffee and black tea are frowned upon in the yoga teachings. There are many wholesome substitutes, such as cereal beverages and herb teas.

RECIPES

Yogi Tea

A wholesome tea that is often drunk in India is made by boiling 6 black peppercorns, 4 whole cardamom pods, 3 cloves, ½ cinnamon stick, and a slice of ginger root in 10 ounces of water for about 20 minutes. Strain. Serve with honey, if desired.

*Fruit Curry**

Fry in 2 tablespoons butter: 2 large diced tomatoes, 3 sliced bananas, 1 quartered and sliced apple, 1 sliced onion (optional), a small handful of raisins, and a handful of sliced almonds (blanched and slightly browned in butter), with a tablespoon of curry powder, 1 stick of cinnamon, 3 whole cardamom pods, 2 cloves, and (if desired) a little ginger. Simmer slowly for 25 minutes. Serve with brown rice. Makes 4 servings.

* *Also good without curry!*

VII. MEDITATION

The conditions of *yama* discussed in this lesson describe some of the attitudes most necessary to correct meditation. Meditation is not a process of mental passivity or blankness. It is a process, rather, that involves seeking *positively* to attune oneself with the subtle vibrations of the Infinite. Like an astronomer bringing his telescope into careful focus on a distant planet, or like a person trying to tune his radio sensitively to one station, and to tune out interference from other nearby stations, the beginning yogi must try to bring all his faculties to bear on the thought of God or of one of His attributes. (Later, when something of God's inner presence is actually perceived, the focus changes from mere imagination to direct experience.) The rules of *yama* are a necessary preliminary to this attunement, like the astronomer obtaining a first sighting on his planet, or the radio operator first moving the radio dial toward the desired wavelength, passing over those stations which do not carry the program he is seeking.

In many ways correct meditation requires a complete revolution in what are commonly looked upon as normal human attitudes. The competitive drive, for instance, implies an assumption that success must always be exclusive, even to the extent of being determined by other people's failures. In this world of relativities it is not possible for everyone to be a millionaire, or the president of a company, or a champion athlete. To compete with others for a high position may indeed help one to develop a high degree of excellence in himself, if self-development is the true motive. More often than not, however, competition merely serves to create an illusion of progress by eliminating one's competitors. Such an attitude will thwart the most earnest efforts to progress in meditation, for it will pit one against the universe instead of harmonizing him with it.

Right attitude is essential to right meditation. The first step in the development of right attitude is to learn to see others, not as rivals, but as friends. This is the principle of non-injury. Even if others, in their own ignorance, should hate you, think of them as your brothers or sisters in God, and bless them with His peace. This is not to say that you should cooperate with them in their ignorance, or offer yourself up as a doormat for their spite, but only that you should sincerely wish them a swift recovery from their disease of personal inharmony. Hatred can be as contagious as the flu; still the greatest sufferer is always he in whom the disease rages. Immunize yourself with extra-strong doses of compassion and impersonal, divine love.

In meditation, examine your heart for any feeling of ill will toward others. Carefully uproot any such feeling, and plant in its stead fragrant flowers of forgiveness. Only when your heart has been softened by universal benevolence may you hope to become receptive to the gentle vibrations of divine love. Do not imagine that you can win God's love until you have developed the power to win the love of man.

Truthfulness, too, is an important attitude for right meditation. Otherwise one's meditations may reinforce rather than banish one's delusions. Inner states of consciousness can be deceptive. Many apparently spiritual experiences are rooted in subconsciousness, not in superconsciousness. Only by the strictest self-honesty can one escape the intricacies of self-deception.

Non-stealing implies another attitude that is essential to right meditation. It signifies a realization that one can never truly possess what is not one's own, and that one's own will surely come to him (a favorite saying of Sister Gyanamata's, Paramhansa Yogananda's chief woman disciple). This is not to say that one should not work hard, but only that one ought not to be anxious about anything. Whose world is this, anyway? God can work best to bring human hopes to fruition through the instrumentality of those persons who keep their minds open to Him by an attitude of perfect trust. When you meditate, offer all of your anxieties up to Him. Tell yourself: "Whatever comes of itself, let it come." Only a trusting, divinely receptive attitude can prepare you to receive, in all their subtlety, the highest states of consciousness.

Non-sensuality in meditation means to realize that real meditation is not possible so long as one remains in body consciousness. One must endeavor to go beyond the senses—to withdraw his energy from them so completely that he is quite literally, as the modern expression goes, "out of this world."

Non-greed as applied to meditation means the nonacceptance of, or non-identification with, anything that might limit one's awareness. When you meditate, mentally relinquish all attachment to places, people, and possessions. Do not even be bound by the *self*-definitions to which you have been so long accustomed to confine yourself. You are not an American or a Frenchman, an artist or a businessman, a man or a woman, miserly or philanthropic, young or old. You are the immortal soul. Even your human virtues are but small steppingstones on the way to an infinite perfection.

To become really settled in any of the principles of *yama,* you must practice all of the others also. They are all interdependent. To be perfectly non-attached (the last of these principles), for example, also implies an attitude of non-injury, for to grasp at anything—even something so elusive as a psychological trait—is always in a sense to harm it. Non-attachment requires also an attitude of strict self-honesty, or truthfulness, and is in turn a necessary attitude for perfect truthfulness. Non-attachment to what one possesses would be a mockery if at the same time one desired what one did not possess, in defiance of the principle of non-stealing. And true non-attachment would be impossible without *brahmacharya,* or mental detachment from the senses.

Perfect non-injury, similarly, requires also truthfulness, or complete recognition of realities other than one's own. It requires a complete respect for the rights of others, which is an aspect of the principle of non-stealing. It requires an attitude of non-sensuality, which is inevitably a kind of taking from life—besides being, of course, injurious to one's own body and nervous system. It requires, finally, an attitude of non-attachment (not, be it noted, of indifference), for only in complete recognition that everything, including one's own life and body, belongs only to God can one put oneself truly in harmony with the universe. Otherwise, egotistically, one will always play his flute out of tune with the symphony of creation.

Perfect truthfulness, similarly, means an attitude of non-injury in the sense of not wanting to punish others (which is to say, of not judging them) for being what their natures have made them. An attitude of non-stealing, or non-taking from life—in other words, of desirelessness—is essential if we would see all things truthfully and without bias. Non-sensuality, finally, gives one that mental poise by which alone one can be completely honest in his perceptions.

Non-stealing, similarly, is refined by an attitude of non-injury, vitalized by truthfulness, brought into clear focus by a deep understanding of non-sensuality, and simplified by perfect non-attachment.

None of these principles can be really perfected until divine perfection is attained. All of them require for their perfection that they be related always to that ultimate perfection. In relation to one's search for God they are all, in the last analysis, simply an effort to make oneself over in His infinite image.

In meditation, mentally cast all your limitations—of thought, desire, and self-will—into a divine fire to be melted and purified into cosmic wisdom and love. Affirm mentally, *"I cast my thoughts, desires, and all past karma into Thy flames of love. Make me whole! Make me pure! Make me one with Thee!"*

It might help you also to build an actual fire, and to place bits of wood into it, or to cast into it grains of rice, feeling each time you do so that you are casting from your heart some egoic imperfection.

Pray to God with love: *"I am Thine; be Thou mine!"*

AUM, *Shanti, Shanti, Shanti!*

Step Five

Niyama

I. PHILOSOPHY

Niyama

Niyama means non-control. It refers to the observances, or "do's," on the path of yoga. The rules listed are five:

1) Cleanliness
2) Contentment
3) *Tapasya,* or Austerity
4) *Swadhyaya,* or Self-Study
5) Devotion to the Supreme Lord

As with the rules of *yama,* those of *niyama* must be understood in a subtle as well as in an obvious sense.

1) Cleanliness means not only physical cleanliness, but also a heart cleansed of attachments, and of the vain preoccupations of a worldly mind.

Cleanliness of body is important for the yogi. Without physical cleanliness there can be no real beginning at self-mastery. The physically unclean person is forced into an awareness of his body that prevents him from soaring to loftier perceptions. The body is unclean not only when physical dirt and other foreign matter attach themselves to it externally, but also when unnatural foods are introduced into it internally—when one cannot properly eliminate waste products from his body.

The heart of man is impure when it longs for anything that is foreign to its own nature. Dirt is not dirt when it is out-of-doors on the ground. There, it is more properly thought of as earth. It is when earth is found indoors that it is considered unclean. To long for the things of this world is a mark of inner impurity not necessarily because the things of this world are impure in themselves (can anything made by God be considered essentially unholy?), but because the soul's true and natural realm is the spiritual. "Father," said St. Augustine, "Thou hast made us for Thyself, and our hearts are restless until they find their rest in Thee." It is the nature of the soul to find fulfillment in itself, in communion with the Highest Reality.

Cleanliness, outwardly and inwardly, physically and mentally, is a necessary step towards freedom from the physical imperatives. Patanjali says that from perfect cleanliness there arises a consciousness of freedom from the body, a disinclination for its natural pleasures. By the same token, he says, one who has reached this state is no longer inclined to seek pleasure from others, physically, nor to commune with them on a physical plane; one's love for them becomes selfless and spiritual. For when the heart has been freed of internal impurities, one is able to see through the veil of matter and to discover in all men the spiritual essence that is his own Self. Once the dust of selfish desire has been removed from the rooms of man's inner consciousness, he is able to see that the things he has desired in this physical world are but Spirit, too, in essence.

The Sanskrit word from which I (and most writers) have taken the meaning, "disinclination" (for one's own body and for contact with the bodies of others), means also, "protectiveness." Protectiveness toward the body, and a sense of protection of the body from contact with others, while more a practice than a result of virtue (Patanjali's actual reference was to the *fruits* of cleanliness), is yet a valid and important aspect of this subject. For the vibrations of every man's consciousness are, in a sense, unique. If he mixes indiscriminately with others, even though desiring nothing from them, there will yet be an interchange of vibrations that may dilute his own personal life stream. The vibrations of other men, though not necessarily bad in themselves, may yet be subtly disturbing to one's own vibrations, to one's own particular line of inner development. To mix with few people, and to try to limit even this association to the company of spiritual people, can be invaluable to spiritual progress. Yogis often, indeed, prefer total solitude during certain sensitive stages of their spiritual unfoldment. (I can offer a personal testimony on this point: I have a spot in the woods to which I go when I want to escape the continual demands that are made on my time. I am always amazed at the inner freedom that I feel, not only in escaping those demands, but in being in a place that has no other human vibrations but my own. It is as if countless psychic strings had been untied, leaving me free inwardly to fly.) There are yogis who will never wear other people's clothing, who eat only from their own dishes, sleep in their own bedding, and who sit down only after first spreading out their own cloths upon which to sit. A widespread custom that has its basis in this same principle is the *namaskar,* a palms-folded greeting (meaning, "My soul bows to your soul") that is the common Indian alternative to the Western handshake.

Worldly people insist that one live

among them, and be as much like them as possible, seeking God (if one must) in the noise and turmoil of the marketplace. It is true, of course, that God is everywhere, and that therefore He can be found anywhere. But to find Him it is important, no matter where one seeks Him, that one weed out of one's heart everything that is extraneous to one's own spiritual nature. If one can go off to a quiet place, where the distractions are fewer, one's progress will be more rapid. Spiritual progress comes not so much by learning to cope with the world as by learning not to *depend* on the world. And while it is true that obstacles may help to awaken in one that energetic determination without which real growth is impossible, there are obstacles enough and to spare in oneself for it to be quite unnecessary to add to them deliberately. Anyone who courts the world in the name of increasing his spiritual strength is more than likely seeking an excuse to indulge his worldly, not his spiritual, inclinations.

Cleanliness on all levels helps to free the mind, that it may soar in the infinite skies. In meditation, approach God with a pure heart, offering up all your desires to Him. In the practice of *hatha yoga,* too, cleanliness must be considered a paramount principle. It is probably the essence of *hatha yoga* practice, involving as it does the removal of toxins and of other physical impurities, of tension, of obstructions to the flow of energy in the body. *Hatha yoga* concentrates less on increasing one's energy than on removing those impurities which prevent one from having the perfect strength and radiant well-being that are his spiritual birthright.

2) Contentment is often praised by yogis as the supreme virtue. If one can oppose with deliberate contentment the tendency of the heart to reach outside itself for its satisfactions, one feels joy inwardly unceasingly.

Every worldly satisfaction is possible only because of a joyousness in the heart. Without inner joy, external fulfillment is impossible. If one has inner joy, however, and knows that it is within that the source of joy truly lies, he can enjoy all things innocently as reflections of that inner consciousness. Purity and cleanliness mean freedom from the need for anything, in the realization that one already *is* everything. This realization brings supreme joy to the soul. The soul realizes that it *is* joy.

But joy cannot be found by merely waiting for it to come, as if it, like outward fulfillments, were hiding somewhere over the horizon in futurity. Joy is always right NOW. Divine states have a way of coming (in the words of Jesus) "like a thief in the night." We should not pray, "Lord, why don't You give me Your joy?" We should pray *with* joy, and we shall discover in the very act of expressing joy that we have opened our channels to Divine Joy.

Do not merely say, then, negatively, that you are not attached to this thing or to that person. Affirm always positively in your heart, "Whatever comes of itself, let it come, but I am ever content in my inner heart." This practice, Patanjali says, leads ultimately to the realization of Divine Bliss in every atom of creation, even beyond creation.

In the practice of the yoga postures, do them always with a sense of quiet enjoyment. Feel almost as if you were smiling while you practice the postures. Learn the rhythm and capacities of your own body, and lead it gently on the pathway to perfection. Western culture is not geared to think that one can be conscientious in doing one's duty, whether to oneself or to the world, and yet remain inwardly happy. The furrowed brow, the compressed lips—these, to the worldly mind, are the price one pays for having serious goals in life. But in fact one can accomplish a great deal more if he enjoys his work. One can advance far more rapidly in yoga, too, if one bears in mind this teaching of great yogis, that contentment is the supreme virtue.

3) *Tapasya,* or austerity, is not a popular word in the West. To the Westerner, a contented life means one that is cluttered with the so-called "good" things: television, fine clothes, the best of foods, the latest in transportation. But these things, as we have already said, rob one of his contentment. The more distractions a person has, the more empty he feels in his heart. It is necessary to weed—indeed, to *thrust*—out of one's life the distractions that reach out coaxingly from every billboard, and from the dancing eyes of people who still hope to find their fulfillment in things.

There is a certain amount of sternness necessary if one is to stem this outward-pulling tide. To the dilettante it will always seem that the creative artist, concentrating silently on his work, is missing half the fun in life. But the artist knows that, unless and until he can channel his energies, he will not be able to create things of lasting beauty.

Patanjali says that from this redirection of one's energies—from external matter to the inner self—one develops certain subtle powers, or yogic *siddhi*s, that are latent in man. Once these powers, no longer spilled and wasted on the sands of matter, are gathered and directed one-pointedly by a consciousness that is in full command of itself, yogis claim that there is scarcely any feat of which one is not capable. It is said that great yogis can create and destroy galaxies. Certain it is that the fulfillment found in the Self is far greater than could possibly be found by a mind that imagines itself to be free in its scorn for self-restraint, while it runs undisciplined through the "labyrinthine ways" of sense indulgence.

Every act of the yogi should be deliberate. He should sit with a sense of setting his body down to rest, rather than of collapsing into a chair. He should move, talk, smile, and eat always with a sense that he is his own master, never with the feeling that his body is running away with him like a car on a hill when its brakes suddenly fail.

When you sit to meditate, discipline your mind to behave. Don't let it run away with you merely because it wants to, because that is its habit. Make the very first minutes of meditation as earnest and deep as the last.

In *hatha yoga* one should be very deliberate, and yet harmonious, in every movement, whether it be only the uncurling of a finger. Austerity, far from implying a grim attitude, is really the concomitant of an attitude of perfect inner contentment.

4) *Swadhyaya* is usually translated to mean, simply, "study" (usually of the scriptures). But *swa* means *self*. The proper translation, then, is "*self*-study." The proper study of man lies not in books or in the gathering of intellectual information; it is the supreme adventure of self-discovery. But again, *self*-study means a great deal more than self-analysis and the probing of one's hidden motives. It means also, in a deeper sense, self-awareness.

It has been said that the difference between true yogic studies and those which are encouraged in school is that in school one seeks to gain learning, whereas in yoga one seeks to lose it. *Self*-study, in a yogic sense, signifies rooting out from one's heart those delusions and false attachments which prevent one from realizing who and what he really is: the Infinite Spirit.

Self-study begins with the careful observation of one's thoughts, feelings, and motives. As one advances in this practice, he discovers that central reality of his being which is beyond thought, form, and substance, which cannot be observed and analyzed, which cannot even be truly defined, though it is sometimes described by its essential quality: JOY.

Patanjali says that when one becomes perfect in his practice of *swadhyaya,* he attains the power to commune with beings on higher spheres of existence, and to receive their help.

Radio and TV programs surround us in the atmosphere, but we cannot enjoy them until we attune our radios or TV sets to those frequencies. Higher beings, similarly, exist, as also do higher levels of consciousness. The worldly man, however, unable to attune his mind sensitively enough to perceive them, can scarcely imagine their existence. By self-study, and the resulting discovery of deep states of consciousness within oneself, one attains those frequency-levels on which it is possible to commune with great souls. If one would be helped by them, he must make himself a fit vessel to receive that help.

This, it must be understood also, is the deeper purpose of yoga postures: not merely to give one a healthy body, but to prepare the body as one would a temple for communion with the Infinite Lord, and with those exalted beings who live always in His light.

5) Devotion to the Supreme Lord, the fifth and last of the rules of *niyama,* may raise the question: "If yoga is not based on beliefs, but only on practices, why then speak of God at all?" Yet no man can rise spiritually who does not have in his mind some thought that there must be something higher than his present consciousness. If a child were to insist that it could learn nothing from its elders, it might remain forever in ignorance. If man rejected every tradition, he would have to reinvent everything for his own use—even the wheel. If, then, the yogi, in reaching out toward higher realities, chooses to call those realities, "God," what is the objection? Man can never understand with his little mind anything so vastly beyond his comprehension as a state of absolute perfection, but that he should be devoted to this ideal is right and proper. Without such devotion, he would stagnate in the shallow pond of egoic limitations.

My great guru, Paramhansa Yogananda, once said, "When you find God, you will know that He is a conscious Being to whom one can appeal, and not merely some abstract mental state." Those great souls who have communed with the Infinite have testified, each in his own language, to the reality of the Infinite Spirit. Though they have described God as man's own Self, they have yet said that this true Self is infinitely greater than the little body and personality to which we presently limit ourselves—even as consciousness, expressed in the billions of creatures in this world, cannot conceivably be limited to their own little brains. To speak of the Infinite as our own self, though it is indeed that in essence, might be to limit it to our present level of egoic self-awareness, rather than to expand this awareness to the farthest boundaries of Self-realization. The yogis say, therefore, that it is good to speak of God as though He were apart from ourselves, even though in fact He is not. (For as Jesus said, "The Kingdom of God is within.")

To have devotion to the Supreme Being is essential for spiritual progress. Without devotion, one can no more advance on the path to God than one would advance on any difficult road in this world, if one had no desire to reach the journey's goal. True devotion is not a slavish attitude. It is only an effort of the heart to lift itself up into that consciousness where Divine Love is felt and known. As with self-study (*swadhyaya*), where one attunes himself to those rays of light on which higher beings move and is thus able to commune with them, so also with this practice of devotion: Patanjali says that by supreme love one enters upon that ray of divine love on which the Infinite Consciousness forever dwells. Without that love, it is not possible to receive the subtle broadcastings emanating from the heart of the Infinite Silence. That is why Jesus said: "Blessed are the pure in heart, for they shall see God."

Even the yoga postures should be done with a sense of worship if one is to receive from them the fullest benefit. They were originated, not by football coaches and P.E. teachers, but by great sages who recognized in certain postures the outward expressions of inward movements of the soul.

II. YOGA POSTURES

No telescope has ever revealed a section of the heavens where angels flit beatifically about their daily duties; nor has any probe into the earth brought up a leering devil along with the oil. Heaven is not really above us, nor is hell down below. For in a cosmic sense, there is no up or down; what is up for us is down for the people in Australia, and vice versa.

Jesus Christ said that the kingdom of God is within. Heaven, too, is within ourselves. In this sense the scriptural teachings can be tested and proved true. According to the yoga teachings, man must raise the energy in his body through the spine to the brain if he would know the fulfillment that he seeks—usually, alas, in a million misdirections. The Spirit is spoken of as One without a second. When the Spirit brought all things into existence, it did not create this universe out of nothing. Everything that is has always existed—but as Spirit, not as matter or energy. The Spirit manifested this universe out of Its own consciousness. It did so by dividing that one consciousness into polar opposites: positive and negative, heat and cold, pleasure and pain, etc. Picture, if you will, a tug of war in which the two groups pulling against each other are evenly matched. They expend tremendous amounts of energy; they may indeed feel that they are working to the limit of their strength; but in fact no overall movement takes place. The stretching of consciousness, similarly, in opposite directions from a state of rest in the center, and the tension that is employed in such a stretch, explains figuratively the nature of creation.

The longer the rope, and the more the people pulling on it, the greater the tension, even though there is no actual movement visible. Similarly, the stronger the polarity away from the state of oneness in Spirit, the greater the tension. All spiritual progress may be seen as a gradual returning from this polar stretch, this outward reaching toward physical manifestation, a final sinking to rest in the Absolute Spirit. In the egotist, and in the worldly person, the tension is greater because the pull away from this central reality is stronger.

In all things one may observe this cosmic principle of duality, or *dwaita,* at work: in heat and cold, in love and hatred, in joy and sorrow, in male and female, in pleasure and pain, in positive and negative. Implicit in everything created is its polar opposite. The attraction between opposites is never so strong as when a great effort is made to go in only one of the two opposite directions, even as the pull of a rubber band becomes stronger, the more one stretches it. As the man who is exaggeratedly masculine is more likely to be attracted to women than the man who finds less need to devote all his time to playing the male role, similarly, one who seeks fulfillment intensively in physical pleasures is attracted irresistibly to physical pains. The person who tries to overcome "blue" moods by external means, such as parties, movies, and loud laughter, only brings himself more under the sway of repeated bouts of depression.

In all of life there is an urge, consciously or unconsciously felt, for the Oneness which is our true and natural state. This Oneness can be found, not by going to some far-out extreme in which at last the opposite to that extreme (pain, for example, as opposed to pleasure) is left forever behind, but rather by returning to the central point within our selves; to the horizon line that rests forever between all opposites; to the state of rest at the bottom of the pendulum's swing.

Modern science, particularly the science of psychology, claims that self-integration can be found only by expressing one's lower nature. Man in his lower nature lives in the state of tension which comes from identification with this world of duality. It is in his higher nature that he can find fulfillment. This higher nature does not imply a state of tension, in which attraction to the one must necessarily bring about the experience of its opposite. The energy that rises in the spine, bringing inner bliss, indicates the one direction in which man may go and actually escape the polar tug of war. The resolution of opposites has already taken place to a large extent before such an upward movement is possible. It is as if two ropes held a balloon from opposite sides to the ground. When these ropes are severed, the balloon can rise to its own natural height. In the case of man, this height is the "Eternal Vacuum" of Spirit, in which no forms or limitations of any kind exist; there is only consciousness.

On the left and right sides of the

spine are two nerve channels, known in Sanskrit as *iḍa* and *pingala.* The very name, *hatha,* refers to the movement of energy in these two channels. *Ha* is the upward movement of energy on the left side of the spine; it is identified with the solar energy. *Tha* refers to the downward movement of energy on the right side of the spine; it is related to the negative, or lunar, energy. As the energy moves up and down in these two channels, man is kept in a state of duality. The upward movement on the left side is associated with health, courage, good moods, laughter. It is also associated with the inhalation of the breath, and is indeed said in the yoga teachings to *cause* the inhalation. The downward movement on the right side is associated with discouragement, with ill health, with death. It is said to be the cause of the exhalation. When the upward movement is strong, the inhalation also is strong; when the downward movement is strong, the exhalation becomes strong. Notice, when a sick person's fever rises to, say, 104 degrees, how the exhalation becomes noticeably stronger than the inhalation. Notice, again, how an unhappy person sighs, while a joyous person inhales deeply as if drawing into himself the wonders of the universe.

These ups and downs are the way of the world. But the yogi, by tracing his mental footsteps back from every effect to its cause (which is to say, in this case, by concentrating on the currents in the spine rather than on the outward identifications that they engender in his mind, and by deliberately controlling and balancing this spinal flow of energy), gradually learns to bring these polar opposites back to a state of rest in the center of the spine. This is a deeper teaching of yoga—too deep for this lesson—but here we may say that when these superficial currents have been neutralized, the energy is freed to rise toward the brain. As it does so, the soul's consciousness is gradually retraced from solid matter, through increasingly subtle states of awareness, until the human being becomes truly divine.

In the postures it is important always to balance every movement with its opposite. When you bend to the left, bend also to the right. When you bend forward, bend also backward. Try through these balanced movements gradually to center yourself in the spine. Then try to raise your consciousness toward the brain.

Be graceful getting into each posture and coming out of it. The more relaxed and graceful you can be, the more you will express the inner harmony that comes when one no longer struggles toward one extreme of consciousness or another. Again, try to do the postures with a consciousness of raising your energy toward the brain. Keep your hands turned up as you come into a pose; notice the difference of feeling, the inward lift that this movement gives to your energy. Do all the postures with the feeling that you are using them almost as gentle breezes to waft your spirits upward.

Ardha-Dhanurasana

(The Half Bow Pose)

"I recall my scattered forces to recharge my spine."

Or: *"Each wave of trials can only raise me to new heights."*

Lie on your front, as for *Dhanurasana* (the Bow Pose). Raise your shoulders, and rest the weight of your upper body on your left forearm, which should be across your body and parallel with the shoulders. With the right hand, grasp your left foot, and raise the left leg completely off the ground. Affirm mentally: *"I recall my scattered forces to recharge my spine."* Or, visualize yourself floating cheerfully over the crests of all difficulties, and affirm mentally: *"Each wave of trials can only raise me to new heights."* Hold this position 15 to 30 seconds. Rest. Then repeat with the other arm and leg.

Benefits: This position is easier than the Full Bow Pose. It also helps to give a certain twist to the spine, adjusting it in a way that the Full Bow Pose does not effect.

The "V" Pose, or Balance Pose

(also known as *Navasana*)

"Within my every breath is infinite power."

Lie on your back, extending your arms down at the side. Come up simultaneously with the upper body and the legs, keeping your head parallel with your feet. Rest your hands on the knees. All the weight should be on the buttocks. Inhale as you come into the position; exhale as you come out of it. Hold the position for 10 to 15 seconds to begin with, gradually increasing the time to whatever length you find comfortable. (One is not likely to overdo this position; it is not that comfortable!)

Benefits: The "V" Pose is excellent for developing a sense of balance, and for toning the stomach and thigh muscles.

Karnapirasana

(The Ear-Closing Pose)

"My boat of life floats lightly on tides of peace."

Go into *Halasana* (the Plow Pose), then drop your knees down to the floor, pressing them against the shoulders and closing the ears. One may affirm mentally while holding this position: "*My boat of life floats lightly on tides of peace.*"

Hold the position as long as you like, but not longer than one minute.

Benefits: This position, once you can assume it comfortably, is surprisingly restful to the brain, as well as to the body. It is an excellent pose for tired businessmen after a hard day's work at the office!

First go into ***Halasana*** (the Plow Pose)

Karnapirasana

(The Ear-Closing Pose)

"My boat of life floats lightly on tides of peace."

Chakrasana

(The Circle Pose)

"I am awake! energetic! enthusiastic!"

To assume the Circle Pose, lie on your back; bring your feet up to your buttocks, and place your hands palms downward on the ground above the shoulders, with the fingers pointing back toward the body. It may help you if you bring your body down a little farther onto the feet. Raise the body slightly, dropping the head back, and arch the spine as far up as it will go. Try to relax the trunk as much as possible; be more aware of your energy in the spine than of the tension of the body.

Hold this position for not more than 15 seconds to start with, gradually increasing the time with practice to one minute. Return slowly to the ground. Never collapse out of a yoga position; always be in full command of your body's movements. Rest in *Savasana* (the Corpse Pose).

As you practice the Circle Pose, feel that you are lifting yourself up out of the long sleep of delusion, of sluggishness and apathy. Affirm mentally: *"I am awake! energetic! enthusiastic!"*

The beginner may have difficulty assuming this position. Some of its benefits can be attained by simply bending backward over the seat of an armless chair.

Adepts may prefer to bend backward from a standing position, their hands over their heads, until their hands touch the ground. To learn this method of assuming the Circle Pose, you may stand with your back to a wall and "walk" down the wall with your hands. The closer the hands can be brought to the feet, the more perfect the pose.

Benefits: Although the position of the body in this pose is similar to that in the Bow Pose, there are certain distinct differences. The backward bend in the Circle Pose involves the entire spine and neck, rather than only the lower back. The relaxed position of the neck makes this pose an excellent one to do after the Plow Pose; the backward bend of the neck offsets any discomfort that may have come from the extreme forward bend of the Plow Pose.

Psychologically, the Circle Pose is marvelous for recharging the body and mind with energy. It is a good pose to do in the morning upon awakening, or whenever one feels tired or sluggish during the day.

Chakrasana is said to be an antidote to obesity. The general invigorating effect of this posture makes it one of the most important of all the *asana*s. *Chakrasana* should not be practiced by women, however, during menstruation, pregnancy, or for several months after childbirth. Persons, also, who are suffering from hernia, "hollow back," or slipped vertebrae, should avoid it.

Simhasana

(The Lion Pose)

"I purify my thoughts, my speech, my every action."

Kneel on the ground, with the buttocks resting on the heels. Place the palms on the knees with the fingers spread outward. Inhale, raising the chest, and open the mouth wide, stretching the tongue outward and downward as far as possible. Open the eyes wide, looking downward. Feel energy in the throat.

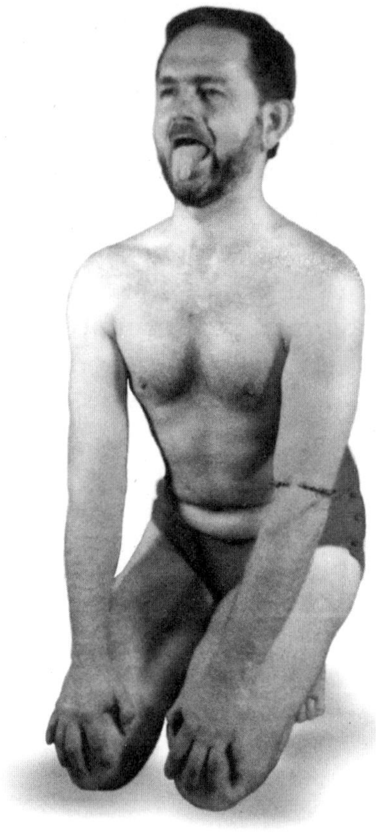

Hold this position for one minute to start with, longer with practice, but never longer than three minutes.

While in the Lion Pose, tense the body as if you were a lion straining forward toward its prey. The sense of springing, however, should be inward, with no thought of anything outward to spring towards.

Benefits: The idea here is to raise all the energy of the body upward toward the throat.

The upward movement of the chest, and the inhalation, should bring energy upward to the throat from the lower body. The downward gaze of the eyes should send energy down to the throat from the brain. In this position, all the energy of the body is converged upon the throat. This is an excellent position for overcoming or preventing sore throats and colds.

Some writers say that while assuming this pose one should exhale and roll the eyes upward. I cannot but feel that this advice is mistaken. The exhalation takes energy downward, away from the throat. The upward gaze sends energy upward, also away from the throat. The main purpose of the Lion Pose is its benefit to the throat. Every movement of the body should be directed with this purpose in mind.

The Lion Pose is also beneficial for the ears and eyes.

III. BREATHING

The basic movements of breathing in *hatha yoga* are called: *purak* (inhalation), *rechak* (exhalation), and *kumbhak* (retention of the breath). The implications here are less obvious than first appearances may suggest. *Purak,* or inhalation, is associated with the upward movement of energy in the spine, and thus with an affirmation of life, of strength, of the joy of living. *Rechak,* or exhalation, is associated with the downward movement of energy in the spine, and thus with the elimination of disease and sorrow, or with an attitude of surrender. When greeting a sunny day joyously, one tends to inhale, as if drawing into one's very lungs the wonders of creation. When one is ill or unhappy, he sighs as if to throw the burden out of his body or mind. The increasing power of inhalation or exhalation is associated with the strengthening of the upward or downward spinal currents. The balance of these two currents results in a state of mental poise, and in a deepening inner awareness. When the two currents are perfectly balanced, even the movement of physical breathing is stopped. Only in breathlessness is one able completely to concentrate the mind. Advanced yogis are able to remain breathless for long periods of time. The practice of *kumbhak,* or forcible retention of breath, is done for brief periods in order to focus one's mind on a particular thought or state of consciousness.

The yogi should combine breathing with an endeavor to expand his consciousness. As you inhale, feel that you are drawing strength, courage, and joy up your spine to the brain. While holding the breath, mentally affirm the positive state of consciousness that you are trying to develop. As you exhale, feel that you are throwing out of your body all opposing states of weakness, discouragement, and sorrow. If you have a specific problem, physical or mental, you may use this technique to affirm the opposite state of well-being, and to throw the negative condition out of your system.

In meditation, however, the exhalation may be used also in conjunction with a feeling, not of negative despair, but of positive surrender into the arms of Infinite Peace.

A breathing exercise that is intended to help balance and harmonize the two currents in the spine (known as *pran* and *apan*) is a technique known as alternate breathing. Close the right nostril, inhaling through the left for a count of 8; hold the breath, counting 8; close the left nostril and exhale through the right to a count of 8. A slight constriction in the throat, so as to make a gentle sound there during respiration, will help to increase the consciousness of the corresponding movement of energy in the spine. Repeat six times.

The proper position of the fingers during this breathing exercise is to extend the thumb and the ring and little fingers, closing the forefinger and middle finger against the palm. Close the right nostril with the thumb of the right hand. Close the left nostril with the ring and little fingers.

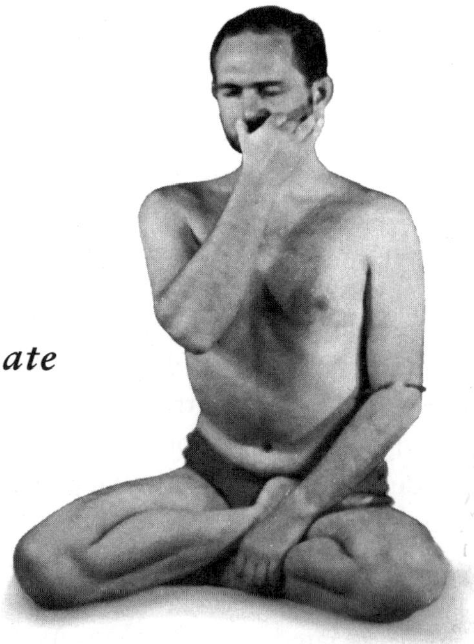

The Alternate Breath

IV. ROUTINE

Sit cross-legged on the floor. Calm your body within and without. Practice the Alternate Breath (as learned in this lesson) 6 times. Rest. Then practice *Sitkari Pranayama* (Step Four) 3 times. Inhale very slowly and deeply, with the Full Yogic Breath, 3 times. Then sit calmly, concentrating your mind at the point between the eyebrows, until you feel completely centered in yourself.

Stand, and practice the Double Breath 3 times. Then practice the following poses:

Vrikasana (the Tree Pose)

Trikonasana (the Triangle Pose)

Chandrasana (the Moon Pose)

Padahastasana (the Jackknife Pose), followed by the Backward Bend.

Savasana (the Corpse Pose), 1 minute.

The "V" Pose, or Balance Pose, 15 seconds, followed by the Corpse Pose for 30 seconds.

Janushirasana (the Head-to-the-Knee Pose)

Paschimotanasana (the Posterior Stretch), followed by the Corpse Pose for 30 seconds to one minute.

Halasana (the Plow Pose), followed by *Karnapirasana* (the Ear-Closing Pose)—approximate total time: 2 minutes. End with the Corpse Pose.

Chakrasana (the Circle Pose), 15 seconds, followed by a 30-second rest in *Savasana.*

Ardha-Dhanurasana (the Half Bow Pose)

Bhujangasana (the Cobra Pose)

End with *Savasana* (the Corpse Pose), for approximately 5 minutes.

Approximate total time: 30 to 40 minutes

V. HEALING

Respiration Troubles

Respiration troubles are among the most serious obstacles to yoga practice, simply because breathing is such an important part of most yoga techniques. Colds and sinus troubles are particularly annoying; they affect the very brain, making it difficult to concentrate and meditate.

Postures that are beneficial for the sinuses are the inverted poses (to be considered in later lessons)—particularly the Headstand. Deep, slow breathing through the nostrils, feeling as one inhales that he is drawing cool air up into the brain, can be beneficial for the sinuses, and also for the brain when it is affected by sinus congestion.

The sinuses, and colds generally, can be helped by taking a teaspoonful of Borax and dissolving it in a glass of lukewarm water. Take enough of this solution to fill a small nasal douche, which may be bought inexpensively at any drug store. Hold the head back and fill both nostrils with this solution. Keep this position for about a minute. Then close the nostrils with the fingers and drop the head forward, until it is more or less inverted. Hold this second position for about a minute. Blow the solution alternately out of each nostril. This exercise may be practiced daily. A saline solution may be used as an alternate, but my guru recommended Borax to me.*

A more difficult exercise for clearing the nasal passages is one that is known in *hatha yoga* as *neti.* I do not recommend that *neti* be practiced without personal supervision, as there is some danger of damaging the sensitive

* Be sure to buy *U.S.P. Grade Borax* (available from a chemical supply house). *Borax* is not to be confused with *Boraxo*, a detergent containing lye and harmful to the nose and sinus cavities, or with *boric acid.*

mucous membranes. If one exercises extreme caution, however, it may be all right. A soft string is introduced into one of the nostrils, allowed to come down behind the nasal passage, and brought out into the mouth. It will be easier to push it up if the first inch or so of the string is slightly stiffened with wax. Grasp the string in the mouth with the thumb and forefinger and pull it out. Then grasp the ends of the string with either hand, and pull it back and forth *very gently* several times. Repeat with the other nostril.

Any inverted position of the head, including the Hare Pose and the Circle Pose, will be beneficial for the sinuses. The Alternate Breath also is beneficial.

An excellent posture for a sore throat is *Simhasana* (the Lion Pose). The Plow Pose also is beneficial. Any forward and backward stretch to the neck will help to relieve tensions there, and to increase the flow of energy that is needed to overcome both sore throats and colds.

This last principle applies also to asthma. The stretching forward and backward of the vertebrae opposite to the chest will help to relieve tension, which is often responsible for attacks of asthma in sufferers from this ailment.

For asthma, practice the following postures: *Sirshasana* (the Headstand)—to be taught in Step Eleven; *Sarvangasana* (the Shoulder Stand)—Step Eleven; *Matsyasana* (the Fish Pose)—Step Ten; *Parvatasana* (the Mountain Pose)—Step Ten; *Savasana* (the Corpse Pose).

Deep, full breathing is beneficial for most respiratory ailments, but it should be slow, never forced. Feel as you inhale that you are freeing all the respiratory passages, driving out congestion by the power of strength and joy. In pleurisy, deep breathing may not be advisable owing to the friction that may be caused between the lungs and the pleura, or lining of the lung cavity. (It might be interesting to consider whether this physical friction is not in some way related to certain mental or emotional "frictions.")

Some Western health writers have stated that colds are Nature's means of eliminating poisons from the body. This obviously is true, but I do not concur with the further thought expressed by these writers, namely, that one should therefore do nothing for a cold, but simply allow it to run its course. Any trouble, physical or mental, may be taken as a means of eliminating some inharmony from the system, but if one passively allows such trouble to work its will on the body, one ends up temporarily cleansed, but in no way stronger than before. If one generates enough energy in the body to overcome a cold, one is not merely suppressing symptoms; one is destroying poisons in a dynamic way. Disease of any kind is the body's way of saying, "You have burdened me too heavily. I must shake off some of these poisons if I am to function properly." But the mind can strengthen the body so that it eliminates these poisons without surrendering its control. In this way, obstacles can be used as a means to develop one's inner strength. As one increases his vitality, he is not only less subject to existing poisons, and able to get rid of them in a way that does not damage the body through its surrender to them; he also destroys the poisons, burning them up in the fire of energy.

Some people find that cow's milk increases the flow of mucus. If this is your case, and if you still wish to drink milk, you may find goat's milk to be better.

With any kind of mucus infection, too much milk drinking, too many starches and sugars, and overeating generally, is to be avoided.

I have found that if I can "seize" a cold just as it is starting, and consciously, with will power, command it to leave my body, filling my whole body with energy as I do so, the cold usually is gone in a matter of minutes.

Cold weather is not a cause of colds, but it may help cold germs to multiply once they have already established a beachhead in the body. The most important prevention for colds is not bundling up and keeping warm, but rather to energize the body with will.

For colds and sore throat, practice the following poses: *Sirshasana* (the Headstand)—to be taught in Step Eleven; *Sarvangasana* (the Shoulder Stand)—Step Eleven; *Jivha Bandha* (the Tongue Lock)—Step Thirteen; *Simhasana* (the Lion Pose).

VI. DIET

Fasting

Fasting is one of Nature's ways of giving the body a chance to overcome disease and return to a state of normalcy. Animals, when they are unwell, will often instinctively fast. There is not room enough here to go into this important subject at length, but it will be helpful to mention that yogis recommend fasting, provided it is not carried to extremes. Fasting is beneficial not only physically, but also spiritually. It helps one to emphasize his freedom from bodily imperatives. Prolonged fasts under expert supervision have often been the means of curing serious physical ailments, even cancer. The student is advised to read books on the subject, readily available in any health food store.

There are different kinds of fasts: total and partial. Partial fasts include the taking of selected foods, or even of only one type of food: for example, carrot juice, or grape juice. Any kind of food intake, while in certain cases good for stimulating the elimination of poisons, will not give the body the complete rest of a total fast. Liquids (apart from water) are still food, and cause the body to work to digest it.

Yogis recommend fasting one day a week, either totally or on water only. They also suggest fasting three days once a month on fruit juices. The stomach, like the rest of the body, needs periods of rest and rejuvenation.

While fasting, try to draw energy into your body by other means. Inhale very deeply, filling your whole body with energy. Yogis recommend also a strange technique that we shall discuss in detail in a later lesson. It is known as *Kechari Mudra*. It consists of joining the tip of the tongue to the uvula (the soft, fleshy lobe that hangs from the soft palate at the back of the mouth), or with certain nerves in the nasal passages behind the soft palate. This position draws energy to the brain and body. Yogis say that bears in hibernation keep their tongues locked in this position, and thereby live through the winter without food. To join the tip of the tongue to the necessary nerves in the nasal passages is more difficult. For now, try simply joining the tip of the tongue to the uvula. I have practiced this *mudra* while fasting, and have found that my hunger disappeared.

Before starting a fast, it is wise to take a gentle laxative so as to eliminate poisons from the intestines that will not be pushed out of the body by any fresh intake of food. On long fasts it is advisable to take a laxative every evening, until all foodstuffs have been expelled from the bowels.

Fasting is not for everyone. Some bodies can handle it easily; others find it very difficult. Yogis do not make a big point of it. The path of yoga is one of moderation in all things. When a disciple of Yogananda's guru, Sri Yukteswar, announced that he was going on a long fast, Sri Yukteswar laughed, "Why not throw the dog a bone?"

When coming off a fast be sure to eat lightly, both quantitatively and qualitatively. Heavy foods should not be introduced at the start. Rather, eat fruits and drink herb teas.

RECIPES

For Prevention and Remedy of Flu and Colds

Boil 5 minutes: 1 quart of water, ½ cup of milk, ¼ cup honey, and 1 teaspoon of powdered ginger. Drink one pint a day, lukewarm.

Halua

This recipe is hardly the best one to include under a section on fasting, but because of its richness it may afford welcome relief after the somewhat bleak consideration of no food at all!

Heat together a cup of water, a cup of milk, a cup of brown sugar (or honey), and a handful of raisins. In a separate pot, melt a quarter of a pound of butter, then fry in this melted butter a handful of pine nuts and a cup of Farina or Cream of Wheat. Stir this mixture for a time, so as to brown the pine nuts and slightly to dry the Farina or Cream of Wheat. Add the liquid from the first pot a little bit at a time, and stir until thick. Pour into a buttered 8" square pan. Cut when cool. This *halua* (there are many kinds of *halua* in India) makes a delicious dessert.

VII. MEDITATION

Superconsciousness

Once, many years ago, I was leading a meditation in a church in Long Beach. A man came in who was evidently the sort of person who feels deep and inspiring compassion for any alcoholic beverage, inasmuch as he cannot bear to see it confined ingloriously in a bottle when it might be freed to fulfill a nobler function. In short, our visitor was grandly, stuporously drunk. Naturally, no doubt, he assumed that, if we weren't as drunk as he was, we must have sought his cherished state of insensitivity by an unworthy shortcut. Staggering up to an usher, and in a conspiratorial stage whisper that filled the room, he demanded:

"What's happened? Are they asleep?"

Obviously, since we weren't fidgeting about we could not be awake. In his view, the only possible alternative was that, by fair means or foul, we had sunk into a state of subconscious stupor.

It is a sad commentary on this age of supposed enlightenment that most people, teetotalers as well as alcoholics, are quite ignorant of the fact that man's alternative to a restless, and often anguished, wakefulness is not necessarily oblivion, but that real release lies in expanding one's consciousness beyond the confinements of thought. This is known as the state of *super*consciousness.

So natural is this state to the fully enlightened soul that I remember my guru remarking once: "Last night I experimented to see how it felt to go into subconsciousness during sleep. It was a most unpleasant sensation. I felt that I was being hemmed in on all sides by thick walls of flesh." Not the least interesting feature of the Master's statement was the suggestion that subconscious sleep was, for him, an unusual "experiment."

What a few persons in this world have achieved, all men may aspire to. The teachings of the great masters of every age emphasize that superconsciousness is man's only *true* state of being, compared with which ordinary outward consciousness is only a sort of extended dream.

In meditation especially, and as much as possible all the time, try to *think superconsciously.*

But be careful, once you forsake the familiar pathways of rational thought, that you do not slip into a vague pseudo-mystical state that regards every passing impression as a revelation straight from heaven. To be superconscious does not mean to take complete leave of one's reason, but more to coordinate the rational faculty with higher levels of awareness.

Man's subconscious impressions and instinctual drives are centered in the lower brain. Here also, in the medulla oblongata, is located the center of all human bondage, the ego. (My guru told me that it is here that the sperm and ovum first unite to begin the formation of the human body.) It is in the frontal section of the brain that man's intellectual, esthetic, and spiritual awareness is centered. Man's ascent to superconsciousness corresponds, physiologically, to a re-centering of his awareness in this frontal section, and particularly in the seat of spiritual vision at the point between the eyebrows. As the consciousness of worldly men radiates outward from the medulla oblongata (observe how the egotist draws his head back, as if in affirmation of his vested interest in this particular area of his anatomy!), so the consciousness of a master is centered in, and radiates from, the Christ center, or *ajna chakra,* between the eyebrows. In point of fact, these two centers of awareness are one: The medulla oblongata is its negative pole, the Christ center, its positive pole. But until divine awakening occurs, bringing with it a harmonious flow of energy through the medulla oblongata to the Christ center, these opposite poles are treated in yoga as separate spiritual centers.

In meditation, try to center your consciousness at the point between the eyebrows. Do not strain. (Some beginning yogis meditate as if their brains were muscles that must be squeezed into the desired attitudes!) Rather, simply channel your awareness calmly, and with a feeling of joyous aspiration, to that point. What you will be doing, in fact, is focusing more and more of the brain's energy there. The greater this concentration of energy at that point, the more powerfully that portion of the brain will be stimulated and awakened, and the more profound will be your spiritual awareness. Paramhansa Yogananda, as a neophyte in his guru's ashram, made it a deliberate practice to keep his mind centered at the Christ center throughout the day, regardless what his other activities were. He told us that in this way divine enlightenment can come very quickly. Because the word "energy" evokes images of strain and tension, however, I suggest you think, rather, of focusing your thoughts and aspirations at this spiritual point.

A major vehicle for the brain's energy is the eyes. Look into the eyes of anyone possessing a strong, vibrant personality (many people's eyes, alas, are spiritually dead), and feel the intensity of this energy-flow. Observe how people's eyes can seem almost to blaze with anger, to freeze in contempt, to sparkle with laughter, to melt with kindness and love. It is only when an abundance of energy flows through the eyes that they manifest these mental states so clearly, but this flow of energy does more than manifest them: It affirms them, and thereby helps to develop them.

Take care, then, that your eyes express only spiritual qualities, for it is literally true that, as you see the world, so you yourself will tend to become.

The eyes, in revealing one's mental states, suggest also the general portion of the brain in which the consciousness at those times is centered. In particular, when the mind slips toward subconsciousness and the energy becomes centered in the lower brain, the eyes tend to look downward; when one is involved in the world, or otherwise active on the conscious level, the energy becomes centered more in the midbrain, and the eyes tend more naturally to look straight ahead; and when one enters a state of superconsciousness, the eyes are drawn automatically to gaze upward.

These directions may be observed to some extent even in normal wakefulness. When a person withdraws mentally from reality, whether in discouragement or in fatigue, he tends to look down. If his withdrawal is for the purpose of pondering something, he may look down and slightly off to the side, as if in partial recognition of the objective world around him. If he desires to relate to the world completely, he will look it "straight in the eye." If he is inspired by something inward, he will tend to look up; if by something outward he may look diagonally upward, as if divided between outward consciousness and superconsciousness.

Much more might be written about the involuntary movements of the eyes. Restless and constantly blinking eyes, for example, indicate a restless mind; quiet, unblinking eyes, a calm mind; staring eyes, a blank (or, sometimes, a veiled) mind. Eyes that look as if pressed inward from the sides suggest mental worry; eyes relaxed at the sides, inner peace; eyes drawn slightly outward at the sides, devotion and a sense of oneness with the Beloved. Shifty eyes indicate untruthfulness—an unwillingness to face reality squarely. Sagging lower lids indicate a downward pull on the mind, whether from ill health, fatigue, dissipation, or despair. Firm and slightly raised lower lids indicate an abundance of vitality, and a radiant inner sense of well-being. A tendency to look calmly off to the side indicates a more-than-usually intelligent person.

Again, the right eye represents a person's rational nature; the left eye, his emotional and "feeling" nature. When reason is uppermost in his consciousness, he tends to think and to express his awareness more through the right eye. When feeling is uppermost, he thinks and expresses himself more through the left eye.

I write these things not so that you may sit judgmentally over your fellow men, but that you may live more consciously through your own eyes. Remember, they are the windows of your soul. Used rightly, they can be made instruments of great blessing and inspiration to others. Just as important, they can help you to affirm and deepen those states of consciousness which you want to develop.

When you sit for meditation, look up toward the point between the eyebrows. I don't mean to cross your eyes, but only to direct their gaze upwards, focusing them at a point no closer than your thumb, when held up at arm's length from your body. You might think of your eyes as being situated only in the upper part of their sockets.

Superconsciousness is a fine line of awareness that divides consciousness from subconsciousness. The Spirit, similarly, rests forever at a point midway between all dualities. Closed eyes denote subconsciousness; open eyes, wakefulness. Thus, half-closed and half-open eyes, with the lower lids relaxed and slightly raised, and the upper lids relaxed and slightly lowered, denote the state of superconsciousness. If you can meditate in this position without becoming distracted by outward visual images, you will find it most helpful to do so. (Your eyelids may quiver at first, but you will find them becoming still as your mind grows calm.) Otherwise, practice this half-open and half-closed position for a time, and then close the eyes, keeping them focused upward. Even with the eyes closed, however, feel that their lids have simply relaxed so completely that they happen to meet.

As you meditate, focus every perception at the point between the eyebrows. (Actually, of course, the frontal point in the brain that you should stimulate by concentration is *behind* the bone.) Every sound that you hear, think of it as emanating from the Christ center, or refer it mentally to that center. Treat every other sensation, every thought in the same way. Direct all the feelings of your heart upward in aspiration to the point between the eyebrows. Gradually, as you come to feel God's blissful presence within you, you will recognize this as the doorway through which the soul communes with Him.

AUM, *Shanti, Shanti, Shanti*

Step Six

Life Is a Battlefield

I. PHILOSOPHY

Life Is a Battlefield

Peace, in the minds of many people, means the mere avoidance of conflict. The peace they long for is a gentle retirement in old age; a simple cottage by the sea; a secured income; and the certainty that any crisis that may come their way will be met with a minimum of effort and worry. They seek the peace of a stagnant pond. As often happens when men retire from a life of intense activity, only (for lack of continued challenges) to sink quickly into the pathetic senility of old age, what begins as peace soon disintegrates in decay. The cottage by the sea, idyllic perhaps for a weekend, becomes a dreary prison of boredom. The life lived with no incident more harrowing than ants in the salad at a church picnic soon leaves a person incapable of thinking further than the sparrows on his front lawn. When one considers the episodes on which people like to reminisce when they converse together, one quickly notices how many of those episodes relate, not to peaceful Sunday afternoons picking buttercups on a meadow, but to some hair-raising event: an operation one once had, an accident, some conflict with the authorities, some heartbreak, or some narrowly avoided calamity in a foreign land. It is almost as if life's bitterest experiences were the spice men needed to make life itself palatable—as if, indeed, there were even joy implicit in its opposite, sorrow.

This is, indeed, the very principle of *dwaita,* or duality, namely, that everything has its opposite, and that in everything its opposite is already implied.

I think in this connection of the Fiji Islands, climatically temperate, having rich soil and an abundance of food. The natives should have lived together with never a ripple of strain or animosity, arms locked perennially in brotherly love. In fact, the Fiji Islander of today seems an amiable enough fellow. But until quite recently (if the missionaries are to be believed) he and his forefathers devoted most of their waking moments to fighting, killing, and eating one another.

I think also of Haiti—a paradise if there be such anywhere on this earth. The one thought of the Haitians seems to be escape from their plodding existence, their dull round of dancing and fruit eating, their dreary glades of delicate forest green and the monotonous flights of colorful parrots, and to embrace the fascinating wonderland of New York traffic, of blaring taxi horns, and of reeking slums. Is it not strange, the perversity of the human mind?

Peace is one of the goals of yoga. It is, indeed, one of the silent aspirations of every heart. The longing for peace is instinctive in all men. But the peace of the soul, dynamic, expanding to the consciousness, the very opposite of stagnation, is too easily mistaken by the worldly mind for sleep and other negative states of being that attend a surrender of one's manhood and of all desire to progress.

Yoganandaji used to recall with amusement one of his brother disciples in Sri Yukteswar's ashram, a spiritually lazy fellow who sought out opportunities for sleep as zealously as others sought out opportunities to meditate. As he arranged himself in a comfortable position preparatory to his daily ashram contribution of heavenly snores, he would grunt comfortably and say, "*Nidra samadhi stithi!*" ("Sleep is *samadhi!*")

Jesus said, "I came not to send peace, but a sword." (Matthew 10:34) The *Bhagavad Gita* describes the entire spiritual path as a battle between the forces of light and of darkness in the consciousness of man. (The battlefield on which the discourse between Krishna and Arjuna takes place is the "field" of man's inner consciousness.) True spiritual peace is not a state into which one sinks passively—a reward for long years of suffering and tears. It is the peace, rather, of victory, of a fight well fought and of the certainty that one has overcome. It is not a wall placed protectively around one to shut out the horrors of life; it is rather a blinding light, banishing those horrors into non-existence, even as darkness is banished from a room when one turns on the electric light.

The path of progress must be seen as an overcoming. No man ever slid downhill into heaven. The path has been described, rather, as an ascent up a mountain, one which may be conquered only after many hardships. The image of Mt. Carmel (so often used in Christian terminology), or of Mt. Meru (used often in India), is most descriptive of the actual ascent of consciousness that takes place in the inner man. It is no mark of spirituality never to be tempted, never to be disappointed, never to fail. These are the marks, usually, of people who have chosen ant hills, not mountains, to climb. But the mark of spiritual growth is that for every setback there is an increased determination to succeed, and that for every obstacle there is an increasing surge of energy, until at last the energy generated suffices to demolish the opposition and allows one to sail forward on the upward journey. "A saint," Yoganandaji used to say, "is a sinner who never gave up."

One of the difficulties of the spiritual path is the fact that, the nature of duality being what it is, even painful experiences have something of joy in them. Though we may not consciously enjoy them when they happen, it cannot be gainsaid that we enjoy talking about them in retrospect, that we even revel in them, once they are over. And although the opposite is true also, that a certain amount of pain lurks in all worldly happiness—the pain of knowing, for example, that a happy day today must surrender to the drabness of a normal, routine, existence tomorrow—nonetheless there is enough enjoyment in the pleasures of the moment to make one reluctant to abandon them. Man is not easily weaned from his attachment to the ebb and flow of this relative, and endlessly contradictory, world. Although spiritual joy is incomparably greater than material happiness, even the devotee is typically reluctant to give up the lower for the higher. He finds it difficult to imagine, what is in fact the case, that the very energy with which he enjoys lesser pleasures is the same that he applies to the enjoyment of undiluted, vibrant bliss in the Spirit. There is no opposite to the state of spiritual joy. There is no boredom there. Yoganandaji described the joy of God as "ever new."

Spiritual awakening is accompanied by a rising energy and consciousness in the spine. In this spiritual state, one may indeed dance, laugh, and sing with unending gladness, wrapped ever in breezes of inner joy, but it will be a happiness quite the opposite of that of those Haitians who look to be acted upon, rather than to initiate any action themselves. All joy lies in giving, in the raising of one's energy, in expansion, in the dynamic application of one's will. All peace, to be true and lasting, lies in this sort of upliftment, not in the passive "flow-with-it" consciousness that is so popular with many people nowadays.

We have said that the practice of the yoga postures must be accompanied by a sense of deep relaxation, never of strain. But this relaxation, too, must be understood in a dynamic sense. Release the tensions in the body, not merely by forgetting them, but by deliberately offering them up into the Infinite Peace. The same energy that may now be keeping your body in an unpleasant state of tension, once you have directed this energy inward toward the brain, can fill your being with a cool fountain spray of peace and happiness.

Why cling to anything? All that man seeks awaits him in his inner Self, not as a result of merely avoiding conflicts, but as a result, rather, of overcoming them. Peace is a mind soaring in the free skies of inner consciousness.

II. YOGA POSTURES

The foregoing may be applied in a practical sense to the yoga postures. One should not wait passively for the postures to give one a deeper sense of relaxation and calmness. Minimal attention will produce minimal results. Mental attitude is almost as important in *hatha yoga* as are the postures themselves. These postures should be, indeed, almost a form of meditation. Practice them with an attitude of peace, even of worship. The peace of Spirit may, as the Bible says, pass understanding (at least so long as man dwells, not in peace, but in turmoil), but spiritual states come not for the mere wishing. One must dwell on the thought of them, imagining peace and whatever he can understand of inner joy, if he would develop these states of consciousness in their higher sense. Joy, in other words, cannot be attained if one waits for it dejectedly, or in an attitude of hopeless supplication. Peace cannot be his who shouts for it with sweating brow and with straining vocal cords. Roses cannot grow on barren rocks; they require a fertile soil. Spiritual states, too, require the fertile soil of a mind that already functions on their wavelength, and that is thus ready to receive their still greater glories. Sunlight cannot penetrate a heavy fog. The air must first be cleared to receive it.

The worldly person may complain that true, spiritual peace and joy are impossible for him, that his life is nothing but turmoil and unhappiness. But every man, being made in God's image, has buried somewhere within him at least a corner of divine consciousness on which he can firmly stand, if he but will. He should dwell on, and identify himself with, this divine part of his being. He should practice the yoga postures with those attitudes that will attune his mind to those higher states. Practicing the postures in this manner, he will find them a hundred times more effective even from a standpoint of physical health, and of course much more so from a standpoint of spiritual growth.

Pavanamuktasana

(The Wind-Freeing Pose)

"I release my spinal energy to rise in light."

To assume *Pavanamuktasana,* squat with the feet flat on the floor, and the thighs pressed hard against the calves. Grasp your knees with the arms, and draw them up toward the chest, exhaling completely. Hold this position as long as you find it comfortable.

You may also get into this position from a sitting pose, gradually tilting your body up onto the feet.

A variant is to lie on your side on the floor, and draw your knees up to your chest in a fetal position, exhaling completely as you do so.

Benefits: Pavana means "wind." *Mukti* is freedom. *Pavanamuktasana* means, literally, the "Wind-Freeing Pose." This pose helps one not only to eliminate gas from the intestines, but also to stimulate proper elimination. Also, *Pavanamuktasana* helps you to exhale completely prior to doing certain other exercises, particularly *Uddiyana Bandha,* which follows next in this lesson.

Uddiyana Bandha

(The Stomach Lift)

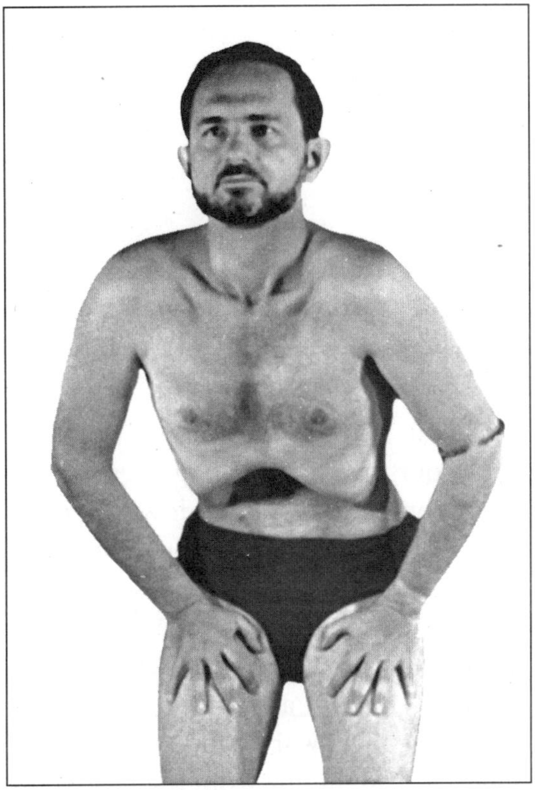

Exhale completely. You may begin from a *Pavanamuktasana* position, then stand up with the breath still held out. Place the palms of your hands on the thighs. Close the throat so that you cannot inhale. Rest the weight of the upper body on the hands, and straighten the middle back somewhat. Try to inhale from below—that is to say, draw the stomach upward into the chest, instead of drawing the breath downward through the nostrils into the lungs. To effect this upward lift, it will help you if you expand your ribs sidewise. This pose should be done on an empty stomach. When it is well done, the entire abdomen will be drawn back tightly against the spine, so much so that it will seem that the abdomen has simply vanished, leaving only a thin coating of flesh against the back.

Hold this pose as long as you can do so comfortably. Exhale, then repeat it several times.

Benefits: This pose is excellent for stomach and liver disorders. It stimulates the digestion. Spiritually, it helps to lift the consciousness and energy from the lower body upward toward the brain.

Ardha-Mayurasana

(The Half Peacock Pose)

Squat down, then come forward onto your knees, spreading them apart. Place your hands palms downward on the floor between your knees, turning them outward and backward so that the fingers point toward the feet. Bend the elbows and place them in the pit of the stomach. Inhale, and gradually extend your feet backward until your body makes a straight line from the feet to the head. All of your weight should be pressing down upon the elbows in the pit of your stomach. In a more advanced version of this pose the legs are brought up, so that the body is parallel to the floor and the whole weight rests upon the elbows. For now, however, keep your feet touching the floor, and hold this pose 15 seconds to begin with, gradually increasing the time to 30 seconds.

Benefits and Cautions: This pose is excellent for stomach disorders and for stimulating the digestion and the liver. It should not be practiced, however, where there is any unaccounted-for abdominal pain.

Vajrasana

(The Firm Pose)

"In stillness I touch my inner strength."

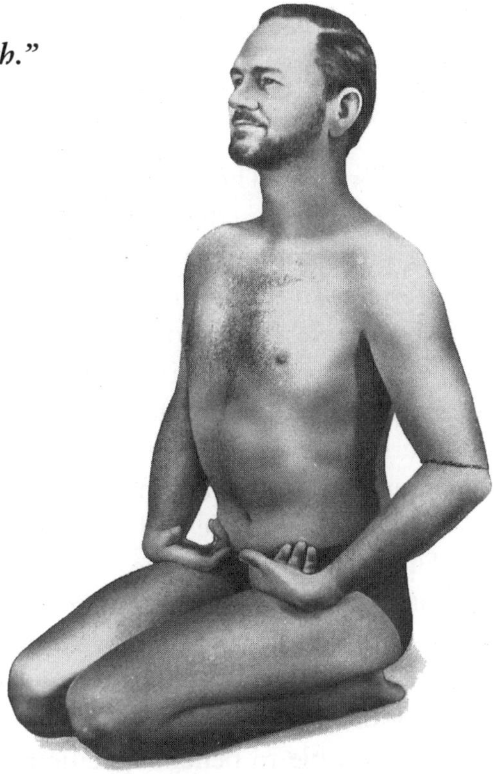

This is the first of several meditative poses. In meditation, one is taught to attain a state of physical steadiness by one of two means—contradictory in approach, but not in effect. One may visualize the body as infinitely light—as composed of nothing but air or space. Having no body to move, one finds his mind soaring to loftier identifications. The other method is to imagine the body to be infinitely heavy, rock-like, and firm. Having a body that is too heavy and solid to move, the mind in this thought also finds that it is drawn to function on levels higher than physical.

Vajrasana is ideal for this second practice. The pressure of the upper body upon the calves suggests to the mind a state of heaviness and solidity. To assume this position, squat down on the floor with your feet outstretched behind you, the right big toe over the left big toe so as to form a sort of cradle for your buttocks. Sit upright; place your hands palms upward on the thighs. Close your eyes, and meditate at the point between the eyebrows. Affirm mentally: *"In stillness I touch my inner strength."* Think of your body as being so firm that you cannot move a single muscle. Breathe normally, and with every exhalation feel as if you were sinking downward into the floor. Gradually you will become aware of subtle energies in the body that move freely even though the body is still; you will begin to identify yourself with those energies, and with your own inner freedom from the body, rather than with the body itself.

Benefits: Vajrasana is an excellent pose for attaining stability of mind. It is good also for flushing blood out of the lower legs. It is said also to be good for the stomach, possibly because of the increase in blood to the abdomen after it has been pressed partly out of the legs, but more probably also because of the sympathetic relationship that exists between the nerve endings in the feet and the different parts of the body. The middle part of the feet (around the instep) is said to be connected with the visceral organs. The ancient yogis no doubt found that the relaxation this pose gives to the instep exerts a beneficial stimulus to the stomach region.

The simple feeling of relaxation in the feet in this position is indeed one of its happiest benefits, particularly if you concentrate on and enjoy this sensation. Try mentally to extend this relaxation upward into the whole body.

The relationship of the feet to the rest of the body is an interesting one. A system of therapy has been developed in modern times called foot reflexology. By pressing on certain areas in the feet, the therapist is able to benefit specific parts of the body. A woman in one of my classes in Sacramento told me that a foot reflexologist, simply by feeling her feet, was able to discover the existence (later verified by x-ray) of a tumor on her left second rib.

How one treats the feet generally can be important to one's physical health. I remember one time my guru telling me not to sit with my toes curled back under them (toward the knees), but to sit in such a way that the toes stretched out, away from the knees. Seeing my curiosity, he remarked that this posture was bad for the eyes! The nerves in the second toe are said to be connected with the eyes. I was interested to note, when I visited Japan in 1960, that an unusually large number of people there wear glasses. This wrong posture is commonly assumed in that country.

III. BREATHING

In the last lesson we discussed something of the relationship between breath and consciousness. Awareness of the breath is invaluable as a means to self-awareness. It is also important as a means to self-transcendence in the breathless ecstasy of *samadhi*.

We discussed in the last lesson the psychological relationships between the inhalation and an upward movement of energy in the spine, and between the exhalation and a corresponding downward movement. Other relationships also may be observed: When you are excited, notice the rapidity of your breathing, and see also how erratic its rhythms become. When you are calm, see how that calmness reflects itself in a slow, harmonious rhythm of breathing. When you are concentrated, see how you tend instinctively to restrain the breath. Yogis point out that, in different states of consciousness, the breath will extend to different lengths from the nostrils, becoming more, or less, forcible.

Swami Vivekananda used, as a young man, to breathe heavily in his sleep. Sri Ramakrishna, his guru, said that this was a sign of a person who would be short-lived. In fact, Vivekananda died at the young age of 39. Yogis sometimes say that man has a certain number of breaths allotted to him. Supposedly, if he breathes quickly, his life span will be shorter. If he learns to breathe slowly, he will live longer. Long-lived animals, like the elephant and the tortoise, breathe quite slowly—as little as four times a minute. One of the secrets of the longevity of certain great yogis is that, being calm, they breathe less than the average man.

Note again how the breath moves differently in the nostrils, sometimes more on one side than the other; and again, sometimes flowing more in the lower part of the nostrils, at other times more on the outer side, or the inner side, or through the upper part of the nostrils. These movements, too, are subtly related to different states of consciousness. The breath on the left side indicates the stronger movement of the *pran* current in the *iḍa* nerve channel; the breath on the right side, the currents in the *pingala* nerve channel. (Yoganandaji remarked that the ideal person will breathe more in the left nostril during daylight hours, and in the right during the nighttime. This current can be changed by closing the opposite nostril and breathing several times on the side desired, or by lying down for a few minutes on the side opposite to that on which you want the breath to flow.) A person who breathes too much through the lower nostrils tends to be somewhat mentally heavy and dull. Such a person may habitually breathe with his mouth open, even though there is no obstruction to proper breathing in his nasal passages. To breathe through the nose, rather than through the mouth, is beneficial for stimulating clarity in the brain. A person who is angry may flare his nostrils outward, like a bull. People who are somewhat reserved, whether from a certain timidity or from aloofness and pride, tend to breathe through the central part of the nostrils, even to the extent of developing a habitual mannerism of drawing their nostrils together. People with strong wills breathe more in the upper nostrils.

Try to become more aware of the different movements of your breath, especially in meditation, when you can focus your mind one-pointedly on the breathing process. By gradually learning to breathe properly, you will be astonished to see how, simply through the breath, you can vitally change your mental outlook.

For the next week practice the alternate breathing exercise, but with this difference: Inhale through the left nostril, hold, and exhale through the right, to a ratio of 1-2-2. As you inhale, mentally count 4; hold the breath 8 counts; then exhale through the right nostril to a count of 8. Repeat not more than 6 times.

IV. ROUTINE

Various sequences are given by different authors for the practice of the yoga postures. The sequence I recommend is based on the importance to *hatha yoga* practice of a peaceful and inward state of mind, and of the awareness and re-direction upward to the brain of the energy in the body. We begin with breathing exercises and meditation, that the postures may be done with the right attitude. We then proceed with standing exercises, to help develop right posture, and to center the consciousness in the spine. We then do various exercises to relax the extremities (the legs and arms)—for example, *Sasamgasana* (the Hare Pose) and *Supta-Vajrasana* (the Supine Firm Pose), which you will learn in the next two lessons. We then concentrate on stretching and loosening the spine, with the purpose of creating a free and open channel for the energy to flow upward to the brain. We then, as will be taught in future lessons, go into the inverted poses so as to use the force of gravity to draw this energy up the spine toward the brain. As we have said, the more the energy can be lifted up the spine into the brain, the more one is in a state of inner harmony and joy—the more, in short, he discovers the truth of the saying that the Kingdom of Heaven is within. A long rest in *Savasana* (the Corpse Pose) follows after these exercises as a means of sinking deep into the inner awareness that has been awakened. After *Savasana,* one may assume any of the meditative poses, and go into deep meditation.

Further rules regarding the sequences are primarily these: One should follow a bend in one direction with a bend in the opposite direction, so as always to return the body to a state of balance, even as the teaching of yoga is that one must neutralize the opposites of duality, and become identified with the one central Reality, the *adwaitic*, or non-dual Spirit which rests forever at the eye of the storm of creation. It is important, also, always to rest after each pose—at least as long as one has held the pose, and longer if the heart has been so activated that it takes more time to return to its normal rhythm.

The routine given in these lessons is for the average person, who presumably cannot easily make time for more than half an hour to forty minutes of practice at a time. Should you wish to devote more time to the postures, you may incorporate more of them, following the guidelines that I have just given. Now that we have already included so many postures in these lessons, it would be impossible to do them all, at least properly, in half an hour. I suggest, therefore, that you do different sets on alternate occasions, either morning and evening, or on alternate days.

Always remember that it is better to do a few postures slowly and well than to do many of them hastily.

Begin both sequences with the Full Yogic Breath, followed by *Sitkari Pranayama*. Then do the Alternate Breath six times, to a rhythm of 1-2-2. Meditate for a couple of minutes, mentally watching the flow of breath in the nostrils. Then do one or the other of the following routines:

Routine A

Vrikasana (the Tree Pose)
Chandrasana (the Moon Pose)
Trikonasana (the Triangle Pose)
Pavanamuktasana (the Wind-Freeing Pose)
Uddiyana Bandha (the Stomach Lift)
Padahastasana (the Jackknife Pose)
Savasana (the Corpse Pose)
Vajrasana (the Firm Pose)
Sasamgasana (the Hare Pose)
Simhasana (the Lion Pose)
Savasana (the Corpse Pose)
Janushirasana (the Head-to-the-Knee Pose)
Paschimotanasana (the Posterior Stretch)
Savasana (the Corpse Pose)
The "V," or Balance Pose
Savasana (the Corpse Pose)
Halasana (the Plow Pose)
Savasana (the Corpse Pose)
Ardha-Dhanurasana (the Half Bow Pose)
Bhujangasana (the Cobra Pose)
Savasana (the Corpse Pose)
Chakrasana (the Circle Pose)
Savasana (the Corpse Pose)—in deep relaxation for 5 minutes

Routine B

(Begin the routine with the breathing exercises recommended at the beginning of Routine A, followed by:)

Vrikasana (the Tree Pose)

Trikonasana (the Triangle Pose)

Utkatasana (the Chair Pose)

Pavanamuktasana (the Wind-Freeing Pose)

Uddiyana Bandha (the Stomach Lift)

Savasana (the Corpse Pose)

Vajrasana (the Firm Pose)

Sasamgasana (the Hare Pose)

Ardha-Mayurasana (the Half Peacock Pose)

Savasana (the Corpse Pose)

Janushirasana (the Head-to-the-Knee Pose)

Paschimotanasana (the Posterior Stretch)

Savasana (the Corpse Pose)

Halasana (the Plow Pose)

Karnapirasana (the Ear-Closing Pose)

Savasana (the Corpse Pose)

Dhanurasana (the Bow Pose)

Bhujangasana (the Cobra Pose)

Savasana (the Corpse Pose)—in deep relaxation for 5 minutes

V. HEALING

Stomach Disorders

The stomach is more important to the average person's physical and mental health than is commonly realized. Many people have the equivalent of a rattlesnake in their intestines—poisons that are trapped there through faulty elimination, and that feed slowly into the system, keeping them chronically weak and tired, a sudden prey to any passing disease. The mind is very much influenced by the stomach, so much so that the fluctuations of a person's moods may often be due only to the presence or absence of poisons in his bowels. Some years ago I read of a man who narrowly escaped committing suicide by discovering that weeks of chronic depression, which had driven him actually to contemplate taking his own life, were due simply to the fact that he was badly constipated.

Basically, what is necessary for all stomach ailments is the elimination of poisons, and the stimulation of energy in the stomach, through fasting, better diet, and right exercise.

CONSTIPATION

Constipation may be overcome partly by the practice of the following postures:

Matsyasana (the Fish Pose) —Step Ten

Uddiyana Bandha (the Stomach Lift)

Nauli—a stomach pose to be taught in Step Twelve

Ardha-Matsyendrasana (Half Spinal Twist)—Step Nine

Supta-Vajrasana (Supine Firm Pose)—Steps Seven and Nine

Paschimotanasana (the Posterior Stretch)

Parvatasana (the Mountain Pose)
—Step Ten
Yoga Mudra—Step Ten
Padahastasana (the Jackknife Pose)
Trikonasana (the Triangle Pose)
Vajrasana (the Firm Pose)

Try not to eat too much starchy food, especially white flour. Don't eat too late at night. Fast one day a week, to give your stomach the rest that it needs to function properly.

LOSS OF APPETITE

Mayurasana (the Peacock Pose)
—Step Twelve
Ardha-Mayurasana (the Half
Peacock Pose)
Dhanurasana (the Bow Pose)
Akarshana Dhanurasana (the
Pulling-the-Bow Pose)—Step Nine

Mental depression is often a cause of loss of appetite. Depression affects the whole body, causing it to slump forward, to restrict its breathing. It sends the body's energy downward, toward the lower centers in the spine. Deep breathing, sitting upright, looking upward, and smiling more, deliberately drawing energy from the base of the body toward the brain—all of these practices help to counteract the depressing influence upon the appetite.

COLITIS

Savasana (the Corpse Pose)

Colitis, like most stomach ailments, is usually associated with some nervous disturbance. Concentrate on curing not only the effect, but also the cause. The postures and breathing exercises, and above all meditation, can gradually restore one to a state of harmony, physically as well as mentally.

DIABETES

Mayurasana (the Peacock Pose)
—Step Twelve
Sarvangasana (the Shoulder
Stand)—Step Eleven
Matsyasana (the Fish Pose)
—Step Ten
Bhujangasana (the Cobra Pose)
Ardha-Matsyendrasana (the Half
Spinal Twist)—Step Nine
Halasana (the Plow Pose)

FLATULENCE (GAS)

Bhujangasana (the Cobra Pose)
Halasana (the Plow Pose)
Dhanurasana (the Bow Pose)
Pavanamuktasana (the Wind-Freeing Pose)

HEMORRHOIDS

Sarvangasana (the Shoulder Stand)—Step Eleven
Mayurasana (the Peacock Pose)—Step Twelve
Aswini Mudra (Anal Contraction)—Step Thirteen
Halasana (the Plow Pose)

HERNIA

Sirshasana (the Headstand)—Step Eleven
Sarvangasana (the Shoulder Stand)—Step Eleven
Viparita Karani (the Simple Inverted Pose)—Step Seven

KIDNEY

Ardha-Matsyendrasana (the Half Spinal Twist)—Step Nine
Chandrasana (the Moon Pose)

LIVER AND SPLEEN

Ardha-Matsyendrasana (the Half Spinal Twist)—Step Nine
Uddiyana Bandha (the Stomach Lift)
Nauli (the Stomach Isolation)—Step Twelve
Janushirasana (the Head-to-the-Knee Pose)
Akarshana Dhanurasana (the Pulling-the-Bow pose)—Step Nine
Sarvangasana (the Shoulder Stand)—Step Eleven
Chandrasana (the Moon Pose)

ULCERS

Deep diaphragmatic breathing in *Savasana,* the Corpse Pose. At night, before going to bed, soak a piece of white bread without the crust in warm milk, and eat it.

VI. DIET

The approach of yoga to the subject of right living is always from a standpoint of what is natural. From a standpoint of diet, too, the emphasis is purely natural. What is the *proper* food for the human body? This is the question asked, not, what are the religious, sentimental, or social considerations? Meat, for example, is obviously the natural food for some animals. Were it not, whole species would reproduce to the point where this planet could not produce enough food to feed them. The question is, simply, whether meat (as one example) is the right food for one particular species, man.

Swami Sri Yukteswar, in his book, *The Holy Science,* points out that the body of man is not that of a carnivore. His intestinal tract, compared to the length of his body, is that of a frugivorous, or fruit-eating animal. Carnivores have intestinal tracts three to five times the length of their bodies; herbivores, 20 to 28 times that length. Frugivorous animals, including man, have intestinal tracts 10 to 12 times the length of their bodies. (Sri Yukteswar points out that when measuring the body of man, one must measure it as one does those of other animals, from the mouth to the anus, not from the crown of the head to the soles of the feet.)

Man's tooth structure, also, is that of a fruit-eating animal. His teeth are not long and pointed like those of carnivorous animals that must rend and tear the flesh they eat. Nor are his teeth flat like those of a horse, which slowly ruminates.

Man, of all the animals, has the mental freedom to develop tastes far outside his own natural instinctual pattern. There are human beings, for example, who actually enjoy eating raw flesh. It cannot be gainsaid, however, that the usual inclination of man is to conceal his slaughterhouses behind high walls, where he cannot see or hear the animals being killed. The thought of killing is offensive to his refined, more sensitive animal nature. When he buys meat, he usually disguises it by cooking it. He refers to it euphemistically, not as flesh, but as steaks, chops, drumsticks, etc. In advertising one never sees pictures of bloody carcasses presented to attract the potential customer to some other product. One *is* likely, however, to see a bowl of fruit.

For man, there is something instinctively attractive in fruit, particularly when the palate has not been abused by years of wrong eating. There is a natural inclination in man for the saliva to flow at the very sight of a bowl of cherries, grapes, apples, or bananas. Fruit is the most spiritual of all foods. It is natural for man, the most spiritually advanced of all the animals, to be instinctively attracted to those foods which are best adapted to developing his spiritual sensitivity.

Because yogis emphasize the natural approach to right diet and right living, they would also point out that the body, through years of wrong living, may not be capable of suddenly adjusting itself to a perfect diet. Dr. Lewis, the first disciple of Paramhansa Yogananda in America, gave up eating meat shortly after meeting the Master. Sometime later, he began suffering mysterious aches and pains in his body. He went to a succession of doctors. None of them was able to diagnose his difficulty. Finally, he asked the Master what the trouble might be. The Master said, "Your body has been accustomed to eating meat. The cells are crying out for it, out of past habit. Eat a little meat once a week, and the pains will disappear." Dr. Lewis followed the Master's advice, and was almost immediately cured. Some years later, he was able to give up his meat diet completely.

If you must eat meat, do try strictly to avoid beef and pork. Pork is an unclean flesh, owing to the eating habits of pigs. Yoganandaji said of beef that he had seen butchers in the slaughterhouses in this country scooping cancers out of cattle after killing them. It is an interesting fact that cancer is far more prevalent in the West, where beef is widely eaten, than in India, where the average Hindu, at least, will not touch it. Yoganandaji said that beef eating is one of the prime causes of cancer. If you must eat meat, eat it less frequently, and try to eat only fish, fowl, and a little lamb occasionally.

We have said that meat eating is unnatural for man. So also is the wearing of glasses, yet men get along fairly well with them. Is there a more specific inducement for limiting one's diet to fruit and vegetables? Indeed there is. Meat eating in general, because it is unnatural, is also the cause of many diseases in man. Certain Western doctors have actually made this statement with no encouragement from yogis. Yogis have always claimed this to be true.

Many friends and students of mine, who, after giving up meat for a time, have gone back to it if only temporarily, have told me that the contrast in the way they felt after returning to a meat diet was phenomenal. They felt much more sluggish and mentally heavy. They had less endurance. They felt easily tired. Much has been made in Western dietary books of the high energy-giving properties of meat. Overlooked are the poisons that prevent the free manifestation of that energy. It is not enough to eat food that is high in energy. It is important also to eat foods that can be eliminated easily from the body, and that keep the body free of toxins. With such food, even a little bit of energy can provide a great deal of strength. There are plenty of proteins available in foods other than meat: Nuts, beans, avocados, and sprouts are valuable sources of protein. Yogis say that cheese—particularly fresh cheeses—milk, and milk products are not only admissible, but actually desirable in the human diet. Though yogis do not generally recommend eggs, Westerners may find it preferable to include eggs in their diet for reasons that we have stated in an earlier lesson.

A final, but important, thought should be expressed on this subject. The food we eat is more than an assortment of chemicals. Essentially, it is vibration. As such, it affects our consciousness. Animals, because of their more developed nervous systems (compared to that of vegetables), feel intense anguish, anger, and fear when they are killed. These emotions fill their bodies with toxins. More than that, they implant in the animals' bodies the vibrations of their strong emotions. People who eat such flesh take into themselves something of these emotions. It is no accident that the more warlike, aggressive nations are also heavy meat eaters, or that the more peaceful nations incline to be vegetarians. For a person on the path of yoga, it is important to give up foods that of their very nature obstruct any effort to achieve inner peace and harmony. For the yogi, a fruit and vegetarian diet is important above all because of the calming effect it has on his mind and nervous system.

I have said that man is a fruit-eating animal. And now suddenly I have recommended a vegetarian, rather than a strictly frugivorous, diet. The reason I have done so is that the bodies of most people at this point in time are not sensitive enough to be able to live on a diet of only fruits and nuts. Some cooked vegetables are necessary for most people, who are in a state of transition from a highly unnatural diet. In more advanced ages, man will be able to give up even such refined foods as fruits and nuts, and live directly from the inner energy, even as certain highly evolved souls have been known to do in our time (the Christian mystic, Therese Neumann, in Bavaria, Germany, for example).

RECIPES

Nut Loaf

1 cup ground walnuts
1 cup finely chopped walnuts
3 cups fresh whole wheat bread crumbs
2 tablespoons tamari
½ cup tomato juice
2 eggs, well beaten
3 tablespoons butter
3 medium onions, chopped fine
1 clove garlic, minced

Mix together the nuts, fresh bread crumbs, tamari, tomato juice, and eggs. Sauté the onions and garlic in butter until golden, stirring frequently. Add the onions to the nut mixture; you may need to add a little water to create the right consistency for a loaf. Press into oiled 9" x 5" loaf pan. Bake at 350° for about 45 minutes. Makes 4–6 servings.

Yellow Split Pea Daal

(an excellent and inexpensive meat substitute)

1 cup yellow split peas
6 cups water
1 cup green beans, cut small
1 cup or more yellow crookneck squash, chopped, or any other fresh vegetable
1 teaspoon salt
½ cube butter
4 tablespoons coconut flakes, unsweetened
1 teaspoon oil
1 teaspoon cumin seeds
a dash of lemon juice

Rinse split peas and add to water. When water begins to boil, pour out and reserve excess water. Add salt and oil. Simmer gently, stirring occasionally, gradually adding reserve water as needed to maintain soup-like consistency. When peas are almost soft, add the vegetables and cook until tender, stirring frequently, until the daal becomes a thick soup. Add lemon juice.

In another pan melt 2 tablespoons of butter. Add cumin seeds and fry briefly. Turn off flame, and add coconut. Add to first mixture. Bring to a boil, and add remaining butter.

You may add a little curry powder and a bay leaf if you like; fry them first in the butter. Serve with rice and a little chutney.

VII. MEDITATION

Raising the Inner Energy

For as long as people have been writing songs and poems, they have fantasized about the moon. For as long as they have known that the moon is another large body of matter like our earth, they have gazed at it and dreamed of someday going there. And ever since the means of actually getting there became known, men worked to make that dream a reality.

In one old poem, by the great Persian mystic, Omar Khayyam, the moon is used to symbolize God, or the divine consciousness in man: "Ah, Moon of my delight, who know'st no wane." Omar was an exception: How common it has been for man through the ages to consider God, like the moon, an impossibly distant ideal!

Some few people, having learned from the timeless testimony of various scriptures that the soul is in essence divine, have looked up from the dusty marketplaces of this world and dreamed of someday approaching closer to God.

But it was not until rocket engines were built with a strong enough thrust to escape the earth's gravity that man actually landed on the moon. Similarly, even after the means of reaching Him, through devotion, yoga practice, and meditation, become known to individuals, it is necessary for them to generate enough upward thrust to break free of the gravitational pull of worldly desires and attachments.

In the last lesson we spoke of concentrating at the point between the eyebrows. This center, known as the Christ center, may be called the inner "moon" in man, the center of his divine awareness. But many a practicing yogi, although gazing long and earnestly at this point in the hope of centering his awareness there, finds his efforts to be to no avail; his consciousness remains anchored firmly to earth. He must deliberately generate more upward "thrust" in his endeavor to transcend matter consciousness.

Anything that you can do to increase the upward flow of energy in your body when you meditate will facilitate your efforts to focus your attention at the Christ center. For your attention IS your energy. That is to say, your measure of concentration depends entirely on how much energy you can direct in the process. Divine awakening depends upon channeling *all* of your energy upward, and focusing it at the point between the eyebrows. That is what Jesus meant when he said, "Thou shalt love the Lord thy God with all thy strength."

The first battle, however, is to generate only enough of an upward flow to break free of the downward, gravitational pull of matter. To accomplish this end, three things are necessary: 1) avoidance of those actions and states of consciousness which pull the energy downward; 2) upward, devotional aspiration; 3) techniques specifically directed toward raising the energy in the body. To understand what it is that pulls the energy downward, it may help you to consider briefly the relationship that exists between matter-identification and awareness itself. For any increase of the one always entails a *decrease* of the other. The boorish fellow and the gross materialist are less sensitively aware even of this world than one who lives primarily in the consciousness of spiritual realities. In the most material manifestations of Spirit—the solid rocks and minerals—consciousness is so reduced as to be almost entirely latent. (This is why the Hindu scriptures make the statement, "God sleeps in the rocks.") In the consciousness of an enlightened yogi, on the other hand, while matter and indeed form of any kind is seen essentially not to exist, yet his consciousness is absolute. To formulate this truth, then, it may be said that *awareness increases in inverse proportion to the degree of one's identification with matter, or form.*

To free your energy from the downward pull of matter, therefore, avoid especially anything that dulls the mind, as well as anything that increases its identification with the senses. Laziness, over-sleep, mental vagueness or lack of interest, boredom, even selfishness, hatred, or pride (which narrow one's perceptions), must be cured by daily mental injections of keen interest and enthusiasm, kindness, forgiveness, and self-forgetfulness in doing things for others. For whenever the former predominate, the energy automatically moves downward, but when the latter predominate, it moves upward effortlessly toward the brain.

It is important also, of course, to be self-controlled, identified less and less with the senses, and more and more with the soul within. For though one experiences pleasure through the senses, and therefore, through them, awareness of a certain kind, it is a fact of life that the more one looks to those pleasures to stimulate his awareness, the more, in the long run, it becomes dulled. On the other hand, increasingly to abandon sense pleasures, far from producing a state of boredom, permits one's awareness so to soar that boredom (so much a part of the sensualist's consciousness) becomes simply unimaginable.

Devotional aspiration can be awakened by chanting, service (or, in meditation, an *attitude* of service), surrender to the Lord, and contemplation of those divine qualities which awaken in one the remembrance of Him.

As for techniques that help one to raise the inner energy, it may, in a sense, be said that *all* the techniques of yoga have this for their aim. But here are a few specific and simple exercises that will help you.

1) Brush your fingers upward lightly on the exposed stomach with a quick, loose movement of the wrists. With deep concentration, the hands can be made to act as powerful magnets. Feel as you brush your fingers upward that they are drawing the energy from the lower part of your body, and flinging it up toward the brain.

2) Then place your thumbs against the head, touching the back of the earlobes and the lower part of the ears. Cup the rest of the hand around your head, without touching it, and with the fingers pointing up toward the top of the head. Stroke the hands forward repeatedly (again with a loose movement of the wrists), and magnetically draw the energy through the brain to the point between the eyebrows.

3) Sit upright in any comfortable meditation pose. Inhale slowly and deeply, and feel that your breath is acting as a magnet to draw the energy up from the lower part of the body to the point between the eyebrows. Concentrate breath and energy at that point to a mental count of 12. Exhale. Then repeat the process, concentrating at the Christ center a little longer (25 counts, if you can do so comfortably); focus your entire being at that point. Exhale.

Again inhale, concentrating still longer (40 counts, if this is not too long for comfort).

Forget the breath and the body, and think only of focusing your energy and awareness ever more deeply at the Christ center, the seat of divine awareness within you.

AUM, *Shanti, Shanti, Shanti*

Step Seven

Affirmations, Part 1

I. PHILOSOPHY

Affirmations, Part 1

Who are you? *What* are you? Superficially, these may seem easy questions to answer. A spiritually unaware person might reply:

"My name is Theodosius Pendleton My father, he was Joe Smith, the First. I was a garbage collector until Sally Schuss, the gossip columnist, discovered me. Now I collect stories for her. I'm a loyal American, 'cause, you see, I wasn't born no place else. And I love good, clean fun—like washing my knuckles off after beating someone in a dirty fight."

Nay, nay, Theodosius, deny not thy secret splendor. For, despite incarnations of evidence to the contrary, *thou, too, art He!*

Man errs when he identifies himself with form. For forms change, yet the inner spirit of man remains unchanging. "This Self is never born," says the *Bhagavad Gita,* "nor does it ever perish. Once existing, it can never cease to be. It is birthless, eternal, changeless, ever itself. It is not slain when the body is killed. . . . This Self cannot be cut by weapons, burned by fire, moistened by water, nor dried by the wind. The soul is everlasting, all-permeating, ever calm, immovable, eternal." (II:20,23,24)

How is it possible for this immortal, divine Self to assume such inglorious disguises as we see everywhere around us? Worse still, why are our own mirrors so unkind to us?

Basically, all is consciousness. For the Supreme Spirit to manifest Itself as cosmic creation, It had to *think* every form in the universe into existence. These vibrations of thought, vibrating more grossly, became energy. This energy, vibrating still more grossly, took on the appearance of matter. The multifarious forms of creation are appearances, nothing more. In reality, everything is Spirit; everything is consciousness.

To the extent that man knows himself as consciousness, and not as a physical body, he, like the Spirit Itself, manifests creative power. Bondage, however, results from the fact that the creative act is an act of *becoming;* it is never a manifestation of something out of nothing. The artist objectifies the vibrations of his own consciousness when he paints. The architect solidifies his thoughts in the buildings he creates. In the act of creating, a man in one sense *becomes* his creation. In the act of doing, he *becomes* his deeds, even to the extent of reflecting them in his own body and personality.

And yet, the essential consciousness of man is not irrevocably committed by any of these acts. Whatever has been done can be undone. The man who, by repeatedly thinking and acting like a criminal becomes a criminal, has only to begin thinking and acting as conscientiously like a saint to become a saint. For we are not to our core the objective roles with which we identify ourselves. We are not, in our inner reality, Americans or Frenchmen, young or old, artistic or practical, honest or crooked. Essentially, we have no sex; we cannot be made well or ill; even birth and death are but seemings. Our consciousness merely *manifests* itself in different ways for a time; that is the sole extent of its becoming. The soul of man accomplishes, in its microcosm, what the absolute consciousness of Spirit accomplishes on an infinite scale in becoming the endless universe. In both cases, our acts of becoming signify but the different molds into which consciousness, like a formless fluid, chooses for a time to pour itself.

This comparison of human with divine creativity is important, for by understanding how the Spirit manifested Itself as creation we may better understand our own acts of becoming, and how, therefore, we might change our habits, or even what appear to be our actual physical limitations. Indeed, because we are ourselves Spirit in essence, if we can penetrate deeply enough to the center of our own being and realize ourselves as pure consciousness, we can manifest this power as perfectly as the Spirit Itself does.

The material universe is, essentially, consciousness. Its beginnings lie not in form, but in thought. Thought is the finest vibration of divine consciousness. Man's physical limitations, similarly, all have their origins in thought.

The universe of thought, known as the causal universe, manifests itself on a grosser level of vibration as energy, the astral universe. Man's inner thoughts, similarly, must be energized before they can be translated into outward action.

Matter, finally, as science also tells us, is only a manifestation of energy. Man's physical circumstances, as well as his habitual behavior, depend similarly on prior operations of energy.

One of my friends in college had an

unfortunate habit of excusing his personal weaknesses, whenever they were pointed out to him, by blaming them on his parents. "I know I'm weak," he would cry, plaintively, "but you see, I had a domineering mother." Or, "How can I have more self-confidence, when my parents always favored my older brother?" It is true that our outer circumstances are often the outcome—the "materialization"—of other people's energies as well as our own. It is also true, however, that we *attract* those energies according to the quality of energy that we first manifest ourselves.

Bernard, a brother disciple of mine at Mt. Washington, was prone to getting involved in car accidents. Our guru would counsel him to be more careful.

"But Master," protested Bernard, self-righteously, "none of these accidents has been my fault! One car crossed into my lane from behind, and hit me. Another hit me when it went through a red light. Twice my car was hit actually after I had parked it!"

"You must be more careful," repeated the Master, unimpressed by these explanations.

Bernard thought the Master was simply being difficult. But one day it dawned on him that he did, at least, have a careless *attitude*. To his astonishment, once he had changed this attitude his seemingly unrelated accidents ceased to occur.

Your life—in the last analysis, all of it—is the outward manifestation of your own consciousness, through the medium of the energy that you generate. Even the unexpected, the undesired, is drawn to you because of *some* attitude in your own mind. For it must be understood that our consciousness functions on various levels, many of them too deep for immediate, conscious recognition.

This is, in fact, the greatest difficulty that we encounter in changing ourselves or our outer circumstances: We are not always aware of those deep currents of consciousness which have made our lives what they are. How, then, can we change those currents?

To become fully conscious of them, by deep meditation, is the surest and most direct method. If you can uncover *all* of the roots of a weed, you will be able to remove every possibility of its growing again. But to dig so extensively is not always easy. For the inexperienced gardener it may be impossible. In that case it will be necessary to apply less direct methods: to pour poison over the general area, for example, or to plant some other kind of vegetation, strong enough to choke out the weed. Indirect methods can be used, similarly, to change subconscious habits, or thought patterns.

In essence, the soul is ever free. Identification with certain patterns of thought does limit its freedom, yet thoughts by themselves can be relatively free-flowing. It is when they become focused enough to generate a flow of energy that the real commitment to a particular kind of self-definition, or self-limitation, begins. When that energy-flow is translated further into outward action, the mental commitment becomes, so to speak, solidified; it is at this stage that it becomes very difficult to break it.

When one wants to destroy a particularly stubborn weed—crabgrass, for example, whose roots go very deep—it is necessary first to destroy the plant at the surface. To destroy bad habits, similarly, one must first of all avoid as strictly as possible their outward manifestations, and whatever might stimulate one to want to express them outwardly. Don't be fooled by people who jeer and say, "Oh, it's all in the mind!" Of course it is! And that's the worst possible place for it to be. It is to change harmful patterns of thinking that one must first avoid their outward manifestations.

Next, the mind should energize itself in fresh, positive directions.

One might ask: "But is it right to repress one's bad habits? Is not such repression a major cause of human suffering?" Well, perhaps it is better to have crabgrass than no grass at all! If one only abstains from a bad habit, without substituting a new and better habit in its place, the field of his life may indeed become bare and uninteresting. For soul-consciousness will not thereby become released to soar in infinite freedom. The old roots of desire will lie dormant. To change the metaphor, the old energies, if prevented from flowing in outward expression, may simply stagnate behind the dam. They may even, if continually fed by fresh thoughts, build up until they burst their dam, rushing out so vigorously into long-shriveled channels of behavior that the ensuing flood is destructive. Had the energy been permitted to maintain a moderate flow through its old channels into the fields of life, it might at least have been kept within narrow bounds.

This is why the great religions have stressed the need for moderation in all things. But the point that worldly people miss is that their worldly qualities do not constitute their true identity. They mistake the energy flowing through the channels of old habits for the habits themselves. The water in a reservoir may be redirected to flow in new channels. The same energy that animates an old, bad habit may be made to animate a good one. In this case, no repression will result. The important thing to remember is that the more your energy can be directed into positive channels, the greater will be your sense of inner freedom and joy.

Action binds the soul to the extent that it constitutes an affirmation *of bondage.* Every time you do a selfish deed you affirm, whether deliberately or not, the thought, "I am this ego, this body." The way out of that thought is to perform generous deeds, which affirm:

"I am *more* than this ego and body! My welfare embraces that of others. My true Self is the Self of all!"

Action, by itself, need not bind. Actions performed absent-mindedly, for example, are not nearly so binding, or self-defining, to the soul as those which are performed with keen attention. A man who works in a bank may move his arm quite as often during the course of a day as he performs the various duties of his job, but because the one movement is automatic, and the other deliberate, he will probably never think of himself as an arm-mover, though he may well come in time to think of himself as a banker. Action, similarly, that is performed without attachment has less tendency to bind.

And so we arrive at a most encouraging discovery. For *most* of our actions lack the full force of a positive affirmation. The man working in a bank is not likely to be heard muttering from one end of the day to the other: "I am a banker. I *am* a banker! I am a *banker!*" Rather, his self-definition as a banker probably steals up on him, as if from behind, over years of steady application to his work in the bank. Selfish, or otherwise worldly, actions, similarly, are usually indulged in for their own sake. The affirmation they entail is not deliberate, and therefore develops strength only through one's repeated association with the actions concerned. Here, then, is the encouraging news:

By strongly and deliberately affirming positive qualities, with full awareness and with deep concentration, one can undo even in a few minutes the negative effects of a lifetime!

This is true even of spiritual states of consciousness. Paramhansa Yoganandaji said: "Just the simple thought that you are not free keeps you from being free. If you could once completely break that thought, your soul would be free forever!"

Daniel, a brother disciple of mine, then inquired, "But Sir, if I said, 'I'm free,' surely I wouldn't be free just like that, would I?"

"Oh, yes!" the Master replied. "But," he added, "the trouble is, you've already damaged your own chances by saying, 'I *wouldn't* be.'" The mind, in other words, must be strengthened in its affirmation of spiritual states by directly perceiving them in meditation. Even after perceiving them, however, it is necessary to affirm, or constantly to dwell on the thought of, one's identity with them. The delusions of many incarnations can be dispelled in an instant, though to accomplish this enormous task the will must be deeply in tune with the all-powerful will of God.

All mental qualities, even particular talents, can be developed by deep affirmation. My guruji asked a well-known artist once how long it had taken him to master his art. "Twenty years," the man replied. "You mean," the Master inquired, "it took you twenty years to convince yourself you could paint?" Indignantly the man said: "I'd like to see you do as well in twice that length of time!" But in a week the Master had produced a painting which the artist himself had to admit was better than one he had done of the same subject.

Whatever you want to become, tell yourself strongly that *you are that already.* To reiterate, avoid as much as possible any influences that might suggest the opposite to your mind. (But do not reject them so strongly as to increase their importance for you. Rather, try simply to be indifferent to them.) Above all, shun the company of weak or negative people, for they will dilute the force of your own affirmations. If, through the force of bad habits, you cannot yet refrain from wrong actions, try to be at least mentally non-identified with them, and at the same time increase the vigor of your affirmations of positive qualities.

Never call yourself a sinner. To do so, Yoganandaji said, is itself the worst sin. Though your delusions be as old as the universe, they are not *you.* Why, then, affirm their reality? If you will cling to the goodness that is in you—even to the slightest glimmer that might be discerned in the midst of darkness—you will eventually be able to banish sin as though it had never been.

Eventually, have I said? Why eventually, if habits can be changed in a few minutes? The problem is that in those few minutes one must be able to generate as much force in one's affirmation as the cumulative force of many years of wrong action. Even if that action was carried on absent-mindedly, its gathered force can be great. And so it is that repeated affirmations over a period of time may be necessary before a delusion can be banished altogether. But the principle holds. The greater the vigor, concentration, and faith with which you affirm whatever quality you want to develop, the more quickly your aspirations will be realized.

One further point needs to be stressed. You've probably met people who, in an effort to impress you with their sincerity, gesticulate wildly, wave their hands emphatically, talk loudly, and swear by everything under the sun. Such people are usually less sincere than those who talk quietly, perhaps with no physical gestures at all. Outward display helps to awaken and channel energy (in oneself as well as in others), but a complete commitment of one's energy must spring from every level of his being. Most of these levels, as I have said, are deep—too deep to be reached by loud noise. Deep concentration alone can penetrate to them. And deep concentration requires stillness of mind and body.

When one has something to say to a room full of noisy people, he may have to shout first to get their attention. But if after they become silent he keeps on shouting, he will only attract their ridicule; they will be too much aware of the noise he is making to listen to his message. Similar is the case with affirmations. For most people's minds are a hubbub of restless thoughts.

Initially, to get the attention of the conscious mind, loud affirmations may be necessary. For affirmations to be really effective, however, they must penetrate to, and alter the patterns of, the subconsciousness. To accomplish this, one must go deeper within himself. Loud affirmations must give way to whispers, then progressively deeper mental affirmations, until the subconscious is reached. Affirmations become potent to the extent that they can be made to resound in inner depths. To be most effective, they must penetrate beyond even the subconscious, to the superconscious. In the next lesson, I shall go further into the practical aspects, the "how-to's," of affirmations.

II. YOGA POSTURES

There is, as I have already said, a connection between physical posture and mental attitude. Many of the postures of *hatha yoga* are related to specific and wholesome attitudes of the mind. All of the postures help in a general way to produce inner peace, contentment, and spiritual harmony. As you practice each pose, do not ask yourself merely, "What do the books say I should be feeling in this position?" Feel, rather, what the total significance of the pose is to *your own* inner consciousness. As you move a hand, feel that your mind is moving with it. Feel, still more deeply, the relationship between outward movement and the inward movements of the soul.

When Buddha preached his first sermon at Sarnath, his first listeners and disciples were fellow devotees of his, who had considered him a fallen soul. He had left the austerities that he had been practicing in their company, and had gone to seek what he later termed the "middle path." When they saw him first at Sarnath it was from a distance. They started at once to leave the scene rather than be infected by the "evil" influence of one who had, as they thought, forsaken the path. It may be said, then, that Buddha preached his first sermon, not with words, but with the vibrant power of his spiritual presence. For something in the way he stood or walked made them want to listen to what he had to say. His first sermon, indeed, was delivered unconsciously, in the natural movements of a body of which the indwelling soul was at peace.

Look at a person's movements sometime, and think of them as a subtle form of speech. This may be no new concept to you. You have probably observed often enough the nervous tension in the hands of a person who is undecided; the upward glance of a person who is happy or inspired; the sidewise, slightly downward glance of an intelligent person in the process of weighing some question mentally. A sensitive person can tell a great deal about others simply by observing the way they walk, stand, sit down, smile.

Every time a thought comes into the mind, there is some message sent, if only a sort of psychic overflow, to the body. Different parts of the brain stimulate different parts of the body. When a particular thought or feeling comes into the mind, it entails a flow of energy to corresponding parts of the brain. This stimulation sends messages, in turn, to related parts of the body. When a person experiences fear, for example, the stimulation of the fear center in the brain sends impulses to the heart, quickening it; it stimulates the flow of adrenalin; it tenses the muscles that may be needed for self-defense or for flight.

A state of spiritual absorption, similarly, focuses energy automatically in the frontal part of the brain. The stimulation of this part of the brain sends messages to the body of a very different nature from those born of fear: The heart slows down, the breathing becomes calm, the whole body becomes relaxed.

The movements of consciousness are reflected in various physical movements. But the reverse also is true: Physical movement in its own turn influences the mind. A nervous person will fidget—one of the signs of a disordered nervous system. His very fidgeting, however, will affect his mind in such a way as to make it more nervous. We see here the build-up of an interactive process similar to the feedback that occurs when a microphone and a loud-speaker are both turned on and left facing each other. It is not that the body has power in itself. The mind becomes more nervous simply because a nervous feedback from the body helps the mind to reaffirm its own nervousness. Merely to hold the body still would do little to improve one's mental condition. If, however, one sincerely desires to improve himself mentally, harmonious positions and movements of the body can go a long way towards helping him in his efforts.

A person who is trying to develop inner calmness may encounter opposition from a body which he has accustomed, by years of nervousness, to remain constantly tense. Though superficially the mind may be affirming calmness, subconscious habits, reinforced by continued physical tension, may effectively block his present plaintive affirmations of peace. Physical tensions will continue to send impulses of tension back to the brain, disturbing the very mind with which he is now trying to rid himself of mental disturbance. This is the great obstacle to all affirmations: The mind is already poisoned with the very delusions that it is trying to deny.

A deliberate effort, then, to harmonize the body along with the mind can be an invaluable aid in reinforcing one's mental affirmations of harmony. This effort must, of course, be deliberate. To expect the body's positions automatically to change one's mental outlook would be naive, since it is the mind that is the ultimate cause. It would be (as I have said in my book, *Ananda Yoga for Higher Awareness*) like trying to placate a cat with milk while continuing to stand on its tail. Where the mental resolution is firm, however, physical posture can be a tremendous aid in that resolution.

Sasamgasana

(The Hare Pose—Full Position)

"I am master of my energy,
I am master of myself."

To assume this position, squat down on your calves and touch your head to the floor close to your knees. Rest your hands down by your side, touching the feet, as you have already been taught to do. Now, grasp the heels firmly with the hands in such a way that the fingers are curled inward, not outward, upon the heels. Raise your buttocks, bringing the weight of your upper body onto the top of the head, until the arms are stretched straight and held taut by the grip of the hands on the heels.

You should feel a stretch in the shoulders, between the shoulder blades, in the front part of the armpits, and down the arms to the fingers. If you do not feel a pull in these parts (if, for instance, your arms are too long to be stretched straight in this position) turn the elbows one way or another until you do feel an actual pull. Be very conscious of it. Affirm mentally: *"I am master of my energy, I am master of myself."*

Return to *Savasana,* the Corpse Pose, and feel the energy withdrawing from your hands, arms, and shoulders to the spine.

Benefits: This pose and the next one offer good examples of the principles that I have outlined above. When the mind is eager to swing into activity, messages are sent to those parts of the body which make outward activity possible.

Tensions appear in the shoulders (especially in the front part of the armpits), between the shoulder blades, in the arms. *Sasamgasana*, by stretching, then relaxing, these parts, helps to free the mind of their suggestion, through feedback, that one should be continuously busy doing things. *Sasamgasana* is a good pose to practice before meditation.

Supta-Vajrasana

(The Supine Firm Pose)

"Energetic movement or unmoving peace: The choice is mine alone! The choice is mine!"

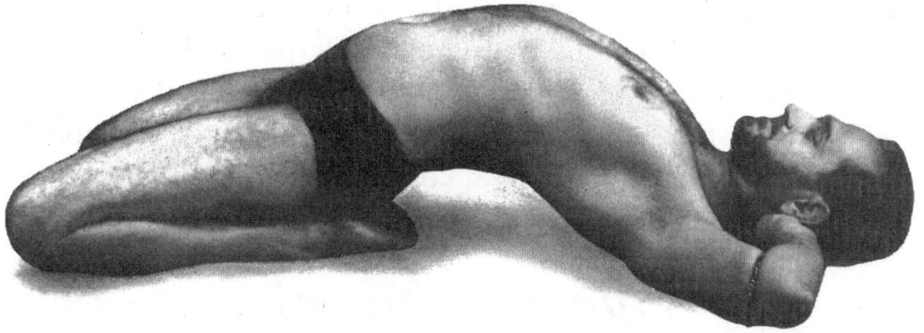

To assume the position, sit in *Vajrasana,* the Firm Pose. Lean backward slowly, using the hands and elbows for support, until the top of your head touches the floor behind you. To go more fully into this position, it is important that you be relaxed. If, therefore, this pose is too difficult for you, it would be well to take the help of a low box on which to rest your shoulders, instead of straining to hold yourself bent back as far as possible. In whatever position you relax, whether resting on the top of your head or on a low box, you will find over a period of 30 seconds or so that you can go back farther still. By progressive relaxation you may find, to your surprise, that the full supine position is not so difficult after all.

To assume the full position, raise your arms and clasp the hands beneath the head. Slowly come down, without raising your knees, until your shoulders rest on the floor. The longer you hold this position, the more you will be surprised at how comfortable it can be!

The knees should be as nearly together as possible.

In this position, affirm mentally, *"Energetic movement, or unmoving peace: The choice is mine alone! The choice is mine!"*

When coming out of *Supta-Vajrasana,* do not sit up again, but roll over onto one hip, extend your legs slowly, and settle back comfortably into *Savasana,* the Corpse Pose. Resting in this position, repeat the affirmation, and feel that you are sinking peacefully into the center of your being.

Benefits: The lower part of the body, too, tends to become tensed as a result of the mind's inclination to be "up and doing." Every such impulse from the mind, no matter how tentative, sends corresponding impulses to the thighs, the shin muscles, the feet. Such tensions often linger even after the mind has moved on to other thoughts. Repeated impulses create a gradual build-up of tension in those parts to the point where, like unruly children, they cry for attention, often drowning out all wishes to the contrary in the conscious mind. The meditating devotee may desire to sit still, lost in inner peace, but tensions in the legs keep shouting at him with vociferous silence to be "up and doing," until at last in despair, he leaves his meditation.

Supta-Vajrasana is a marvelous pose for relaxing the parts of the legs that I have described, and thus for preparing the body for deep meditation. This pose is also excellent for the stomach and for correcting postural defects.

Viparita Karani

(The Simple Inverted Pose)

"Awake, my sleeping powers, awake!"

The Simple Inverted Pose is one of the three basic inverted poses of *hatha yoga.* To practice it, lie flat on your back. Raise the legs slowly until they are vertical. Keeping the legs in this vertical position, slowly raise the hips until you can support them with your hands. In this position, the hands should be pressed against the base of the spine. Because considerable weight is placed upon the elbows when the hands are positioned so low on the back, many who practice this pose succumb to the temptation of bringing the hips a little higher and resting the hands in the middle back. Although this position eases the pressure on the elbows, however, it misses the chief and unique purpose of this pose.

While practicing the simple inverted pose, affirm mentally: *"Awake, my sleeping powers, awake!"*

Hold this pose about 15 seconds to begin with, increasing the time gradually with practice to 5 minutes or longer.

Return slowly to a supine position, and rest in *Savasana.*

Benefits: We shall consider more

Viparita Karani

(The Simple Inverted Pose)

"Awake, my sleeping powers, awake!"

returning your body to a state of balance. Consider how much of the time you spend sitting or standing, thus allowing the blood to accumulate in the lower part of the body, pulled by the force of gravity. It is not only the blood: All parts of the body are affected by this gravitational pull. It is extremely important, then, to your health and general well-being to counteract this pull by occasionally inverting the body.

The primary spiritual benefit of *Viparita Karani* is, with the pressure of the hands, to stimulate the energy at the base of the spine. For the yogi, the awakening of this energy (known as the *kundalini*) is of the greatest importance.

Viparita Karani can also be practiced as a *mudra,* one of those yoga postures which are especially designed for awakening subtle energies, without which spiritual unfoldment would not be possible. We shall discuss this aspect of the Simple Inverted Pose in a later lesson, when we take up the subject of *kundalini.* Because *Viparita Karani* is so powerful as a *mudra,* however, I shall not teach students how to practice it perfectly through these lessons.

deeply in Step Eleven the benefits to both body and mind of the inverted poses. It would be well, however, already at this point to begin practicing holding your body for a time upside-down. This position is important for

III. BREATHING

The breath, too, can be used in conjunction with mental affirmations to help one to develop courage, calmness, self-control, and other wholesome mental qualities. Affirmations can be made most effectively during *Kumbhaka,* with the breath held either in or out (though affirmation is generally considered most effective with the breath held out).

The purpose of affirmations is to send positive thoughts into the subconscious mind, changing its automatic habit patterns. The best times to affirm such thoughts are when the subconscious mind is open and receptive: just as one is going to sleep, for example, or while he is climbing slowly back from sleep to wakefulness. In deep meditation affirmations can be most effective of all. The essential point is that the conscious mind, forever busy with its plans and rationalizations, be lulled into a state where it will not obstruct the flow of suggestions to the subconscious.

Because the subconscious mind is more open during sleep, yogis say that it is important to sleep in a harmonious environment, and among good people. (In my travels around the world I have been interested to observe the extent to which different places may affect my mind during sleep. Though the world of business, for example, has always been very far from my own interests, I remember dreaming one night in a hotel room in New Delhi that numerous businessmen were approaching me with lucrative propositions! On inquiry the next day, I found that this particular hotel was used almost exclusively by businessmen on quick business visits to the capital.)

When the breath is held still (either in or out of the body), the mind tends more easily to become steady, capable of entering deeply into whatever affirmation one has chosen to make. Exhalation, however, is associated with the surrender of the conscious mind—whether into sleep or into superconscious ecstasy. This is why it is generally considered best to make one's affirmations during the rest period following exhalation. (It is also possible, however, to make a positive affirmation during inhalation, and to feel with exhalation that one is casting out all weakness and negativity.)

For the next week, practice the alternate breathing exercise that you learned in the last lesson. This time, however, after exhaling in the right nostril, inhale again immediately in the right nostril, and exhale in the left. Make the rhythm again a ratio of 1-2-2: Count 4 as you inhale, hold counting 8, and exhale counting 8. Practice this cycle a total of 3 times.

IV. ROUTINE

Follow the same routine(s) that you were given in Step Six, following the Half Hare Pose with the Full Position described in this Step, and following this Full Position with *Supta-Vajrasana.* At the end of your practice, just before going into relaxation in *Savasana,* practice *Viparita Karani* (the Simple Inverted Pose).

V. HEALING

Weight Problems

Weight problems are affected not only by the amount of food one eats. I remember reading that the winner in a food consumption contest, a young man whose habitual intake was almost incredible, weighed only 128 pounds. Overweight persons, by contrast, are not always heavy eaters.

In medical science, much is made of such matters as water retention in the body, the rate of metabolism, etc. The yoga science stresses the deeper fact that the body tends gradually (and more or less perfectly, depending on the strength of one's mind) to reflect the inner consciousness of the individual. This relationship goes far beyond the simple and obvious explanation that the mind influences the amount of food that one eats, and, consequently, one's weight. Rather, it is that the mind acts directly upon the body through the agency of the energy. By directing this energy wisely, one can actually think himself into putting on weight, or losing it.

There is no need for me to add to the information that is readily available in the West on fats and other foods that affect the weight in a purely chemical way. Obviously, the less one eats of heavy, starchy foods and other carbohydrates, the less he is likely to put on weight.

One of the teachings of yoga is expressed in the ancient saying, "*Stokum stokum anekoda*" ("Eat a little bit, frequently"). The people on the island of Bali follow this custom. It is an interesting fact, one which I have read about and also observed personally, that no native of that island is overweight. When the stomach is not overloaded, but has its work fed to it piecemeal, it can discharge its functions more efficiently.

This, too, is a reason for fasting one day a week. The stomach needs rest from time to time, if it is to function efficiently.

One's weight is partly determined, certainly, by the *karma* that one has brought over from past lives. One can mitigate this *karma,* however, by right action and right thinking in this life.

A posture that is good for regulating the metabolism of the body, by stimulating the thyroid gland, is *Sarvangasana* (the Shoulder Stand—literally, the "Whole Body Pose"). This pose will be given in Step Eleven.

Another pose, of similar but less pronounced benefits, is *Halasana* (the Plow Pose). In both of these poses, the chest is pulled back against the chin so that the flesh under the chin is pressed hard into the throat. It is this pressure that is beneficial to the thyroid gland. *Sarvangasana,* especially, is beneficial for maintaining the proper weight—for gaining weight, if one is too thin, and for losing it, if one is too fat.

For obesity, another pose that is good is *Chakrasana* (the Circle Pose).

Supta-Vajrasana and *Vajrasana* are good for reducing heaviness in the legs.

It has often been said that one should not drink with his meals, and not for at least half an hour before or after a meal. One reason for not doing so is that this practice tends to cause one to put on weight.

For problems of overweight, the powers of elimination need to be stimulated. *Uddiyana Bandha* and *Nauli* (the latter to be taught in Step Twelve) are excellent for increasing the eliminative powers of the body.

Deep breathing, also, helps to stimulate the peristalsis and thus to eliminate waste products from the bowels.

VI. DIET

Seed sprouts, especially alfalfa and mung, are an excellent source of protein, and for this reason (if for no other) would be helpful especially for persons desiring to give up eating meat. But in fact sprouts have many more virtues than these. Seeds contain the condensed nutrients, the life-essence of the plant. Sprouted seeds bring these essential elements to life; they supply approximately four times the vitamin content of the unsprouted seeds. At no point in its subsequent growth is a plant so packed with energy. H. E. Kirschner, M.D., wrote, in *Let's Live* Magazine: "In the light of both ancient practice and recent research, my advice to you is to make sprouts *number one* on your shopping list."

Sprouts have played a vital role in human nutrition for thousands of years. Today in the West they are beginning to come into their own. Most often seen in American supermarkets are the bleached sprouts generally used in Chinese cooking. Calcium hypochlorite is usually used to bleach these sprouts. It removes the chlorophyll. Though it helps to retard molding, little is left of the real food value of the sprouts.

Alfalfa has been called the "wonder legume." Even now, it is fed mostly to farm stock, not to people. The general public still needs to be educated to its life-giving properties. Alfalfa has been found to contain most of the vitamins needed in human nutrition. It is rich (about 80%) in protein. It contains eight essential enzymes vital to digestion. It also contains important minerals in organic form: calcium, magnesium, phosphorous, potassium, chlorine, sulfur, sodium, and aluminum. Alfalfa is said to stimulate the appetite and to sweeten the breath. All of the above properties are enhanced when alfalfa is taken in the form of sprouts.

Mung sprouts are among the highest of all foods in protein. They are said to help keep a person youthful. The mung bean has long been used in China and in India.

You may buy sprouts in some health food stores. You may also grow your own sprouts. The first problem in the do-it-yourself method is finding seeds that will sprout. It may be that some seeds have been tampered with. Certainly, not all the seeds that one buys have enough life in them to sprout properly.

Several methods are recommended for sprouting seeds. Experimentation as to temperature and quantity of water may be necessary for you. You could place seeds in a thin layer on the bottom of a jar and cover them with water, then cover the jar with gauze (which may be held to the rim with a rubber band). Keep the jar in a dark place. (Vitamin C is said to increase more rapidly in darkness during the early stages of sprouting.) If you keep the jar warm, the sprouting process will be speeded up.

Once the seeds have begun to sprout, move them to a light place. Drain the water and keep the sprouts moist with frequent water changes. The sprouts will be richest in food value if they are not allowed to grow too long.

USES IN FOOD

Sprouts are delicious in vegetable salads, soups, sandwiches, stews, omelets, Chinese and Japanese dishes, curries.

Alfalfa sprouts are especially delicious used in place of lettuce, or in addition to it, in salads and sandwiches. For a delightful sandwich spread, try mashing an avocado with a fork, then mixing it with alfalfa sprouts, lemon juice, and a little mustard (and/or ground cumin) and salt. Or try combining avocado, alfalfa sprouts, lemon juice, salt, and a generous amount of sweet basil.

Spring Salad Bowl

¼ head lettuce
2 stalks celery, cut in sticks
¼ bunch endive
8 radishes, sliced
2 tomatoes (optional)
¼ cup sour cream
1 cup mung or alfalfa sprouts
½ green pepper, sliced
½ bunch water cress

Break lettuce in bowl; tear endive and cress in small pieces. Arrange tomatoes, celery, sliced radishes, and green pepper over top of greens. Pour sour cream over top.

Mung Curry

For a tasty curry dish, fry curry powder with a little ground cumin and turmeric, salt, and mung sprouts in some butter. Add mushrooms and sliced carrots. Garlic may be added to taste. Then boil in a little water and serve with brown rice.

Eggs

Scrambled eggs are delicious with mung or alfalfa sprouts, salt, and lightly sautéed onions and green peppers.

Or try this combination: Fry mung sprouts with sliced mushrooms, in a very little curry, turmeric, and garlic powder. Add salt and pepper to taste. When the mushrooms and curry powder have become a little browned, scramble eggs (not too many) into the mixture.

Daal Purée

1 cup split peas or lentils (soaked 36 hours in 4 cups water, then drained)
¾ cup mung sprouts
1 stalk celery, chopped
1–2 tablespoons oil
½ teaspoon ground turmeric
⅛ teaspoon pepper
½ teaspoon chopped fresh ginger
4 cups water
¾ teaspoon salt
1 tablespoon lemon juice, or to taste

Sauté the celery and spices for 5 minutes or more in the oil, then add water, lentils, and sprouts. Add salt and lemon juice. Simmer for 45 minutes, or until tender. If too thick, thin with hot water. Blend until smooth.

Mung Soup

Sauté 1 clove chopped garlic in 4 tablespoons olive oil; add ½ cup chopped onion, sauté 5 minutes.

Add 2 stalks finely chopped celery with leaves; 1 chopped green pepper; 2 tablespoons chopped parsley; ½ cup green beans, cut in ½-inch pieces; 1 diced tomato; 1 bay leaf; and 2 cups mung sprouts.

Cover pan, bake in 350° oven 20 minutes, then remove and add 4 tablespoons browned white flour (brown in a dry pan over medium heat, stirring constantly until golden). To this dish add 1 quart boiling water; salt to taste. Simmer until tender.

VII. MEDITATION

Meditation on the Elements

In Step Four, I suggested that you visualize (or actually build) a fire, and mentally cast your imperfections into it to be purified. Fire is one of the so-called "elements" of nature, not in the sense that a chemist would use the term, but in a more spiritual sense. There are five such "elements" in all: earth, water, fire, air, and ether. In the yoga teachings they are always given in that relative sequence.

On a universal level we may say that each of these "elements" represents an elemental stage of creation. The consciousness of Spirit, when it becomes condensed grossly enough to enter into material manifestation, becomes the cosmic energy, or "ether," out of which the physical universe appears. This energy condenses into cosmic gases (the "air element"), which in turn condense to form the fiery stars. As fiery matter cools, it becomes molten (the "water" stage of cosmic manifestation). As it cools still further, it becomes solid; thus it reaches its fifth, and final, elemental stage of material manifestation, known as the "earth" stage. When material creation is withdrawn again into Spirit, its dematerialization will follow this sequence in reverse.

These elements also describe the stages of the soul's descent into matter, and, when reversed, the progressive stages of its liberation. In the process of entering the physical body, the consciousness hypnotizes itself into thinking that it has *become* the body. To break this hypnosis, one must identify himself with his inner soul. He will find it easier to retrace his steps Godward if he also, instead of denying the Lord in His lower elemental manifestations, draws what divine understanding he can from *every* manifestation. For God truly has become everything. It is our perception that must be purified to behold Him everywhere.

The yogi must, by ever deeper realization, climb back up the staircase by which formerly he descended into delusion. The "elements" in man signify his varying degrees of worldly attachment. The number of his attachments may be so great as to make it impossible for him to rid himself of them completely, if he works on each of them individually. By the time the millionth attachment has been overcome, the first thousand or so may again seem appealing to him!

The worldly person, by constant association with the things of this world, comes gradually to identify himself with them to the extent that he actually suffers, not only when his body is injured, but when his coat is torn, or when the fender of his car is scratched. This, of course, is the supreme folly of forming attachments: One becomes attached to things, or to people, because he thinks he enjoys them, yet because of his very attachment he sacrifices the power really to enjoy them at all!

I remember once being invited to tea in New Delhi by a certain ambassador. A nice person he was, and interested in Indian culture, but inordinately attached to his worldly goods. He served me tea on what I could see was truly exquisite china. But his pleasure in it was marred by constant anxiety for its safety. As the servant carried in the tea tray, my host cried out frantically to him to be careful. Subsequent conversation was interspersed with frequent references to the danger of entrusting valuable things to untrained servants. Later, as the tea tray was removed, it was followed to the kitchen by a volley of cautions: "Look out! Watch the edge of that carpet! Walk more slowly!" Only *I* was able really to enjoy the beauty of the chinaware!

It is not that possessions are bad in themselves. But to be possessed by one's possessions is slavery indeed. And that is the final sin (or error) of attachment.

You will find it comparatively easy to overcome your worldly attachments if you can cut them off at the point where they all converge: your own self. You will notice, first, that the things to which you feel attached all have certain properties in common. Different objects may be beautiful, for example, each one in its own way, but the simple fact of their beauty is something they share in common. Were it not for your love of this abstraction, beauty, none of these articles would attract you—at least, not for its beauty. Love of beauty, of course, is essentially a spiritual quality; it is not *in itself* a cause of bondage. We must go still deeper into ourselves to discover the true source of our earthly attachments. The resolution, however, of beautiful things into beauty as an essence illustrates the general direction in which we should seek. For if we can trace our attachments back to one, or to a few, essential expectations in ourselves, we may, simply by transmuting those basic expectations, banish all of them at once as though they had never been.

Ultimately, of course, our greatest delusion is to expect any lasting happiness outside of the divine Self within us. Since God is the only Reality, we doom ourselves to disappointment when we seek fulfillment while ignoring Him. But what is it that deludes us in the first place into seeing things in terms of their appearances, rather than in their essential, spiritual reality? The answer is, our own identification with the process of cosmic manifestation. If we can see our identification, like matter itself, in terms of its elemental stages of material involvement, it will be easy for us to break the hold that this world exerts on us.

Our attachment to beautiful things, for example, is partly that they are solid as well as beautiful; we can touch them and feel them. The love of beauty is a spiritual quality, but it can take us into delusion if we add to it the wish to touch it and feel it—in other words, if we add to it the earth element.

Notice how, the greater a person's attachment to "solid realities," the more set his own outlook becomes on life; and how, conversely, the more stolidly materialistic a person, the more his tastes incline to solid, heavy objects: big cars, solid walls in his home, thick, plush furnishings, heavy foods. Mentally, too, he inclines to have a "heavy" outlook on life, to be dogmatic, set in his ways, and rather dull. He is worldly not only because of his attachment to the things of this world, but even more especially because of a certain earthiness in his own consciousness.

This earthiness in man must be dealt with at its elemental source. If one can overcome all inflexibility and mental "heaviness" in himself, the solid properties of objective matter will cease to attract him. For him to rise above these qualities, however, before he has learned their positive lessons, may be as premature as putting a boy behind the wheel of a car before he has learned how to use the brake.

For the earth, and the earth "element" in us, has spiritual teachings also to impart to us. The tendency to remain set in our ways can be developed into *nishtha,* or steadfastness in our search for truth. Stolidity can become *titiksha,* or even-minded endurance in the face of life's dualities (heat and cold, pleasure and pain, joy and sorrow, etc.). Dogmatism can become *shraddha,* or true faith, born of a desire to experience truth directly, and thereby truly to know. Even heaviness of mind has its divine aspect, for it can be purified into *sthanu,* stability, or a consciousness of being always firmly centered in the Self.

If one develops in himself the more watery qualities of human nature—an easygoing, accommodative attitude, for instance, and an ability to flow with life's experiences—before acquiring the virtues of the earth element, he may only become wishy-washy and irresolute. To be dogmatic is, in itself, a human failing, but it is not good on the other hand to be so open-minded that one's brains can be blown away by the first passing breeze of external influence.

It will be good for you, therefore, sometimes to meditate on the thought that you are a rock: immovable, stable, firm. Affirm these qualities in yourself, repeating mentally: *"I am steadfast, determined, unshakably loyal to truth. I endure all things with calm faith in God."*

Inner stability will lead to mental ossification, however, if it is not also allied to a more fluid consciousness, symbolized as the "water element" in man. Without an ability to flow with the currents of grace, spiritual growth would be difficult. Yet this more flowing awareness, when it is directed outwardly toward mere things, constitutes the second elemental cause of man's attachment to this world. For it is not only the solidness and touchability of material objects, but, more subtly, their infinite variety which keeps a man bound to them. If he can trace this desire for change and variety to a certain fluidity in his own consciousness, and if he can overcome the desire for change for its own sake—if, in other words, he can accept change when it comes, yet even in the midst of it remain even-minded—his sense of inner freedom from attachments will increase immeasurably.

The flowing freedom of a person in whom the earth and water elements have been brought into ideal harmony is like that of a skillful surfboard rider; he can calmly ride the crest of every wave of change, and direct his life wherever he wants to go instead of being tossed and buffeted about, and perhaps ultimately broken, when conditions on which he has depended crash around him.

To acquire the virtues of the water element in your nature, try meditating on the feeling that you are flowing freely, fearlessly, with a stream of water; or floating on gentle ocean swells, caring not where they take you, full of faith in the divine will. Yogis sometimes tell their disciples actually to stand in flowing water up to the neck, and to meditate on, and identify themselves with, this flow; or to float on their backs in the ocean or in a lake (usually in *Matsyasana,* the Fish Pose, because it facilitates floating), and to abandon themselves mentally to the flow of divine grace. Whether literally immersed in water, or only meditating on the thought of water, affirm mentally, *"I flow ever freely with the tides of grace."*

The water element in us must be perfected not only by approaching it with the inner stability of the earth element, but also by channeling it into the dynamic enthusiasm for self-improvement that marks, at its best, the fire element in us. Otherwise our surrender to the tides of circumstance, though calm, will yet be passive, and will not carry us forward on the pathway to perfection.

The fire element, when rightly directed, is a necessary aid on the path to liberation. When wrongly directed, however, it too, like the earth and water elements, is a basic cause of human bondage. For attachments arise not only from one's identification with things in their earthy solidity, nor from the false freedom that one feels in their endlessly flowing variety, but also from the sense of dynamic enjoyment which he attributes to them. He enjoys good food, a foreign trip, the company of friends, or an interesting book, as if each were a separate source of enjoyment of which his own enjoyment was but the reflection. In reality, the case is reversed. It is his inner capacity for enjoyment that becomes reflected in outer things. Only when this capacity is great can he enjoy things greatly. Without it, the most beautiful scene, the most exciting "happening" will leave him cold. If he can trace his pleasure in the things of this world back to their common denominator of enjoyment *in himself,* and if he can learn to absorb those pleasures within himself, like tributary rivers of energy, directing their currents upward toward the Spirit, rather than outward toward matter, he will free himself of the last real claim that matter has on his feelings.

The fire element in man, if developed without reference to the stability of the earth element, or to the flowing, more easygoing quality of the water element, can manifest as a certain destructive ruthlessness. For where the earth element is inert, and the water element adaptive, the fire element is creative, a quality that can become aggressive if it is not properly tempered. The image springs to mind here of a warrior riding, screaming, through a village, burning, killing in an intoxication of zeal, unmindful of the suffering that he is bringing to countless innocent people. If the fire element is developed with evenmindedness and sensitivity, however, it can lead outward to great creative deeds, or, if spiritually directed, to dynamic, delusion-dispelling self-control.

In India a widespread custom, reflective of the need to harmonize the earth and water elements with the fire element, is the *yajna,* or fire ceremony, in which rice (symbolic of the subtle seeds of *samskar,* or past tendencies, and also of the earth element in man) and melted *ghee* (clarified butter, symbolic of the pure water element) are offered into fire as an expression of self-purification. By feeding on these offerings, the fire itself takes on symbolic significance, its upward leaping flames becoming the soaring aspirations of the soul for liberation in God.

Without this upward directedness, the fire element in us, even though constructive in its manifestation, will be creative only in an outward way. It may produce wonders, but not the greatest "wonder" of all: soul freedom. Flames that burn by the escape of hidden gases in a log may shoot outward in a variety of directions. Only flames that feed on the surrounding air move always upward. When the creative fire in man, or his capacity for enthusiasm, is directed outwardly, as if in a spirit of imposition on the world rather than of fine kinship with it, one's energies may shine bravely, and yet generally fail to uplift one's own or anyone else's consciousness. The fire element must be offered up into the still finer air element, which in man signifies, as we shall see shortly, a consciousness of the essential kinship of all life. Otherwise, creativity and enthusiasm, whether by one path or another, inevitably lead to delusion and bondage.

Meditation on fire as a means of acquiring, *and of rightly directing*, the mental virtues associated with this element, may be practiced as a purely mental exercise, or with the aid of an actual fire. In either case, the practice should be primarily mental. I have already given this meditation in Step Four. In addition to what I wrote there, you might visualize your own self burning with a cooling and joyous (i.e., not painful) flame, until all the elements of your being become transmuted into pure Spirit, pure Joy and Love.

The air element in man represents that state of awareness which precedes material involvement. It is like the gaseous state of matter before the stars and planets are formed, and therefore before formal distinctions appear to suggest differences between one manifestation of matter and another. At this "air" stage of creation, although the presence of different chemical elements in the gases might preclude our speaking of them as essentially one and the same thing, the kinship between them, at least, is obvious, as it is not on grosser levels of material creation. In man, this air element quickens his sense of *kinship* with life in its countless manifestations.

Directed downward, however, through the lower elements, this sense of kinship becomes particularized. One tends to feel a specific affinity for this person or that thing, and, generally, less affinity for other people or other things. In this way, likes and dislikes gradually develop. By means of his likes and dislikes, the air element in man launches him on his descent into delusion. Ultimately, it is on the neutralization of his likes and dislikes that spiritual realization depends. If he could but overcome them at their source, the other, lower, elements would cease to exert any hold on him. But because he is enmeshed in the material delusion, to work only on overcoming his likes and dislikes, ignoring the elemental channels of earth, water, and fire through which they manifest themselves, might result in too vague an understanding of the nature of his likes and dislikes. To work on developing the air element, moreover, without first developing the virtues of the lower elements, might only make a person apathetic—a condition in which many religious persons in fact dwell, mistakenly believing that by their wan outlook they are demonstrating non-attachment. The air element in us must be rightly developed, not suppressed. It must be stabilized, freed from prejudices, and fired with enthusiasm by the lower elements. It must itself be offered into a higher, divine vision. In this way, human likes and dislikes can be transmuted into disinterested love, which is the positive manifestation of the sense of kinship with life.

It must be understood that at this point, when the evolving soul-consciousness becomes centered in the air element, one finds oneself very delicately poised between divine liberation on the one hand, and further involvement in delusion on the other. For the air element is so refined that in itself—that is, so long as it does not express itself through lower, material attachments—it will seem to be wholly spiritual and pure. The love that one feels for others will seem beautiful, selfless, and serene. One's strong inclination at this point is to pour out divine love to all men *individually*—to love this person for his gentle smile, that one for his humility, still another for his unfailing kindness, and even worldly people for their spiritual naiveté, so like the callow ignorance of a child! But even pure, selfless love has its pitfalls. For once it becomes particularized, no matter how pure the sentiment at its inception, the trend is easily started that leads progressively toward involvement in material distinctions again. Do not trust the freedom that you feel, once this pure love manifests itself in you, but offer it up into the still finer ether element, in which is felt not only one's divine kinship with others, but an expanding, impersonal sense of the essential *oneness* of all life.

Meditate sometimes on the freedom of the vast blue sky. Visualize a balloon. Think of it as symbolizing all your likes and dislikes, all your worldly desires and attachments. Release the string of ego by which you hold this balloon in your grasp. Watch the balloon soar upward, growing smaller and smaller with distance—until only the vast blue sky is left.

Or see the balloon sailing for a time in the skies of divine freedom; consider how insignificant it seems, alone in infinity. Then mentally prick the balloon, and watch it vanish instantaneously into the infinite, blue void. You are that void!

The air element is, by definition, nebulous in character. To associate it specifically with love may prove more difficult for you than the association of the lower elements with their respective mental virtues. It would be well at this time, therefore, to bring out the fact that the elements of which we have been speaking are said in the yoga teachings to have their actual centers of special influence in the human spine. I shall discuss these centers more exactly in a later lesson. Suffice it for now to say that the air element is centered in the dorsal region in the spine—that portion of it, in fact, from which nerves radiate out to, and regulate, the organs that are concerned with the intake of oxygen into the body: the lungs and heart. In this dorsal center, also, opposite the heart, is universally felt the emotion of love, which is why love has always been spoken of in relation to the heart.

Another point must also be mentioned here. I have said that divine awakening is always accompanied by an upward movement of energy and consciousness in the spine. The elements are centered correspondingly lower or higher in the spine depending on the grossness of their material manifestation. To ensure that the subtle air element will be rightly directed, it will help if you meditate on the feeling of divine love in the heart. Then direct its rays, not only outward to all mankind, but especially *upward* toward God. Channel them through the impersonal calmness and expansion that are felt when the consciousness is centered opposite the throat in the spine, in the seat of the so-called "ether" element in man.

This ether element, finally, is too subtle to be itself a cause of material bondage. It contains only the *potential* of worldly involvement, as invisible cosmic energy contains the potential for manifestation as matter. Yet it may be said that energy's potential for material manifestation differs from that of pure Spirit in the sense that it is more dynamic, more actual. The ether element in man, similarly, represents that inner pause in which wrong, as well as right, directions may be determined. Inner calmness, in fact, and the thought, "It's all one to me," so long as the mind is outwardly directed, may soon turn to boredom, and a desire for more active worldly involvement. The sense of the oneness of everything will be spiritual only when it is supported by an upward movement of consciousness from the other elemental centers, and particularly from the feeling of selfless, divine love in the heart center. This expansive sense of oneness, finally, must itself be directed upward to the point between the eyebrows, and to the universal divine vision of which that sense of oneness is only the foundation.

It must be remembered, finally, that although I have written of the spiritual aspects of different elements almost as though the soul needed to meditate on those elements in order to develop their special qualities, all spiritual qualities are in fact rooted in God, and may indeed be developed by simply concentrating at the point between the eyebrows, the seat of divine vision. The reason for thinking of these qualities as they are expressed, and defined, by the so-called elements is only that man, by his descent into matter, has identified himself with them at their own levels. It is not necessary, in other words, once the mind has become uplifted in God, to recall to mind the elemental images with which divine qualities may also be associated. Stability, for example, is an abstract quality; it is only understood more *specifically* when it is identified with the solidity of a rock.

And yet, specific insights are necessary before one can attain a true understanding of abstract realities. In this sense, once the soul has separated itself from absolute wisdom in God, its final descent into matter may be for its ultimate good. No doubt this, too, is why certain scriptures say that even the gods desire human birth.

AUM, *Shanti, Shanti, Shanti*

Step Eight

Affirmations, Part 2

I. PHILOSOPHY

Affirmations, Part 2

Many years ago, before I came onto the spiritual path, I used to smoke fairly heavily. It was an expensive habit to support, and I never liked the lingering taste of stale smoke in my mouth between cigarettes. But it was a habit.

After some time I decided to give it up. Belatedly I discovered the wry wisdom of Mark Twain's words: "Smoking is the easiest habit in the world to give up. I've done it a thousand times!" I *wanted* to quit. But every time I did quit, another part of me wanted to start again.

After a year of repeated, but unsuccessful, attempts, I gained an added incentive. Deep thinking about man's relationship to universal realities had brought me at last to a point where I had begun to think seriously of becoming a hermit. "Who ever heard of a hermit who smokes?" I asked myself. My first step in the new direction, obviously, would have to be to cease depending on unnecessary expenses.

Thus it was that as I lay awake in bed one night shortly before going to sleep, I suddenly decided with calm (not frantic) conviction, that I had already, from that very moment, given up smoking forever. I remember one of the boys who shared the apartment with me coming into the room and my telling him of my decision so matter-of-factly that even he, who had seen me through many past failures, accepted it now not with his accustomed jeer, but as a *fait accompli.*

The following morning I awoke without the slightest thought that I might ever want to smoke again. For two weeks thereafter I carried around in my pocket the remains of my last pack of cigarettes. I passed them out to friends, but I never for a moment thought of wanting one for myself. I can honestly say that, since that moment (it was in the spring of 1948) when I *really* gave up smoking, I have never had even a fleeting desire to smoke again.

The memory of that experience has often returned to me intriguingly, and instructively, whenever I have set out to change other habits. Why, I have asked myself, was that particular effort so spectacularly successful?

Several factors were responsible. I think it might help you if I shared them with you.

1) Though my first efforts to give up smoking were repeated failures, I never allowed myself to think of them as failures. To me they merely meant that I hadn't yet succeeded. Every return to the smoking habit, therefore, was not an affirmation of weakness and defeat, but rather one of simply withdrawing to "regroup" for another, yet stronger attack.

2) My thought of becoming a hermit gave me something I had been needing: a strong incentive.

3) My affirmation, therefore, became positive rather than negative. I wasn't only incarcerating a cherished habit, and standing grimly on guard to make sure it never escaped again. I was relinquishing it for an alternative that I had persuaded myself was more attractive.

4) I took my stand calmly and matter-of factly, with none of the fanfare that often accompanies great sacrifices. Thus, I reduced my adversary from the size of a giant to that of a pygmy.

5) By going to sleep with my resolution firmly in mind, I carried it into the subconscious, where it worked directly on old habit patterns, and, because of the strength of my conscious determination, changed them.

The subconscious mind acts as a receptacle for whatever thoughts and impressions are passed on to it by the conscious mind. In this way it acts quite automatically and indiscriminately, like an echo returning sounds to their sender regardless of whether the sounds are beautiful or ugly. It is a convenient labor-saving mechanism devised by Nature to keep the factory of life functioning in whatever way it has been programmed to function, and to free the conscious mind to deal with new situations as they arise. Were it not for this mechanism, one would have to think his way carefully through each movement every time he tied his shoelaces or tried to walk. Our subconscious mind can be a blessing to us, if we program it properly, but it can also hold us chained to delusions that we reject again and again on a conscious level. For its power to direct human life is enormous. The impressions, or *vasana*s, not of one lifetime only, but of many incarnations lie buried deep beneath the surface of our conscious awareness, subtly influencing our tastes and inclinations, our manner of doing things, the very understanding with which we may seek to change those influences. Man thinks he is free to do just as he likes; he little realizes to how great an extent his very likes are already decided for him by the tendencies (*samskars*) and impressions (*vasanas*) that he has built up in the past. It is like a man being elected to high office on the strength of his campaign promises, only to find that that office has been so firmly committed to its old directions by his predecessors that he hasn't the strength to fulfill a single one of his promises.

Or so it seems, so long as he treats his subordinates high-handedly, as if he had only to speak for his commands to be smoothly and efficiently obeyed. He may, for example, have promised to lower people's taxes, only to find the various departments of government so enmeshed in their commitments that the very mention of cutting taxes is enough to send every department into paroxysms of anxiety and silent rebellion. If he really means to keep his promises, he must search deeply into the workings of every department, and study carefully how its energies might be redirected.

The same is true with the workings of the subconscious mind. It is possible to change them, but merely to issue New-Year's-resolution-type orders from the "executive offices" of the conscious mind may do little more than awaken active resistance from the subordinates below. Hence the common saying, "The road to hell is paved with good intentions." To change one's life truly, one must dig down into his subconscious thought patterns, and redirect them.

This can be a difficult job. I remember an office reorganizing job I once had at Mount Washington, the headquarters of Self-Realization Fellowship. I confidently expected my work to be finished in two weeks. It took a year and a half! The reason for the delay was that I discovered in the departments that I was organizing certain inefficiencies that had their roots in other departments. Those departments, in turn, were hampered by the inefficiencies of still other departments. In order to carry out my relatively simple assignment, I was finally obliged to reorganize the entire office. The case is often similar with the subconscious mind.

Not everyone's subconscious mind is so resistant to change. Resistance to improvement in an office nearly always stems from human egotism. Paramhansa Yoganandaji, in speaking of the human mind, referred to "the thwarting cross-currents of ego." Every human characteristic is like an individual; each has a definite personality of its own. If the different characteristics with which the subconscious has been programmed are all hedged about possessively, or primed to aggressiveness with the thought of "I," the resistance to change, once the order comes from the conscious mind, may assume the nature of an all-out war. Sometimes only great suffering can soften the hard core of egotism, and make it malleable to improvement.

An office, too, that has been allowed

for a long time to go its own way without proper direction will at first resist any efforts to change it. A wise reorganizer will know how to balance diplomacy with firmness. Sometimes, when diplomacy simply won't work, a little stern discipline may be necessary. The illustration remains valid here, too, for the subconscious mind.

I remember a period of months, many years ago, when, try as I might, every time I sat to meditate I found myself drifting helplessly toward sleep. It was discouraging, because in fact I wanted very much to meditate properly. One night I sat down particularly eagerly for meditation. But I had worked hard that day, and my subconscious mind simply did not share my laudable intentions. As I nodded yet again, I suddenly cried: "All right, I've tried to coax you politely, and you haven't listened. Now I'm through with diplomacy. Since you don't even want to stay awake long enough to finish your meditation, you're not going to sleep tonight at all!" By running around, and reading, and typing letters (I was much too sleepy to meditate), I stayed up all night. The following morning I went to my assigned job as usual. To my surprise, the next night I needed only six hours of sleep. And for a long time thereafter the sleep habit ceased to disturb me. Sometimes, as in an office, one must show his subconscious underlings who is boss, otherwise his efforts to direct them may only be treated with passive resistance, even with quiet contempt.

But normally the way for a boss to get the best work out of his employees is to make them *want* to work with him. This he can do by taking an interest in them and in their duties, by making them feel that they are important to the overall working of the company, and by infecting them with his own enthusiasm for any project he undertakes. Generally speaking, he can accomplish far more by drawing them than by bullying them. Indeed, if he only orders them about, they may obey him, but their obedience will lack fire. The work may get done, but the results will be unimpressive.

In dealing with the subconscious mind, similarly, one should familiarize oneself with its ways of functioning, and enlist its constant and friendly support in one's affairs, so that in anything one does he has the enthusiastic cooperation of his entire being, and does not have to walk, as so many people do, as if shackled to a heavy weight of subconscious reluctance and indifference. He should avoid becoming what Paramhansa Yogananda called "a psychological antique." He should deliberately change his habits from time to time, simply to keep them on their toes, and he should constantly streamline them, as one would an office, even eliminating them when they no longer serve any useful purpose. Above all, he will win their enthusiastic support if he affirms every new direction *with joy,* and with faith in their good will.

The greatest mistake people make is to belittle their own power to change themselves. To expect the worst of one's employees is to discourage them, and thereby of course to get the worst out of them. As I said in the last lesson, my guru taught us that the greatest of all sins is to call oneself a sinner, for it identifies one with sin, or error. So hypnotized, one becomes the helpless slave of delusion. No matter how often one fails, he should keep on trying to improve, remembering what Yoganandaji also said: "A saint is a sinner who never gave up." The very season of failure, he further taught us, is the best season for sowing the seeds of success, if we direct the energy awakened by our remorse, not toward self-abuse, but toward reinforcing our determination to do better next time. As with my experience in trying at first unsuccessfully to give up smoking, every time I went back to the habit I did so, not with a consciousness of failure, but with the thought, "Well, I haven't yet won, but maybe next time I will." In this way I strengthened my will ultimately to succeed, instead of allowing every failure to reinforce my self-hypnosis of weakness.

The best times for giving commands to the subconscious are when the door to it is most widely open. As I said in the last lesson, these times occur during deep meditation, and also just as one enters the subconscious in sleep, or emerges from it into wakefulness. Notice how, if you go to sleep feeling exhausted, you usually wake up still feeling exhausted no matter how many hours you have slept, whereas if you make it a point not to carry that thought into the sleepland, you may wake up refreshed even on less sleep than usual. Again, the attitude with which you wake up helps to determine your whole day, which is why people often say of someone who is out of sorts, "He must have got up on the wrong side of bed today." I was fortunate, when I finally did give up smoking, that I made my resolution at bedtime, though I knew nothing at that time of the yoga teachings on this (or any other) point.

Practice deliberately carrying wholesome affirmations into the subconscious. Either at bedtime, or sitting upright in meditation, repeat your affirmation out loud to begin with to generate energy and command the attention of all your conscious thoughts. As I said in the last lesson, your conscious mind must be made awake and ready before it can go deep into the spirit of the affirmation. "I am awake and ready!" is itself a good affirmation to stimulate yourself to complete attention. Yoganandaji used to begin his lectures and services by demanding loudly of the audience: "How is everybody?" Then he would join them in the energetic response: "Awake and ready!"

"How *feels* everybody?" And again, even more vigorously: "Awake and ready!" Sometimes in his younger days, partly to stir people out of their subconscious lethargy and resistance, and partly just because he was himself a man of extraordinary energy and joy, he would actually come running out onto the lecture platform, his long hair and orange robe waving with kindred high spirits.

Remember, then, put your whole self joyously into your affirmation. Then gradually let the words resound from deeper and deeper levels of feeling and awareness. As you do so, you will notice that the outward sound of the words automatically decreases, until it becomes only a whisper. Sink the words down deeper still, until you feel no desire to speak or to chant them outwardly at all, and the affirmation becomes purely mental. Go deeper still, carrying the thought into the subconscious, zealously changing the mental patterns there.

It is unfortunate that the subconscious mind is so often referred to as the "unconscious." This gives the impression that it is an inert thing, needing to be acted upon rather than enlisted in a good cause. Most people are, in fact, so susceptible to impressions from without that they become little more than echoes of the world around them. In their suggestibility they seem almost as if hypnotized. Under hypnosis, a person can be induced to give up smoking, or to overcome some irrational fear, but even under this seemingly desirable influence his suggestibility is increased, with the result that his resistance to subsequent harmful influences becomes lowered. The ordinarily impressionable person, similarly, may act properly when the influences around him are wholesome, but in a hysterical mob he may find himself, to his later bewilderment, screaming for blood. My guruji taught that hypnosis is a spiritual crime. It is not very much better to treat your own subconscious mind as if it were a mindless slave. For it is *not* unconscious. Nor is it even a separate mind from the conscious. Both are parts of one mind—limited manifestations, in fact, of *super*-consciousness. In a universe where divine consciousness is the sole reality, there can be *no* complete unconsciousness, even in the rocks.

The way to treat your subconscious mind, then, is like a friend, not a slave. It is not enough that it merely obey you, passively. Many pleasant, kind, and even spiritual people have no inner fire to burn down the ramparts of their delusions. And sometimes it happens that even a criminal, once converted to the spiritual life, quickly bypasses the vast majority of religious people and becomes a saint, because he has the capacity to put himself wholly into whatever he does.

In feeding suggestions to the subconscious mind, then, do not seek merely to impose upon it. Inspire it rather, to participate creatively in whatever changes you are trying to effect in yourself. Remember, every affirmation is an act of *becoming*. For it to be most effective, you must see yourself *on every level* as a cause, not as an effect.

Finally, for the change to become permanent, your affirmation must be carried deeper still, until it springs from the depths of superconscious bliss.

In making an affirmation, avoid negative statements, such as, "I don't like smoking." A truly creative act is always positive. (That is why we speak of "affirmations," not of "condemnations.") A negative thought is always an affirmation of reluctance, of rejection. As in any office, it engenders attitudes of lethargy and uncooperativeness. Reluctant office workers, even if they cooperate with a dynamic boss in routine matters, will never support him in a creative undertaking.

Keep your mental "office" on its toes by keeping it always *creatively* busy. Don't wait for some rare crisis before instituting a change. Make little changes frequently—giving up a small habit here, assuming another there until your mind becomes so flexible that it can change its habit patterns, willingly and completely, at a moment's notice.

Above all, always say "YES" to life! Do everything willingly, joyously. Have only kind thoughts about people. If you want to get out of this cosmic delusion, don't sit around wanly brooding over how fleeting and empty everything is. For everything is God, also. The difference between delusion and divine enlightenment lies not in things, but in the degree of our awareness. If we can be fully aware at every moment, we shall see God everywhere, no matter where we look. A positive affirmation of life is, in fact, intimately associated with the rising energy in the spine, of which I have already spoken, and without which spiritual awakening simply does not occur. Once all your energies can be focused in a single direction, your power of accomplishment will be, almost literally, infinite.

In this lesson I have left it to you to create your own affirmations, according to your needs. If, however, you would like to receive a book that contains deeply spiritualized affirmations on many subjects, as well as to read further on the subject of affirmations itself, I suggest you write to Crystal Clarity, 14618 Tyler-Foote Road, Nevada City, CA 95959, for a copy of my book *Affirmations for Self-Healing.*

Throughout these lessons, also, many different affirmations are given. For a general affirmation of freedom from all obstacles of delusion, you might like to try the following:

I Am Free

Note: As sung by Kriyananda on the cassette *O God Beautiful*

II. YOGA POSTURES

For every physical posture there is, as I have said, a corresponding mental state. To practice the yoga postures with spiritual feeling is to find that they help to develop that feeling. The yoga postures may thus be seen to be an important aid to spiritual unfoldment. If one enters a pose, not jerkily, but with an inner sense of harmony and peace, the very act of assuming that position can help to develop this *bhav,* or spiritual attitude. How one gets into the postures, the mental thought that he holds during the practice of them, how he comes out of them, and the consciousness of returning to his deepest inner center as he rests between the poses—all of these are an important part of the practice of *hatha yoga.* Without these attitudes, *hatha yoga* becomes, not a discipline of yoga at all, but only a system of calisthenics, beneficial physically, but bypassing completely the depths of discovery that await anyone with a sense of true spiritual adventure.

Some of the postures of *hatha yoga* are designated as *mudras*. I mentioned one *mudra* in the last lesson. A *mudra* is a pose that is designed to increase one's awareness of, and to stimulate the flow of energy in, the body, particularly with a view of directing this energy upward for deeper meditation. All of the postures, however, are in a sense *mudras*, for all of them should be practiced with this deeper purpose in mind. In later lessons we shall consider more of the poses that have been specifically designated as *mudras* because of their special effectiveness in stimulating or redirecting the flow of energy. Prepare for them even now, by feeling your body as spiritual energy moving through different meditative poses expressive of those deep states of peace and inner fulfillment that you hope to attain through your daily practice of this holy science. Make the postures themselves a kind of meditation in action.

Sitting Poses

When the body is full of tensions and toxins, it is difficult to rise above it in meditation. One of the main purposes of *hatha yoga* is the preparation of the body for meditation. The sitting poses themselves are intended primarily for their meditative value; less so for their physical benefits.

The important thing, as far as the body's posture in meditation is concerned, is that the spine be kept straight and the body relaxed. It is all right to sit in a chair, with the feet flat on the floor. There is, however, a definite advantage to sitting in one of the prescribed yoga positions. They exert certain beneficial pressures on the nerves, inducing calmness in the nervous system.

Each of the sitting poses has its own specific benefits. We have already discussed those of *Vajrasana* (the Firm Pose). From a standpoint of meditation, this pose helps to give the mind a consciousness of *nishtha,* steadfastness. Each of the other poses, similarly, exerts its own mental and spiritual influence.

Siddhasana (the Perfect Pose) is considered the classic pose of *hatha yoga. Padmasana* (the Lotus Pose) is said to be the classic pose of *raja yoga.* The difference between these two yogas may, in the present context, be described as follows: *Hatha yoga* uses the body to *push* the energy up toward the brain; *raja yoga* creates a magnet of aspiration in the higher, spiritual nature that *draws* the energy upward to the brain. *Hatha yoga* is not actually a separate science from *raja yoga;* it is merely the physical branch of that spiritual science. Distinctions between the two are, therefore, to some extent academic; in each approach, something of the other will be present. Best, indeed, is a combination of both approaches: an effort to use the body gently to nudge the energy upward, and deep, devotional meditation that must in time draw everything beneath it upward in its wake.

It must be understood that all spiritual effort involves a self-offering of the ego on the altar of God, the Infinite Self. Yogis of both the *hatha* and *raja yoga* schools often make the mistake of thinking that spiritual enlightenment depends only upon the efforts of the aspiring devotee—as if by techniques alone one could harness the Infinite! A right understanding of the yoga techniques, however, in no way contradicts the need for *kripa* (divine grace), as the *sine qua non* of the spiritual path. The highest purpose of yoga is simply to place oneself in a position to receive fully a downpouring of Spirit. If God's grace is not experienced in the average human life, it is not because of divine indifference, but because man's energies and attention are diverted elsewhere.

Siddhasana

(The Perfect Pose)

"I set ablaze the fire of inner joy."

Siddhasana (or the Pose for Attaining Perfection) is practiced by sitting on a blanket in such a way that the feet are pressed in toward the base of the spine. Place the left foot firmly in the crotch. (Men should place it below the genitals.) Take the right foot and place it over the left in such a way that the right heel is aligned directly above the left. (Men should place the right heel above the genitals, preferably pushing the male organ inward upon itself so as to lock the genitals firmly between the heels.) The right foot should then be placed partly between the left thigh and the calf. The left foot should be drawn up, if possible, so that at least the big toe is held firmly between the right thigh and calf.

The hands are placed palms upward on the knees, the thumb joined to the forefinger and the other three fingers extended out straight. Affirm mentally: *"I set ablaze the fire of inner joy."*

If you cannot practice *Siddhasana* perfectly, bring the feet as close to the proper position as possible, even placing the right foot on the floor in front of the left, instead of above it. If keeping the spine straight in this position requires too much tension in the back, place a small cushion firmly under your buttocks to tilt the pelvis slightly forward.

If in any of the sitting poses the legs go to sleep, hold the pose anyway as long as you can do so comfortably. There is no danger involved, merely discomfort. When coming out of a position in which the legs have become numb, you will find the transition very easy if, instead of trying to move about, you place the legs in a new position and hold them in that position for a minute or two. There will then be no pain, no "pins and needles." The legs will return easily and naturally to their normal state, and in less time than they would if you tried to move and massage them.

Benefits: This pose is said to be more beneficial for men than for women, although it may be practiced to great advantage by either sex. The locked position of the feet, even for women, sends energy from the lower extremities to the base of the spine, in a sense pushing the energy upward from the lower regions toward the brain. The position of the hands, similarly, suggests an inward drawing of the energy from those extremities to the spine.

Siddhasana (the Perfect Pose) is so called for its influence upon the spinal centers, the awakening of which helps the yogi to develop *siddhi*s, or yogic powers, and above all to become a *siddha,* or perfected being.

Be conscious of the spine in this technique. Draw the energy upward and focus it at the point between the eyebrows. After 20 minutes or so in this position you will be surprised to see what a calming influence it has upon your body and mind.

Yogis say that, to develop *nishtha* (steadfastness), one should sit in this pose a little *longer* than one likes! That is to say, sit a little *beyond* the point of comfort.

Padmasana

(The Lotus Pose)

"I sit serene, uplifted in Thy light."

Padmasana is, as I have just said, the classical pose of *raja yoga*. In this position the feet are placed soles upward on the opposite thighs, and the hands rested (usually) palms upward, on the thighs or between the feet.

Sit on the floor on a blanket. Place one foot (preferably the right) on the opposite thigh close to the hip. Place the other foot above the first on the opposite thigh, also close to the hip. The hands may be placed in a variety of positions. You may rest them palms upward between the feet, the right hand over the left. The palms may also be joined, with the fingers interlocked. Some yogis sit with the palms turned upward on the knees, or on the thighs, or set in closer to the junction of the abdomen. The important thing is to sit still and relaxed, with the spine straight. Affirm mentally: *I sit serene, uplifted in Thy light.*

If you find the Lotus Pose difficult, but desire earnestly to master it, you may find it helpful to place a pillow under the ankles to give them a little support, and to keep them from bending at an unnatural angle. A pillow under the knees, if they cannot be brought down to touch the floor, is also beneficial for the beginner.

Certain poses may help to prepare the body more easily to assume the different sitting poses:

- *Vajrasana* (the Firm Pose) helps to limber the knees, the ankles, and the feet.
- *Janushirasana* (the Head-to-the-Knee Pose) helps to stretch the tendons under the knees.
- *Paschimotanasana* (the Posterior Stretching Pose) helps to loosen the tendons under the knees, as well as to stretch the pelvis, so as to make it easier to sit straight in any of the sitting poses.
- The "Butterfly" is also helpful: Sit on the floor with the soles of the feet together, knees out. Gradually try to lower the knees and thighs to the floor.
- The inverted poses help to draw an excess of blood out of the legs, making it easier to arrange them into the more difficult sitting positions.
- Massaging the feet and ankles with oil can make them more limber.
- The best limbering exercise of all, however, once you can assume any of these sitting poses, is simply to sit in it. After a minute or two, as one's legs relax into the position, one finds most or all of the initial discomfort disappearing.

Benefits and Cautions: It is important *never* to force the legs into *Padmasana.* One may injure the knees if he does not stretch them gradually, even over a period of months.

Padmasana is the most stable of the meditation poses. Its stabilizing effect, coupled with the upturned position of the feet, is, if anything, more helpful than *Siddhasana* in raising the bodily energy toward the brain. Everything about the body suggests a natural rising upward of one's physical energies along with the upward soaring of the spirit within.

Ardha-Padmasana

(The Half Lotus Pose)

Yogis who find the full Lotus Pose difficult may feel comfortable in *Ardha-Padmasana* (the Half Lotus Pose). In this position, one places one foot only on the opposite thigh, keeping the other foot on the floor under its opposite thigh.

Sukhasana

(The Simple Pose)

Sukhasana refers to any of a number of comfortable positions, even to sitting in a chair with the feet flat on the floor. The purpose of all the sitting poses is to enable one to forget his body and meditate on God, rather than make his aching knees the focal point of his ention. The usual position described for *Sukhasana* is the simple "tailor" position of crossed legs, keeping the knees up.

III. BREATHING

I mentioned in the foregoing section that the general aim of *hatha yoga* is to use the body to push, or gently to nudge, the energy upward toward the brain. There is a danger here, if one goes from gentle nudging to a brutal driving of the energy. *Hatha yogi*s are always cautioned not to use force, nor to practice the postures too long at a time. A million volts sent into a 110-volt circuit would burn up the wires. It is necessary gently to prepare the nervous system to handle the energy as one increases the energy flow.

This warning is particularly important in connection with the breathing exercises. One should not practice violent breathing exercises too long at a time. One should not practice too many breathing exercises at one sitting. When one feels nervous or emotionally upset, he should do only the most gentle of the breathing exercises. Finally, he should always be cognizant of the effects of these exercises upon his general nervous equilibrium. If they have an upsetting, rather than a calming, influence, they should be done for a shorter duration, or even abandoned altogether.

The yogi should especially look out for a feeling of searing heat in the spine. The rising energy in the spine should have a soothing and regenerating effect upon the mind and nervous system. If there is heat, and particularly if this heat is painful, he must cease his practice immediately. If the energy that he feels is in any way disrupting to his peace and to his nervous equilibrium, it should not be encouraged. It is not enough merely to feel energy. The flow of energy must be one that the aspirant's nervous system can handle. Anything that makes him more nervous will be detrimental to his health, and also to his spiritual progress.

With these cautions, practice the

alternate breathing exercise that I have already taught you, to a ratio of 1-4-2. Inhale in the left nostril counting 4, hold 16, exhale through the right nostril counting 8; then inhale through the right nostril 4, hold 16, exhale through the left nostril counting 8. (If this count is too slow, make it 2-8-4.) Do not overdo this practice. Three to six rotations are enough.

IV. ROUTINE

Practice the same routine(s) that you have been following. Sit in one of the yogic sitting poses while doing the breathing exercises and meditation, before the practice of the postures. Sit also in one of them after *Janushirasana* (the Head-to-the-Knee Pose). When your practice of the postures has been completed, and after deep relaxation, sit in any of these sitting poses and meditate as long as you can do so with enjoyment.

V. HEALING

Some years ago I was obliged to give up lecturing for a whole year. I had had to lead a large group of people in chanting for an entire evening, when my throat was suffering from such a case of laryngitis that I could hardly speak. The strain of that occasion affected my vocal cords so badly that they became ulcerated.

I went to a succession of doctors, each of whom gave me some pet remedy of his own, but none of whom helped my condition in the slightest.

After a year, some one suggested to me that I see a chiropractor. I had never heard of chiropractic before, but was more than ready to try a new remedy. To my relief, my condition disappeared almost completely after one or two treatments. Within two weeks I was off on a lecture tour across the country and to Europe.

Many pathological conditions in the body are due simply to an impairment in the flow of energy to the body from the spine. In my case, straining my vocal cords had created sympathetic tensions in my neck that had resulted in a dislocation of my cervical vertebrae. When the vertebrae are not properly aligned, they often pinch on the nerves, drastically reducing the vital supply of energy which those nerves are designed to transmit. Many serious problems, mental as well as physical, have been corrected simply by realigning the vertebrae and relieving pressures that they have been placing on the nerves.

In the situation from my own life that I have just described, yoga postures alone were not adequate to perform the correction that was needed. Sometimes it is necessary to take the help of someone who can manipulate the spine scientifically. In most cases, however, the postures keep the spine relaxed enough never to get out of position, or return it to a normal state of balance if the alignment has not been too severely disrupted.

Try these postures for a stiff or aching back: *Bhujangasana* (the Cobra Pose); *Ardha-Matsyendrasana* (the Half Spinal Twist)—to be taught in Step Nine; *Paschimotanasana* (the Posterior Stretch); *Chandrasana* (the Moon Pose).

For headaches, try *Halasana* (the Plow Pose), or *Sarvangasana* (the Shoulder Stand)—to be taught in Step Eleven; and *Bhujangasana* (the Cobra Pose), or *Chakrasana* (the Circle Pose).

For the bones in general, the irrigation that they receive when the joints and vertebrae are kept limber through the practice of all the yoga postures is extremely beneficial.

VI. DIET

I have mentioned the importance of certain forms of diet (vegetarian, etc.). Something must be said on the subject of faddishness versus the power of the mind to correct almost any physical condition. Many people make such a religion of their diet that they actually weaken the most important element in good health: the mind. "I haven't eaten my kelp today. My spine feels weak!" With such a consciousness, one becomes spineless even if he does manage to get his daily quota of kelp!

It is best to eat as well as one can, conveniently, and then forget it. I have seldom seen so many sick people as I have among food faddists. Their sickly appearance is due partly, no doubt, to the fact that they were sick before they became food faddists (their interest in diet being due to their poor health), but it is also due to an excessive preoccupation with their bodies.

If you tried to arrange cushions on a chair in such a way as to make yourself *perfectly* comfortable, you would never succeed in finding the *one best* arrangement. Similarly with the health of the body, the more one tries to make everything exactly right for it, the more aware one becomes of all the things that are still wrong. There is no end to the search for perfection, so long as one looks for it outwardly. It is only within that perfection can be found.

A strong mind draws energy to the body, keeping it well even under the most appalling circumstances. This is no argument for abusing the body. Though I have seen many sickly vegetarians, I have also seen that, by and large, they tend to be far more healthy than their meat-eating brothers. But to reiterate: Eat well, and forget it! Be cheerful in your mind, and, all other things being equal, you will seldom find anything physically wrong with you.

RECIPES

Ananda Seven-Grain Pancakes

1 cup flour
1 cup seven-grain cereal
2 teaspoons baking powder
2 eggs
2 cups milk
2 tablespoons melted butter
½ teaspoon salt

Warm the milk, then remove from heat. Soak the seven-grain cereal in the warm milk for 10 minutes. Then add melted butter and eggs. In a separate bowl, mix the flour, baking powder, and salt. Stir into the milk mixture. Thin with more milk if too thick. Cook on lightly greased griddle or pan. Serve with maple syrup or topping of your choice.

Curried Cauliflower

Chop cauliflower or separate into florets. Place in a skillet with butter, and sprinkle with curry powder, and a little salt. Fry until brown (5 minutes or so). Add a little water (not even enough to cover bottom of pan). Cover and cook 12 to 15 minutes, or until tender, stirring occasionally. Do not overcook.

Burnt Eggplant

Prick 4 to 5 eggplants, medium size, in several places. Cook thoroughly over an open flame, such as a campfire or a barbecue grill. To broil in an oven, lay the eggplant in a foil-lined tray. Or, to roast over a low gas flame, set eggplants directly on foil-lined burners. Rotate eggplants to char all sides evenly, cooking until the insides are butter soft (about 20–30 minutes). Split open and scoop out the eggplants, discarding the skins. Put 2 garlic cloves through a garlic press, add about ½ cup ghee or butter, and fry until garlic is transparent. Add ½–1 tablespoon onion juice (obtained by finely grating onion), a little garlic salt to taste, and ½ yellow chili, chopped (if desired). Add eggplant to sauce and bring to boil so that the sauce saturates the eggplant. (For a more purely yogic dish, omit the garlic and onion.) Serves 6.

VII. MEDITATION

Prayer, Chanting, Japa, *and* Mantra

"Chanting is half the battle."
—Paramhansa Yogananda

I shall never forget a lesson I received in the difference between affirmation and prayer. It was when our temple at Ananda Meditation Retreat burned down in the early morning hours of July 3, 1970. By mental non-attachment I was able to maintain a more or less cheerful attitude, and not to think of our loss, focusing my energies one-pointedly on the efforts necessary to build a new temple. But that was as far as right attitude could carry me. I felt no gratitude, for example, nor any soaring joy in contemplating the perfection of God's plan in taking our temple from us. In fact, as the day wore on I had to admit that, underneath my cheerfulness, I felt rather numb. No amount of right thinking could change that fact. What I wanted was not only a positive attitude, but *understanding.*

That evening I sat down in meditation and asked God, through the channel of my guru, for enlightenment. Mentally I had already (in fact, long before) relinquished all hold on the temple. Now, however, I held it again in my heart, along with the memory of all the months that had gone into building it, and all the additional months that would have to go into re-building it. I offered all these reflections to God. "What I do," I told Him, "and what happens to the things I do, are not important to me. I have ever worked, and will ever work, only to please You. All that matters is my love for You."

Suddenly God touched my heart. I was flooded with such divine love that, weeping for joy, I prayed, "If losing the temple can bring me such blessings, why didn't You take the Common Dome, too?"

Mental affirmation of some kind is necessary as a means of awakening one's own inner powers. Even at their best, however, those powers are exceedingly limited so long as they are not attuned to the consciousness of infinity. People who think to advance by the strength of their own little egos have simply no conception of their distance from divine perfection, the journey to which has almost for its starting point the relinquishment of the ego. And yet, to expect God to do everything for us is to misunderstand the law also. In the last analysis, what we must learn is, not that we are nothing, but that God is everything, including our own selves. This we can learn, not by passively leaving all efforts to Him, but by doing our own best, while at the same time lovingly inviting His assistance in our efforts.

Affirmation is man's part of the labor of self-transformation. United to the flow of divine grace, affirmation becomes the sort of prayer that alone achieves results. For remember, God has not to be wheedled into doing things for us. He is our own nearest and dearest Friend. The very abundance of the universe would be ours, if His will were the only factor that counted. It is we who have cut ourselves off from that abundance by our consciousness of limitation, of ego-identity. To pray to God like beggars pleading for a rich man's favors only increases our sense of limitation. Such prayer actually holds the door of divine grace closed, even while it begs God to open it. Remember, God's power is everywhere. We must tap it by attuning ourselves to its wavelength. This we can do by acting with a full sense of power ourselves, and then inviting God to spiritualize this power, that its source be, not the ego, but the divine consciousness. Prayer itself, in other words, like a dynamo, is the power that generates the blessings that we seek through prayer. By the intensity of our own concentration and devotion, God's grace is enlisted to make our prayers effective.

I don't mean at all to imply that, because grace flows automatically when our attitudes are right, it is therefore mindless, nor that we can command it, like electricity, to do our bidding as and when it suits us. Divine grace is omniscient, after all, as well as all-powerful. It is we who must adapt ourselves to its ways. It will not conform itself to ours.

Affirmation, as I have said, is most effective when it unites self-effort to a loving call for divine support and assistance. On the other hand, even prayer, to be effective, should contain an element of affirmation. That is what Jesus meant when he said that we should pray believing (Matthew 21:22).

When I prayed for understanding after the destruction of our temple at Ananda, my words were uttered in thought only. Ordinarily, however, unless the inner motivation is deep, it is helpful to combine prayers, and even affirmations, with the uplifting influence of music.

One cannot listen to music sensitively without soon becoming aware that it conveys more than sounds, that it is a vehicle for moods, for states of consciousness. Sound has power. It is vibration. All things created, even subtle phenomena such as thought, are in a state of constant movement, of vibration. And wherever there is vibration there is also sound of some kind, however subtle. Sound, through the medium of the voice, is the channel through which human consciousness flows into outward manifestation. It is the connecting link between the mind and feelings of one person and those of another. All things not only respond to sound; they *are* sound. Vibration, or sound, is the connecting link between *all* phenomena. As the open strings on a piano vibrate sympathetically to notes that are struck on another nearby instrument, so also all things affect one another—mostly on levels far outside the range of human hearing—by the subtle law of vibratory exchange. Because vibrations react on many levels—like piano strings, many of which may respond sympathetically even though only one note is struck on another instrument—normally inaudible vibrations, even of thought and of feeling, can be captured sympathetically through music. By music, in turn, if he impregnates it with the power of his thought, man can sympathetically affect nature in many of its aspects, soothing wild beasts, causing plants to grow more rapidly, even reducing the height of flames in a fire or causing rain to fall during a time of drought.

Some years ago a popular song was banned from the air waves. Too many people, it seems, were committing suicide after listening to it. The song was called, "Gloomy Sunday." I never heard it, but I believe that music may well plunge certain susceptible persons to such depths of depression. For music, perhaps more than any other medium of expression, has the power to influence human consciousness, both for good and for evil. (It would be wise, therefore, never to listen to any music but that which uplifts the soul.)

According to the ancient teachings of India, of all musical instruments the most perfect is the human voice. No other instrument expresses so perfectly the subtle nuances of thought and feeling. The slightest change of mood creeps instantly into the voice: the sharp edge of anger, the bubbling lilt of amusement, the tonal poverty and hardness of greed, the sweetness of compassion. One of the early signs of progress in yoga is a growing sweetness in the voice—the echo, simply, of increasing inner peace and happiness.

Words, more even than mere sound, are man's spirit made manifest on the material level of existence. When words are used rightly as a conscious expression of that spirit, they carry the power to reach into the heart of all things, to perform what worldly people might consider miracles. Through speech, so yogis say, one can command the very elements to do his bidding.

But it must be understood that speech has real power only if it is used to express the true Self, which abides behind the façade of shallow, worldly preoccupations with which men usually identify themselves. Words that are spoken absent-mindedly or insincerely are like piano strings without a piano beneath them for a sounding board: thin and ineffectual. People who speak too much, like people who spend their wealth foolishly, lose their power. It is not only the body that forms a sounding board for the voice, but the heart, the mind, the very Self.

Put your whole being into your speech. Refrain from speaking when speech is likely to become chatter. Speak from a consciousness of inner silence, not of outward gossip. You will find gradually that your very word becomes, as Paramhansaji put it, binding on the universe.

When Paramhansa Yogananda published his book *Cosmic Chants,* he wrote in the "Prelude" to it that each of the chants contained in the book had been "spiritualized." That is, he had sung it over and over until, in the singing, he had received a divine response. Here is a fascinating aspect of music as a vehicle for states of consciousness: Not only do certain kinds of music help to transmit the mental states of their composers; even *after* they have been composed they can be further impregnated with power. This esoteric truth becomes easily understood if we remember that many people can sense in the vibrations of a room or of a building the consciousness—whether happy, or sad, or nervous, or spiritually inclined—of the people who have lived there, and not only the consciousness of the architect. A building is not, essentially, more substantial than a song. All things exist as vibrations. All, ultimately, is consciousness. Matter is not really solid at all. The very rocks are only manifestations of subtler realities. Songs, too, can acquire vibrations according to the uses to which they are put. To sing the spiritualized chants of a master, particularly with a consciousness of attunement with him, can be a very powerful means of attracting his grace.

Attunement is, of course, the most vital factor in fitting oneself to receive any vibration. Even a radio can pick up a station only when it is tuned to its wavelength. Since our attunement is clearest with states of consciousness that we have perceived directly ourselves, Yoganandaji wrote that the greatest benefit comes from spiritualizing a chant oneself, by singing it repeatedly, more and more deeply, day after day until it lifts one into superconsciousness. Thereafter, he said, whenever one sings the same chant it will induce that state of consciousness. This is one reason why it is good to stick loyally to one spiritual path, and to one set of spiritual techniques, instead of trying many paths in the name of "broad-mindedness." For once, by long practice, a specific practice has been "spiritualized" through some form of divine contact, it will quickly induce a divine state of awareness every time it is undertaken again. In the same way, although a variety of chants may be more interesting, and in that sense more inspiring, than sticking to one chant for a long period of time, the way really to spiritualize a chant is to sing only that one for days, weeks, or months together, taking it deeper and deeper into oneself as you have been taught to do with affirmations, until through it one achieves some definite divine contact.

In India this form of continuous chanting is called *japa*. The average person's mind in its wakeful state flows in an unending series of thought patterns, usually expressed in the form of words. Most of these mental words are a mere waste of energy. Some of them (words of anger, frustration, jealousy, fear, etc.) actually help to direct our energy and consciousness downward, into delusion. Constantly to revolve a chant or an affirmation in the mind helps to create a positive vortex that draws all of one's thoughts and energies to a spiritual center.

Yoganandaji told us to chant mentally all day long such words as, "I am Thine; receive me!" or, "I want only Thee," or, "Reveal Thyself!" or, of course, the words and melody of one of his *Cosmic Chants*. To chant in one's own language will probably be more meaningful, and therefore helpful, to most people. Foreign words have a way of twisting and confusing the tongue, even if one utters them only mentally. (When I was teaching yoga in India, I wondered why students often complained that it was difficult for them to count mentally to ten or twenty as I had told them to do. At last I realized what their problem was: They had never accustomed themselves to counting in English!) It is difficult, moreover, to give sincere expression to words which one only half understands. Since Yoganandaji spiritualized his chants, and since, besides, they were born of his own deep Self-realization, they may be used with perfect effectiveness for continuous *japa*.

English, however, though in its own right a beautiful language, is not truly a *spiritual* language. It vibrates with crystal mental clarity, common-sense (as distinct from merely intellectual) logic, simplicity, a keen interest in life, and kindliness. But it does not vibrate with spiritual power. For this quality, probably no other language in the world is so perfect as Sanskrit.

Sanskrit, born as it was during a much more spiritual age than our own, contains in its syllables sounds which the great sages of India have claimed come the closest to the natural sound-vibrations of the astral world. That is why Sanskrit has been known traditionally as *Devanagari,* the language of the gods. Sanskrit seed sounds, or *bij-mantra*s, when correctly pronounced are capable of effecting great changes in the natural order, or in one's own inner nature. Simply to listen to scriptural passages uttered in Sanskrit is to be inspired with a feeling of spiritual power and joy. For Western yoga students who want to make the effort, much, certainly, can be gained from repeating some of the Sanskrit *mantra*s. It is not only that Sanskrit is a deeply spiritual language in its own right. Its *mantra*s have been spiritualized through millennia also by devotees and great yogis.

Much is made in India of the importance of chanting Sanskrit *mantra*s with the correct pronunciation and intonations. The Westerner, certainly, is not likely ever to master this difficult art. Even in India it is rarely that one finds someone who has attained such mastery. In fact, Swami Vivekananda stated that he had once had a vision in which ancient sages appeared to him and chanted familiar Sanskrit *sloka*s (scriptural passages) in a manner very different from that which tradition has passed down as the correct form. From this story one wonders if even the learned pandits of India today can truly master this ancient art according to the original traditions.

There are, however, two aspects to correct pronunciation: exoteric, and esoteric. A brother disciple of mine once wanted to order some split peas for the kitchen at the Self-Realization Fellowship Church in Hollywood. The purchasing agent, a German with a heavy accent, was unable to understand the request until it had been deliberately mispronounced for him. "Oh," he cried, with dawning recognition, "*shplit* peas! Vy you don't shpik Ehnglisch?" This is an example of exoteric pronunciation. Foreigners may say "loff," or "loaf," instead of "love." But even native Englishmen and Americans will often speak the word, "love," in such a way as to convey none of its actual meaning. It is even possible to say, "I love you," with such an intonation as to suggest, "I despise you." And it is possible also to say, "I hate you," in such a way as to convey nothing but love. The consciousness behind one's words constitutes the esoteric aspect of correct pronunciation. Where the state of consciousness, or *bhav,* is strong, correct exoteric pronunciation of the words is of secondary importance, though it may in fact follow automatically.

Specifically, where yoga practice is concerned, it would be well to bear in mind that different states of consciousness actually have their seat in corresponding centers, or *chakras*, in the spine. For example, when we love others, our feeling is centered in the heart *chakra* opposite the heart in the spine. A strong affirmation of will power automatically draws one's energy to a focus at the point between the eyebrows. Vision, though a faculty of the formless soul, has its physical seat in the eyes. Similarly, various mental states have their corresponding psychic seats in the body (to be more exact, in the *astral* body, of which the physical body is the counterpart).

If you will utter any chant or *mantra* with a deep inner consciousness of its purpose, and from the fullness of your own being, the words will be effective even if your outward pronunciation of them is not exact. Of course, it is better still to combine inner sincerity with outward correctness. Sincerity, however, is always more powerful than mere external forms.

And what is sincerity? It is any intention that has the support of one's whole being. As the chest is a sounding board for the voice, so one's inner consciousness is the sounding board for whatever mental or spiritual qualities vibrate in the voice. Specifically, if you will speak or sing from the higher *chakras* (the heart, or dorsal, center in the spine, the cervical center opposite the throat, and the Christ center between the eyebrows), you will make your voice a means both of directing spiritual power and of awakening that power in yourself.

Feel as you sing that you are drawing your voice upward from the heart, through the cervical center, and projecting it outward through the Christ center. To get this feeling, it may help you, while holding a single note, to bring your hand up from the heart and outward in a sweeping motion above and beyond the head, as if offering your tonal purity worshipfully to God. Practice this exercise repeatedly, until you can actually hear love vibrating in your voice as the tone touches the heart center; peace and expansion entering it as it touches the cervical center; and divine power and joy entering it as it passes through the Christ center.

When I studied singing in college many years ago, my singing teacher told me, "The voice is the only instrument that one cannot see. I can't *show* you how to use it correctly. I can only use it correctly myself, and ask you to listen sensitively and try intuitively to absorb my understanding." A truly yogic singing teacher! And how much more I learned from her with this method of teaching than I would have, had her method consisted merely of the vocalizing exercises that comprise the usual singing lesson. For the same reason I might suggest, if you are interested in this aspect of chanting, that you get one of my recordings, and use it as an aid in developing your own capacity to sing and speak from the spinal centers.

What *mantra* should you use? Unless

and until you are given *diksha* (initiation) into one specific *mantra* (*mantra diksha* was not my own guru's path), the choice really is up to you. Many *mantra*s are taught in India. Often those Sanskrit *mantra*s which are used for *japa* (the constant repetition of God's name) consist of twelve or of sixteen syllables, or of half, or of double, those numbers. Just as often, however, the single syllable, AUM, is used for this purpose. AUM is, in fact, the highest *mantra,* attuned as it is to the very essence of all vibrations, the Cosmic Vibration itself. To chant it, pronounce it to rhyme with "home." In English it is usually written, *Om,* to keep people from pronouncing the first letter with a long *a.* Otherwise, it is spiritually more correct to spell AUM with three letters, each letter signifying a different phase of the Cosmic Vibration: creation, preservation, and dissolution. But in English, few vowels are pronounced purely. When we say, *Om,* we are in fact pronouncing *two* principal vowel sounds. Some of us even touch on a few secondary sounds on the way!

Try reciting one or more of the following *mantra*s in your meditations, or before or after your practice of the yoga postures.

"Om namah Shivaya" ("*Om,* I bow to the Lord, Shiva"). Shiva is God in the aspect of Dissolver of the universe, and Destroyer of our attachments and delusions. Normally, *a* is pronounced short, like the *u* in "cut." *Ā* is pronounced long, like the *a* in "arm." If you want to sing this chant, here is a melody that is popular in India:

Om Namah Shivāya

"Sri Ram, jai Ram, jai jai Ram, Om" ("Lord God! Victory to God! Victory, victory to God! *Om*"). This was the *mantra* of a great saint of recent times in India, Swami Ramdas. Its origins are lost in antiquity. Here is the melody that Swami Ramdas popularized:

Sri Rām, Jai Rām

traditional Indian chant

"Om namo Bhagavate Vasudevaya" ("*Om,* I bow to the Lord Vasudeva, or Krishna"). This is the principal mantra of a great Indian scripture, the *Srimad Bhagavatam.* I have written my own melody for it:

Om Namo Bhagavāte

ancient Sanskrit mantra

music by Swami Kriyananda

The Indian *mantra*s that are used for chanting and *japa* usually consist primarily of a repetition of names of God. My guru, in introducing Indian-style chanting to the West, wrote chants that combine the principles of affirmation and prayer: As affirmations, they are prayerful and devotional; as prayers, they are affirmative—"loving demands," as he called them. His chants are a natural preliminary to the simple repetition of God's name, for without first engendering right attitudes in oneself, the mere practice of calling to God may easily cause one to slip into demeaning human attitudes of beggary.

*Mantra*s and other deep spiritual teachings are usually given with an enjoinder of secrecy, not to deprive suffering humanity of their power, but rather so that the devotee receiving them may nourish them with daily practice, until they grow and bear fruit. To tell others what one is practicing in inner silence would be to dissipate spiritual power. It would be like uprooting a seed from the ground before it has had time to sprout. Secrecy is enjoined in all spiritual practices, not to encourage selfishness, but so that the devotee may first grow strong in himself. Once he has acquired inner wealth, he will be in a position to share his wealth liberally with others.

Try incorporating chants and *japa* into your daily spiritual practices. You will soon discover why my guruji said, "Chanting is half the battle."

AUM, *Shanti, Shanti, Shanti*

Step Nine

Energy & Energization

I. PHILOSOPHY

Energy and Energization

In the last two lessons we considered how, with the aid of affirmations, one can change his subconscious reactive processes, thereby enlisting the support of his entire being in anything he undertakes.

What is the nature of this support? Certainly it is no mere acquiescence, but a source of phenomenal power. Initially, it releases for positive use energy that has been held trapped by old habits. Then, as this inner supply of energy becomes directed and focused, it begins to be supplemented by the energy of the surrounding universe. In this simple fact may be found the key to all human greatness. It is from the infinite source *primarily* that all our strength comes, even—and far more so than most people realize—before we attain any marked degree of spiritual development. To endeavor to live more and more by that divine power, even from the beginning of the spiritual journey, will save you from wandering endlessly on bypaths of ignorance. That is one reason Jesus said, "Seek ye the kingdom of God first, and all these things shall be added unto you."

Wisdom, love, joy, peace—all divine qualities, as well as energy, are implied in the flow of divine grace. But they are perceived first, and most easily, in their lower manifestation, as energy. By learning how to attune oneself to the cosmic energy, one learns the secret of divine attunement on all levels. That secret is will power.

Let us suppose to begin with that you have had a party. The guests remained late, so you decided to put off washing the dishes until the next day. But in the morning you had to leave early for work. It was an unusually bad day at the office. Unreasonable demands were made of you by your employer.

Your phone went out of order in the middle of an important call. There were delays, misunderstandings, frustrations. By the time you got home that evening you were exceptionally tired.

Bad enough? Not quite! You had forgotten about that large stack of dishes in the sink. The moment you stepped into the kitchen and saw them, your fatigue increased to exhaustion. "No dishwashing tonight!" you vowed, as you collapsed limply on the couch.

And then it was that the phone rang. An old and good friend of yours, whom you hadn't seen in years, had just arrived in town, and wanted to invite you that very evening to a concert you had been very much wanting to attend, but hadn't been able to afford.

Where did all that sudden energy come from? Five minutes ago you hadn't had enough strength left to sit up. Now you felt eager not only to go out again, but even to stay up half the night!

Obviously, your degree of energy depends not only on the amount of food you have eaten, but upon your measure of will power. People have, in fact, been known to work energetically for long periods of time without either food or rest. The only thing sustaining them was their determination to keep going.

When I was new in the Self-Realization Fellowship monastery, Master, to give some of us an excuse to be with him while he worked on his writings at Twenty-Nine Palms, had us construct a swimming pool. (I think he used it all of once!) To save money, we mixed and poured the concrete ourselves. To avoid seams (though, it turned out, leakage was no problem; water wouldn't even seep out through the drain), we poured the whole pool in one day. It meant working almost non-stop for 23½ hours. But to work willingly for God is a joy. Far from complaining at the long hours, we took them as a chance to show Him what a blessing it was to be serving Him. Every shovelful of sand or gravel went into the cement mixer to the accompaniment of joyous *mantra*s.

One monk, however, after three or four hours sat down, grumbling, "I didn't come here to pour *cement!*" The rest of that day he tried to talk us out of being such "fanatics."

At the end of the day all of us felt full of divine energy and joy—all of us, that is, but one. The reluctant "devotee," though having done nothing all day but complain, was exhausted!

Doctors have often noted that patients who want desperately to live may pull through even medically hopeless diseases, while others, no longer wishing to live, may die even though there seems no medical reason for them to do so.

A friend of mine worked as a physiotherapist in a polio clinic. He told me he had noticed that poor patients, unable to afford a long convalescence, often got well quickly, while rich patients more often accepted their paralysis long enough for it to become a permanent habit. I once met a woman, tall, strong, very active, but poor, who had had polio and had been told by her doctor that she would never walk again. By sheer will power and dogged perseverance, dragging herself on the floor by her hands when her legs refused to obey her, she had been able to overcome her paralysis completely.

I myself had an experience where sheer necessity, born of poverty, hastened my recovery. It was in a hospital in Mexico City, when I was nineteen years old. I had streptococcus, tonsillitis, and dysentery, and had been told by the doctor that I would be bedridden for at least two weeks. My parents, to whom I could have appealed for financial assistance, were in Romania. Discreet inquiries convinced me that a two-week stay there was almost two weeks more than I could afford. In my desperation to get well quickly, I was out of that hospital, cured, in two days.

I read statistics some years ago to the effect that people who are habitually cheerful, who devote themselves to helping others, and who generally keep themselves constructively busy, are less likely to become ill than gloomy, selfish, and lazy people. Mothers, for example, who must stay on their feet to nurse their sick children through an epidemic, are far less likely to become ill themselves. They simply haven't the time to indulge themselves.

Energy, endurance, health—even our actual physical strength—depend on the amount of will power we can bring to bear on any situation. I remember once reading of a woman whose house caught fire. In the desperation of the moment she picked up the piano and ran out of doors with it. (Talk about attachment!) Doctors attribute such displays of strength to a sudden flow of adrenalin, but I have seen cases where no emergency was present, only an extraordinary will to succeed, and in these cases, too, the strength was phenomenal. My guru demonstrated such strength sometimes publicly. Once in Symphony Hall in Boston, though he was short by American standards, he toppled six burly policemen from the stage into the orchestra pit, simply by arching his back as they tried to press him against a wall. These men had come on the stage in answer to his invitation to anyone to test the strength he claimed yoga practice made possible. When the audience saw six such brawny men stride up to meet his challenge, they thought that this time he faced certain defeat, but his victory was apparently effortless. Yogis claim that such feats of strength depend not so much on a flow of adrenalin as on harnessing the natural energy of the body and of the surrounding universe.

"There is enough energy in one gram of flesh," Master used to tell us, "to keep the city of Chicago supplied with electricity for a week." In a recent experiment at some Western university (I think it was Stanford), one human cell was converted into energy. The resulting flash of light was reported to have been many times brighter than the sun.

Yet we complain that we are too tired to do the supper dishes!

We ARE energy. The very atoms of which our physical bodies are made are but energy. All matter is a manifestation of that energy. The more we maintain a consciousness of this reality, the more we can rise triumphant over the bondage of matter. Fatigue, weakness, disease—these have no part of our true nature. Even in little ways, once we learn this truth, we can demonstrate its usefulness. Whenever I feel a cold coming on me, for example, unless it catches me unaware in sleep, I tell it firmly, "Begone!" and in five minutes I am quite rid of it. A brother disciple of mine, fifty-five years old and weighing only 145 lbs., easily performed jobs that a couple of the young monks, 225 lbs. each and ex–weight lifters, found difficult.

Energy is the connecting link between consciousness and matter, between mind and body. For energy is, in its turn, but a manifestation of consciousness. In the last analysis, all things are but manifestations of Spirit. When you will your arm to move, it is energy, not matter, upon which your will acts directly. The energy, in its turn, acts upon the muscles of the arm, tensing them and making them move. If you will your arm to move, but don't send any energy to it, it will remain motionless.

The *amount* of energy flow, as well as the simple fact of its flow, depends on the exertion of will. If you go to pick up what you think is an empty bucket, the energy you exert will not be enough to lift it if in fact it is full. In this case, you must exert more will, and send more energy; you will then be able to lift the bucket easily. To put it simply, *the greater the will, the greater the flow of energy.* There is, literally, *no limit* to the degree of will, and therefore to the measure of energy, that one can summon in any undertaking, simply because a strong will is not limited by the actual energy potential of the body; rightly applied, it draws directly on the energy of the universe. I say *rightly applied,* for to many people an exertion of will power suggests a grim, tense kind of determination, an exaggerated awareness of obstacles and difficulties that implies a "no" vote from the subconsciousness even while the conscious mind is affirming "yes." *Willingness,* then, might better suggest the kind of will power intended here. In this sense, the axiom is as true for man's relationship to the cosmic energy as to the energy of his own body: *The greater the will, the greater the flow of energy.* Remember it. Emblazon it in your mind. Repeat it to yourself several times a day. This single truth can revolutionize your life.

My guru pointed out, in his great book, *Autobiography of a Yogi,* that the principal "doorway" by which the energy of the cosmos enters the human body is through the medulla oblongata at the base of the brain. This, he says, is the seat of the life force in the body. He told me that this is also the seat of ego in the body (notice how often a proud person draws his head back, as if with exaggerated consciousness of this region), and the point from which the united sperm and ovum begin the process of self-division which results in the human body. The medulla oblongata is the only part of our bodies that cannot be operated upon. Were it even touched lightly with a feather, it would produce instantaneous death. This medulla is the doorway through which the body receives energy from the universe. The positive pole of this center is the *ajna chakra,* or Christ center, between the eyebrows. It is through this, the medulla's positive pole, that we *send* energy out into the universe. In both cases—in receiving as well as in sending—the axiom holds true: The greater the will, the greater the flow of energy. The positive, *will* center in the body is the Christ center. By strong concentration at that point, or by centering one's determination there and acting from that point, will power can be exerted to draw a limitless flow of energy through the medulla oblongata.

Athletes have found that if they exert themselves to what seems the limit of their endurance, they develop what is often spoken of as "second wind." It is so indeed, but only in the sense that breath is energy. (In Sanskrit, the word for breath and energy is the same: *prana.*) Those athletes, by their extra exertion of will, have succeeded in tapping the universal source of energy.

I had an interesting experience once, similar to theirs. I was working to build a geodesic dome. It was my first effort to build a home at Ananda Meditation Retreat (the first of three that failed to survive the strong autumn winds). The plans called for stapling plastic onto a large number of wooden triangles. My staple gun was stiff, so unusually so that another person working on the project, a girl, was unable to make it work even once, using both her hands. After about the 500th staple, I felt I simply could not press the release one more time. Then I thought, "But I *must* finish this job before the autumn winds come." (I little knew what those winds would do to the completed dome!) With an extra effort of will, I squeezed the release just one more time, then again, then yet once again. By about the sixth time it began to seem easier. By the tenth time, no extra effort was required at all. I went on stapling almost effortlessly for at least another 500 times. A little added exertion of will, and the energy of the infinite had begun to flow into my hand.

Consciously or unconsciously, all of us live at least partly by this energy. It is, my guru taught, the *direct* source of our energy. Food and oxygen, by contrast, must be converted into energy by the body; the energy they give us comes to us indirectly. Without the direct source of energy to act upon the food, we would not long survive. A car battery needs not only distilled water (which, in our bodies, is comparable to the food we eat), but also to be recharged occasionally. When the battery runs down, no amount of distilled water can reactivate it. Similarly, when a person dies, no amount of food can revive him. Man is a sort of wet cell battery. It is actually possible for him, as several Indian yogis and Western mystics have demonstrated, to live for years by this energy alone. A modern exemplar of this power was Therese Neumann, of Konnersreuth, Germany, about whom numerous books have been written. Submitted to repeated and prolonged medical observation over a period of more than fifty years, she was never discovered to eat a single morsel of food, nor to drink even a drop of liquid.

Many other seeming miracles are possible to yogis, once they have learned to control the flow of divine energy. The energy we send to the different parts of our bodies can also be projected beyond our own physical limitations, to heal others, or to alter circumstances as we choose. This same principle can be used to attract subtler kinds of energy to ourselves: inspirations, answers to our questions, divine blessings and love. These aspects of the subject will be discussed in the next lesson, on magnetism.

But to apply this principle on *every* level, the subtlest as well as the grossest, one more faculty is needed besides will power. This second ingredient is *awareness*. Until sufficient awareness of love, for example, has been developed, it will be simply impossible to direct the will correctly in such a way as to draw to oneself more love. Without some divine awareness, no divine work is truly possible; usually any attempt at such work only manifests itself as fanaticism. *With* such awareness, however, divine work of some kind, if only the steady flow in the heart of divine love and harmony, is inevitable. This, then, is a deeper meaning of the oft-quoted Biblical statement, "Faith without works is dead." St. James was referring to people who pity the naked and the hungry, but who offer them no practical help. Not to express one's pity in some sort of positive action indicates a lack of awareness. (For in fact it is we who suffer when others suffer; we *are* those sufferers.) But St. James's statement is true also on a subtler level. To believe in Christ, for instance, and yet feel nothing of his presence (the inner manifestations of his divine "works"), is an example of dead faith; it is not true Christianity. If one's belief is not accompanied by some sort of definite awareness, it is really nothing but superstition. Any activity based on such "faith" will be merely an imposition on the Infinite Kindness.

"The greater the will, the greater the flow of energy." The greater the will to love, the greater love's flow. The greater the will to joy, the greater the flow of joy. The law governing the expression of energy may be applied on all levels of spiritual truth. But on all levels, awareness also is necessary. To will to express love or joy while one feels no awareness of these qualities will scarcely tap their divine source within oneself, and may, according to one's actual awareness, draw only an added consciousness of hatred or misery. (Consider how often people are prone to make negative wishes, such as: "I wish I weren't so miserable!" Their desire is for joy, but in fact their affirmation, their real act of will, rests on an awareness of misery. It is their misery, not joy, that they are feeding.)

The principle that underlies the energization of the body, then, is vitally important on all stages of spiritual growth. Yet it is easiest to master it on the level of energization. The awareness one develops as a result of this mastery can then be applied on subtler levels. For all spiritual experiences are related to this flow of energy. While it may be difficult even to visualize divine joy, the simple flow of energy in the body is easy to experience. This experience can be made the foundation for increasingly subtle perceptions.

Yet energy itself may at first be a difficult word for beginning yogis to understand. What is energy? How does one feel it?

In higher states of awareness, it is possible simply to see the inner divine light and command it to charge one's body with energy. For the energy of the body is actually a manifestation of that light. In the beginning, however, it is necessary to focus on one of the *results* of that energy flow.

When you move your arm, it is because you have sent energy to the arm muscles, commanding them to become tensed. You are to some extent familiar already with this energy flow. You experience it, for instance, when you stretch your arms on waking in the morning. That "good feeling" in the muscles is the breakfast of energy you are giving them to prepare them for the day's activities.

Even when you cannot feel this flow, you can always feel the tension of your muscles, and can make this feeling the starting point for your developing awareness. By inward concentration on the tension of your muscles, you will gradually become conscious of the *source* of that tension in the flow of energy to those muscles. Muscular tension can thereby be utilized to stimulate the energy flow.

These truths have always been implicit in the yoga teachings, and proved useful long before they were formulated as definite principles, even as the force of gravity was useful to man long before its governing law was discovered. The discovery of the law of gravity, however, made possible the more exact application of this force. Similarly, once these truths relating to the energization of the body had been reduced to exact principles, it became possible for even beginners to benefit from them, and also for more advanced yogis to utilize them more easily, and more completely.

These principles were discovered by my great guru, Paramhansa Yogananda, in 1916. They constitute a priceless contribution to the ancient yoga science, not only because they enable yoga students to recharge their bodies with energy at will, thereby driving away fatigue and disease, but also because they give them an invaluable tool for developing divine awareness in its most subtle aspects.

The stimulation of awareness of the energy by means of physical tension requires a calm, *inward* awareness. Muscular tension is involved in running or in throwing a ball, but here the concentration is engaged in outward movement. It is necessary, for development of an inward awareness of energy as the true force behind muscular tension, that all corresponding physical movements be slow, harmonious, and deliberate. To use this principle for the energization and toning up of the entire body, a complete system of exercises is needed, that every body part receive due attention.

My guru invented such a system. I have practiced it virtually every day since I first learned it in 1948. I have found it truly wonderful. Some days, owing to the pressure of duties, I have omitted doing them in the morning. The rest of that day I have felt as if there were cobwebs in my muscles. And I have thought, "This is how most people must feel all the time. They accept their condition only because they know nothing better!"

I remember one time, many years ago. A group of us went camping in the mountains. I had been told that our destination, a small lake, was an easy twenty-minute stroll from the end of the road. Anticipating no problems, I took with me not only a sleeping bag and light clothing, but a harmonium for chanting, a gallon bottle of fruit juice, and a knapsack full of useful, if unnecessary, things, including a heavy book that I had been reading. Instead of a twenty-minute stroll, unfortunately, it turned out to be a six-mile climb, much of it on steep, gravelly terrain. My daily work was in an office. This climb, at 9,000 feet, was more than my body was prepared to enjoy. Back in the office the next Monday, it was an effort for me even to lift a pencil.

"I *must* think up some excuse," I thought, "to get out of practicing the energization exercises this evening." Being in charge of other people affords certain disadvantages. As the head of the monks, I was expected not only to join, but to lead them in their exercises. Others of them, too, had been with me on the hike. They, too, were sore, though perhaps none of them had been so foolish in burdening themselves as I had. I could think of no excuse that might justify my sitting on the sidelines while they exercised.

As long as I was going to suffer through those exercises, I decided, I might as well put my whole will into the act. This I did, bearing in mind more desperately than usual my guru's principle: "The greater the will, the greater the flow of energy."

Amazingly, after ten minutes of exercise I felt not a trace of pain in my muscles! Instead, my body actually felt better than it would have had I spent the entire weekend at home, resting. As I walked off to meditation, it seemed almost as if I were floating.

I have had numerous other occasions, though perhaps few as dramatic, to demonstrate to myself the value of these energization exercises. I simply cannot recommend them highly enough.

These exercises cannot be learned easily from written lessons, as they are numerous and seem, at least to the beginner, complex. If you want them in written form, you may get them by writing Ananda Sangha at 14618 Tyler-Foote Road, Nevada City, CA 95959 or go to www.ananda.org/energization. In my experience, the best way to learn them is in person from a qualified teacher. You can learn them by visiting *The Expanding Light,* Ananda's guest facility at Ananda Village in California, or else from an Ananda minister.

A happy compromise, if you live too far away to visit Ananda, would also be to learn the exercises from a video cassette tape. We have a tape of them that you can order from Ananda.

For now, and as a good introduction to this system of exercise, let me suggest that you practice tensing the muscles of your body all together, then separately—not hastily, but gradually increasing the tension until the muscles actually vibrate. Concentrate on the *inside* of the muscles—in the center, as it were, of any part you are tensing. Become keenly aware, first, of the sensation of tension. Then try to feel, behind that tension, the causative flow of energy. Repeat mentally as you practice: *"The greater the will, the greater the flow of energy. I will my energy to flow to every cell!"*

II. YOGA POSTURES

The energization exercises form a distinct and separate part of the science of yoga. Yet the principles underlying them can and should be incorporated into the practice of the yoga postures. As you practice the postures, especially those which stretch or tense the body, direct energy to the parts concerned.

Remember that the kind of will power which best energizes the body is an attitude of willingness. It would even help you to practice the postures with an inward smile. (I have too often seen yoga students press their lips together, clench their teeth, and glower as they force themselves grimly into a pose. Such an attitude actually *cuts off* the supply of energy to the body!)

Supta-Vajrasana

(The Supine Firm Pose — Alternate Position, also known as *Ustrasana*, The Camel Pose)

"With calm faith, I open to Thy Light."

Sit in *Vajrasana* (the Firm Pose), then come up on your knees so that you are kneeling straight, as if praying in the Western tradition. Bend backward at the waist until you can rest your hands on your heels. Drop the head back, and thrust the hips out forward so as to form an arch between the head and the knees.

Hold this position not more than 15 seconds to start with, gradually increasing it to a maximum of one minute.

Benefits: This position is excellent for the pelvis, and for toning the muscles in the stomach and the back.

As you come out of this position, sit back slowly in *Vajrasana* (the Firm Pose).

Ardha-Salabhasana

(The Half Locust Pose)

"I soar upward on wings of joy!"

Lie on your front with your arms down at your side. Inhale, and lift the left leg upward from the hip, keeping the leg more-or-less straight and the hip down on the floor. Feel the energy being drawn from the feet and the legs up into the base of the spine. Hold this position about 15 seconds to begin with, increasing it gradually with practice to 30 seconds, or not more than 1 minute. Repeat with the right leg.

Ardha-Matsyendrasana

(The Half Spinal Twist)

"I radiate love and goodwill to soul-friends everywhere."

Ardha-Matsyendrasana is one of only two postures that I know of that have been named after great yogis. Matsyendra lived in ancient times. His full spinal twist is almost impossible for the average person to perform, but the Half Spinal Twist is not difficult for most people.

We have bent the spine diagonally forward, straight forward, sidewise, and backward. This important posture twists the spine sideways—the one movement remaining to complete this series of spinal stretches.

1. Sit with your legs straight out before you. Draw your right foot toward you, *under* the left leg, and place the foot to the left of your body, touching the buttock.

2. Place your left foot *over* your right knee, to the right of it.

3. Twist your body slowly to the left. Place your left hand momentarily on the ground for balance, and bring your right arm to the *left* of your upraised knee. Then grasp your left foot with that hand. Confused?

4. Bring your left arm as far as it will go around the back of your body at the waistline. Keep the palm turned outward.

5. Turn your head to the left, but not so far as to strain your neck.

6. Sit as upright as you can.

If your muscles are tensed in this position, hold it for a few seconds only, increasing the time gradually to a maximum of one minute. But if you can relax in this pose, hold it as long as you feel comfortable doing so. After a leftward twist, relax momentarily in a normal sitting position (*Sukhasana*), then repeat the pose in the opposite direction. One twist in each direction will suffice.

Benefits: The Half Spinal Twist serves a spiritual, as well as a physical, purpose. Physically, of course, it adjusts the vertebrae and exercises the spine, making it more limber. This posture is good, also, for constipation, and for the sex organs. It beneficially stimulates all the trunk organs—the kidneys, liver, and spleen—and is good for a stiff or aching back.

Spiritually, if one can relax in this pose, he will feel that the energy is being forced up the spine into the dorsal region opposite the heart. This region, as everyone knows who has experienced a deep, sensitive love, is the center in the body from which feelings of love radiate. Yogis say that this dorsal center, or *anahat chakra,* needs to be stimulated, its rays of energy directed toward the brain. Divine love is thereby awakened in man.

Ardha-Matsyendrasana, by forcing the energy up the spine to this region, helps to stimulate the *anahat chakra* and awaken the feeling of love. The heart quality experienced in this twisted position, however, does not easily travel farther upward, toward the brain. Rather, its natural movement is outward. It may be felt to express itself as an outflow of compassion, rather than as devotion to God.

If you have even the desire for enlightenment, you have already progressed far on the evolutional path. Look back now, to all those creatures who are less fortunate than you in their understanding of life's purpose. Sitting comfortably in this posture, call them, by the magnetic power of your love, to join you in your search for lasting values. Repeat mentally: "*I radiate love and goodwill to soul-friends everywhere.*"

Akarshana Dhanurasana

(The Pulling-the-Bow Pose)

"With shafts of will I pierce the heart of worries."

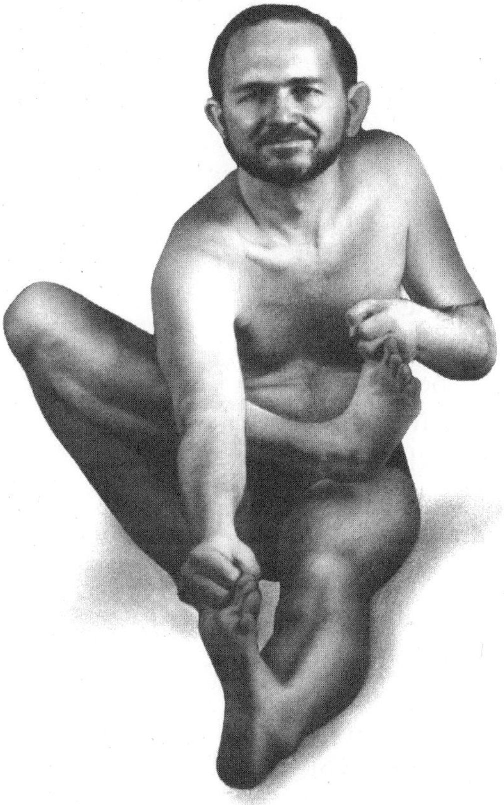

Sit with one leg outstretched before you. Draw the other foot to you, and grasp it by the big toe with the fingers of the *opposite* hand. Stoop forward, and with the other hand grasp the big toe of the leg that is straight; bring the foot as close to your head as is comfortable. Hold the pose 30 seconds or less, gradually increasing the time, if you wish, to several minutes, but not more than 6 minutes. Repeat with the opposite side. Affirm mentally, "*With shafts of will I pierce the heart of worries.*"

Benefits: Akarshana Dhanurasana relieves chronic constipation. It is good for rheumatism in the legs, knee joints, and arms. It tends to remove fat from the middle part of the body. It is good for the digestion, and above all it promotes vitality in the body.

Garudasana

(The Twisted Pose)

"At the center of life's storm I stand serene."

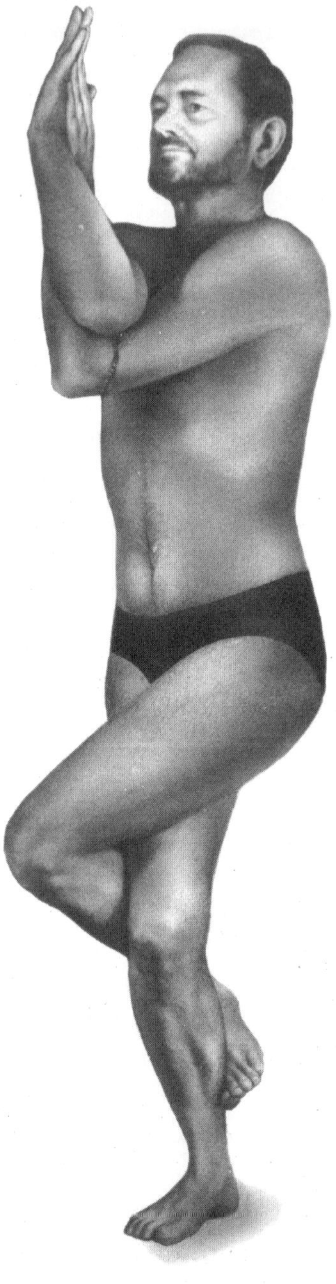

Stand on one foot, and bring the other leg in front and around it as far as it will go. Raise the same arm as the leg on which you are standing, and bring the other arm simultaneously below and around the first so that the elbows are interlocked, and the palms of the hands are together. Stand straight, and feel your consciousness centered in the spine. Feel that, though life twists you outwardly in countless directions, inwardly you remain at peace, centered in your higher Self. Affirm mentally, *"At the center of life's storms I stand serene."* Stand on that leg as long as you find it comfortable to do so, then repeat, standing on the opposite leg.

Benefits: This pose is good for energizing the arms and legs. Its special benefit is psychological and spiritual.

III. BREATHING

Prana is the Indian word for energy, as well as for breath. Breath is called *prana* partly because its inner cause in the body is the flow of energy in the *iḍa* and *pingala* nerve channels in the spine. But breath is also identified with energy because it is an important means by which we draw energy into our bodies. It is also a means by which we send our energy and vibrations to the world around us. When we speak, for example, we send vibrations not only with the voice, as we discussed in the last lesson, but also with our very breath.

Have you noticed how, in the presence of some people, you instinctively back away from them to avoid their breath, even though its odor may not be unpleasant? There are other people whose breath, quite apart from its odor, is pleasing, almost as if it had a soothing or regenerating effect on others. I knew of a saint in India who would heal people by breathing on his fingers, then flicking the fingers toward them as if flinging energy in their direction.

When out-of-doors in natural surroundings, breathe deeply, consciously inhaling the vibrations around you. When in spiritual places, do likewise. Feel that you are filling yourself with rejuvenating influences.

When speaking with others, send your vibrations to them with your voice and with your breath. Bless them as you speak. Bless your environment with every exhalation.

A breathing exercise that is good for strengthening the diaphragm is known as *Kapalabhati Pranayama*. Draw the diaphragm inward sharply, forcing the air out through the nostrils in quick thrusts. Let the inhalation take place automatically; all of your effort should be spent in the exhalation. Each respiration should take about one second to perform. Do this exercise 12 to 24 times to begin with—then more, as you become accustomed to it.

Kapalabhati Pranayama is an excellent exercise not only for the diaphragm, but also for raising the energy to the brain.

IV. ROUTINE

To the routine that you have been following these past two weeks, add this lesson's version of *Supta-Vajrasana* in place of the one that you learned in Step Seven. Do *Ardha-Salabhasana* (the Half Locust Pose) before the Full Bow Pose. Insert *Ardha-Matsyendrasana* (the Half Spinal Twist) at the end of the spinal exercises. Practice *Akarshana Dhanurasana* (the Pulling-the-Bow Pose) in place of, or prior to, *Janushirasana* (the Head-to-the-Knee Pose).

Do *Garudasana* (the Twisted Pose) instead of *Utkatasana* (the Chair Pose).

V. HEALING

Circulation and the Blood

We have already said that most of the postures should not be done by persons afflicted with abnormally high blood pressure. Assuming the heart and blood pressure to be normal, the yoga postures are excellent for the circulation. Their gentle stimulating effect is much more wholesome for the body than violent physical exercise. The slowly changing positions of the body, which alternately fill a particular part with blood, then drain it again, are scientifically devised to keep the blood flowing freely and uniformly throughout the body.

The inverted poses, for example, are excellent for varicose veins, as well as for bringing the blood to the brain.

For the heart, the alternate forward and backward bends of *Halasana* (the Plow Pose) and *Bhujangasana* (the Cobra Pose) are excellent. The standard *hatha yoga* practice of stimulating the heart in an exercise, then resting long enough for the heart to return to its normal beat, is a much better manner of stimulating heart action than prolonged violent activity, as in sports.

For a diseased heart, as well as for high blood pressure, the best posture is *Savasana* (the Corpse Pose).

VI. DIET

Simplicity in All Things

Buddha taught his disciples the Golden Rule of moderation in all things. This rule is important in matters of diet. Everyone knows that it is well not to eat too much of rich foods. Not so many people know that it is unwise to combine too many different kinds of foods. Vegetables should not normally be eaten with fruits. Yogis do not emphasize the process of right food combinations nearly so elaborately as dietary specialists have done in the West, but their emphasis on a simple fare accomplishes much the same results. A simple but effective rule is to eat only one basic kind of food at one time—whether carbohydrate, protein, or fruits. Yogis emphasize foods that are high in energy value, that one may eat less, quantitatively.

You may be interested in learning how I was able to live in the late 1960s, spending only $10 a month for food. Meat, a major item in most people's food budget, was no problem for me; I had not eaten it for more than thirty years. Bread is another costly item; I made *chappati*s very inexpensively, instead. Frying them in vegetable oil, I felt no need to spread them with butter (another expensive item). I omitted eggs from my diet; these too are costly. Milk I prepared from powdered milk at one-third the cost of fresh milk; this preparation required a certain re-education of my palate, but once I had told it to like powdered milk, it obeyed me cheerfully enough. Meat, butter, bread, eggs, fresh milk—omitting these from the diet, one can live inexpensively, indeed.

I also made it a point to eat raw foods as much as possible. When food is cooked, much of its vitality is destroyed. Vegetables are commonly cooked so long that one would do better to drink the water in which they have been boiled, and throw the corpses away.

I sprouted seeds to put in my salads. I ate sunflower seeds and other highly concentrated foods. Ten dollars was quite enough to keep me going with no sense of self-deprivation. I could even afford the luxury, on that budget, of a few desserts.

A good source of protein, and most inexpensive, too, is the split pea daal, the recipe for which was included in Step Five.

Another good, and inexpensive, source of protein may be found in uncooked garbanzo beans. They should be soaked overnight in water, then popped out of their skins and eaten raw.

Here are a few low-budget recipes:

Breakfast Cereal

Soak ¾ cup whole grain wheat 24 hours in 1½ cups water. Drain, rinse, and cook in 4 cups water, adding more if necessary, for 1½ hours, or until most of the grains have popped open. Drain and serve hot, with honey and butter. Yields about 2 cups.

Corn Tamale Casserole

1 cup vegetable burger, prepared according to directions on package for a few minutes, stirring frequently
1 cup corn (canned or frozen is all right)
1 cup tomatoes (canned is all right)
⅓ cup vegetable oil
1 small can chopped olives
1 grated bell pepper
tamari to taste
minced onion (optional)
1 small clove garlic, minced (optional)
¼ cup milk
¾ cup corn meal
1 egg

Mix all ingredients except egg, milk, and corn meal. Cook over low heat for 15 minutes, stirring frequently, then beat egg and milk together and add to mixture. Mix corn meal with a little water, just until it begins to hold together. Stir into mixture; season to taste. Bake in buttered casserole ½ hour at 400°.

Barley Roast

Soak 1¼ cups barley overnight. Bring barley to a boil in plenty of fresh, cold water and cook slowly ½ hour. Strain, and rinse with cold water. Sauté 1 cup finely chopped onion in oil. Add chopped parsley, paprika, tomato, a pinch of salt, and 2 bay leaves. Bake one hour at 375°. Serve with mushroom sauce.

Khicharhi

Fry in butter or olive oil the following ingredients, simmering for a few minutes over low heat, stirring frequently:

½ teaspoon coriander
2 bay leaves
¼ teaspoon turmeric
½ teaspoon curry powder
¼ teaspoon ginger
¼ teaspoon dry mustard
½ teaspoon anise seed
¼ teaspoon salt
½ teaspoon thyme
¼ teaspoon cinnamon

Add to this combination any 3 cooked vegetables such as carrots, potatoes, cabbage, garbanzos, etc., approximately 3 cups. Tomato paste may be added, if desired.

VII. MEDITATION

Concentration

I said in the first part of this lesson that will power, to be effective, must be combined with awareness. If a person tried with great determination, but with little awareness, to jam a thread through the eye of a needle, he would only blunt the thread; he wouldn't get it through the eye. Many acts of will are performed with similar insensitivity. Some people, determined to win their discussions at any cost, end up striking their opponents and losing any chance they might have had of really winning their point. Nations frequently have gone to war, when their disagreements might have been effectively arbitrated. Labor unions, to gain temporary selfish advantages, have paralyzed their country's economy, ultimately hurting also themselves; and industries, competing ruthlessly with one another, have made enemies that later became their undoing.

In the last lesson I mentioned how at one time I used to smoke. I well remember how the habit started. I was at a party, and a friend of mine "generously" showed me how to inhale cigarette smoke. The first puff made me dizzy and sick. "I'll lick this weakness," I decided, "if it's the last thing I do!" Had I been more aware, I would have realized that my real weakness lay, not in my body's revulsion at something so unnatural to it, but in my concern for the good opinion of my peers.

Awareness. What is it? How is one to develop it? For lack of it, how often our very virtues pave the way to our ruin. A satisfactory definition might, conceivably, be found, and might delight the hearts of a few pedants, but it would hardly serve any useful purpose. For we all know what it is to be aware. It takes awareness, for one thing, to delight in pedantic definitions. But two important points may be made. First, we are more or less aware according to how much energy passes through our brains. And second, we are more or less aware according to whether our concentration is focused or diffused.

A dull person, even if focusing all his mental energies on one subject, will be less aware than a bright person simply because his level of energy is lower to begin with. But even a normally vital and aware human being may sometimes be comparatively dull—if, for example, his thoughts have been scattered by excessive worry or preoccupation.

To increase the energy flow to the brain is the chief purpose of yoga practice. For this purpose, many teachings are given, including right diet, postures, and breathing exercises. In the next lesson another aspect of this important subject will be explored, in a discussion of magnetism. But chiefly it must be said that both of the factors determining one's degree of awareness—the amount of energy flow to the brain, and the direction of that energy once it reaches the brain—depend upon one thing only: one's power of concentration. It is as necessary to concentrate one's available energy in the brain as it is to concentrate that energy, once it reaches the brain, on a single object, or state, of awareness.

Concentration is necessary also to the exercise of will power. The will may be described as a single-pointed intention of the intellect, reinforced by energy. The will, the intellect, and the power of concentration all have their center in the *ajna chakra,* or Christ center, at the point between the eyebrows. They are, therefore, interrelated. Concentration applied to the question of what *is,* becomes intellect. Concentration applied to the question of what ought to be (as determined by the intellect), becomes will power. Intellect by itself is a more or less static faculty; generally it reflects one's feelings, and must therefore, on the spiritual path, be purified by devotion. When the will, instead of being focused on doing or accomplishing anything, is united inwardly to the purified intellect in a simple act of *becoming,* divine enlightenment ensues. That is why the *Bhagavad Gita* says that during meditation one should forsake all mental planning. So long as the will is engaged in thoughts of doing, even when the doing seems to be related to self-improvement, the mind will be directed outward from its true center. For we *are already* the Divine Truth itself. We have only to realize our true selves. The very act of *becoming,* spiritually speaking, implies only a complete recognition of, and identification with, realities which the intellect alone might hold impersonally at a distance. But in fact, where the will and the intellect are directed inward toward the soul by the power of deep concentration, their functions are no longer really separable from each other.

On every level of mental activity, *it is concentration that is the key to success.*

The student taking an exam, but plagued with a popular song running through his head; the businessman trying to write an important contract, but worried over an argument that he had that morning with his wife; the judge, distracted by the fact that a teenager to whose defense he is trying to listen bears a striking resemblance to his own son: All of these persons could tell us something of the disadvantages of poor concentration. But I don't suppose anyone really needs to be told that lack of concentration means inefficiency. What is *not* generally known is that a concentrated mind succeeds not only because it can solve problems with greater dispatch, but also because problems have a way of somehow vanishing before its focused energies, without even requiring to be solved. A concentrated mind often attracts opportunities for success that, to less focused (and therefore less successful) individuals, appear to come by sheer luck. A person whose mind is concentrated receives inspirations in his work and in his thinking that, to duller minds, may often seem the proof of special divine favor. Yet such seeming "favors" are due simply to the power of concentration. Concentration it is that awakens our powers and channels them, dissolving obstacles in our path, literally attracting opportunities, insights, and inspirations. In many ways, subtle as well as obvious, concentration is the single most important key to success.

This is particularly true in yoga practice. The mind, in meditation especially, must be so perfectly still that not a ripple of thought enters it. God, the Subtlest Reality, cannot be perceived except in utter silence. Much of the teaching of yoga, therefore, centers on techniques designed specially for developing concentration.

Of these techniques, my guru considered the most effective to be one which involves attentiveness to the natural process of breathing. It is a technique which is well known in India, and is becoming well known also among yoga students in the West, owing to the increasing number of writings on the subject by Indian teachers. This technique has been a favorite among Buddhists since the beginning of their era. It is mentioned in several ancient *Upanishads.* (These authoritative Indian scriptures present the essence of the most ancient scriptures of all, the *Vedas:* The more recent *Bhagavad Gita* presents, in its turn, the essence of the *Upanishads.*) The simplicity of this technique causes many a beginner to ignore it. Yet in its very simplicity lies much of its greatness.

Before discussing the technique itself, let us ask ourselves, What *is* concentration? Concentration implies, first, an ability to release one's mental and emotional energies from all other interests and involvements, and second, an ability to focus them on a single object or state of awareness. Concentration may assume various manifestations, from a dynamic outpouring of energy to perfectly quiescent perceptions. In its higher stages, concentration becomes so deep that there is no longer any question of its remaining merely a practice: The yogi becomes so completely identified with the object of his concentration that he and it, as well as the act of concentration itself, become one. In this way he can even, temporarily, become one with something external to himself, gaining thereby a far deeper understanding of it than would be possible by aloof scientific objectivity, that pride of Western heritage which has the disadvantage of setting man apart from nature, not in harmony with it. But in concentration on our own higher realities, identification with them becomes lasting. For in this case there is no other, more personal, reality to come back to. We *are* those realities. We *are* the infinite light, and love, and joy, and wisdom of God. Even now, our concentration should be developed with these higher directions in mind. And even now, our concentration should be so deep that the consciousness of diligent practice is refined into an effortless process of divine *becoming*.

Obviously, then, the most effective technique of concentration will be one which both interiorizes the mind, and permits a gradual transition from technical practice to utter stillness. The technique of watching the breath fulfills both of these requirements—better, perhaps, than any other technique possibly could. For not only is the breath one of the most natural focal points for the attention, but, as we shall see, the more deeply one concentrates on it, the more refined it becomes, until breathing is automatically and effortlessly suspended in breathlessness: Meditator, the act of concentration, and the object of concentration become one. In the state of breathlessness, moreover, the senses themselves become automatically stilled, permitting an undisturbed continuation of the concentrated state. Once the mind is so perfectly focused, its concentrated power may be applied to any object one wishes. But because attentiveness to the breath involves the will in an act, not of doing, but of inward *becoming* (by concentration on the breath one acquires the consciousness of being air, or infinite space), the natural direction of the mind in this technique is toward superconsciousness. (If the will is not involved at all, the mind tends to slip downward into subconsciousness.)

Why is the breath a natural focal point for the attention? Because it is the most universal *obstacle* to deep attention. Notice how, when you want to concentrate deeply on something, you automatically restrain your breathing. A person holding a camera, and wishing to take a photograph with a slow exposure, must also hold his breath so as to minimize the movement of his arms. Instinctively we all understand, similarly, that the restless breath is an obstacle to holding the mind steady.

A devotee once complained to his guru that he was having difficulty concentrating in meditation. His distraction was a factory whistle that kept sounding near his home. "Since the whistle disturbs you," said his guru, "why not concentrate on the whistle itself?" The disciple found that by doing so his concentration became one-pointed; he became, in a sense, one with the whistle, accepting it now, since it no longer seemed a disturbance. Thus he was able to pass easily from concentration on something outside himself to inward meditation on God.

A restless mind may be distracted by many things. In this condition, it may be necessary for one to command its attention forcefully—by yoga postures, perhaps, and loud chanting. But once the mind begins to grow still, the greatest obstacle to its becoming more so is the breath. By concentration on the breath, mental fixity is attained. Concentration on the breath, unlike other forms of concentration, leads naturally to meditation, which my guru defined as the direction of one's focused attention on God, or on one of His attributes. Concentration on the factory whistle may bring about acceptance of the whistle, but such acceptance is not in itself an inducement to meditation. The whistle remains a whistle. By concentration on the breath, on the other hand, the breath actually diminishes; its gradual refinement leads naturally to an interiorized, meditative state.

The ocean tides that heave with the movements of the moon; the ceaseless cycles of day and night; the seasons; the birth and death of nations and of whole civilizations; the creation of stars and planets, and their final dissolution; the burst of power that brought the universe into manifestation, and the ultimate dissolution of all things into the infinite silence: All reveal a universal rhythm of nature, the ebb and flow of duality without which the creative process could not go on; without which all things would cease immediately to exist, leaving only that Final Reality: *Satchidanandam,* the eternal, changeless bliss of Spirit.

Spirit, in order to create, divided its one consciousness in two through the law of vibration. By movement in opposite directions from a state of rest, it took on an outward *appearance.* At the still center of all things rests the unmoving Spirit. All things created must, to maintain their appearance of separate reality, remain in a state of movement. A bar of iron, though outwardly inert, is composed of electrons shooting about in a microcosm so small that only the most sensitive microscope can detect it. The universe *is* vibration. As that ancient Greek, Heraclitus, put it, "*Panta rhe*": "All is flux."

The manifested universe itself might be called the respiration of Spirit: the appearance and disappearance of all things, His inhalation and exhalation. Because we think of inhalation as a *taking in* of breath, we might associate God's "inhalation" with the drawing of all things back into Himself. On a human level, however, inhalation tends instead to externalize our consciousness. By taking in the air of the world around us we acknowledge its reality, and our identity with it. A newborn baby's first inhalation marks his entry onto the world's stage. In the universal rhythms of nature, too, those associated with inhalation are those which affirm outwardness: day, as opposed to night; spring, as opposed to autumn; the rise of nations, as opposed to their decline. Exhalation is associated with withdrawal; it is, in fact, the final movement associated with death. On the stage of daily life, as well, inhalation is associated with an affirmation of outward realities; exhalation, with denial of them. When we greet life joyously, we inhale deeply. We announce regret with a sigh. As a matter of interest, yogis say that, with inhalation, energy moves upward in the spine; with exhalation, downward. Upward movement in the spine accompanies any mood of life-affirmation; downward movement, any mood of depression, of life-rejection.

To affirm life outwardly is to emphasize Spirit *manifested:* ego, not the changeless soul within. In the constant flow and ebb of nature there is repeated endlessly, in infinite variations, the underlying truth: "I, the manifested self, am He, the Unmanifested." Every "inhalation" of nature, every renewed affirmation of objective reality, becomes offered up with "exhalation" into the Spirit, the final essence of all things. The human breath, too, flows in this continuous *mantra*. In Sanskrit the words of this *mantra,* universal to all creatures, are *Aham saha,* or, reduced to mantric words of power, *Hong-Sau:* "I am He." Yogis say that on a subtle level this is the very sound made by the breath: *Hong* with inhalation; *Sau* with exhalation. To repeat *Hong-Sau* mentally, particularly in conjunction with the breath, is to affirm again and again the truth that the little human ego is one with Brahma, the infinite Spirit: "*Hong Sau!* I am He! I am He!"

Repeat this *mantra,* while watching the breath. Don't try to control it. Let it flow naturally, of its own accord. Follow it all the way in with the *mental* chant, *Hong;* then all the way out with the mental chant, *Sau.*

Perfection in this technique means to pass from breathing to breathlessness. Only in breathlessness can God be fully realized. Elsewhere in these lessons I have pointed out that the breath responds instantly to different mental and emotional states. Even the *way* in which it flows in the nostrils indicates one's state of consciousness. The reverse also is true: As the breath flows, so flows the mind. Heavy breathing can make the mind restless. Calm breathing calms the mind. By concentration on the breath, too, the mind becomes calmer. This greater calmness is reflected in increasingly gentle breathing, which in turn induces still deeper concentration and calmness, a process that continues until mind and breathing both achieve perfect stillness.

There are several explanations for how it is possible to remain breathless for long periods of time without in any way damaging the body or the brain. (Indeed, the rejuvenating effects on the entire being of *superconscious* breathlessness are truly wonderful.) The fact is, once the yogi attains breathlessness in *samadhi,* the body is kept alive by the direct flow of energy from the medulla oblongata. It is possible in this state to remain breathless for days, months, even for years. The body appears lifeless, outwardly, but inwardly one is filled with the consciousness of infinite life.

In 1961 the director of the Zoological Institute in Darjeeling, India, told me of a scientific expedition he had once made in the Himalayas. He and his companions came upon a yogi seated on the ground, well above the snow line, in a state of *samadhi.* The yogi must have been sitting there motionless for at least six months, for his fingernails, very long by this time, had grown into the bark of a tree beside him in such a way that the slightest movement on his part would have snapped them off.

Periods of breathlessness may come to you, while practicing *Hong-Sau,* long before you enter superconsciousness. Don't be alarmed; they can't possibly hurt you, as long as you let the breath flow *naturally,* and don't try to hold it in or out of the lungs by force. When your body needs to breathe again, it will do so. By increasingly deeper calmness, however, you will find that you need less and less fresh air to sustain your body.

The breathing process, as well as the heartbeat, is regulated by the medulla oblongata. The positive pole of the medulla is the *ajna chakra,* or Christ center, located between the eyebrows. Stimulation of the medulla by deep concentration at that center can induce complete suspension of the breath and heartbeat by placing one in perfect harmony with the cosmic energy, and drawing this energy into the body in such abundance that impurities in the body are instantly neutralized.

As you chant *Hong* mentally with the incoming breath, feel that you are affirming not so much the little ego—the John Smith or Mary Green who is unique among human beings—but rather the Universal Man of which *you* are one expression.

As you chant *Sau* mentally with the outgoing breath, feel that you are offering this self into the infinite Self or Spirit.

Imagine your awareness expanding toward Infinity.

Then as you chant *Hong* again, visualize the little self becoming infused with the consciousness of *Sau,* the Spirit, which you have just affirmed. Indeed, some yogis take this concept as their *mantra, So-Hum* (*Hong-Sau* reversed becomes *So-Hum*), practicing it instead of the one I have given, *Hong-Sau.* But Paramhansa Yogananda explained that one can legitimately reverse the *Hong-Sau mantra* to *So-Hum* only after Self-realization has been attained.

When concentrating on the breath, keep your mind focused not so much on the mechanism of breathing (the movement of the navel, lungs, etc.) as on the breath itself. In this way, your mental identification will become at last with air, with space, not with a merely negative cessation of physical movement. But if at first you find that the physical mechanism of breathing intrudes itself too much on your attention, begin by mentally watching the breathing *process:* the movement of lungs, navel, and diaphragm; gradually only, as you grow calmer, shift your attention to the breath itself. At this point, feel it as it enters the nostrils. And even here you may find it natural to go through a transition from physical to more subtle awareness. That is, as the breath becomes finer, feel it gradually higher and higher in the nasal passage.

In the *Bhagavad Gita,* Lord Krishna gives the counsel to concentrate on *"nasikagram,"* "the beginning of the nose." Commentators often interpret this passage to mean "the tip of the nose," since *agra* means "front" as well as "beginning." But no subtle *chakra,* or nerve plexus, exists in the tip of the nose, waiting patiently to be awakened by yogic concentration. It is at the other end of the nose that yogis concentrate. Here is the seat of spiritual vision. Normally, to make it easier to locate, this seat is spoken of as being located at the point between the eyebrows. But where the breath is considered as part of the concentrative process, it is more appropriate to think of this seat as being located at the origin of the nose. In fact, the real Christ center is situated in the frontal lobe of the brain. The breath, as it enters and leaves the nasal passage, passes very close to this point. To visualize the breath passing this point helps to stimulate the Christ center.

As you watch the breath in the nose, then, feel it becoming gradually calmer until you can feel it at the origin of the nose. Relate that feeling to the Christ center. In this way you will find that yoga's two principal techniques for developing concentration—attentiveness to the breath, and stimulation of the Christ center—become one.

Watch the breath as an impartial observer. Don't care whether it flows or remains stationary. Simply remain attentive to whatever it does naturally. *As your practice deepens,* however, particularly *enjoy* the pauses when the breath is not flowing; use them to become more fully identified with the thought: "I am He! I am infinite space!"

Paramhansa Yogananda said that if one wants to be a master in this life, he should practice *Hong-Sau* two hours daily. The great guru himself, as a boy, used to practice it as much as seven and a half hours at a stretch. Really, though in the beginning fifteen to thirty minutes may be enough, there is no limit to how long you may practice this technique.

Never end your meditation with techniques. These are like finger exercises on the piano, which enable one to play fluently but are no substitute for actual playing. Once your mind has become focused and quiet through the practice of *Hong-Sau,* offer yourself calmly up to God. *Hong-Sau* leads naturally to that kind of concentration in which the will, no longer engaged busily in outward planning, is united to the intellect, and uplifted in a single, pure act of becoming. Concentration directed in this way becomes ecstasy. And the twofold meaning of *Hong* and *Sau* combines ultimately in the single—because omnipresent—vibration, AUM.

In the next lesson a more detailed outline of the *Hong-Sau mantra* and technique will be given.

AUM, *Shanti, Shanti, Shanti*

Step Ten

Energy & Energization

I. PHILOSOPHY

Magnetism

You have no doubt met people in your life whose very presence emanated an indefinable power. Perhaps you persuaded yourself that their strange-seeming influence was due to something perfectly ordinary: physical stature, or good looks, or worldly reputation. To speak of a person's aura would strike most people, steeped as they are in the dogmas of a materialistic age, as merely superstitious.

What then of the reactions of animals to human beings? How instantly your own dog may sense the kindness of some people, the animosity of others. There are some people to whom animals flock like filings to a magnet. Other people can hardly get an animal to come near them. It may reasonably be said that animals are not influenced nearly so much by the outward manifestations of human consciousness as by a kind of telepathy. Years ago I was told of one man, slight of stature and not particularly strong, whose very presence made even lions and tigers cower in fear. At the other end of the spectrum, countless tales have been told of saints who, by the sheer purity of their love, befriended wild beasts, and converted hardened criminals to a spiritual life.

I remember once sitting with a group of other monks in the presence of my guru. The conversation was of purely mundane matters, as of course it must be sometimes even in the presence of a master. He was giving instructions regarding some holes that had to be dug (or filled; I forget which) the following day. Since I wasn't directly involved, I sat behind a few of the others and meditated. The conversation itself was an entirely neutral influence. Nor could I have been influenced by anything in Master's gestures or facial expressions: My eyes were closed. Yet suddenly I felt as if my forehead was opening; my consciousness soared out into a freedom it had never tasted before. The uniqueness of this experience lay in the unsupportive circumstances in which it occurred. On other occasions too, though not often so unexpectedly, I and my fellow disciples experienced our guru's uplifting influence. One had only to sit in his presence for a few minutes to feel the weight of problems and worries lift mysteriously, to be replaced by a deep peace. Whenever I meditated with him, I felt as if a strong magnet were drawing my consciousness to the Christ center between the eyebrows. Sometimes he would merely look at me, and a strange power entered my heart, thrilling it with divine love.

It would help you to be aware that your own power, too, is not limited to your command of words or to your outward appearance—that you affect others (more, perhaps, than either you or they realize) by a much subtler quality. I remember a brother disciple of mine who was going through a test, and not taking it very well. He would sometimes come into my room and sit on the edge of my bed for a few minutes, his back bowed in misery. After he left, a cloud of gloom always remained behind him. I could only dispel it by a determined attitude of cheerfulness, and by *japa* (continuous mental chanting).

Reducing these various influences to their simplest possible terms, we may say that some people attract us, while others repel; that some people's power to attract or repel is greater than that of others; and that this power is conveyed not only through the senses, but perhaps even more so by some subtler medium.

In objective nature, the closest observable phenomenon to this may be found in the principle of magnetism. For a long time it was not known why the poles of two bar magnets attract or repel each other. Then it was discovered, as every high school student now knows, that a magnet emits subtle lines of force that can be actually traced by iron filings on a piece of paper. By means of these emanations, the north pole of one magnet will attract the south pole, but repel the north pole, of another. Two south poles also, placed together, will repel each other.

The principle of magnetism affords us more than an analogy. It was long thought that only metals could respond to magnetic influences. Then, in a series of experiments conducted at Northwestern University, in Illinois, it was found that snails are influenced in their movements by the earth's magnetic polarity. The experimenters found also that snails can be made to change their normal patterns of movement if bar magnets of similar magnetic strength to the pull on a compass are buried in the ground, and pointed away from the North Pole. More recently, other experiments have shown that mollusks open and close in rhythm with the movements of the moon, that people's moods may be affected (magnetically, it would seem) by the phases of the moon, and that animal organisms have their own magnetic field very similar to that which has long been known in metaphysical circles as the *aura*. Magnetism, like the power of gravity, is a definite force, and, though not perceived by the senses, can definitely be cognized. The way it operates in the material world is very similar to the way it operates on subtler, spiritual levels, for matter is but a lower manifestation of spiritual realities.

To understand how a living organism may have a magnetic field of its own, we have only to consider the fact that a magnetic field is created every time a current is passed through an electric wire. The nervous system, too, transmits scientifically measurable electrical impulses; in so doing it sets up its own magnetic field. As a matter of fact, electricity is a relatively negligible aspect of this energy-flow, an almost physical effect (gross enough for physical instruments to detect) of energies far subtler, and far stronger. "Electricity," my guru said, "is the animal current in the energy world." The subtler the manifestation of reality, the greater its potential for power on even the grossest material level. Consider, for example, the enormous power that is achieved when atomic energy is released. The more clearly the energy-flow in the nervous system can be perceived, or realized, on its actual, subtle level, the greater one's power to control his life and the physical world around him. Even more important, such realization enables one to control his own spiritual destiny.

The essential feature of magnetism is its power of attraction and repulsion. The material manifestation of this force, in the behavior of magnetized pieces of metal, is only the most outwardly observable effect of a power that is essentially divine—like the janitor in an office, whose function is limited to the simple act of cleaning, and who even in this function acts only on behalf of the office head. Divine love, too, is a kind of magnetism. So also, on grosser levels, are human love, and happiness, and hatred, and fear—in fact, every state of consciousness in active manifestation. For energy, as a vehicle for different kinds of awareness, assumes innumerable aspects, and thereby generates innumerable kinds of magnetism. Love attracts love. Fear excites more fear. If one's energy-flow is directed toward a particular person, and if there exists on any level in that person a similar state of awareness (and therefore of magnetism), one can attract or repel him depending on whether the interchange is sympathetic or antipathetic. Thus, while hatred is negative and might therefore seem to exert only a repelling force, if it is reciprocated in the other person the magnetism between them becomes attractive.

Love, on the other hand, although apparently purely attractive in its influence, if in no way reciprocated can become a repulsive force, causing mutual separation.

In any sympathetic interchange between human beings, a positive-negative interaction may be observed similar to the north-south attraction between two magnets. The most obvious example of this action lies in the attraction of male and female of any species for each other. To speak of the female as the negative pole need in no way imply passivity. Rather, in any sympathetic relationship it is the function of this negative "magnet" to draw *from,* and of the positive magnet to be drawn *toward.* In this way the yoga teachings speak of woman, in relationship to man, as being his *shakti,* or divine energy, for it is her magnetism above all that draws man's energy on every level into outward, creative manifestation. (Therefore it has often been said that no man becomes great in the eyes of the world without the aid of woman. Therefore also the shunning of female companionship by monks whose sole aim it is to direct all their energy and attention toward the divine Self within. Women, too, may shun the company of men if their aim is to draw power only from the highest source, God. Yet it should be added that once the soul is perceived, distinctions of male and female disappear. Put in other terms, it may be said that we are all female before God; it is the soul's function, by divine devotion, to draw grace from the Lord, and thereby to become like Him.)

A magnet does not interact with unmagnetized iron in the same way that it does with iron that has been magnetized; yet it does act *upon* it, drawing it to itself. In the same way human magnetism draws to itself even objects that, in themselves, have no magnetic power, except as man attributes such power to them. A person may feel himself irresistibly drawn to buy a house that he has seen, but of course the magnetic attraction is not in the house itself, but in his own mind. Yet his desire for it may succeed not only in drawing him to the house (which would be the obvious and expected outcome of his energy output), but also in drawing the *house* to *him.* For example, if his desire for it is very strong, the owner may suddenly decide to sell, or an unexpected turn in business may give him the money he needs for it, or any one of a number of things may happen to bring coveted opportunity to his doorstep.

During my sophomore year in college, I developed a theory that luck is more a question of attitude than of blind destiny. "If you want to be lucky," I told my friends, "*expect* to be lucky. Then make your expectation dynamic by going out and meeting luck halfway; don't wait passively for it to come to you." Amazing things started happening to me as soon as I myself began living by this principle. The only chapter, out of many, that I studied for a Greek exam turned out to be the one we were asked to translate. I entered an essay contest for a $100 prize, not because I knew the subject (I didn't), but because I needed the money. The subject was, "The Basic Principles Underlying the Government of the United States"; it must have sounded as formidable to others as it did to me, for ("luckily"!) the history, law, and political science majors among my fellow students kept out of the fray, and I was the only contestant. I also won a $15 first prize in a poetry contest, but that was more in my line. Then with $115 in my pocket, I set off to spend my summer vacation in Mexico. Hitchhiking, I started from Boston. The next day I was offered a ride from Philadelphia all the way to Mexico City—3,000 miles! My benefactor was going to Mexico on behalf of his company, and was kind enough to put me on his expense account as a second driver. And so it went, consistently. Among my relatives, my so-called luck became legendary.

But then my attitude changed. I had gone to Mexico thinking maybe in travel to find the understanding and inspiration in life that I longed for, and that I later did find in yoga. But travel turned out to be, as Emerson called it, "a fool's paradise." Inspiration abandoned me, and with it my luck. For a time, things went poorly. Only the gradual return of positive spirits brought a return of my "luck."

One often hears the expression, "beginner's luck." While I was in Mexico that summer, a family I met told me of an outing they had made to the race tracks. The father went regularly; for the others, it was their first time. To the father's amusement, his wife and daughter bet simply because they liked a horse's color, or its name. "That old nag hasn't won a race in years!" protested the father, as he bet with more seasoned wisdom. Yet he lost, while his wife and daughter won consistently. Surely it was because, in their utter ignorance of the odds against them, they bet with so much cheerful expectation that they actually *attracted* success. Beginners on the spiritual path, too, attract more inner experiences, and advance more rapidly, than many a more seasoned seeker. The reason can only be that they haven't yet any idea how very difficult the path is. If one could only keep the buoyant faith that he felt at the start of the spiritual journey through the plodding "middle ground"—that period of hard, often agonizing work that intervenes between the inspiration born of one's first enthusiasm and that born of dawning divine perception—one might find God very quickly.

Whatever one holds strongly in his mind, that he attracts to himself. This is as true for circumstances and events as it is for things. It is even true for inspirations. "Thoughts," my guru said, "are universally and not individually rooted."

(*Autobiography of a Yogi,* p. 154 in Crystal Clarity Publishers' reprint of the 1946 first edition) If, instead of waiting passively for the muses to smile, one will strike out bravely in the direction of thought that he wants to take, he will find inspiration coming to him from he knows not where, literally drawn to him by the magnetic power of his faith.

It is important to understand that human magnetism of all kinds is never the outcome of mere wishful thinking. Two people may think positively in an undertaking, yet one will attract success, and the other, failure. There are weak magnets, and strong ones. Any current passed through an electric wire will generate a magnetic field, but it takes a strong current to generate a strong magnetic field.

In the last lesson you learned the law of energization: "The greater the will, the greater the flow of energy." To this law may now be appended another: *"The greater the flow of energy, the greater the magnetic field."*

The principles of energization, therefore, apply also to the development of magnetism. When you send out a strong thought, a ray of energy goes out from you toward the object of that thought. This energy-ray creates its own magnetic field—strong or weak according to the relative strength of your will. If your will, and its resultant flow of energy, are powerful, there is nothing that you cannot draw to yourself. You will be able to perform feats that to others will appear miraculous.

But once you understand this principle of magnetism, it is important for you to realize that it can also be *mis*used. Be careful what it is that you want, for wrong desires, even fears, can put this subtle law into operation just as surely. The devotee would do well always to try to unite his will, not only to cosmic energy, but to the divine will. In seeking grace, he should also seek guidance. For one draws divine perception, too, by the magnetic power of his will. The will, when offered confidently to God, becomes faith. If your faith is kept pure and free of any self-interest, you will know when the will is misguided by the inharmony that suddenly develops between your will and its sense of steady development into divine faith.

We influence others by our magnetism, and are in turn influenced by them. It is possible by negative thoughts to harm them, and similarly, in turn, to be harmed by them. To think negatively about another person, especially if one does so with magnetic power, constitutes a grave misuse of the law, and invariably results in far greater harm to oneself as the instrument of such inharmony. (Similarly, to bless others attracts to oneself the greatest blessings.) Nothing would be gained from teaching students how to harm others by magnetic power. Yet much good may come from knowing how to protect oneself against possible harmful influences from others, and this knowledge demands some understanding, at least, of how magnetism can be operated for evil.

Remember, there must be an openness to magnetism of any kind before one can receive it. For this reason, black magicians in various primitive cultures try to instill fear in their victims, or try in other ways to find a vibrational opening for their harmful energies. It is important, then, to know how to close oneself against the wrong kinds of magnetism.

Magnetic self-protection may be accomplished by refusing, on the one hand, to respond on a negative level (for example, with fear, anger, or hatred), and by surrounding oneself, on the other hand, with strong positive magnetism. It may help you to surround your self-styled enemy mentally with divine light. It is possible, however, if his influence is strong, that your very desire to help him will only constitute an emotional opening through which his vibrations can harm you. Remember, *the desire to help must be truly impersonal.* Unless it is so, you may find it better to place a cross of light mentally upon your ill wisher. Imagine that you are using your thumb for this purpose. (Of all the fingers the thumb is the most related to will power.) If you practice this technique with great will and strong faith, any evil coming toward you from others will be arrested at its source, and only good vibrations will be able to reach you. In this way also, while protecting yourself you will not in any way be harming your opponent, though his own negative thoughts may indeed rebound upon him since they cannot reach their intended goal in you.

It may sometimes be necessary by specific thoughts to seal individual chinks, so to speak, in your magnetic armor (for example, to break any attachment that you feel towards a particular individual whose influence you fear). Generally speaking, however, what is most needed is simply to surround yourself on all levels with harmonious vibrations. Remember, no negative energy will be able to penetrate a powerful positive force field, unless indeed you make yourself vulnerable in some particular, to a specific ray of thought or emotion.

Emotion it is especially that creates weakness in one's magnetic "armor." Harmonize your emotions, therefore, by deep meditation. Then, with a conscious effort of will, radiate harmonious feelings outward from your heart center in all directions to the world around you. Another technique for strengthening your magnetic field will be given in the next chapter of this lesson.

Remember also that it is wise always to remain open and receptive to *good* magnetic influences. Do not, therefore, seek to protect yourself against the harmful thoughts of others by assuming an attitude of coldness or indifference to them. Indifference, though it may indeed protect you, will also deaden you to the finer vibrations in the world around you; it will make you less *divinely* receptive. It is better always to respond with a consciousness of light and of impersonal, divine love. Remember, the good thoughts that others send you must also find an opening in you, to influence you. Therefore is it said that spiritual healing requires not only power on the part of the healer, but also dynamic, receptive faith on the part of the person to be healed.

The principle of magnetism, and of energization itself, will be more deeply understood if you consider what it is that magnetizes a bar of iron. Every iron molecule possesses a magnetic polarity of its own. The reason, then, that a bar of iron may manifest no overall magnetism is that its molecules may be turned every which way, in effect canceling one another out. The more these molecules can be oriented in a north-south direction, the more magnetism the bar of iron will manifest.

This simple fact opens up important doors onto the yoga teachings, some of which we shall explore in lessons to come: the need for a guru, and the similarity between a bar magnet and the spine, with its positive-negative polarity in the brain and at the lowest spinal center.

A bar of metal becomes magnetized when it is placed next to an already-magnetized piece of iron. Similarly, to acquire strong magnetism oneself it is important to mix with people who already have the kind of magnetism that one wants to develop. To develop success-magnetism, mix with successful people, not with failures. Mix with artists to develop an artistic magnetism; with devotees, to develop spiritual magnetism.

I remember my guru asking me, on the occasion of our first meeting, how I had liked his autobiography. This book had changed my whole life. Because of it I had crossed America to offer my life to his guidance as a disciple. *Autobiography of a Yogi* was, in fact, the greatest book I had ever read, and still is. I tried lamely to say how deeply it had affected me. "That," Master remarked, simply, "is because it has my vibrations." A new thought to me at that time! It left me fairly bewildered. But over the years I have realized its truth. For words convey more than ideas. They are channels of actual magnetic power by which a writer's soul can touch the souls of his readers. That, especially, is why it is good to read the writings of true saints: Their words convey some of the power of a direct, physical blessing.

Every kind of human activity manifests a magnetism of its own. For success in that activity, the most important requirement is that one develop the appropriate type of magnetism. Once this magnetism has been well developed, indeed, one may achieve success even if his formal training in that field has been limited. (In fact, the greatest benefit from any kind of training—greater even than factual knowledge—is that the confidence born of such knowledge develops in one the magnetic power to attract success.)

Mixing with others to acquire their magnetism requires not physical proximity so much as an attunement of consciousness. Without this attunement, physical nearness may result in little or no true exchange. If such attunement exists, on the other hand, a magnetic exchange may occur even at a distance. In every case the *amount* of the exchange will depend on one's own magnetic drawing power, which in turn depends, of course, on a deep, sincere effort of will.

To draw rightly in this way, don't be a sponge, passively soaking up whatever magnetism you can get. It is possible thereby to deplete another person without truly gaining anything yourself. Remember, as you draw his magnetism you, too, must become a magnet, giving to him in return. The more your own magnetism increases, the greater will be your drawing power, but magnetic development of this kind is always an *interchange.* Forming a broader vortex of energy, it draws to itself increasing magnetism from the surrounding universe, or (if the magnetism is spiritual and uplifting) from God. A teacher with true students gains from the association even as they do.

As the molecules in a bar of iron, when turned every which way, cancel out its overall magnetic effectiveness, so the "molecules" of human desire, when conflictingly directed, cancel one another out, rendering human magnetism ineffective. To will something strongly, one must will it also with one's entire being. To draw anything to yourself, learn to put your whole self into the energy-flow you are directing.

In this way it will be seen that certain attitudes are automatically more magnetic than others. Willingness, cheerfulness, kindness—all wholesome, spiritual attitudes are magnetic. Unwillingness, discouragement, and similar negative attitudes, on the other hand, are like iron molecules turned conflictingly—or like toxins in the nervous system; they impair the free flow of energy. And while hatred and other strong negative emotions can develop a magnetic power of their own, if they are one-pointedly directed, in the end the inner heaviness they produce impairs the free flow of one's energy, and thereby destroys that kind of magnetism.

Even the foods we eat can be magnetically strengthening or depleting. If they load the system with toxins they will impair one's energy-flow, and therefore one's magnetism. If they assist the flow of energy in the body, they may rightly be called magnetizing foods. This aspect of the subject will be discussed more fully in the chapter on diet.

A strong, positive magnetic aura

around your body will prevent not only people's negative thoughts from affecting you, but also negative or harmful circumstances and happenings, even disease, from coming to you. When you yourself are good, only goodness will affect you. Or if, owing to the darkening influence of past karma, anything comes your way that in most human contexts would appear negative, you will find it either minimized, or becoming turned to good account.

Finally, it must be remembered that everything originates in the Infinite Spirit. Magnetism of every kind is born of the magnetic power of God's love. Like the light emanating from an electric bulb, this power is strongest at its source. Like an object held up to a light, and reflecting the light more brightly (even at a distance) the closer it is held to the light, divine power is greatest, even on low levels of manifestation, when its point of origin is closest to the Divine Source. In this material world, the highest realities often appear insignificant. Yet the hidden atomic energy in a bar of iron is far greater than that which one could generate from wielding the bar as a club. Kindness and fair-mindedness, similarly, can solve differences more effectively than can brutal tactics. And divine love, though perhaps the least-known force in the universe, and the one most apt to be scoffed at by men as "impractical, unrelated to mundane affairs, ineffective," is in fact the most powerful—indeed, in the last analysis the *only*—force in the universe. By the magnetic power of divine love, all things can be accomplished—even that most seemingly impossible of all tasks, our salvation from delusion.

What man by his own power alone cannot accomplish, divine love accomplishes easily. And its task, once accomplished, is accomplished forever. The most important thing, therefore, is for us by meditation to attune ourselves to that subtlest ray.

Offer your love to God. You will create a magnetic field thereby which will in turn draw His love to you. In this way, gradually, you will become ever more perfectly a channel for His love, drawing Him to you on higher and higher levels of divine awareness until your love attains perfection in Him. Remember, God's love flows to you always. It is *you,* by your love, who must complete the circuit, thereby generating the magnetism that can draw to yourself the very consciousness of Infinity.

Again, therefore, remember the law governing magnetism: *The greater the flow of energy (as awakened by will), the stronger the magnetic field.*

II. YOGA POSTURES

Your magnetism can be consciously increased, if you understand the principle on which it operates: "The greater the flow of energy, the greater the magnetic field." Magnetic people are always people with a high level of energy.

As you practice the postures, feel with every movement that you are increasing the flow of energy around your body and within it. As you bring your hands up to join them above the head in *Vrikasana* (the Tree Pose), or in *Chandrasana* (the Moon Pose), feel that with your hands you are creating an aura of light around your body. This aura is your magnetic field. It can protect you from harmful influences. It can attract to you good health, true friends, and worthwhile opportunities.

There is a *mantra* that is taught by yogis as a protection against harmful influences, particularly those coming from the astral sphere through the agency of inharmonious disincarnate entities. Modern man, with his hyper-rationalistic attitude toward life, may scoff at such influences as the products of a febrile imagination, but this scorn is not shared by the few souls in every religion who have attained to higher-than-physical vision. Astral possession, many cases of which are recorded in the New Testament, is a fact. Only those persons, however, can be so possessed or influenced whose auras are weak, because their will power is weak.

To practice this technique, join your hands before you, then bring them out to the side and behind you to form a large circle, joining them again at the back. Keep swinging them forward, outward, and backward in a large circle, joining them in front and behind, while reciting this mantra: "AUM *Tat Sat.*" At night, when you go to bed, write AUM three times on your pillow with your forefinger, and feel as you go to sleep that you are resting in AUM. (AUM, as I have said before, is the highest vibration. Nothing can touch you if you remain always in the consciousness of this holy vibration, or even if you simply chant AUM deeply at the point between the eyebrows.)

As you practice the postures, feel that you are deliberately moving in, and at the same time creating, a sphere of protective light. As you walk or go about your daily duties, feel yourself surrounded by this light. Remember, more is required than a pious imagination. The greater the will, the greater the flow of energy; the greater the flow of energy, the greater the magnetic field.

Parvatasana

(The Mountain Pose)

"My thoughts and energy rise up to touch the sky."

Sit cross-legged, preferably in *Padmasana* (the Lotus Pose). Bring the arms slowly upward, extending them straight out to the sides, and keeping the palms turned upward, until the palms become joined high above the head. Press the ears with the biceps. Keep the body very erect. Think of yourself as a mountain, all of your energy rising up toward the fingertips even as the rise of a mountain is focused in its peak. Stretch upward as high as you can comfortably.

Inhale, drawing the abdomen *in,* forcing the air to rise into the upper chest. Imagine that the breath is rising still further up into your fingertips. You will note that the movement of the diaphragm in this breathing exercise is the opposite of normal: Instead of moving downward to draw air into the lungs, it is brought up as it normally would be for exhalation. The purpose of this reverse movement is to reinforce the upward flow of energy and consciousness that is the essence of this pose. You may breathe to a rhythm of 6-12-6, repeating the respiration three to six times, gradually increasing the number to a limit of 30 times.

While holding your breath, affirm mentally: *"My thoughts and energy rise up to touch the skies."*

Parvatasana

(The Mountain Pose)

"My thoughts and energy rise up to touch the skies."

Benefits: Parvatasana is good for the lungs and diaphragm, for stimulating the heart, and for toning up the abdominal organs. It improves digestion, and is said to cure sluggishness of the digestive tract and to remove dyspepsia and constipation.

Spiritually, the Mountain Pose promotes the highest function of *hatha yoga,* namely, the raising of the energy up the spine to the brain.

Salabhasana

(The Full Locust Pose)

"I soar upward on wings of joy!"

This is one of the most strenuous of the poses of *hatha yoga*. Lie on your front, with your hands down at your side as in *Ardha-Salabhasana* (the Half Locust Pose). Clench your fists, turning the palms upward so that the backs of the hands press against the floor. Rest the chin on the floor. Now, inhale, then lift the lower body up with the strength of the arms, back, and legs to form a bow with the body in such a way that nothing below the naval remains touching the floor. Hold the breath as long as you hold the position itself. When you feel a need to breathe, exhale slowly and come down to a prone position. Repeat once or twice, if you so desire.

While in the position, feel that all the energy is being drawn from the legs and focused at the base of the spine. It is difficult to make a mental affirmation in this strenuous position, but the energy that is brought into play can itself be used as a focal point for one's awareness.

Benefits: Salabhasana gives vigorous and beneficial exercise to the diaphragm and the heart muscles. It helps to strengthen the arms and back, and promotes health in the nerves of the lower back and legs. Its deepest benefits, as in most of the yoga postures, are spiritual: the raising of the energy from the lower extremities of the body as a preparation for concentration and meditation.

Matsyasana

(The Fish Pose)

"My soul floats on waves of cosmic light."

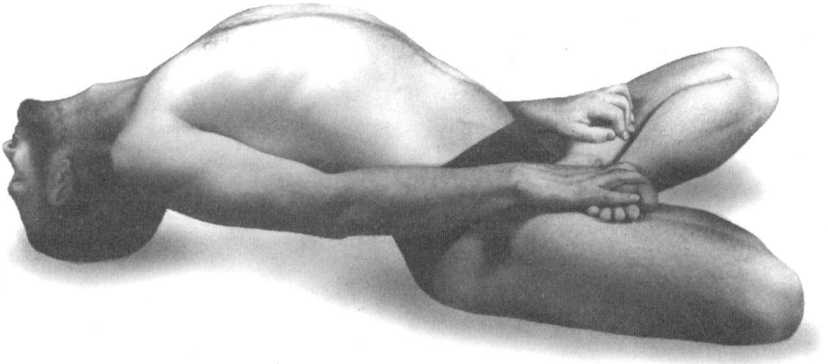

Sit in *Padmasana* (the Lotus Pose). Grasp your feet, and lie back (keeping the knees down) until your head touches the floor behind you. A variation of this pose is to join your hands under the head, bringing the shoulders down to the floor.

Benefits: The Fish Pose is so called because in it one is supposed to be able to float comfortably in water. The reason for floating in water in conjunction with yoga practice is the mental freedom that this practice gives. One should feel that he is floating on waves of cosmic light, completely submissive to the ebb and flow of divine grace.

Rajarsi Janakananda (James J. Lynn), Yoganandaji's most advanced disciple in the West, used to practice floating in the ocean off the beach at Encinitas, California. Rising and sinking gently with the ocean waves, he soon found himself floating in *samadhi* on waves of cosmic consciousness.

Matsyasana is usually practiced on the floor as part of one's regular yoga routine. It may be held as long as one wishes. This pose is excellent as a follow-up to the forward bends, especially *Halasana* (the Plow Pose) and *Sarvangasana* (the Shoulder Stand). It helps to overcome a stiff neck resulting from bending forward over a desk, or while sewing or reading.

Matsyasana helps also to draw energy upward to the spiritual eye, between the eyebrows.

If you cannot assume the full Lotus Pose, some of the benefits of *Matsyasana* may be achieved by simply sitting cross-legged and arching backward until your head touches the floor behind you. While practicing this pose, even on the floor, affirm: *"My soul floats on waves of cosmic light."*

Yoga Mudra

(usually translated to mean "the Symbol of Yoga")

"I am Thine; receive me."

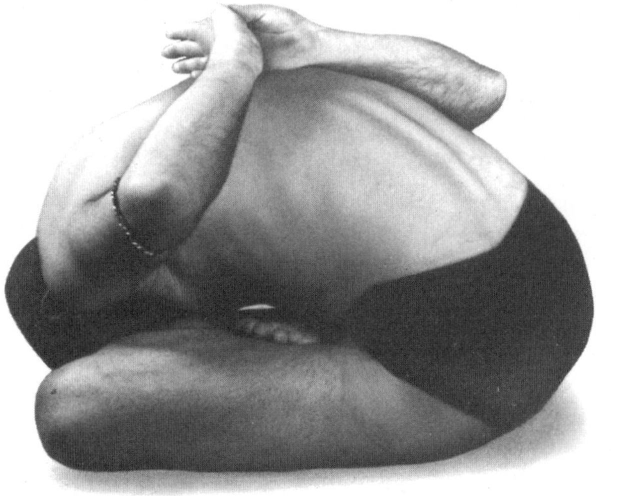

Sit in *Padmasana* (the Lotus Pose); simpler cross-legged positions are permissible, but less desirable. Lean forward until the forehead rests on the ground. Fold your palms together behind you between the shoulder-blades, pointing the fingers upward—or, if you cannot do that, simply hold one wrist behind you with the other hand at the level of the waistline.

Benefits: This posture, according to yoga tradition, helps to develop humility. The student may ask himself: Were the ancient yogis merely "milking" this pose for any conceivable benefits they might draw out of it? Any servile posture, any stoop forward, might as well be said to help develop humility.

Much more, however, is implied in this particular pose.

Paramhansa Yogananda explained that ego-consciousness is centered in the medulla oblongata at the base of the brain. The disdainful angle of a proud person's head is due to tension, ego-induced, in this medullary region. Notice, the next time that you accept someone's flattery, how your energy gathers at the back of the head. Worldly man is ego-centered. Most of his thoughts and activities emanate from, or are in some way connected with, this medullary center. The aspiring yogi should strive always to release his energy from this point, and to center it in the Christ center between the eyebrows. The medulla oblongata represents the negative phase of the brain's function; the point between the eyebrows, the positive phase. Both these locations are, in fact, the two poles of the same center.

Yoga Mudra takes the weight off the back of the neck, helping to reduce tension in that region. The pressure of the forehead on the floor encourages the redirection of one's consciousness to the frontal region. The folding of the palms helps, finally, to induce an attitude of reverent worship. Pray mentally in this pose: *"I am Thine; receive me."*

Yoga Mudra is indeed the "Symbol of Yoga," for in all yoga practice self-effort (which is implicit in the deliberate assumption of the yoga postures) must be combined with loving surrender to the Infinite Power, God. Man's self-effort must be done with a view, not to conquering the divine heights by human power alone, but to opening his consciousness so that God's light may reach down into him.

Dhanurasana

(The Bow Pose—An Advanced Variation)

When practicing the Bow Pose, try sometimes to raise your knees without the help of your arms. Instead of holding the feet with the hands, keep the arms down by your side, and raise them up to the level of your knees as you come up into the position.

III. BREATHING

Many yoga books stress the importance of exhaling more slowly than one inhales. So common is this teaching, in fact, that it is interesting to note that one of the few real masters of yoga in our time, Paramhansa Yogananda, invariably gave a rhythm of breathing in which the inhalation and exhalation were equal. (At least I am aware of no exception in his writings.) In many of his teachings he stressed the importance of balancing the inhalation with exhalation. (The time of retention of the breath in the lungs varies with different techniques.)

Many students have asked me about this apparent discrepancy between his teaching and that of so large a segment of yoga tradition. There is a reason for the difference.

With exhalation, one expels poisons from the body. So long as *hatha yoga* is conceived in a purely physical way, a prolonged exhalation may be seen to be helpful in this eliminative process. When it is understood, however, that the physical breath is intimately connected with the upward and downward flow of energy in the spine, the whole practice of breathing takes on a new dimension.

We shall study this point more deeply in Step Twelve. For now, let me say only that deep spiritual awareness occurs as these two currents become balanced and neutralized. For the purpose of spiritual awakening, it is important that the period of inhalation and exhalation be equal.

In order to stimulate the awareness of the energy that flows in conjunction with the breathing, constrict your throat slightly when you practice the Alternate Breath. Feel that you are drawing the breath up and down the spine with your inhalation and exhalation. When you use the alternate breathing exercise as a means of increasing your inner, spiritual awareness, inhale only through the left nostril, and exhale only through the right. The rhythm should be even: 8-8-8.

IV. ROUTINE

Practice *Parvatasana* (the Mountain Pose) after *Ardha-Matsyendrasana* (the Half-Spinal Twist). Follow it, if you like, with *Matsyasana* (the Fish Pose), then *Yoga Mudra* (the Symbol of Yoga). The Full Locust Pose may be practiced after *Ardha-Salabhasana* (the Half Locust Pose).

V. HEALING

Sex Problems

Sex problems are usually identified with disease or debility of the reproductive system. In yoga, however, sex problems relate also to the obstruction posed by strong sexual desire to the endeavor of the aspiring yogi to channel all his energy upward, to the brain.

Contrary to common supposition, all of one's physical powers, including that of sex, are strengthened, not weakened, when the energy is withdrawn from its outward expression in the senses and gathered in what might be called the rejuvenating dynamo of the spine and brain. Without sleep, for instance, one would soon lose the energy that is needed in work. Although meditation withdraws energy from the senses, the result of this withdrawal, far from starving the senses, is to make them keener. Periodic rest increases one's capacity for sensory enjoyment. Colors become more intense, sounds more pleasing, fragrances more refreshing.

Thus it may be seen that exercises which help to transmute sex energy into spiritual energy are also excellent for helping one to overcome debility, and even disease, of the reproductive system. To use this principle merely to increase one's sexual enjoyment would, of course, be self-defeating in the end, unless one considers a perpetual game of see-saw the true purpose of life.

Postures that are good for menstrual problems include the following: *Sarvangasana* (the Shoulder Stand)—Lesson Eleven; *Trikonasana* (the Triangle Pose); *Matsyasana* (the Fish Pose); *Halasana* (the Plow Pose); *Bhujangasana* (the Cobra Pose); *Paschimotanasana* (the Posterior Stretch); *Padahastasana* (the Jackknife Pose); *Salabhasana* (the Locust Pose).

For sex transmutation, deep breathing is important. It creates a magnet in the lungs, drawing the energy up the spine to the region of the heart. To continue this flow from the heart to the brain, concentrate at the point between the eyebrows, creating a magnet at that point. It is easier to draw energy up from the base of the spine in these two stages—first to the lungs and heart, then to the Christ center between the eyebrows—than in one stage (from the base of the spine straight to the Christ center).

A technique was taught by Lahiri Mahasaya that is excellent for long-range transmutation, but not for use during actual periods of stimulation or excitement. It involves deliberate, but soothing (not exciting) stimulation of the sex nerves, with a view to gently awakening, then withdrawing, that energy to the brain. One cannot redirect the flow of an energy of which one is not conscious. Nor can one easily redirect such a flow, once it is moving too strongly in an outward direction. The stimulation must be completely soothing, inasmuch as sex energy, when wrongly stimulated, manifests itself as heat in the body. Transmutation of this energy makes the body cool (one actually feels a sensation like a cool fountain spray rising up the spine to the brain), therefore the stimulation in this technique should be of a cooling nature.

Place some ice with a little water in an ice bag, and hold it on the closed tip of the male organ, or against the outside of the female organ, and feel the coolness gradually penetrating up the spine to the brain, and spreading outward also to the whole body. Since Lahiri Mahasaya gave this technique to the world, it would be well to use his name mentally while practicing it, invoking his blessings on one's practice. Practice this technique ten minutes at a time, twice daily. Never practice it, however, during times of sexual excitement.

Any action follows as a logical consequence of the first movements of thought and energy toward that kind of activity. The time to prevent any misuse of energy is not halfway along the path toward final misuse, but at the very start of the journey. Success or failure in any endeavor depends primarily on small beginnings. The yogi who aspires to transmute sex energy into spiritual power is advised, therefore, to guard in little matters the directional flow of this energy. He would do well not to look at members of the opposite sex more than necessary, and especially not to look into their eyes, which may be highly magnetic, nor to converse with them more than strictly necessary. To be reserved in one's dealings with members of the opposite sex may seem extreme, and may indeed be impossible in normal social intercourse nowadays, but to assume that one can be completely free and friendly in his actions, and yet remain inwardly unattracted, may be naive. The sex magnetism in the body is exceedingly subtle. The magnetic attraction between male and female, as between the north and south poles of a magnet, exists independently of any natural affinity between personalities. This attraction may be unconscious, or it may inspire only friendship and inspiration. Even in its highest forms, however, unless the sex consciousness of at least one of the persons has been transmuted, the *natural* magnetism (as opposed to any higher kind that may exist also) will tend to pull the energy downward.

It is up to the individual to decide how strictly and how completely he wants to center all his energy in God alone, but if this is truly his desire, he should bear well in mind that it is the beginning movements of thought and energy that he must watch. As Jesus said, "He who is faithful in little will be faithful also in much." Worldly people may mock one for a weakling if he tries to be strict with himself. They do not see how subtle the attraction is, nor how very much bound they already are themselves. A person who is asleep may well dream that he is awake. It is only in actual wakefulness that he can see how very much asleep he really was. An austere attitude is not a sign of weakness. Indeed, it is not even possible without great inner strength.

An excellent technique, also, for sex-transmutation is to meditate on the spiritual light in the sex region and at the base of the spine, and to call on divine grace for help in drawing that energy upward.

Remember, the most important factor in sex-transmutation is mental attitude. And the first step towards right sexual attitudes is not to surround such a commonplace and perfectly natural function with an aura of mystery. Do not give it greater importance than it deserves. If you treat it like a pygmy, it will have only a pygmy's power over you. Treat it like a giant, and it will have the strength of a giant. One time Sri Yukteswar was out walking with a few disciples, all of them young men, when they came upon the sight of a group of young women bathing, unclad, in a river. The disciples tried to look away, but by stealthy glances showed where their minds really were. Sri Yukteswarji ordered them to stop. "Better than guilty glances," he said, "followed by exaggerated memories later on, let us stand here and look frankly." Gazing steadily at the women, the disciples soon realized that what had attracted them was not the women, but their own imaginations. After a few moments, they resumed their walk calmly.

No natural function of the body is inherently evil. To approach sex with a consciousness of shame would be a serious mistake. It has its place in the scheme of things. Without it we would not even be here! The important thing is that this power be not abused or wasted, but used rightly to produce physical children, or spiritual "children" of inspiration and enlightenment. To be free of sex desire is not necessarily a sign of greatness. Great men often have strong sex inclinations. But they must transmute it, for it takes energy to be great. A strong drive in any direction can be diverted to give one great strength in another direction.

VI. DIET

Diet plays an important part in sex rejuvenation and control. Excessively spiced foods, and foods that are heavy in bulk and low in vitality, tend to clog and irritate the nerves, leading to unnatural physical desires of many kinds. Foods that tend specifically to irritate and stimulate the sex nerves include the whites of eggs, and wine. Meat also is an irritant. A diet of raw foods can be beneficial in the practice of sex transmutation.

It is only by repeated, patient effort that any lasting spiritual progress can be made. Every time you make a mistake, simply get up and keep walking toward your goal. Do not waste time and energy in self-accusation. Freedom *must* come to you, eventually, if you truly want it. "A saint," Paramhansa Yogananda used to say, "is a sinner who never gave up."

All foods are considered by yogis to exercise an influence on the mental and spiritual nature of man, as well as on his physical body. Fruits are said to be the most spiritualizing, or *sattwic,* food. Other foods—meats and grains, for example—have an activating, or *rajasic,* effect upon the inner man. Devitalized, or excessively pungent foods (horseradish, for example) have a stultifying, or *tamasic,* influence. All foods are divided according to their essential vibrations: *sattwic, rajasic, and tamasic.* These three qualities—the elevating, activating, and darkening—are said to be inherent in all things created. The whole universe is a product of the mixture of these three *guna*s, or qualities.

Of all material foods, fruits manifest the *sattwa guna* in its purest form. Specific fruits are said actually to help one to develop specific spiritual qualities. Bananas carry a vibration of humility; pears, of peace; grapes, of devotion (turning to lust when the grapes are fermented into wine); cherries, of good cheer (curiously, we have in English the expression, "Life is a bowl of cherries," meaning that it is meant to be lived with an attitude of good cheer). At the end of this section I will append a list of the spiritual qualities of certain foods, as taught by Paramhansa Yoganandaji.

There are people who insist that, if I have any claim to fame, it is for my fruit salads. Perhaps I should share with you some of my fruitarian secrets.

Fresh fruits in season are the first requirement. (Canned fruits, so often served in fruit salads in restaurants, are an insult to the refined palate!) Acid fruits should be blended with bland. A fruit salad consisting only of oranges, grapefruits, and pineapples will be too one-sided; it would be better to eat each of these fruits by itself.

My own favorite combinations include apples, bananas, oranges, strawberries, grapes, a few raisins and/or dates, pine nuts, and almonds. I do not like to chop the pieces too fine, lest the distinctive taste of each be lost in a sort of general puree.

The important thing in a perfect fruit salad is the dressing. This can be made in a variety of ways, to none of which am I consistent. A few general guidelines may, however, be helpful.

Mix in a blender: whipping cream, mango pulp (some specialty grocers carry it), fresh garden mint, and a little honey. If you can pulverize the almonds, these, too, may be mixed into the dressing. (In any case, the almonds should be chopped fairly fine.)

Or try mixing cream with a little lemon juice, ground tangerine rind, fresh mint, and honey.

Or mix cream, lemon or orange juice, half of an avocado (or one full banana), and honey.

Or leave out the cream, and use only avocado with milk or orange juice. Add a little lemon juice and honey.

Or try, with any of the above combinations, adding just a little bit of pulverized coffee—not more than the equivalent of 4 coffee beans.

To all of the above combinations, or to any others that you may conceive, ground almonds are an excellent addition. Cream, incidentally, combines better in the body with fruits than does milk.

QUALITIES OF FOODS

Bananas—calmness and humility
Pears—peacefulness
Grapes—devotion, divine love
Cherries—cheerfulness
Oranges, Lemons—to banish melancholy and to stimulate the brain
Berries (generally)—purity of thought
Strawberries—dignity
Raspberries—kind-heartedness
Peaches—selflessness, concern for the welfare of others
Pineapple—self-assurance
Avocado—good memory
Coconuts—generally spiritualizing
Dates—tenderness, sweetness
Figs—to soften too strict a sense of discipline
Almonds—sexual self-control
Honey—self-control
Maple Syrup—mental freshness
Sweet Corn—mental vitality
Tomatoes—mental strength
Beets—courage
Spinach—a simple nature
Lettuce—calmness
Cow's Milk—enthusiasm and fresh, spiritual energy
Egg Yolks—rajasic, outwardly directed energy
Grains (generally)—strength of character
Wheat—steadfastness to principle
Unpolished Rice—mildness

Rasagulla, a Dessert

One of the most delicious of Indian sweetmeats, *Rasagulla* is time-consuming, but not difficult, to prepare.

Make fresh *panir,* or cheese, by boiling milk and adding 1 tablespoon lemon juice for each pint of milk just as the milk rises to a boil. Stir gently as the milk curdles and simmer for five minutes. Strain through muslin. Hang the muslin bag of curds overnight or until the cheese is very dry. Knead until smooth. Form into balls slightly smaller than a golf ball. Cut each ball in half and put a large pinch of crushed rock candy and 4 cardamom seeds (not pods), in the center. Join the halves and roll them together to make a perfect ball again.

Separately, prepare a pan of syrup by boiling a little honey in water. (Sugar is normally called for, but honey is more healthful.) The syrup should be very thin, and water added if in the boiling of the rasagullas it becomes too thick. A proportion of ⅓ cup of honey to a whole cup of water should be about right.

Simmer the rasagulla balls gently for 5–10 minutes until they swell slightly. After they have cooled, spray them with a little rose water.

VII. MEDITATION

A. Hong-Sau *Outline*

PREPARATION

1. So as to decarbonize the bloodstream, and thereby to calm the body, inhale, tensing the whole body; throw the breath out and relax. Repeat two or three times.

2. Inhale and exhale slowly and deeply several times, making the periods of inhalation, holding, and exhalation the same. (Suggested counts: 20-20-20, or 12-12-12.) Don't strain. Repeat six or twelve times.

3. Mentally check the body to make sure it is relaxed. Periodically, check the body again during your practice of the technique.

4. Begin your actual practice of the technique by first exhaling, slowly and deliberately.

THE BASIC TECHNIQUE

1. When the breath flows in of its own accord, follow it mentally with the sound, *Hong*. Imagine that the breath itself is making this sound.

2. When the breath flows out of its own accord, follow it mentally with, and imagine that it is itself making, the sound, *Sau* (to sound like "saw").

3. If at any time the breathing stops naturally, accept the pause calmly, identifying yourself with it until the breath flows again *of its own accord*.

4. To keep your mind on the breath (or, when you are more interiorized, to differentiate between inhalation and exhalation), it may help you to bring the forefinger towards the palm as the breath flows in, and away from the palm as the breath flows out.

FIRST PHASE

1. If your breath is still restless, you may be more easily aware of the physical movement of your lungs and diaphragm than of the flow of breath in the nostrils. In this case, let the mind follow its natural inclination: Concentrate on the purely physical aspects of breathing—the movement of the rib cage, the diaphragm, or the navel.

2. Gradually, as you grow calmer, transfer your attention from the breathing process to the breath itself.

SECOND PHASE

1. As your attention begins to focus on the breath itself, watch the breath at the point where it enters the nostrils.

2. Gradually, with the progressive calmness of the breath, center your awareness of it higher and higher in the nose. To raise this center of awareness, you may find it helpful if you make a special effort inwardly to relax your nose.

3. As it becomes natural to do so, center your awareness of the breath at the point where it enters the nasal cavity. Feel it in the upper part of this passage, and visualize its movement gently fanning and awakening the Christ center in the frontal lobe of the brain.

THIRD PHASE

1. Become more and more identified with the breath, less and less with your body's need for it to flow in and out. Remember, especially as you grow very calm, that this need may be as much imaginary (the result of deeply ingrained subconscious habit) as actual. Therefore:

2. Particularly concentrate on, and enjoy, the pauses between the breaths. Dwell on the sense of freedom from the tyranny of constant breathing. Beyond enjoying this sense of calmness and freedom, however, do not try to prolong the breathless state by an act of will.

3. Direct the will, rather, toward the thought of *becoming* the air that is flowing in the nose, or of becoming boundless space at the Christ center.

4. As the pauses become prolonged, you may want to engage your attention in chanting AUM mentally at the Christ center.

KEY POINTS

1. Throughout the practice of this technique, look upward so as gradually to raise your consciousness. Do not, however, concentrate at the Christ center until it becomes natural for you to feel the flow of the breath at that point.

2. Sit very still throughout your practice of the technique. Any physical movement (and also any unrelated movement of thought or emotion) will further excite the breath.

3. Every now and then, mentally check the body (especially the nose) to be sure it is relaxed.

4. While chanting *Hong-Sau,* be sure that you are chanting only mentally. Often, the mere thought of a word will produce an involuntary movement of the tongue or lips, or a slight tension in the jaw or throat. Be sure these parts of your body, too, are completely relaxed.

QUESTIONS AND ANSWERS

Q. How long should the* Hong-Sau *technique be practiced?

A. As long as you *enjoy* practicing it. This is one technique (unlike many other yoga practices) that cannot be overdone in the sense of putting a strain on the nervous system. Yoganandaji used, as a boy, to practice it as much as 7½ hours at a time. He once told a disciple that if one wants to become a master in this life, he should practice *Hong-Sau* two hours daily. No technique, however, should be practiced to the point of boredom or fatigue. Beginners, especially, may do better to practice only half an hour at a time, perhaps even less. For others, let *enjoyment* be your key, lest you slip gradually into the pernicious habit of meditating mechanically, without that keen sense of blissful anticipation which is so necessary to any real meditative progress. When your enjoyment of the technique begins to lessen, cease your practice at least for that session. When your enjoyment of meditation itself lessens, stop meditating, or take a break (you might rest in *Savasana* [the Corpse Pose]) before making another effort.

Q. When the Master said to practice* Hong-Sau *two hours a day, did he mean at one sitting?

A. Yes, if possible. But if not, I am sure he would have agreed to your dividing this time into two or more shorter periods. Remember, *no* fixed time can guarantee success in yoga practice. Suggested times should be taken only as general guidelines.

Q. May one practice this technique in idle moments as well, apart from one's prescribed periods for meditation?

A. Indeed, yes! Anywhere, practically: sitting at your desk in the office, or in public places, or at a party when you are not involved in the conversation. Before others, however, don't be obvious about what you are doing. Sit back, and close your eyes as if you were resting them, or look straight ahead, as if reflectively.

Q. What proportion of one's meditation should be devoted to the practice of this technique?

A. It is difficult to advise in this matter, except to say that this is one of the most important techniques of yoga. The longer and more deeply you practice any technique, the sooner you will become proficient in it. It is for you to decide how long, in proportion to other techniques, you want to watch the breath. Regardless what techniques are practiced, however, *at least* the last quarter of one's meditation time should be devoted to simple meditation, without any practice of techniques. As my guru put it, intuition (which he defined as the soul's power to know God) is developed by prolonging and deepening the peaceful after-effects of one's practice of the meditation techniques.

Q. Should one concentrate on the breath and also at the point between the eyebrows?

A. Not until the attention focuses itself naturally on the flow of breath at the beginning of the nose—that is, the point at which the breath enters the nasal cavity in the head. To do so otherwise would constitute a division of concentration which would be self-defeating.

Q. Since Hong-Sau *is pronounced differently in different parts of India (e.g.,"Hung-Sah"), and since much is made in yoga teachings of the correct pronunciation of mantras, is it not important to ascertain which of the different pronunciations is the most classically correct?*

A. No. Pronounced mentally, the variations are so slight as to be virtually indistinguishable from one another, and therefore insignificant. The important thing in the practice of this technique is to deepen one's *consciousness* of peace, and to associate this consciousness with the repetition of the *mantra*. In fact, it is one's consciousness, truly, that determines the most correct pronunciation of any *mantra*.

Q. What if, during one's practice of this, or of any other, technique, one is suddenly lifted into a divine state of consciousness? Assuming that it was the technique that induced this state, should one continue his practice, or abandon it to deepen one's enjoyment of this state of consciousness?

A. That depends on whether the technique actually *induced* the state you refer to, or only prepared you to receive it. Certain divine states, if actually caused by the practice of a technique, may be deepened by continuation of that practice. Otherwise, and generally speaking, the technique should be abandoned in order that you might deepen your enjoyment of, and identification with, the divine experience.

Q. Sometimes I find that my breath, instead of pausing longer and longer at the rest points between inhalation and exhalation, continues its normal rhythm, but becomes shallower and shallower to the point where it virtually disappears. Is this all right?

A. Yes, it is quite all right. In any case you should let the breath follow its own course, instead of deciding for it what rhythm it ought to follow. But such extremely light breathing indicates a satisfactory state of concentration.

B. Magnetism

Regardless what you want in life—things, opportunities, or favorable circumstances; inspiration, insight, or intellectual understanding; ecstasy, divine love, or soul freedom—one thing, and one thing only, will determine your measure of fulfillment; the power and quality of your own magnetism.

Magnetism is an abstract principle. It can be used as an agent of blight as well as of blessing. Be careful what it is that you want, for it is in your own power to win heaven even here on earth, or—even here on earth—hell.

Material desires are the principal cause of man's undoing, binding him to the grossest element in his nature, and blinding him thereby to those inner, spiritual qualities that would free him to soar in skies of untrammeled joy. Yet it is necessary to have enough material prosperity, health, and opportunity not to be a prey to excessive material concern. It takes a mighty spirit in the midst of serious deprivation to think purely of higher realities. The blessings of this world *can* be blessings truly, provided they facilitate our search for inner freedom instead of hindering it. It is not wrong, therefore, to use our power of magnetism to acquire a measure of worldly prosperity, if we do not, in the process, entomb ourselves in our possessions; to acquire health, if we do not become health fanatics; and to cause the doors of opportunity to open for us, if we seek truly worthwhile opportunities, and do not squander our power in detours or in mere diversions. Whatever you need in life, physically, mentally, or spiritually, can be attracted to you only according to the kind of energy you yourself send out. Recognizing this truth, you might as well give some thought to your physical well-being even if your chief desire in life is, as it should be, to find God.

Yet the basis of *all* desires should be the wish to find God, and to please Him. Do not feel that your material desires, being worldly, have no place in your spiritual life. This would be the surest way of directing them to your own detriment, rather than toward your ultimate freedom. Rather, seek even their fulfillment from God in meditation, that the true source of your power be realized, not as the little ego, but as the infinite, divine Self. Seek also God's guidance, that you desire always that which is truly for your own highest good. I do not mean for you to limit your self-effort to meditation, but only to seek in meditation the wellsprings of your strength.

Whatever it is that you desire, formulate in your mind a very clear image of it. Concentrate this image at the will center between the eyebrows, and, calling on the energy of the universe to reinforce your own energy, send a strong thought out through the Christ center. Invest that thought with all the energy at your command. Feel the magnetic power of that outgoing energy, rather than concentrating too much on the particular object that you hope to influence by your desire. Concentrate on your own ideal, rather than on the state of things as they actually are. Above all, make divine peace the channel for your magnetic power, that that power work for harmony, or not at all. Make God your Partner in every such undertaking, and offer the fruits of your self-effort up to Him, seeking to please Him, and acting above all out of love for Him.

In this way you will soon learn that you are in truth a child of the Infinite, and that dominion—not egoic, but in the form of soul-mastery—over all things is your divine birthright.

AUM, *Shanti, Shanti, Shanti*

Step Eleven

Guru

I. PHILOSOPHY

Guru

How is man, lost and stumbling in a darkness of self-perpetuated ignorance, ever to find his way to the clear light of wisdom? He needs a guru. Alone—consider, what path can he safely follow? So many paths have been mapped; their very diversity renders them suspect. Many a well-plotted route has led hopeful travelers windingly to an unbridgeable chasm. Many a broad highway, seemingly sure, has struck off boldly across flowering plains only to spend itself at last, crumbling, in desert sands of unfulfillment. Even those few paths which lead truly over deserts and high mountain passes to the land of divine promise must cross dark regions first; only with great care can they be followed. And everywhere pitfalls of delusion await the unwary; deep ruts of desire lead off into ditches of bad habit.

Man thinks by moral maxims alone to find the way to enlightenment. He might as soon expect to pick his way over a windy plain with the help of a small, unshielded candle! He thinks to find the way by his own strength alone. And then, belatedly recognizing his own helplessness, he waits pathetically to be carried, not even caring who the porter is—priest, soothsayer, palmist—so long as this fellow pilgrim promises to do all his work for him.

Who but the blindest egotist would claim that only by his own power is an electric lamp lit? And who but the merest dreamer would claim that since it is electricity that actually lights the lamp, it is up to the electricity also to turn the lamp on? Man, a creature of the universe, cannot even walk two steps without the strength he derives from the universe. Yet it is up to him alone to draw that strength; nature cannot walk his path for him.

We need help on the path to enlightenment. We need a guru. It is not enough merely to be shown the way—even if, out of countless detours and dead ends, the right way be mapped for us. The pitfalls are too many. We need help, but that kind of help which will enable us, too, to walk surely by our own power.

This kind of help comes neither by egotistical self-assurance nor by passivity, but by understanding and using the very law of magnetism which we discussed in the last lesson.

A bar of iron does not magnetize itself. To become magnetized, it must be placed next to a magnet. Man can, by increasing his own energy-flow, magnetize himself. But this appearance of self-help is often his undoing. Magnetization hinges not on the question of self-determination, but on whether or not magnetism can be created. It cannot. Man can bestir himself to acquire magnetism. But it is in proportion to how well he attunes himself to the universal influences that he becomes magnetized. He is part and parcel of the universe. He has the free will to decide what sort of influences to accept in his life—whether uplifting, or, if his will be perverse, degrading—but he cannot act independently of *any* influence.

Man grows by attracting to himself powers greater than those he already possesses. Unlike the bar of unmagnetized iron, he can attract magnetic influences that emanate not from any specific locale, but that exist generally, as part of the very structure of the universe. Yet man, too, cannot develop such abstract awareness at one leap. We all need specific examples: our Shakespeares and Bachs to help us grow in the understanding of beauty, even though beauty itself is an abstraction, and as such would remain real even if no man were sensitive enough to perceive it. Bach and Shakespeare themselves had specific models for their genius. Infinite awareness may be—indeed, *is*—the divinely appointed goal, but without specific aids along the way all one may hope to attain is a sort of spiritual vagueness.

Hence the value of *sat-sang* (good company). For the beginner, especially, association with others who are firmly on the path is essential. He needs their spiritual magnetism to help him to develop the power to rise above vitiating influences in the world around him, and in himself.

Even ordinarily good people, however, are a mixture of virtues and flaws. Even if, as rarely happens, one were to attract to himself only their virtues, the fact that these virtues emanate not directly from God, but through the filter of ego consciousness, means that they cannot effectively take one to God. At best, ordinary good company can only help one to move forward on the path; it cannot take one to the goal.

The Indian scriptures are therefore unanimous in declaring that the most important thing for any spiritual aspirant is the grace of a true *guru,* or divine teacher—one who knows God, and can bestow upon the prepared disciple the power (which is to say, the magnetism) to know God also. As the Bible says, "As many as received him, to them gave he power to become the sons of God." (John 1:12) A true guru is Christlike in every sense of the word: He has found God. He is one with God. He is a savior, whose sole remaining mission, having freed himself, is to lift other souls from delusion's fogs into the endless skies of Self-realization.

The guru acts like a lighthouse, shining the Divine Light with a mighty blaze of awakening into the darkness of human delusion. Without such a high influence it is impossible for the devotee to rise to great heights. Apparent exceptions have occurred only in cases where a soul was already so advanced that it could walk alone (usually with help from the guru in visions), or where the guru appeared to him on earth, but in secret.

It is not necessary for the guru to be always near his disciples. He need not even be in the physical body to be able to influence them with his spiritual magnetism. It has been said that one must have at least one physical contact with the guru, but this contact, also, can be gained through contact with living disciples. Through those whom the guru has baptized, his power can flow. Subsequent generations of disciples also, having received that power, can act as living links with a God-realized master, whose consciousness is unaffected by the transition from this world to higher spheres. Jesus said: "And if anyone gives so much as a cup of cold water to one of these little ones, because he is a disciple of mine, I tell you this: that man will assuredly not go unrewarded." (Matthew 10:42) His disciples were vehicles for his power. Anyone accepting them as such, he said, would be able to receive his blessings.

To return to a point that was touched on earlier in this lesson, it is often asked: "If God is the true power in this universe, why need man seek any substitute? Why not go straight to the Lord Himself?" There is a story about a priest in Ireland who went to visit one of his parishioners, a farmer.

"What a fine farm you and God have made here," said the priest.

"Well, Father," said the farmer, "you may be right, but you should have seen it when God had it all to Himself!"

The fact is, everything in nature is done through instruments. As the electricity from the power plant in a city cannot be fed directly into a home, but must be stepped down by transformers until its power is low enough not to burn out the wires, so the Infinite Power of Spirit cannot come to man except through the "transformers" of high souls. Man must lift himself up to their state of consciousness before he, like them, can bask unprotected in the Infinite Light.

In India it is held that the most important thing on the path is the blessing of a true guru. It is believed also that such a guru is drawn to one, not by one's own choice, but by the Divine Will—usually because of some karmic link between guru and disciple. Such a bond may last many incarnations, until the disciple is finally free. Sometimes it happens, if the guru has not yet been fully enlightened, that the disciple rises higher, and helps the guru. The spiritual bond, however, once formed, remains through eternity. If the disciple severs it, he can only wait until he is willing once again to accept the messenger that God has sent him. He cannot wander from guru to guru if he would attain salvation.

While seeking one's own guru, however, it is justifiable to take any help that one can find. For, to meet one's own guru one must develop enough magnetism to attract the guru's help. To reject all spiritual influences with the feeble excuse that one is waiting for his true guru is to refuse that aid which would make it possible at last to attract the guru.

One must understand that the greatest help one receives from any teacher is not intellectual, but magnetic. To learn truly in spiritual matters is to sit quietly, not asking a thousand questions, but rather absorbing the teacher's vibrations. This is why Jesus said that Mary, who was sitting quietly at his feet while he spoke, had chosen the better part. (Luke 10:42) To be near the guru physically is beneficial, but by no means necessary. To be near him spiritually is what really matters. Keep his presence in your heart. Call to him constantly at the point between the eyebrows. It is by mental attunement that his true help is received.

But it is not enough merely to call on the guru. There are disciples who wait passively for their gurus to do everything for them. These disciples are the failures. What one must do is call *magnetically,* to draw the guru by the power of one's love, to try always to do his will—in short, to receive him without reservation into every corner of one's life.

I observed in the ashram of my guru that those who advanced most quickly on the path were those who received him completely into their consciousness. In so doing they did not lose their individuality. Rather, he gave them the strength to *uncover* that individuality, by removing the debris of worldly consciousness that makes the vast majority of human beings merely carbon copies of one another, unique in almost nothing, mediocre even in their expressions of joy and love. Those in our ashram, on the contrary, who sought to maintain their mental freedom by not opening themselves fully to the guru's influence advanced more slowly. And those who insisted on maintaining their own opinions in everything never seemed to advance at all. After more than fifty years on the path, I say with greater conviction than ever that the most important thing is to have a true guru, and, having him, to surrender oneself to him wholly—not in subservience or fear, but with total love and trust. Every time that I have been happiest inside has been a time when I was deeply in tune with my guru. Every time that I have trudged in misery has been a time when my attunement was weakened. In times of attunement every step has been easy. When I have not been in tune, no matter how I struggled to advance, every move was like trying to swim in a sea of mud.

There are many God-realized souls in the world, in India especially. I do not wish to dogmatize people, or to tell them that they should seek discipleship only under my own guru, Paramhansa Yogananda. Yet if anyone is drawn to me, it may well be for a reason. Whatever good they may feel in me is not mine to give them. It flows from my guru. Though it is not my purpose to proselytize, I also feel deeply that our line of gurus, and particularly the last of this line, Paramhansa Yoganandaji, are the yoga teachers for this age. Other gurus have come with other messages, but the science of yoga at this time in history has been sent by the Divine in its original and purest form by this particular line. I also feel that Yoganandaji is, in a very real sense, the guru for at least the vast majority of spiritually seeking Americans in this age. He was sent to these shores, not as just another teacher, but as a true *avatar,* or divine incarnation, blessed with the spiritual power to draw countless souls back to God's kingdom. His freedom came to him many incarnations ago. People see very imperfectly when they see him only as a man, or as a humble devotee who brought a few of India's priceless jewels of wisdom to the West. He was no overflow from that ancient culture, but the very cream of Indian sainthood, recognized as such by every living saint that I met in India.

Yoganandaji said to a disciple once, "If you shut me out, how can I come in?" As you have been drawn to these lessons, so experiment at least with this suggestion: Call to Yoganandaji in meditation (you may visualize him from a photograph if you like) and feel his presence in your heart. So may your practice of yoga be but a beginning to a spiritual unfoldment that can carry you to the very shores of cosmic consciousness.

II. YOGA POSTURES

The Inverted Poses

Among the most important practices of *hatha yoga* must be listed the inverted poses. Man has one disadvantage compared to other animals: In his waking hours he is usually upright. The force of gravity draws constantly on his bloodstream, on his internal organs, on his energy. Resultant disorders are common: varicose veins and otherwise sore legs and feet; toxins in the lower abdomen that irritate the colon and the reproductive organs; a general sagging of the abdomen, of the visceral organs, and of the facial muscles, even a general feeling of heaviness in the body that becomes especially pronounced as the vigor of youth recedes before the invasion of middle age.

Not only is the downward pull of gravity unfortunate for the lower body, which receives too much blood and too much pressure from above; it is also unfortunate for the brain and for the organs above the heart, which do not receive their fair share of blood.

From a standpoint of higher yoga practice, it is obvious that the downward pull of gravity works directly against the yogi's endeavor to raise his energy and consciousness to the brain and to the point between the eyebrows.

The obvious solution to this downward drain is to use gravity itself to restore a proper balance to the body. It is for this purpose that the inverted poses were designed. The popular Western equivalent to these poses, the slant board, is not nearly so effective as even the simplest of the inverted poses, *Viparita Karani,* which was given in Step Seven.

The inverted poses should be practiced at the end of one's series of postures, when the spine has been loosened so as to permit the free flow of energy to the brain. One should begin with

Viparita Karani, pressing his hands at the base of the spine to increase his awareness of the energy there, and to encourage that energy to rise upward.

From *Viparita Karani,* proceed to *Sarvangasana* (the Shoulder Stand), to draw the energy up into the upper spine and neck. Finally, practice *Sirshasana* (the Headstand), to bring the energy all the way up into the brain and to the point between the eyebrows.

Daily practice of the inverted poses reduces varicose veins, hemorrhoids, unnatural sex hunger, a sagging abdomen, and other disturbances of the lower body. It flushes and stimulates the brain and the organs above the heart. It refreshes the skin of the face, giving it a youthful appearance. The inverted poses, especially the Headstand, improve one's powers of memory and concentration and increase one's general awareness.

There are yogis who practice the Headstand three hours a day. It has been said that if one practices it three hours daily for six months, the benefits incurred will be permanent. It is not wise, however, for the beginner to remain in the Headstand longer than one or two minutes. Even more advanced yogis should confine their practice to ten minutes.

Though the inverted poses have certain general points in common, each also has its own specific benefits. It is best, therefore, that they be practiced in the sequence given. For a person who cannot practice the more advanced poses, however, even the Simple Inverted Pose (*Viparita Karani*) can bestow many of the benefits of all the inverted poses.

Cautions: These poses should not be practiced by persons with weak hearts, diabetes, chronic constipation, high blood pressure (over 150 mm. in young persons, or over 175 mm. in older persons), or with diseases of the eyes, ears, or sinus. Nor should the inverted poses be practiced when the bloodstream is infected, or impure (for example, as a result of long confinement in a closed room).

A final caution: Don't practice these poses immediately after strenuous physical exercises.

Sarvangasana

(The Shoulder Stand)

"God's peace now floods my being."

Sarvangasana is begun from *Savasana.* Slowly raise the legs until they are vertical. Then raise the hips—again, slowly—until the trunk and legs are vertical, their weight resting as much as possible on the shoulders and on the back of the neck, not on the elbows. Place your hands on your back for support, rest your weight against them as little as possible. The chin should be pressed firmly into the throat—so much so that you could not speak if you tried to.

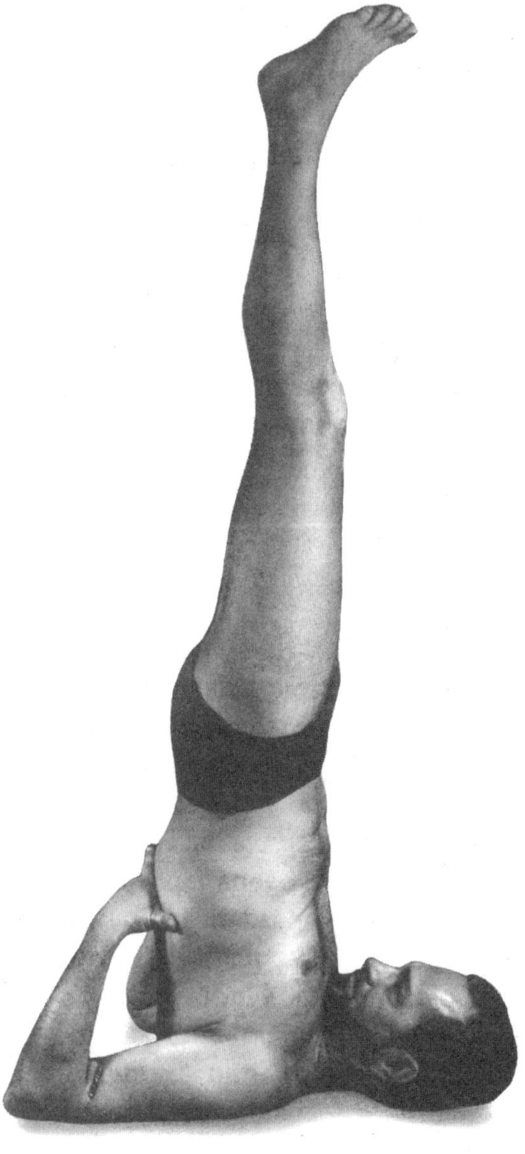

Relax in this pose as much as possible.

Remain in this pose 30 seconds to start with. Increase the time gradually (but never beyond the point of comfort) to several minutes.

Certain writers have claimed that from *Sarvangasana* one should descend into *Sethu Bandhasana* (the Bridge Pose) by lowering the legs slowly to the floor, keeping the hips up so as to form a bow, like a Japanese bridge. (Beginners may find it easier to bring one leg down at a time, instead of both together.) The purpose of practicing the Bridge Pose after *Sarvangasana* is to bend the region of the pelvis in an opposite direction from that in which it is bent

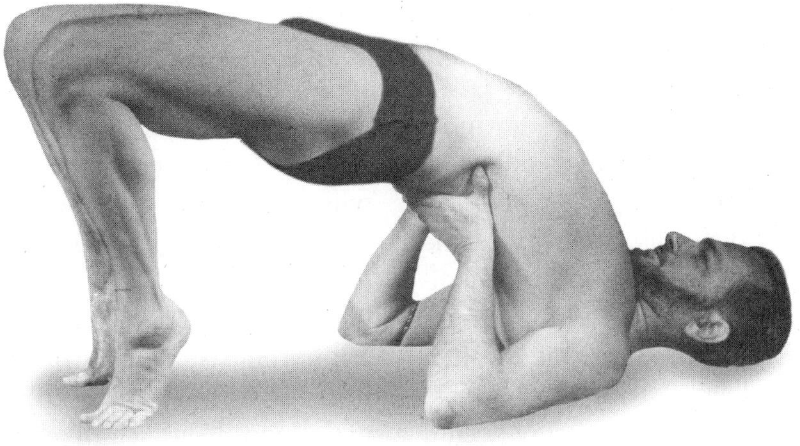

Sethu Bandhasana

(The Bridge Pose)

"I offer every thought as a bridge to divine grace."

in *Sarvangasana.* In fact, however, the real bend in *Sarvangasana* is not in the pelvic region but in the throat. If need is felt for bending the neck backwards, one may find enough of a backward bend in *Sirshasana* (the Headstand), which follows. Otherwise, one may practice *Chakrasana* (the Circle Pose), *Bhujangasana* (the Cobra Pose), or *Matsyasana* (the Fish Pose).

Follow *Sarvangasana* with a rest of at least equal duration in *Savasana* (the Corpse Pose).

Benefits: This Whole Body Pose has been so called mainly because of the gentle pressure exerted by the chin upon the thyroid gland, which regulates the body's metabolism. An additional benefit of this posture is the relaxing effect it has on the neck. *Sarvangasana* helps to relieve nervous tension and "tension headaches." The stretch in the back of the neck also stimulates the medulla oblongata. Because energy is distributed from this neural center to the whole body, stimulation of this center is another reason for the name "the Whole Body Pose."

A final benefit of *Sarvangasana* is the stimulation that it gives to the cervical center at the base of the neck. When this center is harmoniously activated, it radiates deep calmness throughout the body. Concentrate on this center while practicing the pose, and affirm mentally: *"God's peace now floods my being."*

Sirshasana

(The Headstand)

"I am He! I am He! Blissful Spirit, I am He!"

The Headstand is one of the most important, but, alas for many people, one of the most difficult, poses to practice. Because of its difficulty, many students make the mistake of trying to kick themselves up into it, as if it were an exercise in gymnastics—a procedure that, as often as not, lands them flat on their backs! Unless one assumes this pose slowly, and with complete control, he may injure his neck. It is more important in this pose than in most to "make haste slowly."

A compromise with perfection may be necessary to start with. You may use the help of a wall, or better still, of a corner of your exercise room. This prop will give you the confidence gradually to stand on your own. You may also, while learning the pose, make use of the "tripod" position that is common to Western gymnasts, putting the hands on the floor in such a way as to form a tripod with your head. Until you can assume *Sirshasana* properly, however, you will not be able to relax while standing on your head; thus you will miss the fullest benefits of this position.

Sirshasana, Phase 1

(The Headstand)

To assume *Sirshasana:*

1. Kneel on the floor. Interlace the fingers, and place the hands and elbows firmly on the floor, forming a right angle. (It is important not to spread the elbows too far apart; their support is essential for lifting you into the position.)

Sirshasana, Phase 2

(The Headstand)

2. Rest the forehead on the ground at the hairline, placing the back of your head between your hands. Then lift the knees from the floor.

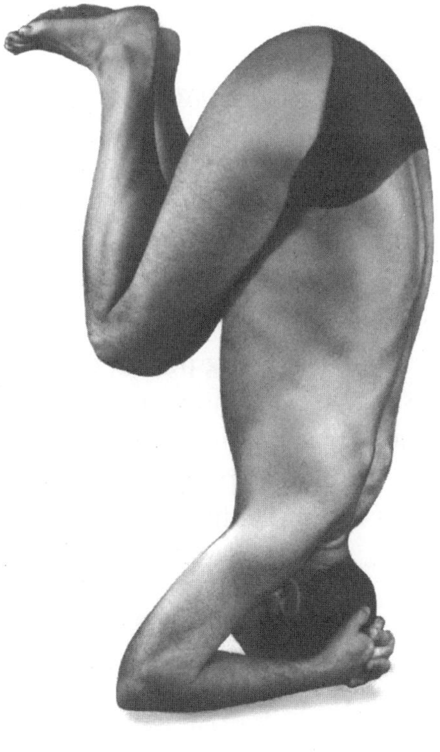

Sirshasana, Phase 3

(The Headstand)

3. Push upward with the legs, walking the feet slowly forward until the trunk reaches a vertical position, preferably with the back arched slightly backward.

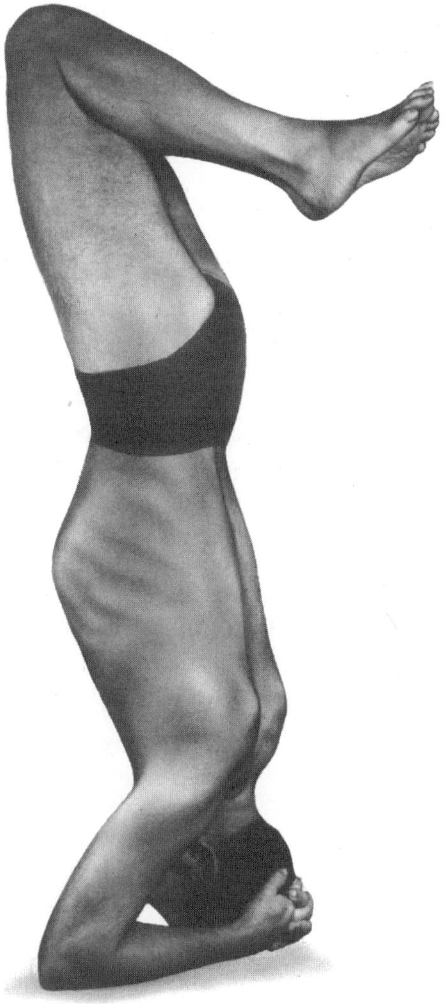

Sirshasana, Phase 4

(The Headstand)

4. You should now be able, with the help of your elbows, simply to lift your body off the ground. Keep the knees folded against the abdomen, with the feet up to the buttocks. When you are balanced comfortably in this position, proceed to the next step.

5. Raise the knees, keeping the legs bent, until your thighs form a straight line with the trunk. Thrust the hips forward to be in line with the thighs and trunk; otherwise you may fall over backward.

6. Finally, straighten your legs.

Once the body can be held perfectly vertical you will find it easy to relax in this position. Concentrate on the pressure of your weight on the forehead. Having brought the energy up the spine, now concentrate it at the point between the eyebrows and at the frontal lobe of the brain.

Affirm mentally: *"I am He! I am He! Blissful Spirit, I am He!"*

After a minute or longer, return very slowly, in reverse order, to a kneeling position. Then stretch out in *Savasana,* the Corpse Pose, and go into deep relaxation.

The duration of the pose should be one minute to start with. It may be increased gradually to several minutes.

In addition to the cautions sounded earlier for inverted poses in general, students will be well advised not to practice *Sirshasana* if they are too heavy, or if their necks are weak.

Variations of *Sirshasana* are often encountered. The most popular of these is *Padmasirshasana,* in which one assumes the Lotus Pose after getting into the Headstand. Some yogis also teach their students to stretch their legs outward, forward, backward, and into a variety of other positions, because in the Headstand one finds it easier to stretch his lower limbs. These variations have more gymnastic than yogic value, however. I do not particularly recommend them.

Benefits: Sirshasana helps the yogi center the spinal energy in the frontal lobe of the brain. Physiologists tell us that this is the most advanced part of the brain. It is this region from which we derive, or in which are centered, the higher aspects of our nature—our conscience, our reasoning power, our ideals. Yogis say that concentration on this area (especially at the point between the eyebrows) develops spiritual insight and conduces to final enlightenment.

Sirshasana, Phase 4

(The Headstand)

***"I am He! I am He!
Blissful Spirit, I am He!"***

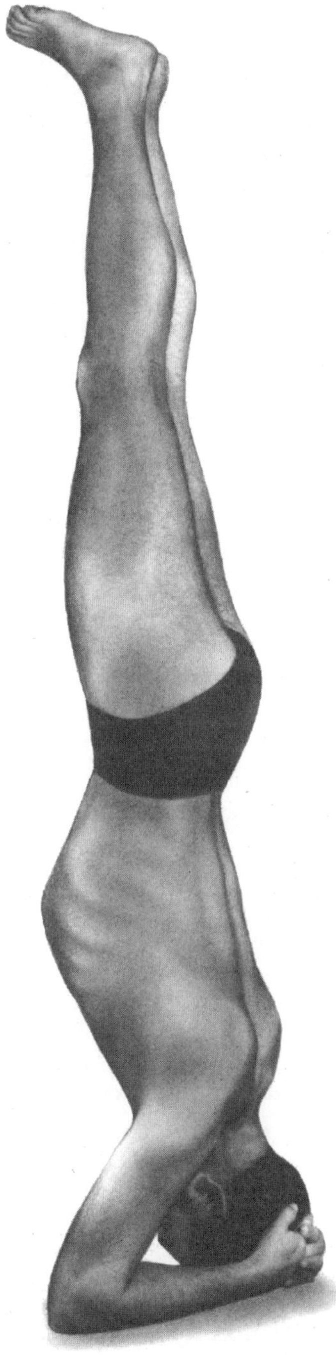

III. BREATHING

You have no doubt been taught since childhood the importance of breathing through the nose. The nose filters dust out of the breath. It also warms the breath, thereby protecting the sensitive membranes of the throat.

There is a further reason, not commonly considered, for nose breathing. The breath, as it comes up through the nasal passages, has a cooling effect upon the brain, refreshing it. "Keep cool," is an expression often heard when one wants to advise someone to remain calm. A cool nervous system, as we have said before, is in a state of calmness and harmony. Heat is a sign of impurities, irritation, or imbalance in the flow of energy in the body and in the brain.

Anger, for example, involving as it does a sudden and inharmonious increase of energy, has a heating effect upon the brain. Under the effect of anger, and of other "heating" emotions, it is difficult to think clearly.

It is important for the brain to "keep cool" if it is to function clearly and vigorously. Normally speaking, as I have said before, people who breathe habitually through the mouth tend to be somewhat dull-minded. Deep breathing through the nose, especially if it is done with a conscious effort to feel the coolness of the breath extending up into the brain, can actually stimulate the intelligence.

Most of the yoga breathing exercises are for this reason done through the nose. Certain exercises, however, involve inhalation through the mouth, though some even of these have as their ultimate aim the same as that of nasal inhalation, namely, the cooling of the brain and nervous system. *Sitali Pranayama* is one such breathing exercise.

To practice it, you must be able to

curl your tongue into the form of a tube. Some books teach one to stick the tongue far out in this exercise, but actually the tongue should be placed at the lips, not protruding beyond them. Inhale through the tube of your tongue, and concentrate on the coolness that you feel at the back of the throat. Exhale through the nose, and feel this coolness spreading out into your nervous system, and particularly up into the brain.

The rhythm of this breathing should be to a ratio of 1-4-2.

Do not practice this exercise more than 6 times at a stretch. Don't do it when the weather is very hot or very cold, nor on a full stomach, nor when unwell, tired, or excited. The inhalation should be gentle, not forced, so that most of the coolness is felt at the tip of the tongue, and the coolness at the back of the throat is caused not so much by the gush of air into the throat as by the extension of feeling from the tip of the tongue.

Sitali Pranayama is said to be a good exercise to practice for cooling the body in warm weather. But remember, the mind plays the principal role in this technique, as in most others. Unless you use the imagination to feel the coolness of the breath extending soothingly through the nervous system, the automatic benefits of the technique will be insignificant. You may understand the power of your mind to influence the body's temperature from the following true story:

Paramhansa Yogananda one day was traveling in a train. It was summertime, and the temperature was well into the hundreds. This was before the days of universal air conditioning, and everyone was suffering from the heat. Yoganandaji, too, was perspiring. He said: "Let me show you what influence the mind can have on the body. I will meditate on the thought of icebergs."

Five minutes later he held his arm out for people to feel. It was quite cool.

IV. ROUTINE

Do the inverted poses at the end of your posture practice, just before deep relaxation, and in the following order: *Viparita Karani* (the Simple Inverted Pose); *Sarvangasana* (the Shoulder Stand or Whole Body Pose); *Sirshasana* (the Headstand). If you cannot do all of these, do what you can. To include them, it may be necessary to omit some of the earlier exercises from your routine so as not to take too long a time to do the postures. Poses that might be omitted in such a case would include:

Trikonasana (the Triangle Pose); *Utkatasana* (the Chair Pose); *Padahastasana* (the Jackknife Pose), followed by the Backward Bend; the second version of *Supta-Vajrasana,* taught in Step Nine; *Ardha-Dhanurasana* (the Half Bow Pose); *Salabhasana,* and *Ardha-Salabhasana* (the Full and Half Locust Poses); *Ardha-Mayurasana* (the Half Peacock Pose); *Chakrasana* (the Circle Pose), *Parvatasana* (the Mountain Pose); *Matsyasana* (the Fish Pose); *Yoga Mudra; Akarshana-Dhanurasana* (the Pulling-the-Bow Pose); *Garudasana* (the Twisted Pose); *Pavanamuktasana* (the Wind-Freeing Pose); *Simhasana* (the Lion Pose); the "V" or Balance Pose; and *Karnapirasana* (the Ear-Closing Pose). Do as many of these as you wish, in the order given previously, and omit as many as you wish.

Let me point out again that it is better to do a few poses slowly and well than many of them hurriedly.

V. HEALING

Headaches

Certain yoga postures are beneficial for certain kinds of headaches. The sinuses, for example, which are often a cause of headaches, may be greatly benefited by *Sirshasana,* the Headstand.

Headaches caused by impurities in the blood may be overcome by deep yoga breathing, feeling the air coming up close to the brain, cooling it. *Sitali Pranayama,* taught in this lesson, may also prove helpful in such cases.

Many headaches are due to pressure on the nerves in the neck. A chiropractic adjustment may sometimes be indicated, but a variety of yoga postures may serve the purpose as well. Specifically recommended would be: *Halasana* (the Plow Pose); *Sarvangasana* (the Shoulder Stand); *Bhujangasana* (the Cobra Pose); *Chakrasana* (the Circle Pose); *Matsyasana* (the Fish Pose); *Supta-Vajrasana* (the Supine Firm Pose); and the first position of *Sasamgasana* (the Hare Pose).

It may help you to stimulate energy in the brain by rapping the skull all over with the knuckles, drawing energy mentally from the medulla oblongata. You may also rub the scalp briskly, stirring up energy in the cells while affirming, *"Awake, my sleeping children, wake!"*

Yogis say that long hair draws more energy to the brain. They describe the body as an inverted tree of which the spine is the trunk, the nervous system the branches, and the hair the roots. This is why many yogis let their hair grow long. When I was in India, I allowed my hair to grow until finally it reached halfway down my back. I discovered with long hair that I was subject to fewer headaches than I had been before.

There are pressure points on the skull that can be felt, subjectively, on the sides of the head, in the forehead, and at the back of the skull. On the sides, these points are located about an inch above the ears. In the forehead, the pressure point is in the middle of the forehead. In the back, it is about an inch above the depression at the base of the skull. If you can help someone to find these pressure points on your head, and to press inward upon them with the heels of his palms (or with his fingers), he may help you to overcome certain headaches. He should feel, as he presses, that he is forcing the pain up through the top of the head and out of your body.

Sometimes, in meditation, the practicing yogi feels an uncomfortable pressure in the brain. It may be only at the point between the eyebrows, or it may extend through the whole cerebrum. If at the point between the eyebrows, the pressure is probably due to a tendency to "think" with the body. You will notice how some people frown when they concentrate. Some people, similarly, tend to strain physically in meditation, whether by actually frowning, or merely by pushing the energy with a certain mental tension toward the point between the eyebrows. Many headaches are in fact caused by the tension resulting from this tendency to "think" with the body. They can be overcome by a deliberate effort to relax mentally. Thought is much clearer in a relaxed than in a strained state of mind. Instead of driving the energy forcibly to the point between the eyebrows in meditation, simply feel that all your thoughts and perceptions originate there, or refer them repeatedly to that point. *Absorption, not strain, must be the keynote of all meditative effort.* Yet it must be added that a feeling of pressure at the point between the eyebrows is not necessarily always bad. Sometimes it is simply a result of focusing one's energy at that point, without tension, and may even help to concentrate there more deeply.

Sometimes the feeling of pressure can extend through the entire brain. In such cases, strain may not be the only cause. Too much reading, intellectual work, or even meditation without proper physical exercise may sometimes be a cause. Excessive sex dissipation, or too many thoughts in this direction, are also a common cause. Remedies include some of the practices that I have outlined above, notably deep, slow breathing. An excellent breathing exercise for this particular difficulty is to stand out of doors, if possible facing the wind. Practice double breathing: Inhale short and long through the nose, then exhale short and long through the mouth and nose. As you inhale, bring the hands in to the chest; as you exhale, extend the arms out in front to their full length, palms downward. Rest between the breaths as long as it is comfortable to do so, concentrating your mind and your gaze at the point between the eyebrows. Repeat this exercise several times.

Almond oil is an excellent remedy for this general pressure in the brain.

The oil may be rubbed into the scalp. If the condition is serious, wash the hair every night and rub almond oil into the scalp. (You may need to protect your pillow with a towel.) Almonds are good for the entire nervous system. They may be eaten whole, or ground up in a blender with a little lime juice, honey, and water.

If the pressure is too strong, meditate less for some days, and do not meditate late at night. Wear a hat in the sun, and try, if possible, to avoid deep thinking. Avoid reading and problem solving. Simply divert the mind until the pressure diminishes. Physical exercise out-of-doors will be invaluable at such times, especially if you can get down to the seashore or up into the mountains. Indeed, it is astonishing how clear the brain of the city dweller may become when he gets off to the open countryside even for half a day.

Another practice may prove helpful in case of pressure in the brain: Sit in *Vajrasana.* Clench the fists, and put them in the stomach at about the level of the navel. Bend forward in *Sasamgasana,* resting your head on the floor, and remain in this position for at least a minute.

Headaches are often caused by alimentary disturbances such as constipation. The stomach should be kept clear and functioning well for the sake, not only of the stomach, but of the head and of the whole body.

VI. DIET

Fruit, as we said in Step Ten, is the most *sattwic,* or spiritual, of all foods. Compared to subtler forms of energy, however, even fruit is gross. Advanced yogis and mystics of various religions have been known to go for long periods of time without physical food. It is not that they went without sustenance, but only that they knew how to draw energy from the atmosphere, from the sun's rays, and from the *prana,* or cosmic energy, in the surrounding universe.

"The greater the will, the greater the flow of energy," the principle so often emphasized by my great guru, may be applied here also. One can draw several times as much energy from the sun's rays, for example, if one concentrates on that energy as he feels the warmth of the sunlight on his body. A friend of mine, an elderly disciple of my guru, and a vegetarian, was told by his doctor that he was so anemic that if he did not go back to a meat diet he would certainly die. This person's brother, a doctor also, even more urgently insisted on this renunciation by my brother disciple of his strict vegetarianism.

This disciple had, however, a determined character. Instead of eating meat, he sat every day by the window, letting the sunlight fall upon his body. Using his hands to emphasize his awareness of the solar energy, he would stroke his arms very slowly, commanding them to absorb all the energy they could. Within a few months, he was completely cured. The doctors, of course, attributed his remarkable comeback to his obedience to their instructions! My friend said nothing to them on the subject of his actual treatment.

Air, too, is full of *prana,* or energy. If you breathe in very slowly and deliberately, concentrating upon the energy in the air as it comes into your body, and filling your body from the toes up to the head with this energy, you will find that you can develop tremendous vitality simply by breathing.

Kechari Mudra, "the tongue-swallowing" technique that I taught in Step Five, creates a cycle of energy in the head that generates enough magnetism to draw great amounts of energy from the universe around you. This energy is actually experienced in the mouth as a slightly sweet, and very pleasant, taste that has been described (accurately, in my experience) as resembling a mixture of *ghee* (clarified butter) and honey. This is what is known in various mystical writings as "the nectar of the gods." A whole *Veda,* the *Sama Veda,* has been named after this spiritual nectar, or *sama.*

The important thing is to realize that the energy and vibrations that one draws from Nature depend chiefly upon one's readiness to receive them, and upon one's *will* to receive them.

This principle, as I shall discuss in the next lesson, should be applied also to the consciousness with which one eats his food.

RECIPES

Bircher Muesli

This recipe, well-known to health food enthusiasts in America, was originated by a famous Swiss physician, Dr. Bircher-Benner. I use it frequently for breakfast. It is a full meal in itself.

1 banana
2 or 3 small apples, or 1 big one
1 tablespoon walnuts or hazelnuts or almonds (ground or chopped)
1 tablespoon oats—soaked beforehand for 12 hours in 3 tablespoons water
1 tablespoon condensed milk
juice of ½ lemon
handful raisins or currants

Mix the condensed milk and lemon juice with oats. Grate apples quickly (using the whole fruit), adding to oat mixture. In order to prevent apples from turning brown, stir them immediately; always prepare them just before serving. Mash 1 banana; whip with fork, and add. Sprinkle nuts and a few raisins or currants at the last minute.

Dried fruit may be used if fresh fruit is unavailable. In this case, first wash the fruit in hot water, then soak it in cold water for 24 hours, thereafter reducing it to a pulp as much as possible with a fork. Two to three ounces of this soaked dried fruit is the portion for one person. Serve with milk and honey.

Nut Patties

Blend ½ cup each ground almonds and ground raw peanuts with 2 tablespoons rice flour. Add a well-beaten egg, chopped parsley, and seasoning to taste. Make into patties and bake in an oven, or fry in hot oil.

VII. MEDITATION

To some people, meditation is merely a state of mental abstraction. To others, it is a sort of intellectual exercise in which one endeavors to "figure out" the mysteries of existence. But no amount of meditation can enable one to *create* valid answers to the problems of life. Those answers exist already, on high planes of consciousness. It is for man only to reach up to those planes and to *perceive* their truths. Imagination alone will not take him there.

Armchair travelers may spin all sorts of lurid fancies about the places of their dreams. Practical travelers, however, will generate the energy necessary to visit those places and find out about them in person.

The kind of energy most needed for success in any undertaking is the *active desire* for success. This desire, in terms of spiritual involvement, translates itself in terms of devotion. God is not another wonder of the world—a mere esthetic or intellectual curiosity. God's nature is the fulfillment of all man's deepest aspirations. He is Love. He is Peace. He is Joy. To find God one must awaken in oneself those heart qualities which will draw one into practical attunement with these divine mysteries. Without devotion man cannot take a single step on the path to enlightenment.

As much in yoga as in any other approach to the Infinite, one's meditation must be filled with the sweetness of longing, and of love. It has been said that God has all things—all wisdom, all knowledge, all power—that there is only one thing He lacks: our love. It is in our power to give or withhold this gift from Him.

Some yogis, over-preoccupied with techniques, postures, and *pranayama*s, with subtle energies and psychic centers, forget that without love all such efforts are wasted—like a mountain stream that loses itself in a vast desert. Love is the prime necessity. All one's efforts in yoga should be directed with love, and offered on the altar of devotion.

The egotistical attitude, "*I* can conquer all!" is self-defeating. An attitude of humility and surrender must be the guiding force in every self-effort to advance. As Arjuna said to Lord Krishna: "Guide me; I am thy disciple."

Yoganandaji exclaimed once, "Why *should* God reveal Himself to people? He knows they only want to argue with Him!" In the *Bhagavad Gita,* Lord Krishna says: "To you who are free of the carping spirit, I reveal these truths." An attitude of respectful, loving attention is necessary if one would draw a response from the heart of the Infinite Silence.

Feel in meditation that your heart center (situated in the spine opposite the heart) is like a flower with its petals turned downward. Mentally turn these petals upward so that they point toward the brain. Feel rays of energy flowing up from the heart toward the point between the eyebrows. Awaken love in the heart, and channel all this love upwards, as if to the altar of God, in deep meditation.

This is the end of chanting and *mantra*s, of *pranayama,* of all self-effort, when the heart's love flows upward in silence, with "wistful yearning" (to use my guru's lovely phrase), toward the heart of God.

MEDITATION ON THE GURU

Call to your guru in meditation. If you have no guru, call to Jesus, or Krishna, or Yogananda, or to any of the great masters. At the start of your meditation, ask one of these great souls to help you in your meditative efforts. After your practice of the techniques, ask him to help you go deep in the Spirit, or to give you a clear perception of truth, or a solution to some spiritual problem. Above all, pray to him, "Introduce me to God." Draw from him, by the magnetic power of your devotion, the power to become like him—an awakened child of the Infinite.

Concentrate on the guru's image, especially on his eyes, visualizing him at the Christ center. Call to him there deeply. The Christ center is the "broadcasting station" in the body. If you send your thoughts out strongly from this point to any divinely awakened being, he will receive them, and will respond to your loving call.

The "receiving set" in the body is the heart center, or *anahat chakra,* opposite the heart in the spine. Feel the guru's responsive presence there. When the awareness of his presence comes to you, it will be very distinct. It will also be distinctly different from that of every other guru. The presence of Jesus conveys a feeling of infinite love and compassion; of Yogananda, one of divine love and joy; of Sri Yukteswar, one of deep wisdom. Even love or wisdom, when felt from different masters, will be perceived differently. Yet each ray of an individual master's grace is but his effort to awaken within you a consciousness of *your own* divinity.

Thus, in fact, the blessings of a guru will be received and interpreted differently by each of his disciples. For as the guru acts as a filter for the unimaginably subtler, because undifferentiated, consciousness of Spirit, so also the disciple acts as a filter for the guru's vibrations. In one sense, all true disciples express a certain divine quality in common, because of their attunement with the same guru. (I have often known just from the look in a person's eyes who his guru was. The tone of his voice also has told the story.) In another sense each disciple of one guru, by his attunement, shows his guru in a different light.

If a disciple can become so immersed in the thought of his guru as in some subtle way even to look like him, one might wonder if there was danger, through discipleship, of reducing oneself to a mere spiritual echo of another human being. There is not. In fact, quite the opposite happens. A true guru's influence is magnetic, not hypnotic. He does not *impose* his vibrations on others, but *offers* them—as one would extend a hand to someone floundering in a ditch, only to help him to lift himself up. Disciples that keep the guru constantly in mind—even imagining that they are seeing with his eyes, tasting with his tongue, etc.—quickly find themselves rising out of human bondage to that plane wherein alone the will becomes truly free. If in the process one assumes to some degree the outward personality and appearance of his savior (which of course does imply a sort of imitation, and does not in itself constitute self-discovery), it should be remembered that one's personality is in no way the true Self. It is only a *vehicle* for self-expression, and a *channel* for self-development.

Saints in India, in fact, realizing the superficial nature of the human personality, sometimes make a game of it, treating as a mere plaything that which to most people seems the quintessence of selfhood. I read recently of one such saint who, in personal fun at the typical attitude of materialists, would sometimes demand a rupee before answering people's spiritual questions. He never explained his joke, though I imagine not a few people were put off by it. In effect, he was challenging people to meet him on his own true level, to receive his spiritual vibrations or, if they were not sensitive enough to feel them, to leave him alone. A saint can never be truly understood in the light of his personality, however inspiring that may be, but only by the subtle vibrations of his spirit.

As your inner attunement with your guru deepens, you will find answers coming to your most mundane questions. He may even appear to you in vision, to instruct you as he would do were you with him physically. To the true disciple, indeed, such inner attunement is infinitely more precious than mere outward proximity.

The ultimate goal of discipleship is to expand one's relationship with the guru from personal, divine friendship with him to the infinite, impersonal reaches of divine love. This is the greatest gift that he has to bestow on you.

Through your attunement with the guru, may you approach ever closer to the shores of Divine Bliss.

Bhawa teetam, triguna raheetam,
Sadgurum tuam namami.

(Beyond all thoughts and qualities,
My true guru, I bow to you.)

Hari AUM, *Tat, Sat*

Step Twelve

The Anatomy of Yoga
Part 1

I. PHILOSOPHY

The Anatomy of Yoga, Part 1

The other day a friend of mine was discussing some repair work that was needed on his car. Not a mechanic myself, I got lost somewhere around the third sentence. And I thought to myself, "Here we are, speaking the same language, and discussing an object that is almost as much a part of our daily lives as clothes and food, and yet I don't understand a thing he's talking about!"

How many things there are in this world, even those nearest and most familiar to us, that we know only superficially, or from one facet only. A mother thinks she knows her son; hasn't she been with him since his birth? Yet she will be surprised to see how many changes can take place in him after only one semester away at college. Potentials that she never suspected were simply waiting within him for an opportunity to express themselves.

When Master was a schoolboy, he often meditated in the classroom instead of paying attention to the teacher. One teacher, seeing him in meditation at the back of the room, told the young yogi to come forward and sit right before him. Yoganandaji did as he was told, but then continued his meditation. The teacher had noticed his inattentiveness in the back row, but here, under his very nose, he observed nothing. Master was free to meditate as long as he wished.

Similar is the case with our physical bodies. Familiar with them though we are, we know almost nothing about their inner workings. Their very closeness to us leaves them all but unnoticed by us, as our gaze wanders at a distance to the surrounding world.

Every field of study has its esoteric aspects. The automobile, familiar to us though it is, has given rise to a veritable jungle of expressions, hopelessly obscure to the layman, but quite necessary to anyone desirous of really understanding what makes a car run.

Similarly with the science of yoga. Though rooted in experience and common sense, it contains many subtle aspects that, in the eyes of the layman, make the whole science look like some elaborate system of primitive mythology. But yoga deals with realities that are in every way comparable to the mechanical workings of a car. The facts of man's inner, spiritual world are quite as specific as those of the objective universe. There is nothing vague about the path to God. What strikes the worldly person as vagueness in spiritual writings is so only in the sense that a conversation between two mechanics about cam shafts and distributors will seem vague to a person like me, to whom it seems a miracle that all I need do to start a car motor is propitiate it, by turning a key.

What takes place in the body as the consciousness of man unfolds is as universally true as the use of his physical eyes for vision. This lesson and the next, then, are intended to help you understand something about people's, including your own, spiritual "motor works."

> *"Men travel to gaze upon mountain heights and the waves of the sea, broad-flowing rivers, and the expanse of the ocean and the courses of the stars, and pass by themselves, the crowning wonder."*
>
> —Saint Augustine

What a puny thing seems man! A cut on the arm, a careless slip in the bathtub, and he may die. What mighty efforts he must sometimes expend merely to open the honey jar! And how frantically the slightest turn in the weather sends him running to turn up the heat, or the air conditioner. Amid a universe of wonders he rejoices only that his baldness is less advanced than that of a few of his neighbors. Faced with tragedy in the lives of others, his first, perhaps his only, thought is to be annoyed that his dinner hour must be delayed.

It is very easy to expose human self-importance for what it is: pusillanimity self-betrayed. The literary market today is fairly monopolized by self-styled realists whose sole contribution is to push noble dreams, beauty, and human worth aside scornfully with the slender cane of cynicism. Their pride is a delusion. Theirs is only the first stage of realism.

The true realist sees more deeply. For behold: This same "weakling," man, has leaped across space to the moon. He has probed universal mysteries. He has offered his own life heroically for the sake of others. Weakness and pettiness may hinder the development of his highest potentials, but there are individuals everywhere who have scattered hindrances aside, and who have proved that, potentially at least, greatness is the truest measure of man.

It is *within* that man's greatness lies. Outwardly, he is puny indeed. The greatest hero or genius is a mere bundle of bones, flesh, and skin that must be pampered constantly merely to remain alive. Small, too, his inner dimensions appear from without. But seen from within, how different even this "puny" physical body!

One evening our guru remarked to a few of us: "I see all of you as light. You have no idea how beautiful even your physical bodies are, behind their outward appearances!" The yoga student must learn to dwell more and more on this inner reality. He must visualize himself as light. He must feel himself as energy.

I have already pointed out elsewhere in these lessons that all men understand, if only instinctively, that there exists a relationship between their contrasting mental states and the movement of energy in the spine. Many of the expressions they commonly use ("I feel uplifted," "I feel downcast") betray this understanding. The soul's destiny is to realize its true state as infinite, divine Bliss and Freedom. Like the upward leap of a bird taking wing, soul-aspiration is invariably accompanied by an upward soaring of consciousness, and by a corresponding upward surge of energy in the spine. The opposite movement takes place in the spine when the mental tendency is toward materialism, that most limiting of all states of consciousness into which the soul can fall. Worldliness is invariably accompanied by a downward flow of energy—by vague "sinking feelings" for which no outward explanation can be found.

Man normally seeks those experiences which he associates, consciously or unconsciously, with an upward lift, and shuns those which, by his own expression, depress him. If the path to enlightenment involved nothing more, there would be no need for yoga or for spiritual instruction of any kind; temptation would not be tempting, and the earth would be populated only by civilized human beings, and not by well-dressed, well-fed, and well-housed barbarians. The trouble is that any upward flow of energy that flows also *outward,* away from man's center, involves him in the world's dualities, and leads inevitably to a downward flow again. Such is the law.

There is an old Hindu legend to the effect that when Brahma first created man, he created him wise. The first thing man did, being wise, was to sit in meditation and merge back into the Infinite. It was then that Brahma made what, for us, seems to have been a very poor decision. Yet, obviously, he had to do *something* to keep his creation viable. On his next try he increased the power of his *maya* (delusion) to draw man out of himself. This time, man, caught in the ceaseless ebb and flow of duality, mistook for ecstasy that which could give him merely passing pleasure. In seeking endless repetitions of ephemeral pleasure, he was obliged also—for such is the law of duality—to experience pleasure's opposite pole: pain. Battered ceaselessly back and forth between these contrasting dualities, he forgot God, the sole Reality. It was a sorry trick to play on us, no doubt. But then, most people wouldn't really have it any other way. And I guess that is a way of saying that man, too, is Brahma. Perhaps we all wanted to add the joy of creating to that of simply Being.

Well, anyway, it's just a story.

Yet, story or not, it contains a number of important truths. For duality does form the basis of cosmic creation. It is to their identification with this simple fact that all creatures owe their bondage. For man, at least, this needn't remain so. The objective dualities of nature—heat and cold, light and darkness, positive and negative, etc.—would have no effect on man if he remained neutral to them. Like a shopper who, not content with merely making a necessary purchase, devotes days to exulting over its advantages to him, and brooding over its possible disadvantages, man reacts emotionally to the dualities of objective nature. In so doing, he becomes caught up in them.

Man's likes and dislikes are the key to his involvement in delusion. They take him outside of himself. His upward surge of enthusiasm, when things go well, is no sign of ultimate fulfillment, for it relates to things that do not really affect *him*. He is like a mountaineer who after enormous effort reaches the top of a difficult climb, only to have to turn around and come down again. In the realm of duality, every up is followed, sooner or later, by a down. The two must, and do, cancel each other exactly, for the Truth exists only and forever at the midpoint between opposites. All the striving and the dreaming, the laughter and the tears of countless incarnations add up at last—outwardly, at least—to nothing gained, nothing lost: a neat zero. The happiness of acquisition will be balanced in one way or another by the pain of loss. Fulfillment cannot be found outside oneself any more than one man's success can be a complete triumph for his neighbors. The achievements of a mountaineer become meaningless to him once he realizes that climbing mountains serves no great or lasting purpose—a point he must certainly come to sooner or later, if only with the discovery that man's one true duty is to realize the indwelling Spirit.

The most basic dualism that we need to overcome is inside, not outside, ourselves. It is the sense of our own separateness from Spirit. Man is a house divided. While he can never escape the spiritual nature that is his true essence, yet he fears to surrender his individuality. The satanic power in man is a reality: Lucifer, the fallen angel, rebellious against God's all-consuming Light, hoping to escape the awful summons by fleeing into utter darkness.

Ah, blindness! Sees he not that in

that consumption, so foolishly dreaded, he would *become* the Light?

There are two poles in man, a positive and a negative. The soul in us says, "I can fulfill myself only by uniting myself completely with God." The Lucifer in us replies, "I can fulfill myself only by gratifying my animal needs." The soul says, "I can attain freedom only in absolute consciousness." Lucifer cries, "Ah, no, so great an awareness would be too demanding! I can attain true freedom only in sleep and unconsciousness."

Many modern thinkers proclaim that our true self owes its allegiance to the mud of nescience out of which we have evolved. Thus speaks the Lucifer in man. The other, and the only true, view is that we are the immortal soul. The deepest incentive for progress, on the animal as well as on the human level, is not the mere struggle for survival. It is the soul's longing to retrieve its lost paradise of divine perfection. Man can never find fulfillment by wallowing in the senses in defiance of his higher nature. In this sense, thank God, the dice are loaded: Man *must,* sooner or later, discover his only true nature as a ray of the Infinite Light.

The positive pole of man's nature has its actual physical seat at the top of the brain. The negative pole is seated at the base of the spine. Divine transformation is literally accompanied by an upward flow of energy from the negative to the positive pole. When, in rejoicing at anything, we feel a corresponding upward flow of energy, we become at least dimly aware that in this general upward direction lie our freedom and awakening. But alas, we see not that when this upward flow is also a flow *outward,* it takes us away from our true Self and into the world of endless diversity and change. Worldly satisfactions are the perennial rainbow of promise, at the end of which one finds, never the hoped-for pot of gold, but always that zero. The further away one draws from his own center, and the more materialistic and sensual in consequence a person becomes, the more he dances up and down like a yo-yo between laughter and despair. The straight and narrow upward path to God, which can be found only at man's center, has been missed; his focus on the true goal has become blurred.

As there is an actual, central channel, the deep spine, through which an upward flow of energy accompanies the process of divine awakening, so also there is an actual spinal "by-pass" through which the energy, and with it the consciousness, become tricked into accepting a mere outward semblance of true, upward transformation. On either side of the spine there exist two nerve channels: *iḍa,* which begins and ends on the left side, and *pingala,* which begins and ends on the right. (On the way up and down they intertwine with the spinal *chakras*.)

The negative pole at the base of the spine is the result of the soul's own personal, inward tug-of-war with God: its assumption of a separative consciousness with respect to Him. The movement of energy in the *iḍa* and *pingala* nerve channels represents the soul's further involvement in the *outward* dualities: its (or rather, at this stage, the ego's) deluded preference for an infinite number of limited relationships over one solitary, but infinite, relationship with God.

The energy travels upward through the *iḍa naḍi,* or nerve channel. This upward movement, taking place as it does outside the deeper channels of self-unfoldment in the spine, signifies an affirmation of temporal, not of eternal—of external, not internal—values. With this upward flow, the breath is automatically drawn into the lungs. As a result, the mind is drawn outward to the world of the senses. (Notice how instinctively you associate inhalation, as well as an upward surge of energy and consciousness, with life-affirming attitudes.)

The energy travels downwards through the *pingala naḍi.* Its movement is related to a negation of external, rather than of internal, conditions. This downward movement is accompanied by physical exhalation, which is why, when you feel negatively inclined toward things, you exhale more heavily than normally.

As I said earlier, it is not the world itself, but our reactions to it that involve us in delusion. Liking some aspects of it, and disliking others, we become enmeshed in its dualities. The upward surge of affirmation in the *iḍa* must in time be followed by a downward wave of rejection in the *pingala.* The rhythmic sequence may be irregular: One's likes, after all, follow no smooth, steady rhythm, but crowd eagerly to express themselves, and struggle to maintain their ascendancy. ("The thwarting cross-currents of ego," Master called them.) As a result, their contrasting dislikes may be long deferred. Yet they will certainly come in time.

The yogi, realizing that his dualistic involvements spring only from his own reactions to the world around him, and observing further that these reactions are always accompanied by upward or downward movements of energy in the spine, concentrates not only on improving his mental reactions, *but also on controlling and neutralizing those inner movements of energy.* In this esoteric technique lies an amazingly useful key. For specific likes and dislikes are so numerous and varied that it is almost impossible to root them all out and correct them. But they do have one thing in common: their link to the energy-flow in the spine. If this energy-flow can be brought under control, specific likes and dislikes will be more easily tamed also.

To demonstrate the truth of what I've just said, try a simple experiment.

The next time you feel moody or depressed, try first to *think* your way out of your mood. You'll find that that isn't so easy! Next, try sitting upright and inhaling several times, vigorously and deeply. If that doesn't work, try raising your hands high above your head, looking upward, and inhale several times more. The combination of deep inhalation with a thought of upward motion should at least make you feel better. If you practice this simple exercise with enough will power, your gloom will almost certainly vanish. And it will do so without your addressing yourself at all to the particular thoughts that made you gloomy in the first place!

The yogi sees in the upward and downward flow of energy (the *pran* and *apan* currents, as they are called) in the *iḍa* and *pingala* one of the most potent of all methods for the attainment of soul freedom. For by controlling this flow he much more easily masters his likes and dislikes, and turns his consciousness inward to its true center.

The reactive process itself is a function of the *chitta,* or feeling, the psychic center for which is opposite the heart in the spine. It is through this dorsal plexus, so-called, that energy flows out to the lungs. The medulla oblongata (which, as I mentioned in earlier lessons, is the seat of the ego) is responsible for the *regulation* of the breath. Impulses from the medulla flow to the lungs through the dorsal plexus. On a spiritual level, similarly, impulses from the ego affect the breath through the likes and dislikes of the heart. This outward flow of energy to the breath, and through the breath to the world, draws man out of himself.

The farther one travels from any source of power, the weaker its influence becomes. The consciousness of people who seek their center only outside themselves—in other people, or in mere things—grows dull to the point of chronic apathy. No longer even conscious of the true source of their strength within themselves, and therefore incapable of replenishing their strength, worldly people look farther and farther afield for happiness and dominion, only to spend their forces at last in frustration and disillusionment.

It might seem that the cure for excessive worldly involvement would be to try to *arrest* the reactive upward and downward flow of energy in the *iḍa* and *pingala* nerve channels. But first the sheep have to be called back into the fold. Instead, therefore, the yogi concentrates on *increasing* the strength of this spinal energy-flow. His aim is to create a magnetic field so strong as automatically to draw the outward-flowing energy back to its inner source. When this aim has been accomplished, and the breath thereby becomes calm, the entire reactive process becomes traced back to a point of sheer movement in the spine. Focused no longer on any outward consequences of that movement, the yogi finds it a natural next step to renounce altogether the dualism suggested by that movement. He can now focus all his energies on the one true, divinely appointed task: the conquest of his own pristine urge for separation from God.

The real spiritual work begins only when the energy has been withdrawn into the deep spine. The task is not merely to overcome our attachments to the world. Even more deeply, it is to overcome our age-old, delusion-inspired resistance to total surrender to God.

Fortunately, this task is not so endless as it may seem. By deep devotion to God, the whole process can be very much shortened. "Seek ye first the kingdom of God . . . and all these things shall be added unto you." (Matthew 6:33) Best of all is a combination of devotion with a right knowledge of the path.

The *iḍa* and *pingala* branch out from the medulla oblongata, to meet again at the base of the spine. (They also pass to the nostrils and to the *ajna chakra,* or Christ center, but that is secondary to our present consideration.) At the base of the spine they meet the central spinal channel, the *sushumna,* or deep spine. If the downward flow of energy in the *pingala* can be caught at this point and directed into the *sushumna,* interrupting the normal process that would send it rising again in the *iḍa,* the soul can at last truly begin its ascent toward the Spirit.

Through the medulla oblongata energy enters the body from the cosmic source. Positively directed, this energy flows into the brain and to the point between the eyebrows. Negatively directed (away from the consciousness of divine union), it flows downward to the base of the spine. *Outwardly* directed, as we have already seen, it flows into the *iḍa* and *pingala,* there to assume the secondary positive-negative flux of superficial likes and dislikes. The ebb and flow of energy in the *iḍa* and *pingala* is really only an echo of the much more powerful contest between the positive and negative pulls in the brain and at the base of the spine. Whatever energy flows in the superficial spine, even by deep yoga practice, is as nothing compared to the *immense* reservoir of energy waiting to be tapped at the base of the spine.

This energy is spoken of in the yoga teachings as *Kundalini,* "the coiled," named also the Serpent Power. *Kundalini* represents the entrenched vitality of our mortal delusion. But *Kundalini* is also man's greatest single key to enlightenment. Only by arousing this force from its ancient resistance to divine truth can the soul hope to reunite itself with the Spirit.

Divine enlightenment is the soul's awakening from cosmic delusion. *Kundalini,* by contrast, represents the soul's blind pull toward darkness and unknowing. *Kundalini* is therefore said to be asleep. This negative power is both the dragon of ancient legend and the vast treasure about which it was said to sleep, coiled protectively. The fire it breathes is the emblem of its great energy. The dragon deals certain death to all who would steal its treasure for selfish gain—who think, in other words, to squander the soul's power for worldly ends—for it is from man's very ego-centeredness that this monster derives all its power. The dragon can be slain only when mortal selfishness is overcome. Then it is that the gems of soul-joy and wisdom are retrieved in the secret lair of divine communion.

The dragon's occasional, fitful stirrings were said in the old tales to send tremors throughout the entire mountain. *Kundalini* likewise, though asleep, yet stirs enough to affect the body and mind of man in countless vital ways. Every time a man thinks selfish, unkind, or otherwise soul-darkening thoughts, subtle waves of energy flow downward to the base of the spine stirring *Kundalini* to coil herself more deeply, more ego-protectively, in darkness. Such is her magnetic power, that at such times, man's whole being is drawn down with her just a little bit further into the deep sleep of delusion. And every time a man thinks kind, generous, or otherwise soul-awakening thoughts, fine rays from *Kundalini*'s storehouse of energy shoot upward, bestowing, to however slight a degree, gifts of life, health, and happiness on the entire system. For the dragon has shifted in its sleep, uncoiling slightly to admit a fleeting glimpse of its shining treasure.

Kundalini is always referred to in yoga treatises as feminine, for it represents the negative polarity in the body, and the soul's separateness from the one positive principle, *Purusha,* the Supreme Spirit. Saints have even personified *Kundalini* as a goddess. (The gods and goddesses, or *devata*s, in the Indian scriptures are equivalent to the angels of Christian tradition.) But she is man's supreme temptress as well as his salvation. Swami Muktananda, a saint who lived in India, described a vision he once had for several days in a row of the goddess *Kundalini.* She appeared to him at first as a naked woman of extraordinary beauty, seeking to tempt him to indulge in sexual enjoyments. When he had succeeded in resisting her repeated appeals, she appeared to him at last as the ideal woman, modestly clothed, gentle, tender, serene—as that aspect of femininity, in short, which is the inspiration and upliftment of the human race. With the appearance of this second vision, his inner *Kundalini* was awakened at last, and the process of divine enlightenment was begun in earnest.

In the *Holy Bible,* too, we read of Eve, the woman, tempting Adam. First it was she who was tempted; her evil counselor, interestingly, was a serpent. To the student of these lessons, the basic symbolism here must be obvious. Eve represents the feminine principle, or negative polarity in every man. When Eve lived truly as Adam's helpmate, mankind remained in a state of grace, his every thought flowing upwards in joyous divine communion. But the coiled serpent of egoic separativeness had yet to be wholly slain. Lucifer tempted mankind to sink back into delusion. As the Bible puts it, man elected to become "like" God, affirming a separate reality of his own apart from the Lord. Thus he became enmeshed again in the dualities of phenomenal existence.

The specific avenue of humanity's undoing, as Paramhansa Yogananda explains at greater length in *Autobiography of a Yogi* (pp. 177–179), was sexual desire. Man's urge was reawakened to create on his own, egotistically, giving up his seemingly secondary role as a pure instrument of the divine creative energy. In reawakening his latent sexual drive, mankind's ego became strengthened, and the entire reactive process of egoic likes and dislikes was started again. For the ego, struggling to affirm its own worth, entered the ceaseless contest with objective reality.

The sex nerves are the first to be stimulated by the downward flow of *Kundalini,* situated as she is at the base of the spine. The sex drive is therefore the strongest of human instincts, next to that of self-preservation itself. The feminine principle in every human being is his (or her) greatest foe, if it is allowed to pull the consciousness downward, toward sexual desire and away from the true Self. It is also humankind's greatest friend, if it inspires pure, self-*giving* love, in which case it lifts one toward God.

Women, who are the objectification of this feminine principle, should understand that their role in this world is, similarly, a dualistic one. If by their sexual magnetism they seek to draw men egoistically to themselves, they strengthen the grip that duality has on human minds—and on their own minds most of all. They thereby perpetuate the degradation of the human race. But if women see themselves primarily in their higher role as mothers and sisters, and if they seek to draw others, not to themselves, but to lofty ideals and principles, they become the salvation of mankind.

Men, too, should look upon women in their exalted earthly role, honoring, even revering them as living instruments of the Divine Mother of the universe. In this way men can learn from women important attitudes for their own growth. And women can draw from men the strength of purpose to grow themselves. For when God is placed first in people's minds, the age-old battle of the sexes ceases, and men and women truly help one another to grow towards eventual unity in Him.

It is not my point, however, to suggest to serious yoga students that they rush out to find some ideal man or woman with whose help to grow spiritually. If we have to mix with people, it is of course better to mix with them in the right way. But remember, God is the soul's one, *true* Beloved. Only when He is loved first can there be true harmony in human life. That is why I have stressed the egoless nature of true friendship even between the sexes. If you would conquer your own ego, try not to see others, either, as realities separate from God. Seek the Lord first. Be impersonal, even somewhat distant from others. That is the road to freedom. Remember, all that you are seeking can only be found in your own Self.

Most important of all is it for each individual, whether man or woman, to realize that the feminine principle exists as an inner reality *in himself,* waiting to be lifted Godward. *Kundalini* must be awakened and drawn up through the *sushumna,* to be united with her positive pole at the top of the brain.

Kundalini is said to be sleeping *coiled* at the base of the spine. Hence her metaphorical identification with the serpent. I do not know exactly to what extent this coiled energy has been described literally, and to what extent metaphorically. Certainly it is not an actual serpent. Nor, to my knowledge, has any coiled passageway been found in the bone at the base of the spine, though physical counterparts have been found for the other features of our yoga "anatomy." I am inclined to think (but I offer it only as an opinion) that the so-called coils of *Kundalini* refer to her magnetic action. The magnetic field that is created when electricity passes through a wire follows a circular pattern around the wire. Similarly, as *Kundalini* begins her powerful upward surge a circular motion is felt. Very possibly, then, the coiled passage through which *Kundalini* is said to move is only a metaphor for this circular magnetic current.

Whatever the case, as *Kundalini* moves upward she gathers force from tributary streams of energy along the way. At last she becomes a river mighty enough to rule the universe. But that is not, or it should not be, her goal. For if it be she will only fall again, and will have to struggle once again to reach the heights.

Perfect spiritual safety is reached only when *Kundalini* becomes united at last with her positive pole. Only then is the storm of duality finally stilled, and the self, no longer in rebellion against God, merges completely into the Infinite Self, *becoming* the Infinite. This, and this only, is the state of salvation, of final liberation from all the bondage of delusion.

(To be continued)

II. YOGA POSTURES

Advanced Poses

One of the gratifying things about the yoga postures is that some of the easiest poses are among the most beneficial, while the most difficult ones are not always the most beneficial. The following poses, however, are unfortunately as beneficial as they are difficult. They would be excellent to learn if you feel so inclined.

Nauli

(The Stomach Isolation)

Nauli (the Stomach Isolation) is an excellent exercise for the entire stomach region. It helps to promote peristalsis and to exercise all the organs of the abdomen.

Practice *Uddiyana Bandha* (the Stomach Lift) as it has been taught in these lessons. Pressing on the heels of the palms and straightening the back slightly, bring out the *rectus abdomini* muscles (the long muscles that go upward on either side of the navel from the pubic bone to the ribs) by drawing the navel outward away from the spine. There should be a sense of vacuum in the whole abdomen, as in the Stomach Lift. The outward movement of the *rectus abdomini* muscles works against this vacuum. Draw these muscles out and in several times, with the breath held out. Concentrate on awakening energy in the region of the navel.

Now try separating the left *rectus abdominus* muscle from the right by pressing on the left thigh with the heel of the left palm. Alternate the isolation of the left and right sides several times.

Finally, rotate these muscles by making the alternation between them continuous.

There are small little muscles on the sides of the abdomen, the external and internal oblique muscles. These, too, can be isolated with practice.

The stomach poses should always be done on an empty stomach. If any sharp pain is felt in the practice of them, they should be discontinued until the cause of the pain has been ascertained.

Nauli is said to be beneficial for women suffering from menstrual disorders. One negative point may be considered: Certain persons have been known to develop high blood pressure as a result of too much practice of *Nauli*. This would be true only of persons who are already susceptible, and who are no longer young—say, over forty.

An easier version: If you cannot practice *Nauli* correctly, you can achieve some of its benefits by simply pushing the entire stomach out, then drawing it in again, repeating this practice several times during one exhalation.

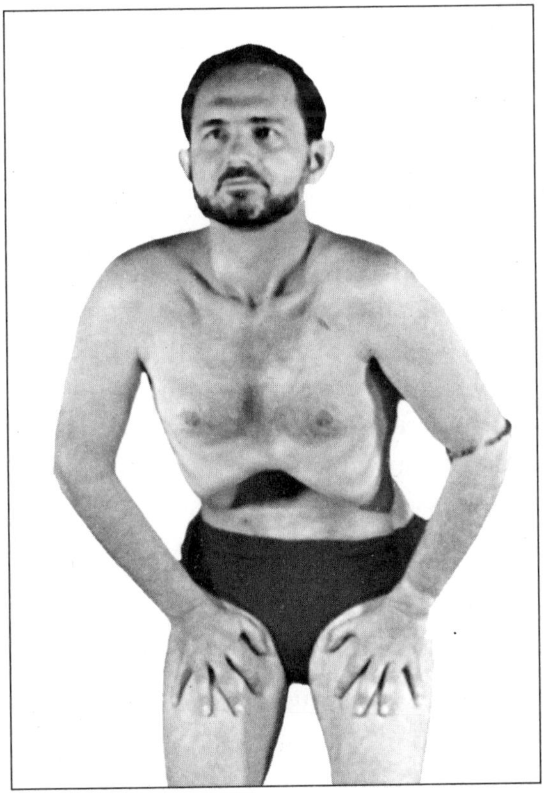

Uddiyana Bandha

(The Stomach Lift)

Mayurasana

(The Peacock Pose)

I have already given *Ardha-Mayurasana* (the Half Peacock Pose, also known as *Hamsasana,* the Swan Pose) in Step Six. The preparation for the full Peacock Pose is the same.

Squat down on your knees and toes, spreading your knees apart. Place the hands between the knees, palms downward, turning them *outward* until the fingers point back toward the feet. Bend the elbows, and press them into the pit of the stomach. (Women may find it necessary to push their breasts inward so that they do not become pressed uncomfortably between the upper arms and the chest.)

Inhale, and gradually extend your feet until your body makes a straight line from the feet to the head. Now come forward, slowly, until you can balance your entire weight on the hands. Lift the legs up, and remain balanced in this position for 5 seconds. Gradually increase this time to 30 seconds.

A variation of this exercise is to get first into the Lotus Pose, and from that position, resting the weight on the knees and hands, gradually lift the knees up until the whole weight of the body rests on the hands.

Benefits: Mayurasana is said to be good for diabetes, and also for piles (hemorrhoids). It is excellent for the appetite and for increasing the digestive power. It is good for the liver and the lungs. And it helps to cure constipation. *Mayurasana,* for those who can practice it, is an excellent exercise indeed.

III. BREATHING

There are numerous breathing exercises in *hatha yoga*. It is by no means necessary, or even desirable, to practice all of them. To do one or two deeply is better than to skip eagerly through a long series of them. Indeed, one may well interfere with his progress by too great a variety of techniques. It is an interesting fact that universal consciousness, which is the goal of all spiritual endeavor, is attained by *restricting* one's consciousness, one's loyalties, and one's practices—by becoming one-pointed, instead of scattering his forces. Cosmic consciousness is attained not by spreading oneself thin over the surface of life, but by going deep at one point. Reaching the heart of reality at that point, he finds the one reality which lies at the heart of all phenomena. Finding all there is to know about even one atom would give one perfect knowledge of all other atoms in existence.

It is up to the individual, however, to choose his own way. Since other breathing exercises than those which I particularly recommend are very much a part of the science of *hatha yoga,* I shall include a few of them in this lesson and the next.

Surya Bedha Pranayama

One such exercise is *Surya Bedha Pranayama*. Sit in any meditative posture. Close the eyes. Then close the left nostril and inhale slowly through the right. Next, close both nostrils, and press the chin firmly against the chest, holding the breath. Mentally chant AUM at the point between the eyebrows.

The breath should be retained as long as it is comfortable. Then exhale slowly through the left nostril, keeping the right nostril closed. Repeat this exercise several times.

Surya Bedha will increase heat in the body, perhaps because the inhalation through the right nostril works against the normal relationship between the flow of energy in the spine and the breath. (Normally, inhalation is associated with the upward flow on the *left* side, which is related to the breath in the left nostril.)

Surya Bedha is said to be good for the lungs and heart, as well as the sinuses. It helps to draw energy into the deep spine, or *sushumna*.

IV. ROUTINE

How much time should a person practice the yoga postures? And how long should he meditate? The question is, of course, a personal one; it depends on the individual's interests and on the time he has available. If his interest is purely physical, his meditation will be a token gesture; most of his time will be devoted to the postures.

Many persons of deep spiritual aspiration, however, imagine that for spiritual progress they should spend so much time doing the postures that little time remains to them for meditation. There is also the tendency to prolong whatever one is doing at the time. Since the postures come first, to prolong them in order to include as many as possible in one's daily practice may well entail cutting down too much on the time remaining for meditation.

For devotees in search of spiritual enlightenment, *at least* half their daily practice should be devoted to meditation. Two-thirds of the time would be a better proportion. Thirty to forty minutes of yoga postures, and another hour for meditation, would make a good proportion if one has that much time at his disposal. If one has more, a full hour of postures would be better. If less, it might be well to practice the postures more, proportionately, early in the day, and less or not at all later in the day—meditating more in the evening than in the morning.

The sincere aspirant should meditate at least an hour and a half a day, if he can find the time to do so. He could do a half an hour in the morning and an hour at night, or vice versa. Any amount of time that is spent in meditation, however, is better than none. Nor should the amount of time that one can spend really be made a measure of one's sincerity. There are persons with very little time to spare for whom deep sincerity is needed to be able to meditate at all. It is not so much in any case the time that one spends as the *intensity* with which one meditates that helps him to progress spiritually.

V. HEALING

The Eyes, Ears, and Teeth

THE EYES

The eyes have often been called "the windows of the soul." We speak almost as much with our eyes as we do with our words. I have always thought it a pity for this reason that people must wear glasses, for they express much less than they might, could they communicate visually.

Everything one does should be a conscious and heart-felt expression of what one *is*. The eyes should express the vibrations of the heart and mind. The energy in the eyes should be developed to its full potential. One exercise for developing this potential is amazingly effective also in curing weak vision. It strengthens the flow of energy through the nerves to the eyes. Indeed, this exercise is primarily a cure for faulty vision. Here is how it is to be practiced:

When the sun is close to the horizon—within half an hour of sunrise or sunset—gaze into it deeply. (At this time its harmful rays are filtered out, and the tremendous healing power may be drawn into the eyes without injury.) Gaze unblinking for one minute to start with, gradually increasing the time over several weeks to a maximum of 9 minutes. By the force of your will, draw the sun's healing rays into your eyes.

Then turn your back to the sun, and blink your eyes fairly rapidly for about one minute. Close the eyes, and cover them first with the right hand, then with the left (so that the left hand covers the right), and gaze into the after-image that you see. The sun's rays should strike on the area of the medulla oblongata. The light that you see in the after-image will be partly due to the energy flowing into the eyes from the medulla oblongata.

The more deeply you concentrate, the more this flow of energy will be strengthened.

Gaze into the after-image as long as it lasts. Then turn your eyes far to the left, up, right, and down. Repeat this rotation three times. Then squeeze the eyes tightly, sending energy to them as you were taught to do in the lesson on energization. Open the eyes, and stare at an object. Repeat this squeezing and staring process three times.

You will be amazed to see how, in a comparatively brief time, your vision improves, and also how much more *alive* your eyes feel.

Yoganandaji said that the sun represents the Fatherhood of God; the moon, the Motherhood. He said that at one period of his life he gazed into the sun at sunset every day for two months, and that he received tremendous inspirations of Wisdom thereby. (It is interesting in this connection to consider how many love songs have been written about the moonlight.) When you gaze into the sun while practicing the eye exercises, try to be sensitively aware of its ability to heal on levels more subtle than merely physical. Brahmins in India, while gazing into the sun at sunrise, mentally recite the *Gayatri Mantra*.

Postures that are good for the eyes include especially *Sirshasana* (the Headstand), and any of the inverted poses; *Simhasana* (the Lion Pose); and *Trikonasana* (the Triangle Pose).

It is also helpful to gaze upward toward the point between the eyebrows—not with the eyes crossed, but rather converged gently as if on the thumb when the hand is extended to a point about 18 inches in front of, and slightly above, the head. This position is extremely beneficial for the eyes if practiced with complete relaxation, not with visual strain.

THE TEETH

Master taught an excellent exercise for the teeth. Take the thumb and forefinger of the right hand, and massage the gums by pressing on either side of the gums above each tooth, and drawing the fingers downward over the tooth itself. As you squeeze with the fingers, feel that you are sending energy through them to the gums. Repeat 6 times over each tooth. The gums and teeth may also be stimulated by alternately clenching and relaxing the teeth, sending energy to them.

THE EARS

The ears may be stimulated similarly with energy, thereby improving the hearing faculty. Listen intently, as if in the ear drum (first in one side, then in the other) to whatever sounds you hear. Send energy to the ear drum.

One practice, said to be a cure for deafness, is to peel three cloves of garlic, and chop them fine. Fry them in 4 tablespoons of *mild* mustard oil (olive oil may do) until they turn brown. Strain the oil through a cloth. After it cools, and at night before going to bed, half fill the affected ear (or ears), sealing the oil in with a piece of cotton, and leave the oil in all night. Repeat twice a week.

Postures that are good for the ears include *Simhasana* (the Lion Pose); *Sirshasana* (the Headstand); *Chakrasana* (the Circle Pose); *Sarvangasana* (the Whole Body Pose, or Shoulder Stand); and *Jivha Bandha* (the Tongue Lock)—to be taught in Step Thirteen.

VI. DIET

Paul Brunton, in his fascinating book, *A Search in Secret India,* mentions a man he met in India who was fasting because, he said, his cook had gone away for a few days, and he would not trust anyone else to cook his food for him. The important consideration, in his mind, was that he knew her character, whereas the character of another person might contain hidden weaknesses, the vibrations of which could affect him through the food.

The great master, Sri Ramakrishna, would not accept food from the hands of worldly persons. Sometimes, if such food was given to him without his prior knowledge, he would feel that his whole body was burning.

Are these merely quaint oriental superstitions? or have they some basis in objective reality? Here in America, much is made of "good home cooking." Mother's cooking epitomizes many people's dreams of happiness. Why? There are millions of mothers in this country; can *all* of their cooking be so good? Habit must, obviously, have something to do with it: The diet on which a person has been raised will exert a natural attraction. But I think more is involved in the very special appeal of Mother's cooking. The love with which she cooks for her family is a vibration. As such, it permeates the food which she prepares. It has been my experience that any food that has been cooked with love is somehow more deeply satisfying than the gourmet dishes served in high-class restaurants.

I remember one such occasion. It was Christmas, and everyone was filled with the Christmas spirit. Joyously, we cooked a banquet for all the monks in the SRF monasteries. Later, I'm afraid I ate much more than my normal capacity. (Everyone was laughing at my "prowess" that day!) But, strange to say, I did not feel heavy or sluggish afterwards. Indeed, I had a wonderful meditation. And I remember awakening the following morning to the sound of inner voices chanting, "O God Beautiful!"

In India, much is made of the vibration with which food is prepared. Cooks are normally *thakurs*; that is to say, they come from the priestly, or Brahmin, cast. Many saints cook for their disciples as a means of blessing them.

I remember, in contrast to this teaching, something I read years ago in the *Reader's Digest.* It was about a woman who baked bread whenever she was angry. The kneading of the dough helped her to work out her frustrations. Her "mad bread," as she called it, was said to be delicious because it was so well kneaded. To spiritually insensitive persons this bread may have tasted good, but I doubt that yogis would have cared for it!

Have you noticed how some food, though tastily prepared, sits heavily in the stomach? Have you noticed how, sometimes, a full meal can leave you feeling physically unsatisfied, because not truly energized?

According to the teachings of yoga, it is important to cook food with an attitude of blessing. If you cook for others, and find yourself one day in a bad mood or in any way upset emotionally, it would be better not to cook at all. (You see: I have given you a good excuse for insisting to your husband that he take you out to dinner!)

The consciousness with which one eats is important, also. In India, many people observe strictly the practice of silence at meals, in order that they may concentrate on their food and draw from it the energy and spiritual vibrations that it contains. When food is ingested with conscious attention to its vibrations, one draws more from it than if he eats absent-mindedly.

The place where one eats is important, also. At the time of eating, one is opening himself to the inflow of vibrations from without. If the vibrations of the room in which he eats are harmonious, they can be helpful, but if not they can affect one more adversely than at other times. Paramhansa Yoganandaji did not like for us to eat in public places, amid the heterogeneous vibrations of worldly people. In India, *sadhaks* (spiritual aspirants) will seldom, if ever, eat in public places.

From what I have said on this subject so far, it will be evident why the scriptures say that food should be offered to God before it is eaten. The *Bhagavad Gita* calls it a sin to eat food that has not been so offered. Bless your food before you eat it. By so doing you will help to transform any negative vibrations that it contains.

RECIPES

Cheese Cake

Graham Cracker Crust:

11 graham crackers—crushed fine
6 tablespoons melted butter
1½ tablespoons granulated sugar

Combine ingredients and pat them into a 9-inch pie pan.

Filling:

3 3-oz. packages Philadelphia cream cheese
1 cup sour cream
½ teaspoon vanilla
½ cup sugar
½ teaspoon grated lemon rind, plus juice
2 eggs

Blend the cream cheese until creamy; add sour cream and blend. Beat eggs slightly; add sugar and vanilla. Add to cream cheese mixture along with lemon juice and rind. Blend, pour into graham cracker crust. Bake in preheated oven at 375°, 20 to 25 minutes. Remove from oven and cool.

Topping:

1 cup sour cream
2 tablespoons granulated sugar
½ teaspoon vanilla (add a little lemon juice)

Combine ingredients, spread on cooled pie filling. Bake in preheated 475° oven for 5 minutes. Chill.

Samosas

(or Singharas, as they are called in Bengal)

Set aside extra time to prepare these delicious pastries.

Filling:

1½ boiling potatoes, medium size
1 tablespoon *ghee* (clarified butter)
½ medium onion, chopped fine
A little golden ginger, grated if fresh
½ teaspoon curry powder
1½ teaspoons coriander seeds
½ teaspoon salt
¼ teaspoon chili powder
1 small tomato, diced
½ cup fresh peas
1½ teaspoons lemon or lime juice

Boil potatoes in their skins until tender; cool. Skin and dice into small cubes. In a large pan, fry the onions in *ghee* until soft, stir in ginger, curry powder, and herbs, and fry briefly. Add salt, chili powder, and tomato. Stir well and fry for a few minutes. Add peas and cook gently for 10 minutes, stirring frequently. Add potatoes and lemon juice and cook until almost dry.

Pastry:

1½ cups flour (not whole wheat)
1½ tablespoon *ghee*
¾ teaspoon salt
9 tablespoons thin yogurt or warm milk

Sift flour into mixing bowl, heat the *ghee* and pour it over the flour; add salt. Stir in yogurt or milk a little at a time until dough can be formed into a ball. Divide into 9 pieces and roll into balls. Roll out each piece into a thin round with a little flour. Cut pastry rounds in half and place a small amount of filling in center, leaving ¼ inch around the edge. Moisten edges with a little milk and fold over, pressing edges together with fingers to seal. The edges may be crimped with a fork for a better seal. Fry *samosa*s in 1–2 inches hot oil. Makes 18 *samosa*s.

*Samosa*s are usually served hot with chutney as a teatime savory. They may be re-heated in an oven if desired.

VII. MEDITATION

Attitude

Because the science of yoga deals so much with the awakening of subtle energies, many yoga students imagine the entire process of spiritual evolution to be a mere mechanism. They think by technique alone to find God.

In so thinking, they of course err greatly. But a technical age like ours predisposes people to commit such an error. Is it not the common belief that everything is a mechanism? Even the mind is approached mechanistically. One well-known psychology professor at a leading university tells his students, "If anyone here thinks he has a soul, I must ask him please to leave it outside the door when he enters this classroom."

Yet mankind has always been somewhat prone to mistake technique for inspiration, forgetting that technique is merely a vehicle for inspiration. Even in religion, what method is usually recommended for the attainment of salvation? No herculean labor of self-transformation, no pure, self-giving devotion, but only that one join the right church, subscribe to the right beliefs, and, preferably, donate the right amounts to the right causes. Mechanisms!

Yoga, which approaches the path to salvation more scientifically, offers at the same time a stronger temptation to confuse method with something infinitely more important on the path: right attitude.

Remember, technique is only a vehicle. What good is a car in the hands of a driver who has no idea where he wants to go? And of what use is it to be a technically skilled driver, if one's driving *attitudes* are anti-social? The fact that yoga practice accelerates one's spiritual progress only *increases* the need for right attitude. Socially responsible attitudes are more important for automobile drivers traveling at high speeds than for bicycle riders. Concentration on yoga techniques alone, without developing right attitudes, can prove dangerous. For spiritual progress can never be forced, any more than one can force the delicate mechanism of a watch. If nothing else, too technical an approach to yoga practice will strengthen the ego to the point where one's true, divine Self becomes almost hopelessly obscured.

In the first chapter of this lesson I discussed *Kundalini*, the tremendous power that lies dormant at the base of the spine. A forceful awakening of this power, especially by violent breathing exercises and by certain physical postures, but without any corresponding effort to develop spiritual attitudes, can be exceedingly dangerous. Remember, the subtle energies of the body with which yoga deals are not mechanisms, essentially, but manifestations of consciousness. If you were to ride a horse as though it were a machine, you might easily get thrown. The enormous power of *Kundalini* can actually destroy the nervous system, if the ruling force in its awakening is not devotional aspiration, but an egotistical presumption that the heights of spirituality can be scaled by power alone.

Do not try to awaken *Kundalini* only by techniques. Vitally important to its awakening is a spiritualized consciousness. As I mentioned in the first part of this lesson, every time you express pure love, or think high thoughts, or associate attentively with spiritual people, *Kundalini* is already inspired to send advance emissaries of light upward to the brain. And every time you think selfish, sensual, or otherwise darkening thoughts, or delight in worldly company, *Kundalini* moves downward, drawing light from the brain and leaving the mind a little bit darker than it was before.

Before *Kundalini* can be fully and properly awakened, it is necessary to gain a measure of control over more superficial energies in the body, particularly those flowing in the *iḍa* and *pingala* nerve channels outside the main channel of the deep spine (the *sushumna*). By working with these energies, one learns something of the attitudes necessary for the proper awakening of *Kundalini*. Especially, when working with this energy, do not treat it as though it were an inanimate object to be acted *upon*. It has its own consciousness. Invite its cooperation, rather, as though it were a friend. Approach it with joy, with calm, magnetic enthusiasm.

Magnetic is a key word in the right use of the will for awakening energy in the body. Yet to be magnetic there must be a flow of energy in the first place. If it takes energy to produce the magnetism one needs to acquire energy, one may seem to be facing certain defeat. For all progress then is a circle!

Yet a circle describes quite simply the nature of the spiritual path. Progress of any kind, in fact, never takes a straight line. When it seems to do so it is because we can see only such a small segment of it at a time—like our flat-seeming view of this round earth. The circle—in this case, magnetism-will-energy-magnetism—generates its power by revolving, so to speak, like a dynamo. Progress in a straight line, by comparison, would be rather like a shopping spree: gaining, perhaps, in acquisitions, but not in power. That is why Jesus said: "He that hath, to him shall be given: and he that hath not, from him shall be taken even that which he hath." (Mark 4:25) This was a favorite quotation of my guru's. It must also have been a favorite saying of Jesus, for we find it in four other places as well: in Matthew 13:12 and 25:29, and in Luke 8:18 and 19:26. These Biblical passages seem eminently unfair until one thinks of spiritual growth, not as a linear progression, but as a revolving wheel—moving nowhere, but drawing power to itself as into a whirlpool, and expanding slowly outward to infinity.

The main problem with such a self-enclosed cycle is, of course, how to enter it in the first place. And the solution? It is not so difficult as one might think. For it lies simply in finding one's center not outside, but within, oneself. Most people define themselves only by reference to the world around them. They have virtually no inner life. If you tell them that will power determines the flow of energy, they may reply, "Oh, I do understand! That means I must keep on finding fresh things to excite me, so as to stimulate my will." Then they add, dubiously, "The trouble is, I find that fewer and fewer things excite me anymore." Or if you explain how an abundance of vitality increases one's magnetism, they may wait passively for that sunny day, or that occasional good mood when their vitality seems higher than usual. Then they wonder why their magnetic appeal (their effect on others will probably be all they can understand of magnetism) seems to be decreasing with the years. "I guess it's just that I'm getting old," they tell themselves, not realizing that, if a person lives wisely, his magnetism only *increases* with age. And if you point out that for the will to be truly effective it must first be magnetic—expressing itself, for example, as willingness and a cooperative spirit, not as a grim sense of obligation—they may answer, "Well, I'd like very much to show a more friendly attitude than I do, but I find that when a person seems too cooperative, other people take advantage of him." And so it is that the little they have of will or energy or magnetism gradually becomes lost to them. It need not have been so, had they not sought their center outside themselves.

For the fact is, we cannot *enter* the magic circle. We are already at its center. Rather, we *are* its center; we have only to live more inwardly. And how are we to do so? By right attitude. *The ability to live more inwardly is the hallmark of right, spiritual attitude.* Right attitude is the force that sets the wheel of spiritual evolution turning in the first place. Right attitude is what keeps it turning, drawing more and more divine power to itself. Right attitude it is, finally, that keeps the whirlpool of Self-realization expanding outward to infinity, instead of becoming locked in a narrow cycle of ego-limitation.

But many are the paradoxes on the spiritual path. This inward attitude is not easily comprehended by the worldly mind, for the world has its own power to draw anyone who embraces it. Boredom-fatigue-reluctance-boredom is a self-perpetuating cycle capable of generating its own negative energies. For the beginner, therefore, an extra impetus may be needed initially to spark the right, inward attitude.

An electric generator needs a strong spark from a battery to get it started. The wheel of inner development, similarly, usually needs a strong stimulus from without to get it going. Hence the need for contact with other devotees, and particularly with saints. Since saints are not easy to find in this world, and not easy to get close to once one does find them, one would do well also to meditate on them from afar. Study their photographs. Try to draw into yourself their magnetic, divine attitudes.

It would be no exaggeration to say that attitude, in the last analysis, is everything. One may have right attitude and know nothing of yoga or of meditation, and still reach God, eventually. But without right attitude, lifetimes of yoga practice may develop nothing but spiritual pride, and an outward focus thereby for one's energies.

The world, steeped as it is in delusion, often upholds as the best attitudes those which would most surely enmesh us in further delusion. Egotism, for example, is often prized by ignorant people as a sign of strength. Self-seeking is mistaken for practicality; miserliness, for thrift; restlessness, for a proof of inner vitality; and loud laughter, for a sure sign of inner joy.

Look, then, to the saints. But since probably you must mix with worldly people, too, and may have to be more with them than with saints, look to them also. But *study the end results of their attitudes.* For even in a worldly sense, those attitudes bear the sweetest fruits which spring most purely from an inner source: self-giving, rather than possessive, love; a wish to correct oneself, not others; an inner freedom in every undertaking, and in every human relationship; an impersonal gaze that can enjoy even the world without constant reference to one's own standing with respect to it.

The developed yogi sees in all things the one, divine Self. But the beginning yogi needs to cultivate, in addition to a divinely impersonal outlook, a more intimate, devotional attitude towards the Lord. This attitude is expressed in the awakening of *Kundalini,* and is a necessary step towards that awakening.

Kundalini represents, as I have said, the negative, feminine pole in everyone's nature. It would be a mistake to think of *Kundalini* as a blind energy; it (or she) represents an integral part of humanity's total being. Essentially, man's nature is androgynous, for the soul has no sex. Masculinity and femininity are but the poles of duality by which the soul manifests itself in a limited form. The closer one approaches a realization of the essential oneness of all life, the less polarized one's consciousness becomes. Paramhansa Yogananda combined the compassionate, all-forgiving nature of a perfect mother with the impartial wisdom of an ideal father. It was even difficult for many people to tell from a glance whether he was a man or a woman. Anandamayee Ma, a great woman saint in India, seemed truly a physical embodiment of the Divine Mother of the universe. Yet when she walked it was often with the deliberate tread of a general, and her conversation was so much at ease in the deepest questions of abstract philosophy that the foremost scholars of India sought her out for clarification of difficult points.

The practicing yogi, too, should strive always to "depolarize" himself. He should think of himself not as a man or a woman, but as the all-unifying soul. He should see others similarly, but at the same time he should take care that his view of them is also, as the soul's is, impersonal, lest age-old desires trick him through philosophy into once again accepting physical substitutes for divine union.

It would be preferable in the beginning to think of oneself as androgynous—as both the ideal man and the ideal woman—than as the soul really is: sexless.

Kundalini, as I said, is a feminine energy. To awaken her we need to develop what are essentially feminine attitudes: devotion, surrender, servicefulness, receptivity, and humility in our approach toward God; kindness, compassion, forgiveness, and cooperation in our dealings with other people. Rugged, masculine types who see women only as sex objects, otherwise ridiculing all feminine qualities, merely betray the fact that, in them, *Kundalini* is so fast asleep as to be completely unconscious. Women, too, who find themselves attracted to such men are experiencing what can only be termed, spiritually speaking at least, a kind of death wish.

Kundalini's energy is essential to spiritual awakening. Because the vibrations of this energy are feminine, women are more naturally attuned to it than men are. That is why women are more naturally inclined to the spiritual path than men, and why so many men shun religion as an activity for women. (Even the reproductive organs express the natural upward directedness of *Kundalini* in women, and its outward directedness in men.) In fact, because all mental alertness and physical vitality are associated with at least *some* upward movement of energy from *Kundalini,* it would seem that women are more apt to be alert and energetic than men. Study people. I think you will find this to be the case.

No man can succeed truly in life who scorns to develop the feminine side of his nature. And no woman can succeed who does not resolutely develop her masculine side, thereby assigning herself goals that are not only definite, but impersonal. But neither can succeed unless he awakens the feminine side first.

Kundalini represents the deepest, all-but-unconscious pull in human nature to separate itself from the Spirit. On a more conscious level this pull is cognized in the heart center, with its likes and dislikes. The pure feminine consciousness associated with *Kundalini* awakening, too, is most easily perceived in the heart center. To develop divine qualities of devotion, receptivity, surrender, and the like, concentrate in this center, not in the region of *Kundalini.* The energy in the heart will then become a magnet that will draw *Kundalini* upward from those nether regions in which she has remained, drugged by the sleep of ages.

Concentration on the heart center, however, is quite secondary to concentration on those *qualities* which are associated with an awareness of that center. Meditate on those divine qualities.

Swami Sri Yukteswar says in his book, *The Holy Science,* that the necessary basic attribute for developing them is firmness of moral courage, which amounts to the ability to follow the principles of *niyama,* the "do's" of the spiritual path that were outlined in Step Five of this course. This ability, Sri Yukteswarji writes, "when attained removes all obstacles in the way of salvation. These obstacles are of eight sorts, viz., hatred, shame, fear, grief, condemnation, race prejudice, pride of pedigree, and a narrow sense of respectability, which eight are the meannesses of the human heart. By the removal of these eight obstacles, *beeratwam* or *mahatwam* (magnanimity of the heart) comes in." (p. 49)

Meditation on divine qualities is particularly successful in association with stories from the lives of saints and masters. Jesus, for example, in his great compassion asking forgiveness for his enemies even while he was on the cross. Or Yogananda, when someone asked to be forgiven, replying, "Well, what else can I do?"—or, when encountering a self-styled enemy who for years had been slandering him, saying gently, "Remember, I shall always love you."

Sabari, a girl, lived in a forest

surrounded by the huts of many stern ascetics. Everyone in that forest was a devotee of Rama. Everyone but Sabari practiced severe ascetic disciplines by which he hoped to please Rama. But Sabari's heart was too full of love to be drawn to such dry practices. Her understanding of philosophy was too simple to rejoice, as the others did, in long discourses. Every day, rather, she lovingly swept the forest paths—hoping to make the way easier for the Lord when He passed that way, as she never doubted He would.

What need has the Lord for smooth pathways? He who can pass freely everywhere? He who already *is* everywhere? But there is one path He cannot take: He cannot walk on the heart-ways of people whose pride blocks the way. Sabari, by sweeping the forest paths, swept a clear path in her own heart as well. And at last Rama did visit that forest. And when He did so, He by-passed all the huts of those great ascetics. It was in Sabari's humble dwelling that He chose to stop.

Sri Chaitanya, a great saint of medieval India, was once attacked by ruffians. In return for their striking him, he gave them a taste of his divine love. "You have drawn blood from this body," he said. "Now I shall draw 'blood' from your hearts!" Their lives were completely changed by the encounter.

My guru was once accosted by three hold-up men. He willingly gave them his money, then said, "But there is something else I have that you can't take from me unless I choose to give it to you." "What's wrong with *him?*" they asked one another, sneeringly. Suddenly he flooded them with the magnetism of divine love. Overwhelmed, and in tears, they returned his money to him, vowing that they could never again live as they had lived until then.

One time Master underwent a severe trial. A disciple said to him, commiseratingly, "How cruel of Divine Mother to treat you so, when She knows you live only for Her!" "Don't you *dare* speak a word against Divine Mother!" replied Master, indignantly. Complete surrender to God's will was, for him, an absolute principle.

The devotional, soul-uplifting attitudes of which I am writing must be directed above all to God Himself, in prayer and meditation. It is good to have a serviceful attitude towards others, but it is even more important to meditate with an attitude of serving God, of self-giving with no thought of any reward but His pleasure. It is good to be compassionate and forgiving towards others, but it is still better to be, in a sense, compassionate towards God. For consider how long He has hungered for our love! How long He has called to us! To renounce our millennial indifference to Him, our soul's rebellion against His all-consuming love, to forgive all the hurts that we have imagined to have come from His hand (when in fact it was we who created them, our inharmonies all springing from our soul's ancient resistance)—these are the attitudes by which the soul, repenting of its follies at last, can begin the long climb back to its eternal home in God.

(To be continued)

Hari AUM, *Tat, Sat*

Step Thirteen

The Anatomy of Yoga
Part 2

I. PHILOSOPHY

The Anatomy of Yoga, Part 2

The upliftment of consciousness which occurs when the energy rises in the spine is not only one of general direction: There are also specific stages of development along the way. At certain definite points along the spinal journey new insights occur, like a succession of vistas opening out as one climbs into the mountains, and sees below him first the smog-filled city, then green but still-hazy hills, then a sea of smog in which a few hills nestle here and there like islands, then nothing but the free, blue sky, majestic peaks, and blue-green, solitary valleys.

Yet there is also a wonderful difference between this spiritual voyage and any earthly journey: One need not wholly embark on the voyage to experience at least something of the wonders that it holds along the way. When *Kundalini* rises to the area of the heart, for example, great love is felt for the Divine; but *any* upward flow of energy in that general region bestows *some* feeling of love. And other flows of energy there, if not upward, produce at least emotions of some kind, which are but lower manifestations of love. By concentrating on directing energy upward through that center, one develops devotion. Complete "awakening" of that center requires that *Kundalini* be raised past that point, but some, at least of the insights that result from the awakening of that center can be achieved long before *Kundalini* has been awakened at all. The same is true for the other spinal centers.

The spinal centers, or *chakra*s, are found at those points where tributary streams of energy join the upward flow of *Kundalini* in the *sushumna,* or deep spine. In man's unawakened state, when the main energy-flow is downward away from the brain, energy is drawn away from the *sushumna* at these *chakra*s to perform various outward functions. Thus, in the physical body these spiritual centers correspond simply to the spinal plexuses, from which nerves branch out to provide energy to the different body parts.

There are six of these centers in the spine, acting as substations, or transformers, for the main dynamo of energy in the brain.

Kundalini, in her unawakened state, rests below the lowest center at the base of the spine, the *muladhara chakra,* or coccyx center. From this center radiate the nerves that go to the lower parts of the body: the anus, and the legs.

An inch and a half above the *muladhara* is the *swadisthan chakra,* or sacral center. The nerves from this center operate the reproductive system.

Opposite the navel in the spine is the *manipur chakra,* or lumbar center, the nerves from which operate the digestive system.

Opposite the heart in the spine is the *anahat chakra,* the dorsal, or heart center, from which nerves go out to the heart, lungs, and chest, and into the arms.

Opposite the throat in the spine is the *vishuddha chakra,* or cervical center, from which nerves radiate to the throat and neck.

The highest center in the spine is the medulla oblongata, of which the positive pole is the Christ center, or *ajna chakra,* at the point between the eyebrows. The medulla oblongata is, as I have said before, the center through which cosmic energy feeds the entire body.

But to speak only of the physical functions of these spinal *chakra*s would be like defining a great yogi in terms of the food he eats. Everyone, moreover, is at least potentially a great yogi. In even the most worldly person the *chakra*s exert some of their subtler, psychological or spiritual influences. Less so in the case of the worldly man, however, floundering as he is in the downward-flowing stream of consciousness.

The more worldly a person, the lower what we might call his spiritual "center of gravity." The more spiritual a person, the higher that spiritual center. In this way, the lower three *chakra*s may be understood to relate more strictly to worldly consciousness; the upper three, to spiritual consciousness. If one wants to spiritualize his consciousness, he should try to center his energy increasingly in the upper three *chakra*s.

The student might wonder, "How are the lower spinal centers to be awakened, if one's concentration is directed exclusively to the higher centers?" The answer is that concentration on these higher centers generates a magnetism that attracts the energy to flow upward at the lower ones. It is this upward flow of energy at the *chakra*s that constitutes their awakening. By concentration on the lower *chakra*s, the natural tendency would be for the spinal energy to flow downward. (In this case, it would be the lower *chakras* that generate the greater magnetism, drawing down toward themselves the energy in the upper *chakras*.)

But in any case it is not a question of *exclusive* concentration. In relation to each other, the upper triad of centers deserves more attention than the lower. But each *chakra* in relation to its own various outward functions can be spiritualized better by concentrating at its source than on the outward effects of its energy-flow. Thus it is a good practice in meditation to chant "AUM" mentally three times at each of the *chakras*, moving up and down the spine several times. In this way the energy becomes somewhat withdrawn from the outer body to the centers. Once the energy is felt in the centers, draw it upward by concentrating your attention on the upper centers—especially on the Christ center between the eyebrows.

The vibration that is felt when the energy becomes focused in the dorsal center, or *anahat chakra,* and directed upward from that point toward the Christ center, is one of divine love.

When the energy is focused in the cervical center, or *vishuddha chakra,* and directed upward from that point, one feels deep inner calmness and a sense of expansion.

When the energy is focused deeply at the point between the eyebrows, one experiences divine joy and soul-consciousness.

Even the lower centers have their spiritual aspects.

The more the energy is withdrawn from the coccyx center, or *muladhara chakra,* the more one develops the power to follow inwardly, as well as outwardly, the rules of *yama* (control)—the "don'ts" of the spiritual path. As I mentioned in Step Four, the more perfect one becomes in these rules, the more he manifests their positive fruits. The fruit of perfect non-injury is that even wild animals and ferocious criminals become tame or subdued in one's presence. The fruit of perfection in non-lying is that one develops the power to attain the fruits of acting without even acting. When the third rule of *yama,* non-stealing, becomes firmly rooted, one finds wealth coming to him whenever he needs it. When non-sensuality, the fourth virtue in this series, becomes firmly rooted, the yogi attains great vigor. And when non-greed, the last of these principles, becomes established even to the extent of non-identification with one's own possessions and body, one acquires the power to remember his previous identities in other bodies.

The more the energy is withdrawn from the sacral center, the more one develops the power to follow inwardly, as well as outwardly, the principles of *niyama,* the "do's" of the spiritual path. Perfection in these principles as one continues to advance spiritually confers upon one, as I mentioned in Step Five, subtle rewards also. From perfect cleanliness arises a disinclination for the pleasures of the body. From contentment one develops the power to realize divine bliss. Through inward austerity one develops the so-called miraculous *siddhis*, or powers. Through self-study (*swadhyaya*) one develops the power to commune with beings on higher spheres of existence. And by devotion to the Supreme Lord one develops the power to commune with Him.

But most of these powers imply at least a degree of awakening of the higher centers as well. Thus it is only when the energy begins to be withdrawn from the lumbar center, or *manipur chakra,* that one develops truly dynamic, "fiery" self-control.

Spiritual progress is not strictly an A-B-C thing. There is a general *direction* of development. There are also definite stages on the path of development. But like an advancing army, different parts of one's nature reach these various stages at different times. Some people, as soon as they feel a little energy in a particular *chakra,* or feel a touch of the state of consciousness that yogis have attributed to that *chakra,* imagine that they have already fully awakened it and are free now to move on to the next stage of development. Unfortunately, the matter is not quite so simple. An army's advance on one front does not imply its victory everywhere. Very often, high achievements in certain sectors of the spiritual struggle are accompanied, temporarily at least, by disappointing performances elsewhere. Even highly advanced yogis may not yet have shed pride, or jealousy, or intolerance. In a state of final perfection, of course, such weaknesses are not to be found, but the path to that highest state is long. Until the end has been reached, there are degrees of awakening—even for each *chakra.*

In fact, a spinal center may not truly be said to have been awakened until *Kundalini* has passed through it in full force. It is not enough for mere spurts of energy to have shot up from the base of the spine; these are but advance scouts from *Kundalini,* testing the terrain so to speak, and preparing it for later invasion. There is a great difference between these relatively minor flashes of upliftment and the mighty upward flow of *Kundalini* herself, a river swelling with the addition of each tributary stream of energy joining it at the *chakra*s.

The spinal centers correspond, as I mentioned in the meditation section of Step Seven, to what are called the basic "elements" of matter: earth, water, fire, air, and ether, representing not the elements of chemistry, but the elementary stages of material manifestation—from subtle cosmic gases to solid matter. As nature may be properly understood only by retracing its manifestations back to their subtlest essence, so man, too, may be understood by retracing his identity back to the Spirit of which he is but a manifestation.

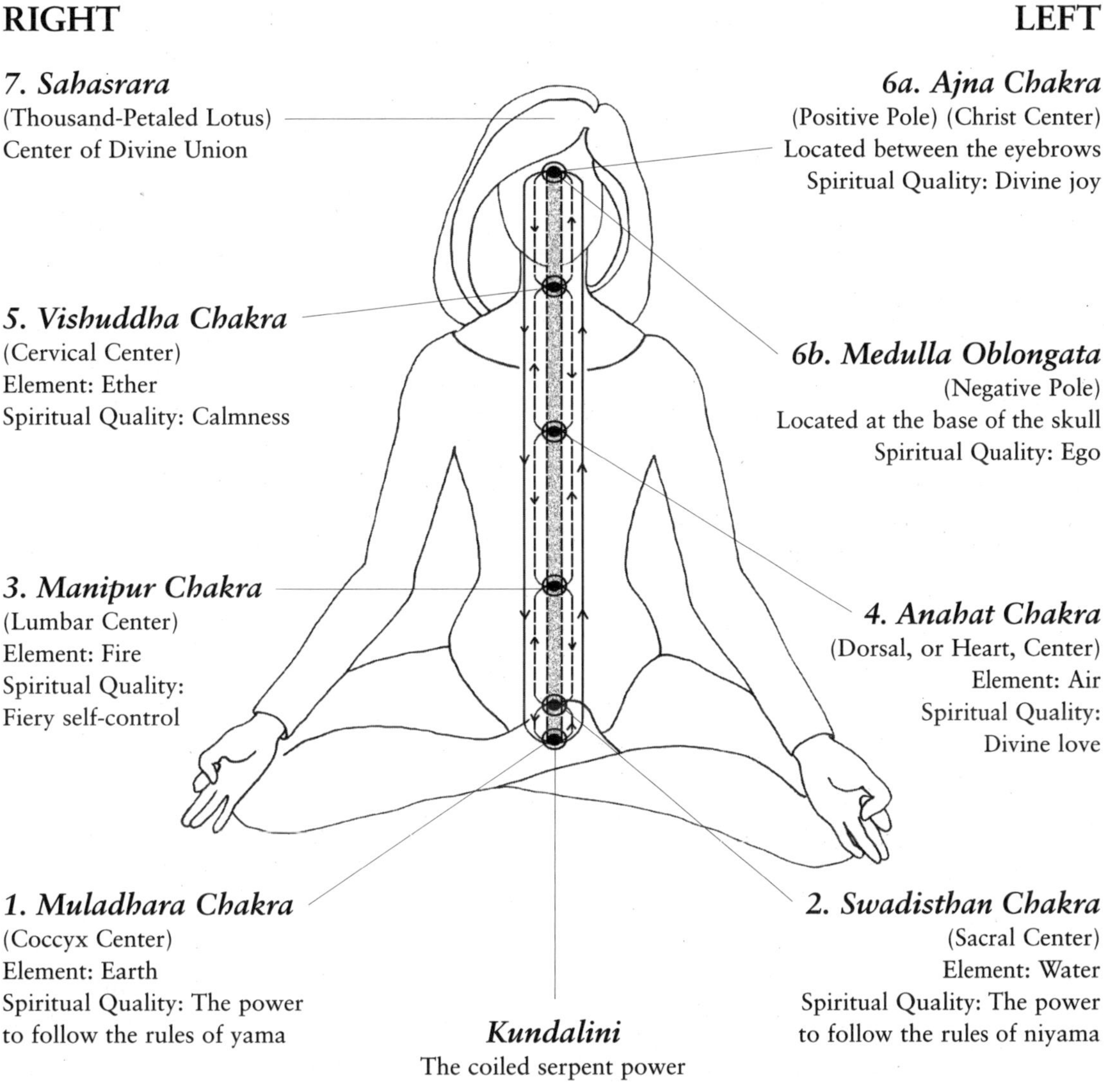

Chart showing spinal nerve channels (*naḍi*s) and centers (*chakra*s). Solid line arrows indicate general direction of movement of energy in the *iḍa* and *pingala* *naḍi*s, respectively. The central channel is the sushumna. Dotted lines indicate actual path taken by *iḍa* and *pingala*. For simplicity's sake their complicated pattern is under-emphasized in these lessons; one's experience of them is of a straight, not a wavy, flow.

Each of the spinal centers represents a different so-called "element." Thus, the lowest center represents earth, the grossest element. The sacral center is associated with the water element; the lumbar, with the fire element; the dorsal, with the air element; and the cervical, with the ether element. As each of these centers becomes fully awakened, the yogi understands the subtle principles of which its respective element is a manifestation. In this way he gains power—even in an objective sense—over that element. Though the yogi is warned not to use his spiritual powers for outward display lest he succumb to the temptation of pride, the manifestation of these powers at least affords him an objective test from which to determine whether his inner experiences are truly superconscious, or are merely the subconscious products of an active imagination.

But these seemingly miraculous powers* develop only with the full awakening of *Kundalini* and of the spinal centers. Are there other tests to determine whether a center is at least being stimulated in the right way? Corresponding changes of consciousness may be too subtle to be readily recognized. The mere focus of energy in a *chakra* is no guarantee that the energy's flow will be upward. Often, especially with respect to the lower three *chakras*—and even to some extent to the heart center—an unusual gathering of energy signifies a downward, rather than an upward flow.

Generally speaking, one is safe if the *general* flow of energy in the spine seems to be upward. But there is also a more specific test. The harmonious stimulation of each center is accompanied (albeit not invariably) by subtle sounds. These sounds are heard properly within the right ear. With the stimulation of the coccyx, the sound of a bumblebee is heard; of the sacral, the sound of a flute; of the lumbar, that of a stringed musical instrument being plucked; of the heart, or dorsal, that of a deep bell; and of the cervical, the sound of wind, or of rushing waters. Heard less perfectly, some of these sounds have the following variations: The bumblebee (with the stimulation of the coccyx center) may sound like a motor; the flute, like crickets, or like trickling water; the bell, high-toned instead of like a deep gong.

All of these sounds are manifestations of the Cosmic Vibration of AUM. Communion with these sounds, and above all with AUM, is a vitally important aspect of the higher practices of yoga. This technique is available from Ananda as a written lesson with audio or videotape. Call Ananda Sangha for details (1-530-478-7560). To study in person is always best, where the yoga techniques are concerned. Audio and videotapes are a good substitute, if one

* Rightly understood, of course, nothing is a miracle—unless indeed *everything* be called a miracle.

cannot visit Ananda's retreat facility, *The Expanding Light,* or one of our other churches or communities (or if one cannot attend lectures from Ananda ministers when they are out traveling on lecture tours). Something—a certain subtle energy—is conveyed in this format that is less easily received in written format.

Meanwhile, try listening intently in the right ear during meditation for the sounds I have described. To tune in to the Cosmic Sound of AUM (pronounced *Om*), chant *Om* at the point between the eyebrows while at the same time listening with deep concentration.

The seventh and highest *chakra,* located at the top of the brain, is known as the *sahasrara,* or thousand-petaled lotus. Albeit the highest center, it must be approached through the Christ center. By prolonged meditation on the spiritual eye—the circular field of blue light, surrounded by a ring of gold, that appears of itself when the mind is deeply concentrated at the Christ center—a subtle passage opens up from that center to the top of the head. To attempt to approach the *sahasrara* by any other route would be futile; it has even been said to be dangerous.

I was interested to learn from a Roman Catholic scholar and priest that St. Teresa of Avila, somewhere in her writings (I have never come upon the passage myself), stated that the soul has its seat at the top of the head. Sincere seekers in every religion cannot but discover spiritual realities for themselves as they advance on the path, even when no official tradition has prepared them to encounter those realities.

Actually, we may say that the *sahasrara* represents the soul in its aspect of Perfect Being, that highest state when the little self has become merged in the Infinite. "Soul" is a somewhat vague word, however. It signifies the long bridge over the chasm between ego-consciousness and God-consciousness. Generally one thinks even of the ego in its more worshipful moods as expressing an aspect of soul-consciousness. But it is not these lower aspects of soul-consciousness that have their center in the *sahasrara.*

The seat of ego, as I have said elsewhere, is in the medulla oblongata. This ego-consciousness must be transformed into soul-consciousness by prolonged concentration at the Christ center, until one's actual center of consciousness shifts to that point. An enlightened master always acts, thinks, and lives from that center. His consciousness becomes centered in the *sahasrara* only when action ceases, and his soul merges with the Infinite in *samadhi.* The Christ center, then, also represents an aspect of soul-consciousness: the spiritualized ego—the soul in its state of active manifestation. For practical purposes, and for all but the fully enlightened soul, we may say that the Christ center represents the *sahasrara* as the seventh *chakra.* For not only is it the positive pole of the sixth center (the medulla oblongata); it also serves in place of the *sahasrara* as the seat of soul-consciousness in the aspiring yogi.

O yogi! Strive always to act, think, and live from the Christ center in the frontal lobe of your brain, between the two eyebrows. Do not wait to become a master to live as a master lives. It is by living in a divine way *even now* that one becomes divine. Renounce ego! You are not that little self. Dwell always in the thought of your soul's freedom, of the soul-guidance that emanates in soothing rays from your own Christ center.

For you are the immortal *Atman.* You are Spirit. The very universe, vast as it is, is inferior to your soul's majesty. Stars and planets, like your own body, are manifestations of spiritual realities that you can discover on deeper levels of your own inner being. The very physical universe is but a symbol of those higher realities; it is the lesser always that symbolizes the greater, never the reverse. Since those realities can be realized only in the Self, it is not wrong to say that the universe is the outer symbol of man's inner world.

In this way my guru said that the sun is the symbol of the spiritual eye—not the reverse.

The moon too is a symbol—of the human ego. As the moon only reflects the sun's light, so the ego has no reality of its own, no light but that which it reflects from the soul. Hindu deities are sometimes depicted with the moon in their foreheads to show that their ego-consciousness (normally centered in the medulla oblongata) has been transformed into soul-consciousness at the Christ center. Lord Shiva is even depicted with the moon in his hair, in the area of the *sahasrara,* to show that his ego is totally merged in the Infinite Spirit.

Hindu astrology, which evolved, as yoga did, in a more spiritual age, is really but an extension of the inner yoga science and its "zodiac" of the spinal centers. The constellations and planets were considered in ancient times to express, objectively, deep *subjective* truths of man's nature. But unfortunately, most of this lore has been forgotten.

I used to wonder why writers sometimes claimed that an understanding of astrology is invaluable for a deeper understanding of yoga. With this question in mind I studied a little astrology, only to find that astrologers themselves are not generally overburdened with spiritual insight. Finally, the only thing left for me to do was meditate on the subject. In meditation, answers came to me that seem inescapable. At least one other person, a scholar and advanced yogi from India who is deeply versed in the ancient lore, has approved of my correlations. So perhaps I should record my "discovery" here, hopefully, lest it become lost for lack of any other opportunity for expression.

Paramhansa Yogananda stated in *Autobiography of a Yogi* (p. 246) that the six spinal centers, becoming twelve by polarity, correspond to the twelve signs of the zodiac. The spinal centers are polarized by the upward and downward movement of energy through the *iḍa* and *pingala* nerve channels.

Can these spinal centers be correlated more specifically with the zodiacal signs? Interestingly, they can exactly so. And not with the signs only, but with the planetary rulers for those signs, and with the traditional positive or negative polarity of each sign. Nor is this correlation a mere intellectual curio. An understanding of it may help you to deepen your own understanding of the *chakra*s.

We must begin by correlating the constellation Aquarius with the coccyx center at the base of the spine. Aries, not Aquarius, is the usual starting point of the zodiac, but for reasons which it would take too long (in relation to their importance) to explain, Aquarius is the sensible starting-point for the spinal "zodiac." From this point, moreover, we find everything else fitting perfectly into place. The intertwining of *iḍa* and *pingala* with the *chakra*s puts all of the positive signs on the left side of the spine (where they belong), and all of the negative signs on the right side. The planetary rulers for the different signs turn out in each case to relate to the same *chakra* going up and coming down the spine: Saturn, to the coccyx, Jupiter to the sacral, Mars to the lumbar, Venus to the dorsal, and Mercury to the cervical. The sun and moon, which relate to the positive and negative poles of the medulla oblongata, are given in astrology the rulership of only one sign each.*

Rahu and *Ketu,* moreover, in Hindu mythology the head and tail of the dragon, and in Hindu astrology the north and south nodes of the moon, correlate perfectly with the upward- and downward-flowing currents through *iḍa* and *pingala.* This correlation is enhanced by the fact that *Kundalini* is symbolized, as we saw in the last lesson, by the dragon itself. *Iḍa* and *pingala,* as the head and tail of the dragon, branch upward in opposite directions from the base of the spine. And again, *iḍa* and *pingala,* as the north and south nodes of the moon, join at the medulla oblongata, the moon's physical seat in the body.

Venus's position in the heart center will be better understood once it is realized that the traditional Hindu name for Venus is *Shukra,* mythical guru of the demons. The "demons" in man are his emotions, and thus relate naturally to his heart center. The ancient Latin name

* It should be noted that the planetary rulerships I have ascribed to the different signs are those traditional to Hindu astrology. Modern Western astrology assigns as the rulers of some of these zodiacal signs planets that have been more recently discovered: Uranus, Neptune, and Pluto.

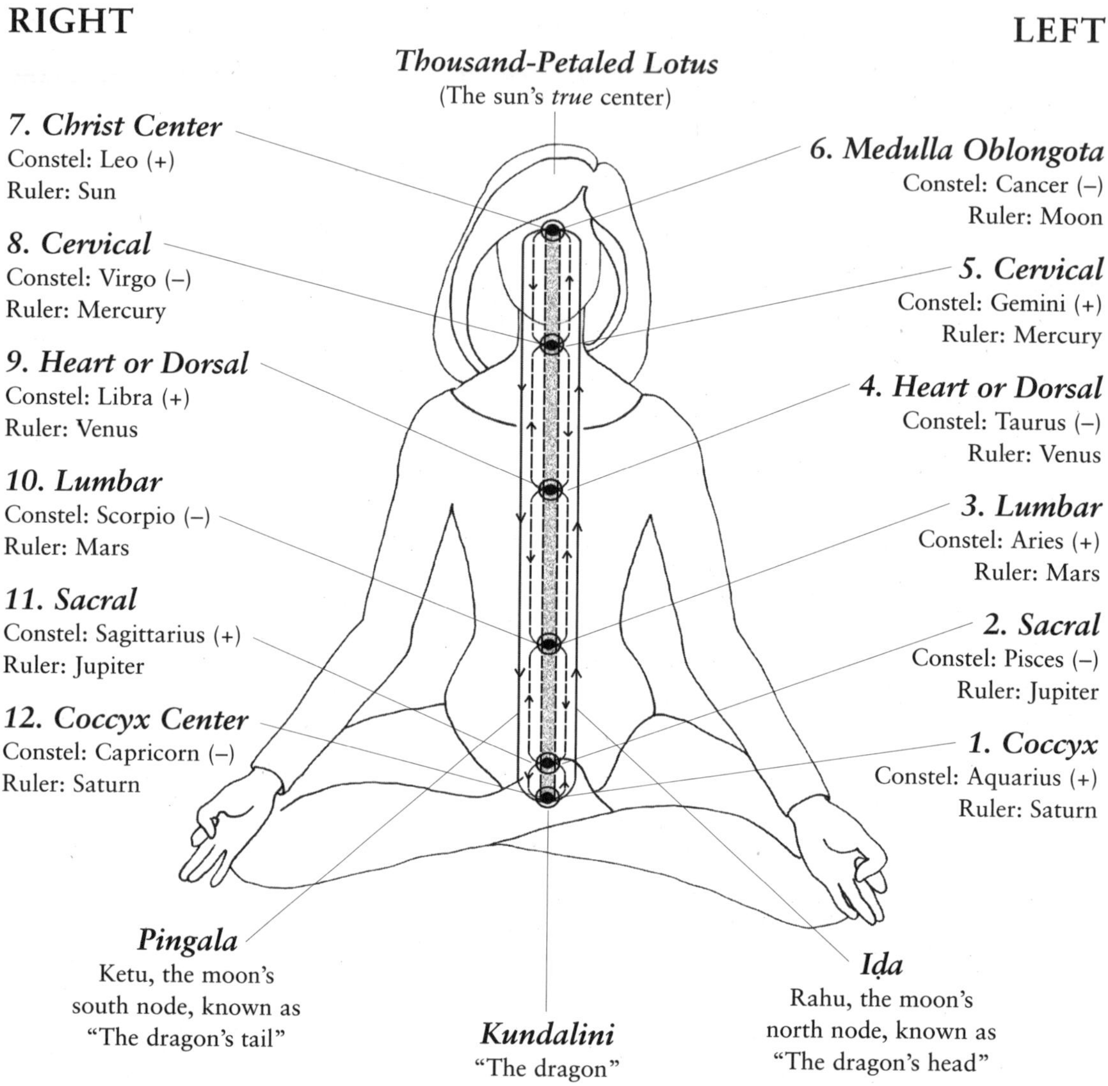

The inner "zodiacal constellations" and their rulers as a key to the essential qualities of the centers. Solid line arrows indicate the general direction of movement, dotted lines the *actual* path taken in the *iḍa* and *pingala* nerve channels respectively. *Iḍa* stands for *Rahu* (in mythology, the dragon's head); *pingala*, for *Ketu* (in mythology, the dragon's tail); *Kundalini* stands for the dragon itself.

for the planet Venus, incidentally, was Lucifer.

Once divine awakening occurs, the inner "moon's" natural center becomes the point between the eyebrows; the "sun's" becomes the *sahasrara,* the thousand-petaled "lotus" in the top of the brain.

Mars, the so-called "fiery" planet, is a fitting symbol for the lumbar center, seat of the fire "element" in man.

Saturn, with its supposedly constricting influence, is the perfect symbol for the coccyx center, in which the constricting principles of *yama* (the "don'ts" on the path) have their seat.

Mercury, whose traditional mental restlessness, when spiritualized, resolves naturally into its opposite—deep mental calmness and expanded awareness—is a good symbol for the rays of consciousness emanating from the calm, non-matter-involved cervical center.

And Jupiter, the divine teacher and impersonal broadener of our horizons,* fittingly symbolizes the sacral center and its association with the principles of *niyama,* the "do's" of the spiritual path. It is interesting that Krishna, the cosmic guru, is usually depicted playing the flute. The flute, as I just said a few paragraphs ago, is the sound that emanates in meditation from the sacral center.

If any planet is weak in your own horoscope, you might try to improve its influence on you by meditating on its relative *chakra* in your body, and harmonizing the vibrations there. But if it is one of the lower three *chakra*s that is involved, don't meditate on it, but on the relatively positioned *chakra* in the upper triad: on the heart center to harmonize the vibrations in the coccyx; on the cervical center to harmonize the sacral; and on the Christ center to harmonize the lumbar.

In my book, *Your Sun Sign as a Spiritual Guide,* I have gone into the more general question of how the practice of yoga can increase one's sensitivity to universal influences, thereby to augment the good influences and minimize the bad ones. Ultimately, however, by ever deeper meditation one must reach a point where he receives influences from God alone. The deeper purpose in understanding the relative influences on us of the signs and planets is to realize that the outer cosmos is, as I have said, only a symbol of the inner. It is also to help us to realize that within ourselves is the whole universe of truth that we are seeking.

The planets also symbolize various outward aspects of the spiritual path: Saturn, our *dharma,* or spiritual duty in life; Jupiter, our own personal guru, or spiritual guide. I am not trying to

* In Hindu astrology Jupiter is called *Brihaspati*, the guru of the gods. The word *guru* comes from the Sanskrit root, *gur*, to raise, to uplift.

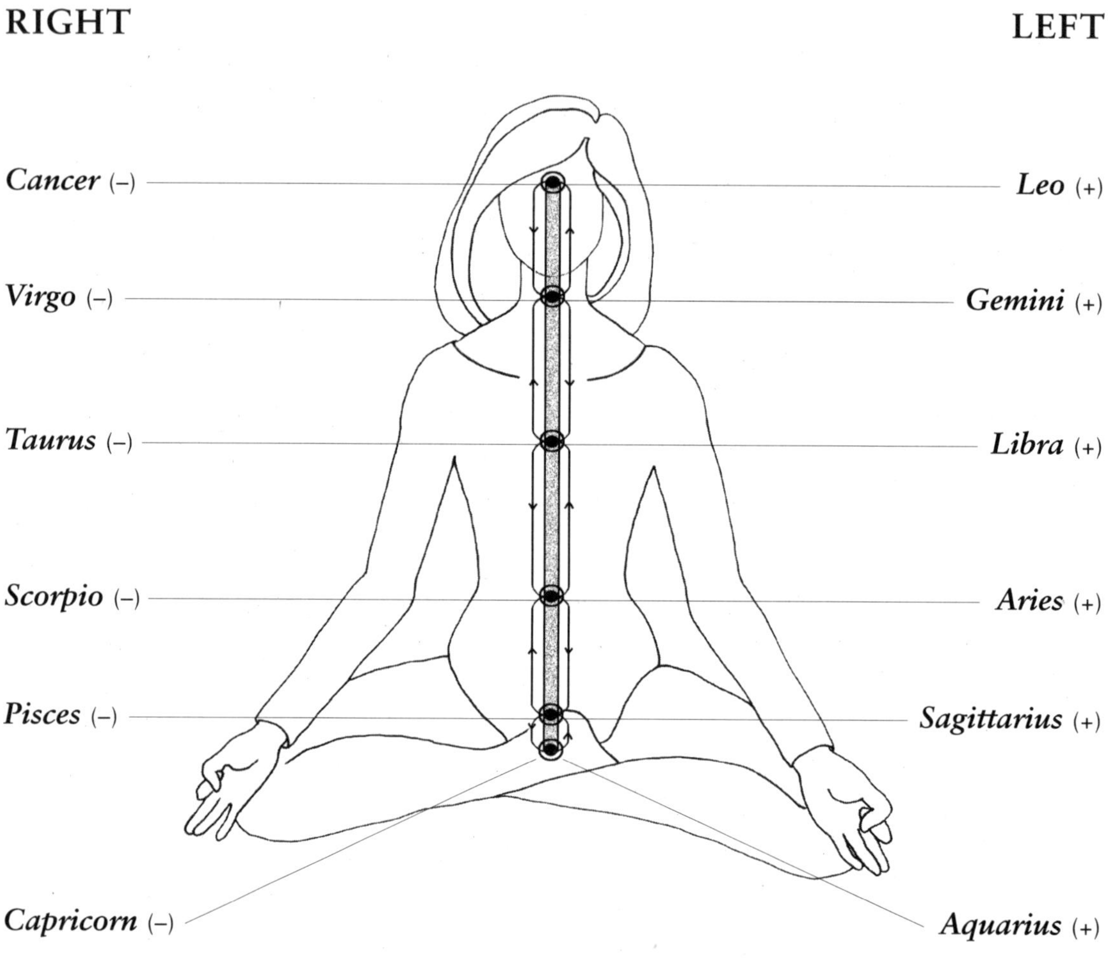

Chart showing *actual* movement of the currents in *iḍa* and *pingala* and their resulting polarization of the *chakra*s (positive as the currents flow left, negative as they flow right).

include a course on astrology in these lessons, or I could say much more to correlate the stellar science with the inner science of yoga,* but this one last point (the relation of Jupiter to one's guru) ought perhaps to be included here.

The Hindu scriptures state that man moves forward in his spiritual evolution by 12-year cycles. (Examine your own life and see if the ages of 12, 24, 36, 48, etc., were not important years for you, spiritually.) Twelve years is the length of time Jupiter requires to make one complete cycle of the zodiac. Although the outer heavenly movements are fixed, inner currents of energy relative to those external movements can be influenced by our own spiritual efforts, and by the grace of our guru. This twelve-year spiritual cycle, especially, can be greatly speeded up by intensifying the *pran* and *apan* currents in the *iḍa* and *pingala*—particularly if one adopts as the real key to his practice a deep, devotional attunement with his guru.

The technique *par excellence* for intensifying these spinal currents, and thus the most truly central technique in all of yoga, was introduced in this country by my great guru, Paramhansa Yogananda. Initiation into *Kriya Yoga* is available through Ananda. For information about how to prepare yourself, write to the Ananda Kriya Ministry at the Ananda address.

As I said in the last lesson, the upward and downward currents in *iḍa* and *pingala* relate directly to the waves of our own reactive process—the likes and dislikes which form the basis of our delusion. By concentrating on these inner currents rather than on the specific outward objects of our likes and dislikes, we can gradually bring our entire reactive process under control, ultimately neutralizing it. In the last lesson I therefore suggested that you try to bring the current up the spine (through *iḍa*) with a consciousness of life affirmation, and down the spine (through *pingala*) with the thought of excluding from your life all negativity and mental bondage. These mental attitudes will help you to control those currents. So long as you do not know *Kriya Yoga,* try simply watching the breath in the spine; feel it rising with the inhalation, and descending with the exhalation.

As one's consciousness of the spinal currents deepens, however, they can be used not only to neutralize one's inner reactive process (his likes and dislikes), but also to stimulate the upward surge of *Kundalini.* For if the upward current in *iḍa* relates to our affirmation of outward life, it is only because it approximates the joy we experience inwardly when the energy in the deep spine (the *sushumna*) rises toward the brain. In the same way, the downward current in

* Interested students would find much useful information in my book, *Your Sun Sign as a Spiritual Guide.*

pingala approximates the ego's withdrawal into itself which accompanies the downward flow of energy in the deep spine. But whereas this downward flow of energy in the deep spine reflects the ego's pull away from God, and *in relation to Him* therefore is not something we want to emphasize further, in relation to the outer world this egoic withdrawal is the first step towards self-offering to God. In the practice of *Kriya Yoga,* as well as of more rudimentary methods of controlling the spinal currents, try following this suggestion:

Once you feel the currents flowing strongly in *iḍa* and *pingala,* endeavor to use the ascending current through *iḍa* to stimulate *Kundalini*'s upward movement; then sink ever more deeply into the *sushumna* with the descending current through *pingala.*

This technique has a further value. It helps to free one of the *samskar*s (subtle tendencies) that block the upward flow of *Kundalini.* These *samskar*s—the "seeds" of karma, as they are called—are the result of repeated actions (*karma*s) of the past—not only of this life, but of many past incarnations. Each *samskar* constitutes a subtle vortex of energy. There are countless such vortices in the spine.* Until the energy in them has been released to flow upward, *Kundalini*'s upward movement will be slow, her progress impeded.

In fact, *Kundalini* in her upward surge gradually "roasts" these karmic seeds of *samskar*s. Once "roasted," they can never again sprout into outward actions; instead, their energy becomes freed to join *Kundalini* in her upward journey. This "roasting" process, as yogis call it, is made possible by the fact that a strong flow of energy creates a powerful magnetic field. A stronger magnetic field will break down any weaker magnetic field with which it comes in contact, and will bestow on it its own magnetism.

The work of rechanneling, or repolarizing, the energy that is held trapped by old, dormant tendencies can be greatly assisted by intensifying the energy-flow in *iḍa* and *pingala.* As the breath is used in various yoga breathing exercises (and especially in *Kriya Yoga*) to intensify the flow of energy in *iḍa* and *pingala,* so also the so-called "astral breath," which is the flow of energy in *iḍa* and in *pingala,* is used to magnetize the *sushumna,* and thereby to intensify the upward flow of energy there. The downward flow of energy in *pingala* is helpful in this respect also, if one uses it to sink his consciousness more and more deeply in the *sushumna.* For remember,

* If you find it difficult to imagine vast numbers of such vortices in such a narrow-seeming channel as the spine, it may help you to realize how large your body really is. On a scale of size between the smallest atom and the largest star, the human body belongs close to the midpoint.

success in the transmutation of past tendencies depends on the extent to which one can work on them *from within.* It is only from the very seat of Being that all delusion can at last be dispersed.

Intensifying the currents in *iḍa* and *pingala,* finally, can help in redirecting the flow of energy in the spinal *chakra*s. The *chakra*s are described metaphorically in the yoga writings as "lotuses," their rays of energy forming the "petals."* These petals are normally turned downward; that is to say, their rays of energy flow out toward the senses. By yoga practice one must turn the petals upward, so that they point towards the brain. *Kundalini* is the main force by which this energy in the *chakra*s becomes redirected, but the intensified flow of energy in *iḍa* and *pingala* also can hasten this process.

O yogi, strive therefore to live more in your spine. Remember, all you are seeking in this world will be found in your own Self. Relate every inhalation to an upward "breath" of energy in the spine, through the *iḍa naḍi.* And relate every exhalation to a downward "breath" of energy in the spine, through the *pingala naḍi.* Use your physical breath to prime the pump, so to speak, of your astral breath in the spine. O yogi, live more in the spine!

And then strive, by ever deeper meditation, to plunge your consciousness into the deep spine, the legendary river of baptism. There coax *Kundalini* to flow upward in final surrender to the feet of God.

Remember, to raise *Kundalini* you need not keep your mind focused on the region of *Kundalini.* Nor need concentration at the Christ center imply a divorce from the rest of your body. Feel, rather, in concentration at that highest point, that you come with the support of your entire spine—and of *Kundalini* as well—in your devotional act of self-offering to God.

* Each *chakra* has a different number of such "petals": the medulla oblongata, two (*iḍa* and *pingala*); the cervical, sixteen; the dorsal, twelve; the lumbar, ten; the sacral, six; and the coccyx, four.

Yoga Teachings in the Bible

The teachings of yoga relate not to untested dogmas, but to the actual discoveries of great yogis as they advanced on the spiritual path. Truth is one. Yoga teaches universal truths, corroboration for which will be found in other great scriptures. And while nowhere else do we find yoga's special insights into reality explained in such a wealth of detail, the wise teachers of other religions shared those insights, as we may see in many passages of their teachings.

The Holy Bible, far from being a stranger to these truths, is full of them. Here are a few passages that relate to some of the yoga teachings presented in the last two lessons.

THE SPINE

The Hindu scriptures, as I have mentioned elsewhere, speak of the body as resembling an upturned tree, with the spine as its trunk, the hair as its roots, and the nerves spreading outward from the spine as its branches. This truly is the tree of life, through the trunk of which flows the sap of divine awakening. The Bible in several places refers to this "tree."

In Genesis 3:24 we read of "the tree of life." The reference is to the spine. Again in Revelation we find it referred to: "To him that overcometh will I give to eat of the tree of life, which is in the midst of the paradise of God." (Revelation 2:7) The "paradise of God" is man's inner, spiritual world.

And in Revelation 22:14: "Blessed are they that do his commandments, that they may have right to the tree of life, and may enter in through the gates into the city." The "gates" are the *chakra*s, and especially the *ajna chakra,* or Christ center.

The three spinal channels (*iḍa, pingala,* and *sushumna*) and the seven *chakra*s are referred to in Zechariah 4:2,3: "And [the angel] said unto me, What seest thou? And I said, I have looked, and behold a candlestick all of gold [the *sushumna*], with a bowl [the *sahasrara*] upon the top of it, and his seven lamps [the seven *chakra*s] thereon. . . . And two olive trees [the *iḍa* and *pingala*] by it, one upon the right side of the bowl, and the other upon the left side thereof."

Again we find the seven *chakra*s referred to in the first chapter of Revelation, the analysis of which is contained in my guru's correspondence course. A reference to the six spinal centers (twelve by polarity) is made in Revelation

22:1,2: "And he showed me a pure river of water of life, clear as crystal, proceeding out of the throne of God and of the Lamb. ["The Lamb" refers to the Christ consciousness within.] In the midst of the street of it, and on either side of the river, was there the tree of life, which bare twelve manner of fruits, and yielded her fruit every month. . . ." The "river" is the *sushumna.* The tree of life in this instance refers to the *iḍa* and *pingala* ("on either side of the river"), for St. John speaks in this case not of six *chakras* ("fruits"), but of twelve, which is how the *chakras* are thought of with respect to the polarizing effect that the upward and downward currents in *iḍa* and *pingala* have on them.

Ezekiel refers to a vision of the *chakras*: ". . . [T]hou wast upon the holy mountain of God; thou hast walked up and down in the midst of the stones of fire." (28:14) The "mountain of God" is a universally used mystical symbol to suggest the heights of divine attainment. The "stones of fire" relates to a vision of the astral light blazing in each *chakra.*

KUNDALINI

Kundalini is referred to in Numbers 21:8,9: "And the Lord said unto Moses, Make thee a fiery serpent, and set it upon a pole: and it shall come to pass, that every one that is bitten, when he looketh upon it, shall live. And Moses made a serpent of brass, and put it upon a pole, and it came to pass, that if a serpent had bitten any man, when he beheld the serpent of brass, he lived."

Two kinds of serpents are spoken of here: ordinary serpents, which relate to the downward-moving *Kundalini,* drawing man into worldliness; and the "fiery" serpent, or "serpent of brass"—that is to say, the brilliant light of the upward-moving *Kundalini.* The radiant, awakened *Kundalini* alone has the power to cure man of the "poisonous bite" of delusion.

Jesus also referred to this *Kundalini* awakening: "And as Moses lifted up the serpent in the wilderness, even so must the son of man be lifted up." (John 3:14) The son of man in this instance signifies not Jesus, but the physical body of man as opposed to his soul. This physical consciousness must be "lifted up" with the raising of the serpent force, *Kundalini.*

AJNA CHAKRA

The *ajna chakra,* or Christ center in the forehead, is referred to in several places. Revelation 22:4,5 speaks of it in these words: "And they shall see his face; and his name shall be in their foreheads. And there shall be no night there, and they need no candle, neither light of the sun; for the Lord God giveth them light: and they shall reign for ever and ever."

Jesus spoke of the spiritual eye in a passage that has been translated differently in recent editions of the Bible because no one could make any sense out of the image of a "single" eye. Yet to the yogi the image is perfectly clear. The passage occurs in Matthew 6:22: "The light of the body is the eye: if therefore thine eye be single, thy whole body shall be full of light."

The spiritual eye in the Christ center has not been described in detail in these lessons, but in the center of it a silvery-white star is seen. It was this star that the wise men saw "in the east," and followed to the manger where Christ had been born. The expression, "in the east," refers to the forehead. The word for *east* in ancient Hebrew was *kedem:* "that which lies before." It was therefore natural to use the word, east, to refer also to the forehead. But the forehead is also referred to in other mystical traditions as being the "east" of the body, for the reason that the sun of awakening, the spiritual eye, is seen here.

"And the Lord God planted a garden eastward in Eden; and there he put the man whom he had formed." (Genesis 2:8) Much scholarly labor has been devoted to trying to find out where the garden of Eden was located. We have not to look any farther than our own spiritual eye!

"Afterward he brought me to the gate, even the gate that looketh toward the east: And, behold, the glory of the God of Israel came from the way of the east." (Ezekiel 43:1,2)

Jesus said: "Say not ye, There are yet four months, and then cometh harvest? Behold, I say unto you, Lift up your eyes, and look on the fields; for they are white already to harvest." (John 4:35) Earthly fulfillments must always be sought in the future. Only God lives in the Eternal Now. Look up into the white light in the forehead. It is only there that eternal fulfillment lies.

The counsel to "look up" is found frequently in the spiritual writings of the ages, for it is in this position that the eyes behold the inner, divine kingdom.

"I will lift up mine eyes unto the hills, from whence cometh my help," said the psalmist. "My help cometh from the Lord." (Psalm 121)

II. YOGA POSTURES

Of all the techniques for awakening *Kundalini*, the best is the *Kriya Yoga* technique of Lahiri Mahasaya, which Paramhansa Yogananda brought to the West.

Techniques that are taught in *hatha yoga* include the following:

Kechari Mudra

A *mudra* is a yoga position that is designed especially to awaken spiritual energies in the body. Of all *mudra*s, *Kechari* is one of the most important. Unfortunately, it is also one of the most difficult.

The tongue must be brought back behind the soft palate so that its tip connects with certain nerves in the nasal passages. If the tongue cannot be brought back so far, its tip may be placed against the uvula (the soft fleshy appendage that hangs from the soft palate at the back of the mouth). I have already mentioned that this *mudra* is excellent for drawing energy into the body when one is fasting. Its chief purpose is to awaken the *Kundalini.*

Kechari Mudra may be practiced as long as one likes. It is definitely worthwhile to master it if one can. The chief obstacles to its practice will be the shortness of the average tongue, and of the phrenum (the cord that ties the tongue to the floor of the mouth).

The tongue can be stretched by "milking" it with a damp cloth. Pull it outward and downward several times.

You should be able at least to touch your nose with the tip of the tongue. Adepts of this *mudra* have been known to touch the tip of the tongue to the point between the eyebrows.

The phrenum may be stretched by turning the tongue back, and pressing the base of it against the roof of the mouth. It may also be softened by pulling the tongue out and gently rubbing the phrenum left and right upon the lower teeth. (Under no circumstances should the phrenum be cut, as certain unscientific writers have proposed. The phrenum was put there by nature to prevent us from swallowing our tongues. To cut this phrenum might also sever the nerve that goes to the tongue. It may take longer to stretch it than to cut it, but to hasten this process with a razor blade would be foolish and dangerous. I would not even have mentioned the practice, had it not been for the fact that certain writers have advised their students to do exactly that. Yoganandaji spoke severely against this practice one time, when one of his students had, on the advice of such writers, begun to cut his phrenum.)

You may meditate in *Kechari Mudra* as long as you like. There is no limit to the length of time prescribed for this technique.

Benefits: The positive and negative energies in the tongue and nasal passages (or uvula), when joined together, create a cycle of energy in the head which, instead of allowing the energy to flow outward to the body, generates a magnetic field that draws energy upward from the body and from the base of the spine to the brain. It is said that the tongue turns back of itself in *samadhi*. The assumption of this *mudra* helps to hasten the advent of deep spiritual states of consciousness.

Aswini Mudra

(Anal Contraction—also known as *Mula Bandha*)

Sit in any meditative pose, but preferably in *Siddhasana*. Contract the anal muscles, and feel that you are drawing the energy upward from the coccyx center (the *muladhara*) through the center of the spine. You may repeat this contraction several times. Draw the stomach in also, if you wish, as if to force the energy up into the region of the heart.

This exercise is often done in conjunction with the following pose:

Jalandhara Bandha

(The Chin Lock)

Press the chin firmly into the chest, as close to the throat as possible. Inhale slowly, and hold the breath throughout the time that you hold the position. Feel that you are drawing the energy up the spine into the cervical center, or *vishuddha chakra,* and from there to the brain. (*Jala* means the brain. *Dhara* signifies the upward pull of energy to the brain.)

Jivha Bandha

(The Tongue Lock)

Turn the tip of the tongue back toward the uvula; pressing it hard against the soft palate, move it forward across the roof of the mouth until it rests firmly against the base of the front teeth. Press the entire tongue up into the roof of the mouth in such a way as to fill the entire roof with the tongue.

This exercise is sometimes done in conjunction with *Simhasana* (the Lion Pose), and with *Viparita Karani* (the Simple Inverted Pose). With *Simhasana,* the mouth should be kept open; with *Viparita Karani* it should be kept closed.

Benefits and Cautions: The Tongue Lock used in conjunction with *Viparita Karani* comes closer to making this position a powerful *mudra,* one that should not be practiced for too long. The pressure of the tongue against the roof of the mouth exerts a powerful upward draw toward the brain of the subtle spinal energies.

III. BREATHING

The subtle breath, and the inner cause of the physical breath, is, as I have already said, the energy that flows in the spine. It is on this subtle, astral breathing process that the supreme science of yoga, *Kriya Yoga,* is founded. Since in this lesson we have talked of the importance of awakening the spinal centers, through an intensification of the flow of this spinal energy, and since we have also considered various *mudra*s and *bandha*s for the stimulation of these currents, let us emphasize in this lesson those aspects of breathing which are especially related to this teaching.

Practice *Jalandhara Bandha,* locking the chin as much into the throat as possible, and concentrate on drawing the energy up the spine to the brain as you inhale. Combine this technique with *Aswini Mudra,* also drawing the stomach in as you inhale, thereby forcing the air into the upper part of the lungs. Chant AUM mentally at the point between the eyebrows. After inhalation, relax all contractions, exhaling, and start again. The total duration of this practice should be about one minute to start with, increasing the time gradually to two or three minutes.

Next, raise the chin up as high as possible, and feel that with the backward bend of the head you are again raising energy up from the heart center to the brain. No breathing is connected with this pose. Simply chant AUM at the point between the eyebrows for about a minute to begin with, gradually increasing the time to about two or three minutes.

Relax, and sit comfortably in any meditation pose. Imagine a current coming up the center of the spine very slowly from the base to the medulla oblongata, and then through the brain to the point between the eyebrows. (The duration of this ascent should be not less than one minute.) Feel each *chakra* as you draw the current through it; chant AUM there, if you like, and visualize the rays from that *chakra* turning upward toward the brain. Practice this third phase of the technique only once to begin with. Later on, repeat it two or three times if you like.

Next, practice *Ujjayi Pranayama.* Inhale slowly through both nostrils, keeping the throat slightly constricted so as to make a gentle sound that will help you to feel the breath in the throat rather than in the nostrils, and draw the current of energy up the spine. At the top of the breath, practice contracting the anus and locking the chin, and hold the breath for the same duration as the inhalation. Relax, raising the chin to its normal height, and exhale slowly through the left nostril to the same count as your inhalation.

IV. ROUTINE

The *bandhas*, as well as the breathing and other exercises that have been taught in this lesson, should be practiced after one's routine of yoga postures, as a preparation for meditation. Practice the postures first, then deep relaxation in *Savasana*. Then sit for meditation, and begin your practice with *Aswini Mudra,* the Anal Contraction. Add to it the drawing upward of the stomach, *Jalandhara Bandha* (the Chin Lock); follow with *Jivha Bandha.* Then practice the succession of exercises given in the foregoing section on Breathing. If you like (and if you can!) practice *Kechari Mudra,* while drawing the energy very slowly up the spine in the exercise that was described in the last section.

Don't overdo these techniques. Even with all the techniques that one practices in meditation, at least a quarter, preferably longer, of one's time for spiritual practice should be given to the enjoyment of the peace that one feels, and to the simple devotional aspiration of the heart for its Cosmic Beloved.

V. HEALING

The Legs and Feet

Discomfort in the legs and feet is one of the common ailments of our age, in which a great deal of time is spent sitting or standing, but not nearly enough in moving about with sufficient vigor to keep the legs properly exercised and the blood flowing in them as it should. Sore feet can have a tiring effect upon the whole body. Indeed, it is amazing how easily the fatigue of a long day's work can be removed simply by assuming one of the inverted poses and allowing the blood to drain from the lower extremities.

Poses that are particularly good for the legs include all the inverted poses; *Vajrasana* (the Firm Pose); *Supta-Vajrasana* (the Supine Firm Pose); *Janushirasana* (the Head-to-the-Knee Pose); *Paschimotanasana* (the Posterior Stretch), concentrating on the stretch in the tendons under the knees; *Salabhasana* (the Locust Pose); *Padmasana* (the Lotus Pose); *Utkatasana* (the Chair Pose); and *Pavanamuktasana* (the Wind-Freeing Pose).

All of the exercises given in this lesson for raising the energy in the spine help to draw energy from the legs and to relax them.

One of the troubles that people have with the postures is the cramps that they get in the feet and in the legs. A deficiency in calcium is sometimes the cause, for which more calcium is the obvious cure, but cramps in the feet may be helped also by standing up, turning one foot back, and resting one's weight on the back side of the toes as much as possible, so as to bend the foot back further. Cramps may also be overcome by assuming any inverted pose.

For flat feet, try rising up as high as you can on your toes, then bending your knees and stooping down, remaining high on the toes, then standing up straight again. Repeat this movement several times vigorously.

Varicose veins, as I have already said in former lessons, may be greatly helped, if not cured, by the inverted poses, especially *Sirshasana*.

Gentle pressure on the feet with the thumbs can be extremely soothing and refreshing to the whole body. It is difficult to do for oneself. If you can, get someone else to apply this pressure very gently and slowly to every portion of the feet, including the toes. Let him also massage the soft area above the heels, including the tendons. The pressure may be alternated with a gentle, circular motion of the thumb. The circular movements in this case should be small enough to cover only the particular area that the thumb is engaged in massaging at that moment.

Sometimes one leg is found to be shorter than the other, not because of an actual shortening of the leg itself, but because of a displacement of the vertebrae in the spine. In such cases, a simple chiropractic adjustment is often helpful.

The person should be told to lie on that side on which the leg seems longer. The lower leg should be straight, and the upper leg bent in such a way that the knee dangles forward and the ankle rests on the lower knee. The upper arm should be placed in such a way that the elbow hangs backward, with the hand on the chest close to the shoulder.

The person doing the manipulating should place his hand at the base of the spine, and rest his forearm on the hip. His other hand should be placed on the "patient's" shoulder. He should be facing this person from the front. A simultaneous push back on the shoulder with a forward pull on the hip will effect an adjustment that should help to equalize the length of the legs.

A good pose that may help to effect this same adjustment is *Ardha-Matsyendrasana* (the Half Spinal Twist), with the knee of the leg that is to be lengthened pointed upward. This adjustment is also good for pains in the lower back.

VI. DIET

The knowledge of ancient India branched out into many fields. Yoga was the name given to one aspect of that culture: the science of spiritual development. This science has its physical aspects, particularly in *hatha yoga.* Even *hatha yoga,* however, was developed primarily for its usefulness to spiritual growth. The science of yoga was not an isolated, unique phenomenon of India's ancient culture. It was the application to one phase of life of an insight that penetrated into all of life's phases.

The medical science of ancient India, for example, is closely related to the teachings of yoga. It was known as *Ayurveda.* This is a vast, highly complex, and exceedingly sophisticated science that will in time prove worthy of detailed investigation by medical science.

The basis of *Ayurveda* is, in a sense, the same as that of yoga. The emphasis is on the strengthening of the life force, or energy, of the body, rather than on the mere mechanical functions of its organs.

The teachings of *Ayurveda* on the subject of diet, while not necessarily part of the yogic lore, are yet compatible with the yoga teachings. It might be well here to touch on them lightly.

According to *Ayurvedic* teachings, there are subtle magnetic currents in the atmosphere that affect the body variously at different times of the day. Thus, it is important to harmonize the bodily functions with these universal, natural influences.

Much is made of the different times of the day in relation to the position of the sun. For three hours after sunrise, for example, one is not supposed to eat solid foods. A light breakfast may be taken of orange juice and ground nuts (preferably almonds). The best time to eat a solid meal is between 9:00 a.m. and 12:00

noon. Food taken in the afternoon is said to be not easily digested, and therefore harmful to the body. From noon until evening, liquids only should be taken (but note the four-hour lapse mentioned below), or, if one is hungry, fruits and fruit juices.

The evening meal, according to *Ayurveda,* should be taken between 7:00 and 8:00 p.m., or at least not before 6:00 p.m.

For four hours after a meal, no water should be taken. If water is taken during the time of digestion, it will disturb the digestive process, and will tend to produce indigestion and gas.

RECIPES

Pampered Peas and Potatoes

1 pkg. frozen peas (or an equivalent amount of fresh peas)
4 cups diced, cooked potatoes
6 tablespoons butter
2 tablespoons curry powder
½ cup cream
chopped parsley

Cook peas; drain. Melt butter in skillet and mix in curry powder. Blend cream with butter-curry mixture, salt to taste; add peas and potatoes to sauce. Heat through. Garnish with parsley.

Lenten "Meat" Balls

2 cups cracker crumbs
½ cup walnuts—finely ground
¼ lb. sharp cheese, grated
3 eggs
salt, pepper, cumin, sage, oregano, and soy sauce to taste

Mix in food processor cracker crumbs, walnuts, and cheese. Season with salt, pepper, cumin, sage oregano, and soy sauce. Fold in 3 eggs beaten until light, adding a touch of water if needed. Form into 16 balls and set aside until firm.

Sauce:

1 quart tomato juice
2 teaspoons soy sauce
1 quart water
⅛–¼ teaspoon savory powder
4 stalks celery
4 carrots

Braise the "meatballs" in hot oil and put in boiling sauce, to which have been added 2 stalks of celery and 2 carrots, finely chopped. Simmer the meatballs in sauce for 1½ hours.

VII. MEDITATION

Attitude *(continued)*

Bali was a great king of ancient, legendary times. He was an *asura* (demon), which was how the ancient sages described worldly people, in whom ego and the pride of possession are still strong. (Most, perhaps all, of the ancient legends of India are deep, spiritual allegories.) But Bali was also a good man, as even worldly people often are. In fact, he was not worldly at all in the sense commonly understood in this dark age. He was a devotee, who undertook long and severe austerities until he received God's grace. His worldliness consisted only in the impure motives for which he sought that grace, and in the use he made of it once he had obtained it.

Protected now by the Lord's blessings, he extended his dominion over the three worlds, vanquishing the very gods, and dethroning their king, Indra. (This was only a way of saying that, like many imperfect devotees, Bali attributed the divine grace he had received in meditation to the power and splendor of his own ego.) As he proceeded on the inner path of self conquest, it was always with the delusive thought, "*I* and I alone am the conqueror!" It is possible to advance very far on the path, and to develop great mystical powers, and yet not know God, while remaining caught in egotism. The joke is that even though spiritual pride may cause us to consider as wholly ours whatever inner power we may have acquired by our meditative efforts, the power always is God's alone. That is why Jesus prayed, "*Thine* is the kingdom, the power, and the glory forever." But Bali was not so wise. He was an *asura*.

Naturally, the gods (his own higher tendencies) were offended at his presumption. But what could they do? It was with God's own power, even though misappropriated by ego-consciousness, that Bali had grown so powerful. Aditi, the mother of Indra, was especially distressed over the defeat of her son. (Bali's "feminine," devotional quality, in other words, "mother" of the inner light, was particularly grieved by his arrogance.) She prayed deeply to God, who finally blessed her, consenting to be born through her into this world. He came as a dwarf. (Even so, humble and seemingly insignificant, do the first glimmerings of true insight ever steal into our souls.)

Some years later, Bali held a great sacrifice, and invited all Brahmins to attend it. The Dwarf Brahmin, as Aditi's son had come to be known, appeared at the sacrifice, his countenance shining with inner light. Bali, inspired by the Dwarf's radiant features, asked him if there was anything he wanted.

"Only as much land," the Dwarf replied, "as I can cover in three steps."

"I freely grant your wish," Bali said. "But why is it that you wish so little? I could as easily give you a large estate, and would be most happy to do so."

"Three steps are quite enough for me," replied the Dwarf.

"Your Majesty!" cried Bali's guru, Shukra. "You do not realize what an enormous boon you have granted. It will mean nothing less than the sacrifice of your entire kingdom. Don't you see that in this little Brahmin shines the very effulgence of the Infinite? What is even one footstep to Him? With it he could cover the entire world!"

"So be it," said Bali, quietly. "I have pledged my word."

The Lord began suddenly to expand in all directions to infinity. With His first step He covered the entire earth; with His second, the heavens. His form filled the universe. To Bali He then said, smiling, "How can you fulfill your promise to Me now? There is no room left for Me to take My third step."

"There is, my Lord," said Bali, humbly at last. Prostrating himself in perfect surrender, he explained, "There is still my head. I entreat You to place Your foot upon it, and to keep it there forevermore."

The ability to surrender, as I mentioned in the seventh section of the last lesson, is essentially a feminine virtue. But devotion, service, surrender, and other essentially feminine attitudes, necessary as they are on the spiritual path, achieve their perfection—as Bali's did—in the abandonment of all personal attitudes, of all sense of distinctions of any kind, in the vision of God as the Sole Reality. This impersonal outlook is essentially masculine.

One's personal feelings, in other words, should not be directed downward, toward an increasing consciousness of distinctions, but upward, toward a vision of cosmic unity. Likes and dislikes should be dissolved in all-embracing love.

Mankind's "masculine" characteristics, similarly, should have for their direction an upward-flowing, ever-broader vision of unity. Reason that sees only distinctions everywhere will inevitably be guided downward, away from truth, and into that separative consciousness which is the essence of *maya* (delusion).*

Feeling, to be rightly guided, must flow upward, toward reason—must in that sense be led by reason. And reason, to be progressive and not merely theoretical, wisdom-guided and not desire-oriented, must grow out of calm feeling—must have the *support* of feeling.

When the direction of human consciousness and energy is downward in the spine, toward *maya,* reason (centered in the *ajna chakra*) becomes guided instead by feeling (centered in the *anahat,* or heart, *chakra*). That is why, when you want some thing intensely, no matter how obviously harmful it may be to you, reason is more likely to show you why you should have it than why you should not. It is the subtle reason why advertising is, more often than not, directed toward our emotions: For people generally understand that if human feeling can be converted, reason is more likely to tag along quietly.

When the direction of human consciousness and energy is upward, on the other hand, feeling becomes guided by reason. That is why, when your feelings are pure,† they support and don't tug against whatever your impartial reason shows you to be right. It is why women themselves usually turn to men for guidance on matters involving impartial reason, duty, or justice. It is also the subtle reason why outward positions of power have always been given preponderantly to men. For although there have been many excellent women rulers through history, and although it is women often who actually determine the course of human events, anthropologists have found no evidence to suggest that any human society, past or present, has ever been a full-fledged matriarchate, or mother-ruled society.

From the standpoint of meditation, these thoughts are important primarily as a guideline for the right direction of our spiritual attitudes. Many devotees, charmed by the inner sweetness that accompanies feelings of devotion and divine surrender, mistake the path for the goal. They envision themselves spending eternity singing to God, their Cosmic Beloved, or serving Him, or otherwise acting in the separate role of worshiper rather than merging into and becoming one with Him.

Mirabai, a woman saint who lived in the Sixteenth Century in India, was a great devotee of this kind. Her songs to

* Literally, *the measurer*—that which appears to separate the One Reality into innumerable segments.

† Open, for example, to receive, instead of clutching at things and at people with selfish desire.

Krishna are still popular today. The path of *gyana* (wisdom) was not for her; she considered it enough for eternity simply to sing God's praises.

There was another Indian woman saint, Gauribai, who lived three centuries later. Gauribai, too, wrote devotional songs. Unlike Mirabai, however, she also sat for long periods immersed in the oneness of *samadhi;* sometimes for fifteen days at a stretch she would remain motionless in that impersonal state. Interestingly, her guru told her that she was an incarnation of Mirabai. He said that Mirabai had failed to perfect herself in *gyana* and that it was to correct this saintly shortcoming that she had been reborn.

The consciousness of separate existence is born of delusion. The *Bhagavad Gita* says: "To the truly wise, a learned brahmin, a cow, an elephant, a dog, and an outcaste are all one." (V:18) And again: "He is said to be a fully Self-realized yogi . . . to whom a clod of earth, a stone, and gold are the same. That yogi stands supreme who regards with an equal eye well-wishers, friends and foes, relatives and strangers, those who are impartial to him and those who hate him, righteous people and evildoers." (VI:8,9)

A saint once was set upon and badly beaten by a band of ruffians. His brother disciples later found him, lying unconscious by the road. They carried him back to their ashram and nursed him lovingly back to consciousness. One of them was pouring a little milk into his mouth, when the saint started to open his eyes.

"Do you recognize who it is that is feeding you?" his brother inquired, gently.

"Yes," said the saint with a blissful smile. "The same One who beat me earlier!"

Rare is that wise sage who sees God in everything, and everything in God. It is to his state of consciousness that every devotee should aspire.

O yogi! Learn to be impersonal not only with others, but also with yourself. Understand that you are only an instrument of the Divine. Of yourself you are nothing. Of yourself you can do nothing.

The goal of all spiritual striving is to merge the little self in the Infinite Self. In that state, separate existence is abandoned forever. The ego will put up a mighty struggle to resist what to it seems but self-annihilation. But how wonderful is the Infinite! In it all things exist. In it nothing is ever lost. As the *Bhagavad Gita* puts it, "That which *is* can never cease to be. That which is not can never come into existence." (II:16) Self-awareness can never be obliterated. On the one hand it simply becomes expanded, in cosmic consciousness, to infinity. On the other hand, having once existed in a limited state, it retains this identity too—as an eternal, undimmable memory. The Infinite always remembers that it was, for a time, John Smith. Because there is no past or future in the Eternal Now, the memory of John Smith is a *living* awareness.

In meditation it is good, in addition to devotional thoughts, to meditate on your own true, formless state. Think of a blue light (since blue is the color of the Christ consciousness). Visualize this light gradually expanding, filling your body, then the room in which you are sitting, your city, your country, your continent, the world. Visualize this light expanding beyond the world, filling the solar system, our galaxy, the entire manifested universe. See all things glimmering in this infinite light. The scriptures say: "*Tat tuam asi!*" "Thou art that!" Dwell on the thought of your own infinite freedom. Why always affirm your temporary littleness? Patanjali said that divine realization is attained by awakening *smriti,* divine memory. In meditation the devotee at last remembers who and what He really is. *That* is the state of enlightenment. Any thought that feeds that divine memory will help to bring you back more and more to a recognition of the highest of all truths: "*Aham Brahm asmi!* I am Brahman!"

Hari AUM, *Tat, Sat*

Step Fourteen

The Yogic Scheme of Life

I. PHILOSOPHY

The Yogic Scheme of Life

Primitive peoples live in a world of miracles. To them every tree, every flower seems potentially a sign from heaven—perhaps even itself a deity. The twinkling stars at night betoken the lively fascination of gods and goddesses with the affairs of men. The raindrops may be God's tears for human sin and suffering.

How our modern enlightenment has changed all that! Now everything has a scientific explanation, or, if it doesn't, we feel sure it soon will have. Apparent signs and wonders are "coincidences." Flowers serve no other purpose than to attract bees, and through them to propagate their own species. The stars are much too far away to be concerned with human affairs, and of course would not be conscious of them even if they were closer. And the rain, as everyone knows, is a purely meteorological phenomenon.

I once heard a story about a man who went out duck hunting on a lake. As he shot his first duck, his dog jumped out of the boat to fetch it. But instead of swimming, the dog ran across the water.

The man couldn't believe his eyes. When his dog ran out to fetch a second duck, the man decided that perhaps his beer had been somehow "enriched."

The next day he took along a witness. Again, as he shot his first duck, his dog jumped out of the boat to fetch it. Again it ran across the water. The man looked at his friend to catch his reaction. There was none.

"Am I losing my mind?" wondered the hunter. He shot a second duck, and again his dog ran out to fetch it. This time, too, his friend took in the scene with no sign of interest.

"D-d-did you see what my dog just did?" asked the hunter, anxiously.

"I saw," replied his friend. "The stupid thing can't swim."

What makes this story amusing is not the friend's dullness in failing to recognize a miracle when he saw one, but rather his exaggeration of an attitude that has become so common these days: one of studied indifference to anything unusual or wonderful—an inbred assumption that everything can be explained in terms of the utterly commonplace.

Modern science it is, of course, that has fostered this attitude—science, with its cool insistence on accepting only what it can test and prove. But yoga, too, demands proofs, not assumptions. Like modern science, yoga proceeds from the known to the unknown, from the demonstrated to the still-sought-after. In both sciences, the mundane and the spiritual, there is a definite risk of projecting onto the vast universe of unexplored realities a gray vision of mediocrity—as if an Englishman were to see the greatness of Einstein in terms of his ability to serve good tea. It is not only scientists and the people influenced by their approach to life who tend to see everything in terms of the prosaic. Many yogis, too, especially in the West where yoga is only beginning to become known, define their science in terms of its ability to cure their sinus trouble or their insomnia. Many yogis of the more intellectual kind, even in India, refer somewhat slightingly to high states of consciousness, as if *samadhi* were but a hop beyond ordinary, human consciousness.

Science is limited by the fact that, while it may know generally where it is, it cannot know where it is going. Yoga suffers from no such disadvantage. Great yogis in every age have reached the ultimate goal of yoga practice. Their vision, described in the ancient *Vedanta* philosophy, forms an important adjunct to the "how-to" approach of the yoga science.

For India's ancient seers understood, as modern man so far has not, that man lives as much by his philosophy of life as by his practical knowledge. Everything he does expresses, in a sense, this philosophy. The very way he moves his body reveals to the sensitive eye whether he sees life as a series of contests with threatening but nameless foes, or as a perpetual shopping expedition for familiar ideational antiques, or as a brave and joyous adventure into the shining unknown. Man simply cannot think and have no philosophy at all.

The *Vedanta* philosophy describes the true goal of yoga practice, lest yoga practitioners address themselves to scaling molehills, not mountains. It is a philosophy based on the actual experiences of enlightened yogis, and is therefore not a *separate* system of thought, but the same system with merely a different emphasis. *Vedanta* and yoga form two legs of a tripod.

The third leg is supplied by the system known as *Sankhya*. Where *Vedanta* describes the Ultimate Reality, and yoga presents the science by which that Reality may be realized, *Sankhya* examines man's present state, and his need to seek a higher one.

Yoga is as closely tied to its sister philosophies as modern science is to the cultural attitudes of which it is a part. In fact, we are really talking of only one basic life view seen from different angles. Since in these lessons we have approached that essential vision through the teachings of yoga, I think it will be less confusing to the student if we refer to the different aspects of this basic view as *yogic*. The masters of India, certainly, waste little time in separating one philosophy from another. To them, such distinctions are merely academic. Basically, the three systems are one.

Patanjali's *Yoga Sutras* (Yoga Aphorisms) begin with the sentence, "Now [we take up] the study of yoga." Swami Sri Yukteswar, my guru's guru, explained that that word, "now," was intended to imply a continuation of philosophy: The science of self-development could be pursued sincerely only after the student had become convinced of his own deep, *personal* need for something higher. Yoga, in other words, was not intended for armchair philosophers. The foundation for right yoga practice must be those insights into life's transitoriness which are the special emphasis of *Sankhya* philosophy. Since we have already explored many of those insights in these lessons, however, let us now view the whole yogic scheme of life from the other end of the funnel—the cosmic.

The Hindu scriptures offer an interesting slant on the story of Creation: Instead of creating the universe, they say God *manifested* it; He *became* it. This is not to say that, in becoming something new, God's nature in any way changed. Nor does it mean that God Himself evolves as His manifested universe evolves. The *Bhagavad Gita* states explicitly that the Spirit, though dwelling in the heart of all things, is unaffected by them. Where there is anger or hatred, it is God's power alone that is expressed, there being no other power to express; yet God, while thus manifesting as anger, is not angry, and while manifesting in the universe as good and evil, is neither good nor evil.

This is perhaps the most difficult aspect of the yoga teachings for the human intellect to understand. Christian theologians have pounced on it (gleefully, alas) as proof that Hinduism has not dealt *responsibly* with man's need to combat evil and to seek goodness, and holds out no vision for him of Ultimate Purpose. But since scriptures don't get written to rob men of their incentive to be good, nor to undermine whatever sense of purpose they may naturally feel in their lives; and since, even if anyone were to write such a book and call it a scripture, people certainly would not resort to it for thousands of years, quoting from it hopefully in their hours of darkness and despair, we may confidently say that those theologians have missed the boat.

Even a novelist, when "creating" a villain, is not necessarily villainous himself for having done so. A novelist's creation too, if it is perceptive, is a manifestation of himself, born of an inner identity of sorts with his character. Yet the novelist may in fact be a better, more compassionate man than most people for his empathy, not a worse one. God, too, brings all things into outward expression out of His own consciousness. God is not a man, nor a person of any kind, but an infinite Spirit—infinite, not in the sense of being too vast or too ancient for finite space and time to hold Him, but rather in the sense of belonging to a level of reality where space and time simply do not exist. God, or Spirit, is like an ocean, in relation to which the manifested forms of creation are like waves. The waves may be large or small, but we may not say that the ocean itself has thereby become large or small: The total amount of water in either case is the same. A part of the ocean takes on the shape of its waves; yet in no way can the ocean itself be defined in terms of its waves. It is not more an ocean for having them, nor less so for not having them. If one wave crashes violently (let us say, angrily) against another one, the ocean has not to this extent become violent or angry, for it is itself both of those waves: the oppressor and the oppressed. A consciousness of opposition can spring only from a consciousness of essential distinctions. It cannot exist where one's view of reality is complete.

Again, if one wave towers high above its fellows, a corresponding trough merely appears in the water elsewhere. Everything in the overall view must balance out so that the median ocean level remains constant. Even so the Spirit, in manifesting the phenomenal universe, did so by the principle of *dwaita* (duality). The one consciousness of Spirit, moving a part of Itself in opposite directions from a state of rest in the center, took on an appearance of innumerable separate existences. But these existences are an appearance, merely, like the waves on the sea. They have no essential reality of their own except as the sea itself is real.

A close view of the ocean surface reveals not only large waves and small ones, but wavelets upon larger waves, ripples upon larger ripples, their complexity increasing the more closely one studies them. Duality, too, is no simple, single movement left or right or up or down from, but still fairly suggestive of, the central, unmoving Spirit. There are movements within movements, dualities within dualities, oppositions within oppositions, until the essentially still nature of things is completely lost sight of in a welter of complexity.

Everything manifested has its opposite: love and hatred, pleasure and pain, heat and cold, light and darkness, positive and negative, male and female—and yes, good and evil. Within each of these opposites there are relativities—gradations of light and darkness, for instance, within the overall phenomenon of darkness, and gradations of good and evil within the general movement of consciousness towards evil.

What, indeed, *are* good and evil? Evil is that movement of consciousness and energy which obscures the essential reality of things as the Infinite. Good is that which helps to clarify that reality. The reality itself simply *is*. There is no other reality in relation to which it might be termed *good*. But in relative existence, which is the state of things in the manifested universe, evil is evil because it obscures the true state of things and thereby induces progressively the bondage of delusion (*maya*), of limitation of all kinds, of inharmony, and enmity, and hatred, which are signs, simply, of identification with one expression of reality (one's own ego) to the exclusion of all others.

The movement of consciousness toward this state of progressive duality is an actual force—necessary to bring the universe into manifestation. It is what is known as the satanic force. God, the Supreme Spirit, is not directly responsible for the delusions and sufferings that result from the existence of this force. To manifest creation at all, it was necessary to produce a separative movement of consciousness, but the further ramifications of this movement developed as a result of that force itself assuming the delusion of a separate existence, and seeking to perpetuate its own consciousness of individuality—if we may consider individual an all-but-infinite consciousness, unlimited by form of any kind. Satan—not a man in a red suit with horns, tail, and cloven hooves, but an omnipresent, conscious force—is a reality, one to which every master has definitely testified. It is not merely a subjective thought in the minds of men, but a universal stream of magnetic power into which men may be drawn by their own active interest in, and desire for, the endless variety of manifested phenomena rather than the one all-dissolving consciousness of Spirit.

The opposite stream of consciousness—from complexity to divine oneness—is necessary also to the cosmic balance. Man can enter this stream, too. The choice is up to him. Each stream of consciousness has power to affect only those who enter it of their own free will. Assuming that most people, out of ignorance, have already entered the negative stream, it is possible for them, by changing their own interest, to come out of it and enter the positive stream.

Nothing is farther from God or closer to Him than anything else, but some things *appear* farther or closer according to whether they express more of the delusive quality of distinctness, or more of the divine qualities of unity and harmony. The closer one's consciousness is to the divine ocean, the more he senses the inner unity of all things, and the more naturally therefore he lives at peace with the universe. The more one's mind is drawn to the ceaseless play of duality, the more he beholds everything in conflict with everything else, and consequently the less harmony he finds in himself and in others. Low waves, close to the ocean bosom, are more suggestive of the calm ocean depths than tall waves crashing together in a storm. The consciousness of humble, spiritual people is still a part of universal duality, but the love and joy they express is a self-giving love, a joy not in specific things, but in the Self. The more, however, one concentrates on the storm of duality, the more the divine quality of love becomes broken up into numberless desires and attachments, and joy into a host of petty enthusiasms. Where the waves rise high, their corresponding troughs are deeper by that much. Where love is broken up into many worldly desires, it will also manifest as antipathies: Likes are inevitably balanced by dislikes. If one's likes are intense, one's dislikes will be intense also. And the same also for joy: The more one's joy is centered in things rather than in the inner Self, the more things one finds also to make him miserable. Deluded people think by a multitude of fascinations to increase their awareness, but in fact excessive outward stimulation only dulls the awareness. The person who excuses an erratic life style by saying, "Well, at least I'm *living!*" offers the best possible disproof of his own claim. Over the years he becomes jaded, cynical, leaden-eyed, and insensitive. The balanced, inwardly centered person on the other hand, far from sinking slowly into a bog of apathy, becomes only more vitally joyous and aware over the years.

The gradations of apparent divine unity and delusive disunity, of the sense of union with God and of separateness from Him, are called in Hinduism the three *guna*s (qualities): *sattwa* (elevating, or spiritualizing), *rajas* (activating, or energizing), and *tamas* (darkening, inertial, or stultifying). These *guna*s represent not only different stages of cosmic manifestation, but also the different *directions* of thought and energy that result in those manifestations. Thus, even on a level of *sattwa* there is *some* consciousness of distinctions as opposed to cosmic unity. (Were it not so, even *sattwa guna* would cease to exist, and the soul would merge back into oneness with the ocean of Spirit.) This consciousness represents the *rajasic* and *tamasic* aspects of *sattwa guna*. It may only manifest itself as an eagerness to help others; nevertheless, this consciousness of their distinctness from oneself might, if continually emphasized, carry the mind gradually so far out of itself that it would become lost in the darkest pits of *tamo guna*.

Even in the depths of *tamas,* on the other hand, there cannot but be *some* urge toward higher things. The wish, at that stage, to uplift oneself by work, or to get along better with one's neighbors, or even to steal more cleverly, represents the *sattwic* and *rajasic* aspects of *tamo guna*. If such a person will continually emphasize these positive *directions* of awareness in himself, he will gradually rise toward spirituality.

The whole universe is thus a mixture of these three *guna*s. The *tamasic* quality represents the pull away from Spirit, and thus (though I have never actually heard it identified as such) the satanic force. The *sattwic* quality represents the divine urge in all beings to achieve union with God, the one Source of all life. Between these two opposites, like the neutral gear on a car in which the motor spins but can't move the car either forward or backward, is the *rajasic,* or activating quality. Under the influence of this *guna* the mind seeks diversity rather than definite direction. In this attachment to diversity it may drift toward a greater affinity for things and people, and thus toward that sense of underlying unity with them which is *sattwic;* or it may drift more and more toward a sense of distinctions, of rivalry and oppositions, and thus sink gradually into the spiritual chaos of *tamas. Raja guna* gives objectifying power to both *sattwa* and *tamas*. For *tamasic* people, it represents the necessary steppingstone to *sattwa guna;* for *sattwic* people, it represents the first pull away from spiritual reality, carrying them into worldly involvements that in themselves are more or less neutral, but that can also develop into that kind of ardent dedication to self-gratification which is the main entrance, so to speak, to the outward-moving stream of *tamo guna*.

In *sattwa,* as I have said, there is also a touch of *rajas* and *tamas,* and in *tamas* there is a touch of *rajas* and *sattwa*. In *rajas,* too, the other two *guna*s are present. All things, I said, are a mixture of the three *guna*s. It is the *predominance* of one *guna* or another that defines a thing as basically *sattwic, rajasic,* or *tamasic.*

The very stages of creation express these three *guna*s.

When the Spirit first manifested the universe, a portion of its consciousness moved in the form of thoughts. Out of these thoughts evolved the causal, or ideational, universe—a universe not of forms, colors, and textures, but of pure ideas. Being closest to the Spirit in its manifestation of pure consciousness, the causal universe expresses primarily *sattwa guna.*

Spirit then vibrated Its thoughts more vigorously. Like a person sleeping, his thoughts gradually forming to become a dream, so a portion of the manifested ideas of God became the astral universe, a universe of lights, shapes, and colors—all in the form of pure energy, and hence a manifestation of *rajo guna*.

Finally, the Spirit vibrated a portion of this astral universe more grossly still, and energy took on the appearance of solid matter: the physical universe. Scientists nowadays state that matter is really nothing but energy. Its solidity and other material properties, as yogis anciently claimed, are an appearance, merely. Of the three levels of creation, this physical universe is a manifestation primarily of *tamo guna,* the quality of inertia. Yet on this level, too, the other *guna*s may be discerned. Whole galaxies, in fact, were said by my guru to express predominantly *sattwic, rajasic,* or *tamasic* qualities—of course, within the relatively *tamasic* medium of matter. Whole galaxies, that is to say, are spinning vortices of negative energy, whose planets are peopled primarily with evil beings. Other galaxies—including our own—are vortices of *rajo guna;* their planets produce, at their highest life-levels, people who are primarily worldly-minded—i.e., not markedly either spiritual or evil. And other galaxies there are that, in relation to the other galaxies in this physical universe, contain at the pinnacle of their evolution predominantly *sattwic* beings.

Each of the other universes, too, contains its own mixtures and gradations of *sattwa, rajas,* and *tamas*. The astral universe, for example, contains dark hells as well as shining heavens. (The causal universe, being primarily *sattwic,* has no such extreme contradictions.) The vastness of cosmic creation simply staggers the mind. Even in this relatively small physical universe, astronomers estimate that there are about 100 billion stars. If national budget statistics have inured you to thinking in such astronomical terms, it might help to underscore the vastness of this figure to consider that, if you wanted to count to only *one* billion, and counted one number every second without ever stopping to eat or sleep, it would take you approximately thirty-three years to reach this figure. Someone has estimated that if you counted the numbers by *naming* them ("one thousand, two hundred and three," etc.), to reach one billion would require over 3,000 years.

As if this were not enough, the Hindu scriptures state that this vast cosmos is manifested by God, then (perhaps after some trillions of years) dissolved by Him back into Himself, repeatedly. These are the Days and Nights of Brahma—vast stretches of time beside which one human lifetime seems almost too brief for serious consideration!

Before creation was manifested, the

Spirit alone existed—"One without a second." In manifesting Itself, It, too, assumed in a sense a role relative to Its creation. Though untouched by creation, and essentially unchanged, seen from the standpoint of creation itself the Spirit appears as the Creator—God the Father, *Sat,* the pure essence of reality. Spirit also is creation itself; a portion of Its consciousness has manifested Itself as the infinitely varied forms of creation. And Spirit is still-ly present in the heart of even the restless atoms. As the creative power that manifests the universe, God is spoken of as AUM (*Om*), the cosmic vibration. And as the still Presence at the heart of all phenomena, the reflection (so to speak) of the Spirit beyond creation, God is spoken of as *Tat,* or *Kutastha Chaitanya,* the Christ Consciousness.

AUM is the sacred Word, or Holy Ghost, of the Christian scriptures. The Spirit, in setting Its consciousness into movement to manifest the "waves" of cosmic creation, created a vibration with power and intelligence of its own to continue the act of creation to all its subsequent levels of manifestation. ("The Word was with God, and the Word was God." (John 1:1))

Reflected, or present, in the heart of all this cosmic activity is at the same time the undisturbed consciousness of God—the ever-present, though silent, judge and witness. These three aspects—the Spirit as non-involved Creator, as creation itself, and the Spirit also present *in* creation—form the Trinity of Father, Son, and Holy Ghost, or *Sat Tat* AUM as it is called in the more ancient Hindu scriptures.

AUM, though a divine intelligence, is also intelligence *in action.* Where there is movement of any kind, even of thought, there is also sound. The sacred sound of AUM can be heard by the yogi in deep meditation. Where the forms of creation represent the outward-flowing power of AUM, and thus represent Nature in Her aspect of Satan, the sacred sound of AUM heard in meditation represents the inward-flowing stream of consciousness—Nature in Her aspect of the all-compassionate, all-liberating Divine Mother. Man's duty as a child of the Infinite is to overcome his fascination with AUM in its outward expressions—the endless variety of the manifested universe—and to enter the Godward-flowing, purely *sattwic* stream of AUM as divine sound, love, and bliss.

There is nothing in the universe that is not living. There is nothing that does not manifest divine consciousness. The very rocks contain the germ of life and consciousness. Evolution is not a blind thrust upward from below, a mere incident in the struggle for survival. Still less is it, as modern theorists hold, an accident. It is consciousness, inherent in all things, reaching out to reclaim its own. All things are divine; sooner or later they must realize their own divinity.

I can imagine a cartoonist having a good time with this concept: depicting a rock, perhaps, in the process of muttering blissfully to itself, "I and my Father are one!"; or a man gravely engrossed in a game of chess with a cabbage plant. But of course, for consciousness to express itself effectively through the medium of matter it must have a suitable vehicle—a highly developed nervous system—just as, for energy to express itself as power in a material way, it must use the principle of leverage. The intelligent life force that is locked up, so to speak, in lower life forms must find higher and higher channels through which to express its intelligence. This it can do only through a process of repeated reincarnation. As a child grows out of one set of clothes and must be given a new set, so the life force that animates one combination of chemicals (in the form, say, of a beetle) must find a higher combination (in the form, say, of a bird) once it has outgrown the beetle stage.

The soul is individualized Spirit. Individuality is one of the properties of every atom; no two snowflakes are completely identical. (One is reminded here of the scriptural saying, "The Spirit is center everywhere, circumference nowhere.") The soul, having been placed at the start of the race, must run its course before it can get off the track.* This it must do through a long succession of physical bodies, evolving to ever higher forms until it reaches the human level. Evolution of the soul up to this level is a more or less automatic climb; the intelligence reaches out for continually greater awareness, but is not yet sufficiently developed to become caught in the countless bypaths that open up to a more inquiring mind. The Hindu scriptures state that it requires from five to eight million lives for the soul to evolve to the human level. Once on this level, the soul finds itself equipped with all the physical tools it needs to achieve freedom from bondage to matter—a highly developed brain and nervous system, and a body that can respond efficiently to the commands of its brain. But it also has an intelligence sufficiently refined to pursue side interests: those not concerned with its own ultimate freedom. These it pursues with a vengeance.

Theoretically, it should be possible for the soul, once it reaches the human level, to realize its true, spiritual nature fairly quickly. In practice, alas, the process invariably is a very long one. When the soul is first born into a human body, it feels no pressing need to realize any deeper reality. It carries with it into the human form much of its previous

* *Why* it ever entered the course in the first place is an academic question, now that we are here. Our present problem is how to get out. But we may safely assume that, at some time in our past, we did "that which we ought not to have done," accepting the rules of bondage in preference to those leading to liberation.

animalistic outlook. Primitive peoples often fall into this category, but so also do others. (I recall a Hindu couple that I met in New Delhi. The husband insisted that his wife had been a cow in her last life—hardly a compliment, I thought, even granting the Hindus' ingrained love of cows. But in response to his remark his wife would only give a most bovine smile. It was easy to suspect that her husband just might be right!)

Evolution is not a straight line, but a spiral. Primitive peoples, like certain animals, often have keen intuitions of a certain limited kind, but intuitions nevertheless which they may not recapture until, much later, they begin to develop spiritual awareness. They know what is happening to their relatives at a distance. They often sense the future. A few of them even exercise a certain control over the elements. (I know of several cases, for instance, where such people by their thoughts or prayers brought rain.) They also have a notable mastery over their bodies, comparable to that found otherwise in highly advanced souls. Though their senses are more refined than those of civilized people, they can ignore physical pain of the most severe kind. A doctor friend of mine who worked with primitive peoples once told me of some of them who would come into his clinic after a Saturday-night fight, perhaps holding their intestines in their hands. "Don't bother to give me an anesthetic, Doc," they would say. "Just shove them in and sew me up!"

Yet these same people, close as they are on one level to perfect mastery over their bodies, think only of enjoying the world as they have found it. It is quite possible that they have not a single abstract thought in their lives! Talk to them of God, and you may have to describe for them an old man in a white palace in the sky for them to grasp anything of your ideas at all. Speak to them of a higher purpose in life, and you may find your hands full just getting across that this concept includes not killing people merely because they belong to a neighboring tribe. I do not mean that primitive peoples are devoid of wisdom. Nor do I mean that advanced souls are never to be found among them; such souls may indeed be born among them, if only to uplift them. But by and large the innocence and the surprising insight alike of the savage are marks of the soul's first foray onto the human plane—before the ego has had time to develop "complexes."

It is one of the strange paradoxes of life that, while the ego is the greatest barrier to divine attainments, one needs a well-developed ego to long for those attainments. The animals have very little ego sense. The very real greatness of primitive peoples is due largely to the unobtrusiveness, or at least the relative simplicity, of their egos.

As man progresses through the long

spiral of incarnations, however, seeking happiness and fulfillment in one material channel after another, and repeatedly being disappointed, he begins to become painfully aware of his own personal frustration and inadequacy. Consequently he begins gradually to develop a desire to find deeper, personal, solutions. The desire to seek something deeper demands this sense of *personal* need. The ego, therefore, though in the end our enemy, is for a long time our greatest friend.

What carries man through incarnation after incarnation of delusion is the outwardly propelling force of desire. Wisdom is the realization that everything we are seeking may be found truly in the Self alone. But for many incarnations the soul seeks itself in outward reflections, and projects onto mere things the joy that is its own nature. How many are the channels it explores! How many the bitter disappointments, the fleeting satisfactions, the subsequent losses and bereavements! How long the path—through so many eons of time! through so many myriads of circumstances! on how many planets! Could even millions of years suffice to tell the tale? The great age and vastness of a galaxy have their counterpart in this finite-seeming, but equally infinite soul!

Why, one may ask, when the physical body dies, does not the soul merge back into the infinite? The reason is that the body, like the physical universe, is only the grossest stage of manifestation for the indwelling spirit. Behind the physical body, animating and directing it, is the astral body—a body of light and energy. Behind that is the causal, or ideational body. When the body of man dies, the astral body lives on. His desires live on also, for these, forming as they do vortices of *energy*, belong not to his physical, but to his astral body. But because desire directs energy, so long as his desires are for worldly enjoyment they draw him again and again into physical incarnation. After death he goes for a time to the astral plane, but his time there is limited by the strength of his physical desires. Only to the extent that matter has loosened its hold on him (which is to say, of course, to the extent that *he* has loosened his hold on *it*) can he find a home for himself on the astral plane.

Indeed, not only is the length of time he spends in the astral universe determined by his degree of material attachment. Even the extent of his awareness of that universe depends on his material involvement. The very worldly person is conscious only dimly, if at all, of his astral visits between earthly incarnations. His perceptions may be more in the form of dreams—pleasant, or otherwise! The more refined a person becomes, however, the more sensitive he is after death to the infinitely more beautiful astral world. Its subtlety no longer eludes him, for he has learned that the essence of true beauty *is* subtle.

The astral universe contains many different vibrational spheres. Unlike this physical universe, where people of many different kinds are thrown together, in the astral world the different planets attract only people on their own vibrational "wavelength." Where on earth there is disharmony and discord, in the astral world—except in its lower regions, or hells—there is harmony and peace. Yet, strange as it may at first seem, it is here in this physical world that the greatest spiritual progress can be made. The harmony of astral existence offers no real incentive to further progress. Like the delight felt by the ego on first experiencing the relative freedom and expanded awareness of a human body, the astral world offers such rare delights—beautiful scenery, compatible companions, satisfying labors, and exquisite feelings; this world is only a poor copy of that one!—that the ego is too easily drawn once again to seek its fulfillments outside the Self. Therefore it is said that even the gods consider it desirable to be born in a human body. With all its limitations, this physical world offers the best battleground for spiritual progress.

True yogis, indeed, shun the astral world as but another trap. It is not necessary (though perhaps it is usual) for the soul to evolve by slow degrees through the astral world before attaining the greater freedom of the causal, or even of cosmic consciousness (*nirbikalpa samadhi*). Strange as it may seem, even animals have attained to the highest consciousness, at least after death, by the special grace of great masters. Wherever one finds himself on the evolutional scale, he can realize God then and there if he will but offer himself unreservedly to that highest Truth. For at no time is the soul less a part of God than at any other.

When in meditation one attains a state of ecstasy, it is in his causal body that he is functioning. The yogi, therefore, by striving to be always bliss-minded, lives more and more on a causal level, and bypasses the grosser attractions of the astral spheres.

All sin, and all virtue, may be summed up in terms of these principles. That is sin which obscures one's nature. That is virtue which helps to reveal it. Hatred, jealousy, violence, and similar affirmations of one's own separateness from others are obvious causes of ignorance in the ego, for the Divine cannot be found in ourselves if we deny Him in others. But even a seemingly innocent enjoyment of the world, so long as it contains the germs of attachment and desire, cannot but lead to bondage. Not only is it a question of mistakenly placing our center outside ourselves. It is also that, placing our reliance in the fickle storm of *dwaita* (duality), we must suffer a balancing pain for every outward pleasure. The soul seeks bliss because its own nature *is* bliss, but in seeking the false comforts of duality it finds itself increasingly tossed between the oppositions of reward and disaster. It is not earthly pleasures in themselves that must be shunned so much as slavish identification with them, for, as the *Isha Upanishad* states, "One should live in this world without attachment, doing his duty, and, so doing, should wish to live for 100 years." The entire emphasis of this truth is positive. What one must learn, quite simply, is to be positive in the right way, and about the right things!

Egoism is the sole cause of bondage. It is because of ego that desires infest the heart. My guru defined the ego as the soul identified with the body. So long as this identity persists, every action by the body will be viewed as an action *by oneself*. So long, therefore, will the body (or its successor in a future incarnation) have to bear the consequences, good, bad, or indifferent, of that action. Such is the law of *karma,* the counterpart, on a subtler level, of the physical principle of action and reaction. Soul freedom consists essentially of banishing this sense of ego by realizing that we are not the body, but the Infinite Spirit.

In the first stages of liberation, the state of *jivan mukta,* this realization is reached; the ego cannot acquire any new *karma,* for to all practical purposes it has ceased to exist. One's past *karma,* however, must still be worked out, for it is one thing to realize that from now on God is the Sole Doer in one's life, and quite another to free oneself of the memory of actions already performed in a limiting state of ego-consciousness. It is not so much a question of unraveling *all* the tapestry of past *karma,* but of finally convincing the soul that it is free even of its actions (*karma*s) and self-definitions of the past. Once this state has been reached, and not until then, final liberation is attained. The individual wave of bliss merges into the vast ocean of *satchidanandam* ("existence-consciousness-bliss," or, as my guru described it, "ever-existing, ever-conscious, ever-new bliss"). All that it retains now of its individuality is the memory that its own Self, the Infinite Spirit, existed for a time as a certain ego. But the memory will be of something that happened, merely; it will have ceased to be in any way a self-definition.

Can such a soul ever reappear in a physical body to help others? Yes. If he does so it will be as an *avatar,* a divine incarnation. That is what Paramhansa Yogananda was, among other great masters. That is why he often said, "I killed Yogananda long ago. No one dwells in this temple now but God."

And that should be the goal of yoga students: not to find God selfishly for themselves, but to find Him that they may give Him to all.

II. YOGA POSTURES

The highest goal of yoga practice is to reach a state of *sahaja* (ease), where the yogi no longer finds it necessary to engage in formal meditative practices, but remains always in a state of divine union even while going about his normal physical activities. One of the goals of the yoga postures, similarly, is to reach a point where one's every movement expresses the same grace as he expresses through the practice of the postures themselves. That is to say, the yoga postures should lead one out of the narrow confines of a specific group of poses to the realization that all of his movements can in a sense be yoga postures. The poise with which he moves into a yoga position should be translated into his daily life as the poise with which he rises from a chair, plays with a child, breathes, or greets a stranger. Every act of life should be deliberate, a conscious expression of inner peace and harmony.

Now that you have learned so many formal yoga postures, try also to incorporate the attitudes behind them into a few specific, everyday movements of your own. Don't make only a general resolution to be more yogic in all of your movements. Back up that vague intention, rather, with specific actions: the way you walk to work, perhaps, or the way you wash the supper dishes—something that you can keep your mind on while you're doing it, and preferably something that permits continuous, flowing movements.

Then try gradually to extend this practice to other actions. Remember, your feeling of peace must flow *from within*. It should not be done with a consciousness of its effect on others. The purpose of this suggestion is not to compete with the charm schools, but only to help you to feel inwardly more in tune with life.

In this connection, you might also try this technique for meditation in action:

A question often asked is, "How can I keep the peace of meditation, and the inspiration that I feel then, when I am at the office, or in the factory, or hurrying to get my shopping done and return home in time to cook dinner?" The bridge between peaceful meditation and the daily bustle of activity is, especially for the neophyte, a flimsy one: Often, simply to cross it safely, he feels that he must leave his peace behind—lest by driving too peacefully on the freeway, for instance, he fails to relate realistically to some other driver who just doesn't know what great things meditation can do for one. But the yogi must learn in time to preserve his inner peace without acting as though he had just been hit by a falling beam. In fact, inner peace should make one's reflexes *faster,* one's common sense even more realistic. It's a question of habit.

For any new state of consciousness to become a habit, it should be practiced deliberately. Meditative peace will inevitably seep into all your activities over a period of time. But why be satisfied with a mere seep? To feel peace in action more quickly, and more fully, it needs to be brought into outward expression consciously and deliberately.

What is needed to develop the habit of preserving one's calmness is some activity that will entail less involvement in activity as such, so that the mind may be free still to cling to the peace of meditation. We need a bridge to take us over the gap from inner peace to outward preoccupation. Once the peace of meditation has been practiced in moderate activity, it will be easier to keep it when one's activity becomes intense. It is like a child learning to tie his shoelaces. If you tell him, "Come on Johnny, tie your shoelaces, we're in a hurry!" he will run to catch up with you with his shoelaces untied. He must learn to tie them slowly before the act of tying them can become so automatic that he can perform the task quickly, while yet talking of other things.

I have found it exceedingly helpful to pass from meditation to *slow* movement, in which I try to accomplish nothing, movement in which my mind is on the action itself, rather than on the accomplishment of any particular goal. I may walk, for example, moving quite slowly, not hiking. I feel the movement of my muscles, the swing of my arms and legs. I feel that I am bringing peace and joy into my whole body. Then I gaze around me, and become aware one by one of specific things in my environment: perhaps the flutter of a leaf, or the nodding of the grass before a breeze, the ripple of sunlight on a patch of water, the barking of a dog, the laughter of a child, the honking of a distant car horn. Each one of these I perceive in turn, and reach out to it with my peace, blessing it as it were, and in turn feeling as if God were conveying to me through that phenomenon some special, personal message. At last I feel that all these sights and sounds and inner movements of my body are joined in harmony to some great symphony of life, that the peace within and the peace without are one.

From this state it is easy to proceed to activities that demand more of my attention, and yet to cling to this sense of oneness and inspiration that make quiet meditation the most wonderful part of the yogi's daily life.

A final word on the postures: In the science of *hatha yoga,* many variations are taught for every basic pose. I cannot but think that the reason for so many variations is that each person, unique in his own humanity, must express himself in some ways uniquely. Basic, universal teachings can be offered to all men, but once the principal purposes have been understood, each man may feel a certain freedom to express them in the ways that are most natural to his own body.

Natural development is a basic part of the yoga teachings. Try to capture your own body's rhythms, and in so doing, make this science truly your own.

III. BREATHING

Transcendence is the goal of life. Rest is the goal of action. Breathlessness is the final goal of all breathing exercises. Spirit is the eternal silence out of which all sound and vibration are born. Deep yoga practice is not possible until superficial movements, including the movements of breath, have been stilled, leaving the mind free to soar in superconsciousness.

That the breath can be stilled may be seen from the fact that man breathes in proportion to his body's need to cleanse itself of broken-down cell tissues. After running a race, or while experiencing intense emotion, one breathes more heavily. The body's need for oxygen is greater at such times. In deep sleep, on the contrary, the breath becomes slow because the body's need for it is slight.

You may already have observed in meditation that there are times when your breath ceases to flow. At such times the beginner is often afraid. There is no need for such fear. One has simply relaxed so deeply that very little carbon is being formed in his body, to be thrown out by the lungs as carbon dioxide. When the yogi becomes calm within, he can remain breathless (and more fully conscious than would be possible in a normal physical state) for long periods of time.

Hatha yoga teachings often stress *kumbhaka,* or the forcible retention of the air in the lungs. This is artificial breathlessness—unscientifically, and sometimes even injuriously, induced. Breathlessness should be, rather, a perfectly natural outgrowth of complete inner calmness and relaxation.

After practicing the breathing exercises, go into inner stillness. Feel the connection between your breath and the Cosmic Breath, as if your breath were but a function of the breezes of cosmic consciousness. In your breathing, as in your working, feel that you are an instrument of the Divine.

IV. ROUTINE

In keeping with what I said in this lesson under Postures, it is important that one's routine, too, be personalized. The poses that you, personally, find most helpful are those which you should practice.

But do not take this advice as an excuse to practice only those poses which are easiest for you. Understand that if, for example, you cannot easily bend forward, this is a sign that you should give *more* emphasis, not less, to the poses that will help you to overcome this deficiency. A limber spine is necessary both for good health and for a more vital awareness.

Bearing in mind the body's needs, however, select those poses in which you yourself find the most enjoyment.

V. HEALING

One indication of the health of the body is the skin. Boils and other eruptions are an obvious sign of impurities in the bloodstream. A pallid complexion is a quick indicator of a low vitality. Smooth, soft skin is a sign of good health.

The yogi's body is very soft in repose. The muscles of a strong man who practices yoga may feel like those of a woman. But when the yogi chooses to send energy to his muscles to tense them, they become hard, like steel. The softness of a yogi's body has a resilience to it; it is not flabby. His skin is soft, but not sagging or spongy.

The palms are a good indicator of one's health and vitality. Soft, flaccid palms are not a sign of good health, or of dynamic vitality. Hard hands are a sign of tension throughout the body that in time must result in breakdowns, inviting disease. The palms should be resilient to pressure from the fingers. A certain rosiness in the color of the hand will be an indication of good health.

When I met my guru, Paramhansa Yogananda, he told me that when giving interviews he did not even feel his body below the chest; so great was his relaxation. The yogi, no matter how hard he works physically, must be able to withdraw the energy from his body, to become relaxed and soft when the body's need for energy ceases.

Exercises that are good for the skin include all the bending exercises, the headstand, and those poses, especially, which tense and relax the muscles, and which gently exercise the heart (as in the Plow Pose and the Cobra Pose).

It is excellent for the skin for one to get out of doors into the fresh air for at least part of every day. Expose as much of your body as possible to the elements, especially to the rays of the sun. Too much exposure has been said by some people to be harmful, but I remember an unusually healthy group of people whose exposure was constant, and, usually, total. They were a band of *sadhus* (holy men) at a *Kumbha Mela* (religious fair) in India, in 1960. Normally they wore no clothing, though for the fair they had donned simple loin cloths. They were what is known as *naga sadhus*, or naked ascetics. Their total disinterest in the modern world was in itself interesting. One of them asked me what country I had come from. "America," I said. With mild curiosity during the course of further conversation, one of them asked, "By the way, where *is* America?" Another hazarded the opinion that America might be somewhere up in China. A passer-by then explained that America is that country which is referred to in the ancient epic, *The Ramayana,* as *Patal Desh* (the country on the underside of the world). When reminded of this description in the ancient story, the *sadhus* brightened with recognition. Now they knew where America was! Whatever their grasp of modern so-called realities, however, their grasp of eternal principles seems in certain ways to have been far in advance of our own. I asked them whether, with their life of constant exposure to the elements, they were ever unwell. They assured me that illness was a thing unknown among them.

Do not, when bathing, submit your body too long to hot water. Hot baths are demagnetizing. It is well always to follow a hot bath or shower with a thorough rinsing of cold water.

Much of the air that we breathe is drawn into the body through the skin. Keep the skin clean. It is well to invigorate it by rubbing it briskly all over with the hands, recharging it with divine energy.

A healthy skin is far more attractive than one that has been made soft artificially with a variety of creams and lotions. (Certain lotions, however, if applied temporarily, can be beneficial. Mud packs, for instance, are considered extremely beneficial.)

Vaguely related to this subject—only because the skin is, so to speak, the "port of entry"—is that of stings from poisonous insects. For lack of a better place to consider them, let me discuss this subject here.

The commonest of stings are those from mosquitoes. I have found, interestingly, that if I refuse to scratch a mosquito bite for five or ten minutes after I first receive it, the swelling all but disappears, and the discomfort is forgotten. If I scratch it, on the other hand, the swelling may endure for two or three days, and be uncomfortable all that time.

For scorpion stings, my guru taught me to dissolve a teaspoon of salt in a glass of lukewarm water, and then to pour as much of that water as the ear would hold into the ear that is *on the same side* of the body as the sting. Close the ear with cotton, and hold the water there for some 10 minutes or so.

A fascinating cure, though one which I have never tested for its validity, was taught to me by a retired doctor of the Indian Army, a Colonel Dass at Abbot Mtn., in the Almora district of the Himalayas. Colonel Dass told me that he had learned this technique from another Indian Army doctor when they were both stationed in Palestine. The troops were working on a road at that time, and very frequently a soldier would be stung by a scorpion as he lifted a rock. Colonel Dass assured me that his friend's cure had proved infallible in every such case. An English doctor in the same regiment scoffed at these cures, calling them mere superstition—effective only because of the ignorant faith of the soldiers. But one day, it seems, this doctor was himself stung. No anti-serum was available. While they waited for it to arrive, the Indian doctor offered to try his "cure" on the Englishman.

"I don't believe in it," the Englishman said between clenched teeth, "but try it anyway. What have I to lose?"

The cure worked on him, too.

Dr. Dass told me that he, too, had used it effectively on numerous occasions.

With these recommendations, I offer for your possible experiment one of the strangest nostrums that has ever come my way.

You must use an old nail, preferably a rusty one. Ask the patient where the line of pain is. Normally it will travel from the point of the sting upward toward the heart. Start somewhat above where the pain ends, and draw a pentagram on the skin with the nail, but without breaking the skin. Come down *without lifting the nail from the skin,* and make another pentagram. Keep moving downward, following the line of pain until you reach the point of the sting itself. Here make the pentagrams smaller and smaller, until you cannot reduce them any further.

At no time may the line be broken. The nail should be in contact with the skin at all times. The direction of the diagram should always be the same as in the drawing on the next page.

In nature there are cures for every ill, even as, in this world of duality, everything has its opposite. One of the leading religious figures of India, Swami Bharati Krishna Tirth, told me something that I hope I never have occasion to test. In the tail of a cobra, he said, there is a nectar which, if sucked, can neutralize the cobra's venom. Again, as with the pentagram above, I am passing on information that I have not tested, but that I find fascinating enough to share with you.

I have been made aware in many years of exposure to these teachings of yoga that there are countless mysteries in Nature and in the human body. One such mystery that may be included here, in this treatment of the skin and of the surface of the body, is the value of wearing certain gems or metals next to the skin. A chapter titled "Outwitting the Stars" in *Autobiography of a Yogi* describes this ancient and subtle therapy.

All things are made of vibrations, and have their own magnetic properties. Certain pure gems and minerals emit radiations that are beneficial to the body of man. One such "bangle" made of gold, silver, and copper was recommended by Sri Yoganandaji for general use. He said that this bangle had more than physical value. (I remember his advising a disciple, who was prone to having accidents, to obtain and wear one of these bangles.)

A number of people who own these bangles have told me that, during times of physical illness (and, perhaps, of mental depression), their bangles have become so hot on one arm that they had to move them onto the other. I myself have felt a person's bangle when he said that it felt hot. It was, in fact, much hotter than the arm itself—so hot that it almost hurt my fingers to hold it.

Persons may write or call Ananda Sangha for details on how to obtain such bangles. According to the teaching of great yogis, the value of these bangles should not be underrated. It can be very great.

Pure, unflawed gemstones of not less than two carats may also be beneficial, if worn next to the skin. An armlet of general usefulness, but one that is too costly for the average person to buy, is the so-called *navaratna,* or nine-stone bangle. It is composed of the following stones, each of them two carats or more: diamond, emerald, yellow sapphire, chrysoberyl cat's-eye, blue sapphire, garnet (or, more properly, "gomed"—a stone unknown in this country), coral, pearl, and ruby. Each of these stones stands for a different planet. A knowledge of one's own horoscope, and of the right stones to wear in order to strengthen weak planets and to offset the vibrations of inauspicious planets, is believed to be beneficial. If all you need personally is one or two stones, you may be able to afford such a bangle even if you are not rich. But you must convert your horoscope from the normal Western tropical to sidereal, and preferably to Indian sidereal, if you want to make proper use of this *Indian* science of gem therapy.

For serious therapeutic purposes, I would not recommend the common birth stones that are listed in Western writings on this subject. Your own horoscope is unique, and must be considered as a whole, not only with reference to your sun sign.

In an age when newness is made the chief criterion for the validity of every claim (one is forever hearing the phrase, "a new breakthrough"), it is interesting to consider the possibility that India, just because of her antiquity, may have discovered and preserved through the ages certain truths that have as yet remained unsuspected in our scientific age, basking as it does in the harsh glare of a merely rationalistic view of reality.

VI. DIET

Diet for Meditation

Deep meditation requires a calm breath and heartbeat. It is carbon in the blood that forces them into activity. Physical exertion, tensions, and emotions feed carbon into the blood and force the lungs and heart to increase their activity. (Note, for example, how you pant after running a race.)

But certain foods also have the same effect. Carbohydrates especially are to blame. The excess of carbon in the body from too many sweets forces the heart to beat faster, and the lungs to work harder. For this reason, the yogi should not eat too many sweets, nor too many starches and other carbohydrates. For the same reason he should avoid the use of stimulants, which speed up the heart. Tea and coffee are not recommended in the yoga teachings.

Overeating can place as much of a load on the heart, however, as any stimulant. Here again the reason for the yogic teaching, "*Stokum stokum anekoda*—(Eat a little bit, frequently)."

It is well to eat more raw foods, especially fruits and nuts, and not to eat for three hours prior to any long meditation.

A strong mind can force a reluctant body to do its will, but if the body is brought into harmony with one's spiritual aspirations, the resulting teamwork can be a tremendous aid on every level—physical, as well as mental and spiritual.

RECIPES FOR HEALTH

The banana has wonderful curative properties when properly prepared. It should be carefully mashed and beaten, or crushed through a sieve, and served with cream or milk. Such a combination will heal and tone up the intestines, for when the acid of the banana is mixed with milk it becomes soothing as well as healing to the alimentary tract.

Undiluted juice of orange or lemon combined with a pinch of powdered garlic is effective in removing a tendency to rheumatism, gout, and neuritis.

To remove mucus: Take portions the size of a small pea each of cayenne and ginger with a dash of white pepper in a glass of hot distilled water. Use it so hot that it requires to be spooned.

Use a dash of cinnamon, mace, or nutmeg to bring out the medicinal qualities of tropical fruits. They will assist in eliminating heat from the system, and will thus also help to prevent fevers.

VII. MEDITATION

Signs of Spiritual Progress

One day a brother disciple of mine was asked to dig a deep hole for a septic tank. He dug all day, never stopping to see how far he had come. At the day's end, much to his own and everyone else's surprise, the hole had been finished.

"That," Master said, "is the way to find God. Keep on digging and digging, never worrying how far you have come. Then suddenly, one day, you will find yourself *there.*"

Master used often to say, "If you plant a seed, then keep digging it up to see how it is doing, it will never be able to grow. You must leave it in the ground, and water it daily; then it will surely grow in its own time. So also with the path to God: Plant the seed of divine aspiration; don't dig it up constantly to see how it is doing, but water it daily with meditation and with divine actions. See also that you surround it with a protective hedge of good company. In time, your little seed will grow into a mighty tree of Self-realization, affording shade and shelter to every passing wayfarer. But remember, if you dig up the seed constantly you may only succeed in killing it. Doubt is one of the greatest hindrances on the path to God."

Yet Master said that doubt also has its constructive aspects. His caution was against indulging in destructive doubts—the "Hamlet," or fence-sitting, complex for instance ("Shall I? Shan't I? Will meditation *really* help me? Should I try serving in a hospital instead?"); or the attitude of self-judgment, which insists on "keeping an open mind" to every discouraging idea ("I'm sure I haven't got what it takes to get anywhere on the path. Maybe I'm practicing the techniques all wrong, and going backwards instead of forwards. What if this path is only a snare for the unwary, leading them not to enlightenment, but to confusion?") How many—alas, how *very* many!—devotees I have seen, not only on this but on every spiritual path, wandering dazedly in a fog of such doubts as these. Master, in referring to such people, sometimes quoted from the *Bhagavad Gita:* "The doubter is the most miserable of mortals."

Destructive doubts are their own undoing. It is not possible to advance in any field of action until these mists have been cleared away. They are the fruit, merely, of bad *karma*s of the past. They must be dealt with vigorously, and not accepted passively in the name of fair-mindedness. A wise person will not offer the hospitality of his home to criminals. Why open your mind to the invasion of thoughts that come only to rob you of your inner peace?

Constructive doubt is quite another matter. It is a positive quest for solutions to problems, not a negative suspicion that no solution exists. A runner in a race hasn't time to consider such questions as, "Maybe I shouldn't be doing this," or, "What, I wonder, are my chances of losing?" But he may consider more practical questions: "Shall I lengthen my stride now? Is it time yet for my final sprint?" The true devotee, like the true athlete, concentrates on doing the very best he can. With such an attitude defeat is impossible; there can be only varying degrees of success.

The signs of spiritual progress, then, can be considered constructively only as guidelines to present endeavor, and not as depressing reminders of how far we still have to go, nor as ego-balm for the semi-enlightened.

Remember, the surest guideline of spiritual progress is the growing sense that God's is the only power in life—a *growing* sense, because this understanding must be dynamic, not passive. (Too many devotees shrink from acts demanding courage and initiative, out of fear of strengthening their own egos. But how can one realize God as the Sole Doer, when nothing ever gets done?)

One of the saddest, and most common, mistakes on the spiritual path is to equate progress with psychic phenomena of various kinds. This error has grown especially prevalent since the discovery of hallucinogenic drugs as a supposed short-cut to *samadhi.* When these drugs first began to be popular, I felt some empathy for the people who used them, though I felt no temptation to try them myself. What impressed me was that these people talked so earnestly of how their drug experience had convinced them of the delusion of egotism. It made no sense to me that anyone could develop wisdom with a pill, but I thought that perhaps they had developed this much understanding in a former life; in this case, drugs might help to shock them out of attitudes that had been imposed on them by their present environment, and might thereby bring out their old *samskar*s (tendencies). It was a reasonable theory. *Something* must awaken those old *samskars* to bring people onto the path. Often it *is* a shock of some kind—illness, perhaps, or bereavement. Perhaps, I thought, drugs too work in this way.

But if they do, it is by unnaturally forcing the door open. Observation of drug users over the years has convinced me that they have only abandoned one form of egotism for another. Indeed, theirs is the more insidious. The aggressive person at least relates to the objective world, though not attractively. But by drugs people seem to retreat to a subjective island where even love and their so-called expanded awareness give them no genuine compassion for, or active interest in, others. Their lack of interest in relating to others, except purely subjectively, denotes not freedom as they believe, but only an excessive involvement with themselves.

Whether by drugs, or simply by wrong understanding, one of the delusions on the spiritual path is the thought that progress consists in being merely entertained. Visions, voices, and other mental or psychic phenomena are no sign in themselves of genuine exaltation of consciousness. Swami Sri Yukteswar said that many devotees renounce worldliness only to seek it again on the subtler level of astral phenomena.

The basis of all true progress is right attitude. If you are becoming more kind, more self-giving, more calm, you may be sure that you are progressing whether you see visions or not. If you are succeeding in relinquishing your likes and dislikes, and are learning to accept even-mindedly whatever experiences life sends you, then you have much cause for rejoicing. If you find that you have fewer and fewer desires for the things of this world, know that you are truly finding freedom. And more important still, if your love for God is growing ever deeper, know that you are fast approaching Him. And if through all the trials of life you always feel joy inwardly, a joy that nothing can shake, know that you have Him already to a wonderful degree.

Yes, *samadhi* is a wonderful thing, ardently to be desired. But once one's attitude is right everything else will fall into place automatically. On the other hand, because of some imperfection in their attitude, saints have been known to fall even from a state of *samadhi.**

But remember, right spiritual attitudes cannot come merely by affirmations and positive thinking. They are a natural by-product of divine contact in meditation, of divine grace.

"But *my* attitude seems to be improving," you may argue, "and I certainly

* But not from the highest degrees of *samadhi*. In *nirbikalpa samadhi* the ego becomes totally merged in God. From this state, impossible to attain without supremely right attitude, the soul, now a *jivan mukta* ("freed while living"), can never fall again.

can't boast about my 'divine contacts' in meditation!"

My friend, this kind of negativity is the very thing I warned against at the outset of this chapter. Digging up the seed to see how it is growing—remember? You'd better give thought first to *that* attitude, lest it cancel out all the others!

How do you *know* that you have had no divine contacts in meditation? The very fact that your attitude is improving is sign enough that *something* is happening. What then have you been expecting? Lightning? Thunder? Parting curtains, and a chorus line of angels? Jesus Christ said that God comes "like a thief in the night." Greater things than what you now experience will surely come to you in time, but know that one's very love for God in meditation is already a sign of His presence. That's just His way: He likes to steal in by the back door.

One of the most difficult things for people to do, so doctors tell us, is correctly to diagnose their own illnesses. How much more difficult is it to assess correctly one's own spiritual delusions! People hardly can determine for themselves whether their illnesses are improving or worsening. ("Doctor, how am I doing?" is the first question they generally ask when they visit their doctors.) How much more difficult it is to determine for oneself whether or not one is advancing spiritually. The gains are very rarely evident from one day to another, but become felt rather over periods of months, even of years. Do not allow yourself to become overly impressed when someone says to you, "I attended this spiritual gathering yesterday, and the inner growth I experienced was *fantastic!*" Life's peak experiences must be balanced against the subsequent troughs before a true assessment can be made. Sometimes there *are* days, even moments of sudden growth, but it isn't usual, and even when it occurs it is usually because the ground has been long and carefully prepared beforehand.

Much time is wasted in any case, as I said earlier, in analyzing one's degree of spiritual progress—time that might have been better spent in meditating and advancing still further. The most important thing to bear in mind is that what truly matters is not what God is giving you, in terms of visions and consolations, but rather what you are willing of yourself to give Him. Often it happens that a weak and worldly soul, more in need of encouragement, is given more experiences than one who is purely self-giving. In any case, don't seek experiences for their own sake. I don't mean not to be grateful when they are given to you, for a grateful heart is one of the best signs of right attitude. I mean only not to seek such experiences, not to be attached to them. As Master said, "The path to God is not a circus!"

If I seem to be slighting deep, meditative experiences (as distinct from merely psychic phenomena), it is because right attitude must be the foundation of such experiences. Every path to God has its own pitfalls. The special pitfall on the path of *raja yoga* is the temptation to spiritual pride as a result of one's meditative insights or new-found miraculous powers. Yet to talk only of right attitude and ignore the soul's *inner* unfoldment would be a mistake, too—an invitation to the devotee to rest comfortably on his oars, and be content with a journey but started. Right attitude itself should lead one to want to come ever closer, consciously closer, to God.

Master met a monk once and asked him, "Do you ever see lights or angels in meditation?"

"When God wills it I shall see those things," replied the monk.

"That is not so," Master told him, severely. "When your devotion is right you will see them. God has hidden those things from you, not because He wants to, but because your own devotion is still lackluster."

Once pure love, and not a desire for miracles and phenomena, becomes the basis of our spiritual search, we may expect certain phenomena to attend us even though we desire them not. If they remain too long absent, it is a sign that something is lacking. Pray then for more devotion, not for those mere fruits of devotion, lest you fall into the error of the starving man who prayed for a large stomach, instead of a full one.

But again, bear in mind how subtle the inner world is, and don't wish for lights merely because others see lights, when God is already showering you with another kind of abundance. Many are the inner paths to God. Some people advance very far and never see lights of any kind. Master's words to the monk therefore should be taken in part as personal counsel, directed to him alone. The important thing is that God's presence be actively *experienced* in one form or another.

God comes to the soul in different ways—as light, or sound, or love, or peace, or intense calmness, or power, or wisdom, or divine joy. One may advance by any one of these paths or by several, but one seldom advances by all of them together until the higher stages of *sadhana* (spiritual practice) have been attained. One who sees lights may have visions of saints or angels, or of the astral world. One who hears sounds may hear astral music, or the sounds of the spinal centers. One who feels love may find tears flowing inadvertently in meditation. One who feels peace will feel as though he were drinking it in pure, life-giving draughts. One who feels calmness (the positive aspect of peace) may feel his consciousness expanding as if into a vast hall. One who feels divine power will be made intensely aware that God alone is the Doer, that man's own power is simply non-existent. One who experiences wisdom may develop deep insight into any question he asks of God, or he may know himself inwardly as the undying Self. And one who experiences divine joy will never want for anything else.

But to go deep into any of these experiences, the little ego must be forgotten. So long as one still has the consciousness that he is meditating on them, his meditation will be imperfect. The meditator, the act of meditation, and the object of meditation must become one. For this condition, the first requirement is that the mind be held steady. (A state of excitement renders deep inner experience impossible.) The next requirement is that the breath become calm—indeed, motionless. Once the breath ceases (not by holding it, but as a natural consequence of physical and mental calmness), the thoughts, too, must cease altogether. Until this state is reached, deep spiritual experiences will not be possible.

One who sees light should concentrate not so much on visions as on entering the light himself. Concentrate on the *center* of whatever light you see at the point between the eyebrows. If you see the spiritual eye (a circular blue field surrounded by a golden halo, and having a white, five-pointed star in the center), that will be better still. Concentrate on the star if you see it, or in the center of the field of blue. Gradually the gold will expand and form a tunnel. Passing into this tunnel, you will consciously enter the light of the astral world. In time, the blue light will form a tunnel. Entering that, you will enter the light of the causal world, the Christ Consciousness. When you can penetrate the star in the center, you will enter the Spirit beyond vibratory creation.

I have described elsewhere the sounds of the spinal centers. It is better to hear these sounds than to hear astral music, and better still to hear the sounds of the higher centers than those of the lower. But best of all is it to hear, and merge into, the great sound of AUM.

One who feels love should seek perfect union with the Divine Beloved. Devotion (*bhakti*) will not develop into divine love (*prem*) until it expands beyond ego-consciousness.

And so also with the other experiences of God: Always they should be offered up to Him, that they take one ever deeper into His consciousness, lest one rest satisfied on a mere ledge, and never reach the mountaintop.

Above all, never compare yourself with another, lest you fall into either discouragement or pride. Don't even dwell too much on the signs as I have described them here. I have but scratched the surface. God, who is infinite, can come to the soul in an infinity of ways—as exquisite smells, as a thousand sweet tastes crushed into one, as divine instruction, as the purest divine merriment, as the tenderest imaginable forgiveness. Each soul's relationship with the Infinite is unique. Compare yourself not with others, but only with your own self: Do you love God more now than you used to? Are you developing even-mindedness? Are you more inwardly contented and joyful—or at least happy? Are you renouncing self-will? Do you want to serve and please only God? If your answer to these questions is *Yes,* and if you can add to your answer the wish to grow daily in these sublime virtues, know that God and Guru must be well pleased with you. Offer yourself into their arms. They will bear you surely and swiftly to the Divine Shores!

A Farewell to the Student

And so, dear friend and student, we reach the end of these lessons. I feel, for all my diligent work on them, as though I had offered you but a thimbleful of water from the great ocean of Truth. Most of that ocean, certainly, must be discovered by you personally by plumbing its depths. Yet as I write, how much more I wish I might say!

Many people already have begged me to lengthen this course, or to write a new one. But alas, for now at least that may not be. Merely to revise these lessons has taken me almost a year and a half, and at least a year longer than I ever expected it to. Some of this time, to be sure, has necessarily been spent on other things. (To be the director of a large community of devotees is not to be utterly without responsibilities!) Yet even so, a great deal of this time has been devoted to these revisions. Many other things remain for me to do.

It was my wish in any case to lead you to the teachings and blessings of my guru. He is the fountainhead; I am only a trickle, surviving but by his power. If you have benefited from these lessons, it is by his grace, not by my wisdom. I pray that you turn to him, and receive into your heart that grace which has flooded mine. Whether or not you take him as your guru is quite another matter. In any case he can help you to the extent that you allow him to. Would it not be folly itself to turn from the gift of such divine love?

And, dear friend, if in any way I myself can serve you further on the path, please give me the chance to try. For me it would be a blessing and a privilege.

May God and Guru bless you always.

In their love,
your own Self

Swami Kriyananda

ABOUT THE AUTHOR

Swami Kriyananda (J. Donald Walters) has been since 1948 a close, direct disciple of the great yoga master, Paramhansa Yogananda.

Swami Kriyananda has shared his guru's teachings in many countries throughout the world for more than fifty years. He has given thousands of lectures and classes, written over seventy books, composed more than 400 musical works, and recorded numerous albums of his music.

Swami Kriyananda is perhaps best known as the founder and spiritual director of Ananda Village near Nevada City, California. In existence since 1968, Ananda is generally recognized as one of the most successful alternate-lifestyle communities in the world. There are some 800 resident members living at Ananda Village, and in its branch communities in California, Oregon, Washington, Rhode Island, and Italy.

INDEX OF BIBLE QUOTATIONS

INDEX OF RECIPES

GENERAL INDEX

AN OVERVIEW BY SUBJECT MATTER

Each of the fourteen lessons is divided into seven sections, as outlined below.

I. YOGA PHILOSOPHY—Guidelines for personal, spiritual growth. Includes the ancient teachings of Patanjali's *Yoga Sutras,* as given to Kriyananda by Yogananda in his lectures on these subjects.

- Step 1. The History of Yoga
- Step 2. The Paths of Yoga: *bhakti yoga* (the path of devotion); *karma yoga* (the path of action); *gyana yoga* (the path of wisdom); *raja yoga* (the path of meditation); the correct attitudes for attaining perfection in each path
- Step 3. The eight stages of Self-realization, according to the ancient yoga exponent, Patanjali
- Step 4. *Yama* (the spiritual "don'ts")
- Step 5. *Niyama* (the spiritual "do's")
- Step 6. Duality; the basis of manifested reality
- Step 7. Affirmations (Part I); the magnetic power of thought
- Step 8. Affirmations (Part II); the power of *mantra*s (seed sounds)
- Step 9. Energy and Energization; how to awaken energy in the body, tapping the infinite source of magnetism
- Step 10. Magnetism; how to develop your natural magnetism for physical, mental, and spiritual success
- Step 11. The need for a *guru*; how to find your own *guru*; the laws of true discipleship
- Step 12. The Anatomy of Yoga (Part I); the movements of spirit in human beings; the power of *kundalini*; the signs of spiritual development
- Step 13. The Anatomy of Yoga (Part II); the spinal centers (including a chart); inner astrology (including charts); Christ consciousness; yoga teachings in the Bible
- Step 14. The Yogic Scheme of Life; the three *guna*s: *tamas* (darkening), *rajas* (activating), *sattwa* (spiritualizing); *AUM* (Amen) explained

II. YOGA POSTURES FOR HIGHER AWARENESS—The yoga postures presented as tools for improving your mental outlook, achieving a harmonious emotional life, and fostering your spiritual progress.

Hatha yoga, the physical branch of *raja yoga,* stresses the relationship of physical well-being to right meditation. Over 50 postures are given, with photographs of Kriyananda and others demonstrating the poses and detailed instructions on how to practice them. In addition to the physical benefits, special emphasis is given to their spiritual and mental effects.

III. BREATHING PRINCIPLES AND TECHNIQUES—"Breath mastery is self-mastery." Learn to master the breath for improved physical, mental, and spiritual well-being. The general principles covered in this section include:

Breathing in conjunction with the yoga postures
The science of correct breathing in normal life
Using the breath to clarify one's thinking
Breathing as a source of energy and healing power
Different subtle movements of the breath, and their effect on physical, mental, and emotional states
Gentle (natural) vs. violent (unnatural) breathing exercises
Breath as vehicle for sending or receiving vibrations
Breathing to cool the body and nervous system
Breathing to warm the body
Breathing to cure various physical disorders
Breathing and breathless ecstasy

IV. ROUTINE—Each step suggests a personalized daily routine of yoga postures and yoga breathing exercises, which can be adapted to fit your schedule. This section also includes:

Suggested duration of practice for each posture and breathing exercise
Recommended sequence for the poses
Alternate suggestions for students with more (or less) time available for practice
The relative importance of various poses
Suggestions for balancing one's time between postures and meditation
The need for personalizing your yoga practices

V. HEALING PRINCIPLES AND TECHNIQUES—Learn to take charge of your own health. This section gives yoga teachings for the cure of various ailments, and includes recommendations of special yoga postures. Subjects are:

Step 1. Insomnia
Step 2. Integration vs. Disintegration
Step 3. Hypertension and Nervousness
Step 4. Chronic Fatigue
Step 5. Respiratory Troubles (including colds)
Step 6. Stomach Disorders
Step 7. Weight Problems
Step 8. The spine as a source of physical problems
Step 9. Circulation and the Blood
Step 10. Sex Problems
Step 11. Headaches
Step 12. The Eyes, Ears, and Teeth
Step 13. The Legs and Feet
Step 14. Cures for stings; skin care; astrological bangles; the science of curative gems

VI. DIET AND NUTRITION FOR TOTAL WELL-BEING—A natural and holistic approach, including dietary principles and newly revised vegetarian recipes. Subjects discussed are:

Step 1. Foods and Insomnia
Step 2. Foods that calm the nervous system
Step 3. The importance of natural foods
Step 4. Harmonious vs. stimulating foods
Step 5. Fasting

Step 6. Meat-eating vs. vegetarianism
Step 7. Seed sprouts—their benefits and how to sprout them
Step 8. Common sense vs. faddishness
Step 9. Simplicity as a dietary principle
Step 10. The psychological and spiritual vibrations of different foods
Step 11. Air and sun "diets"
Step 12. The importance of right vibrations in the preparation of food; special susceptibility to vibrations at the time of taking food
Step 13. *Ayurveda*—ancient India's naturalistic science of medicine; the best hours for eating, according to *Ayurveda*
Step 14. Diet for Meditation

VII. MEDITATION—Specific instruction for focusing your mind, calming your emotions, and discovering inner peace and joy; includes:

Step 1. Meditation: a universal need
Step 2. How to find time for meditation
Step 3. Preparing a place for meditation
Step 4. Right attitudes for meditation
Step 5. Attaining superconsciousness; how to redirect the flow of energy in the spine; the eyes as windows of the soul
Step 6. Raising the Inner Energy
Step 7. Meditation on the primal elements: earth, water, fire, air, ether
Step 8. Prayer, Chanting, *Japa,* and *Mantra*
Step 9. Concentration, will power, and awareness
Step 10. A basic technique of concentration; closing psychic doors by which our powers are drained, and opening up revitalizing channels
Step 11. Attunement with the *Guru*
Step 12. Awakening *Kundalini;* masculinity and femininity, their spiritual basis
Step 13. How to balance feeling and reason; meditation on the light
Step 14. Signs of Spiritual Progress; true and false states of consciousness; using meditation to transform daily life

FURTHER RESOURCES

Works and Words of Paramhansa Yogananda

Autobiography of a Yogi

Original Edition, 1946,
Paramhansa Yogananda

Named one of the "hundred best spiritual books of the century," this book is recognised by followers of many religious traditions as a spiritual masterpiece. Rarely does a sage of Paramhansa Yogananda's stature write a firsthand account of his life experiences. Vividly he reveals the fascinating and little-understood subtle laws by which yogis perform miracles and attain complete self-mastery.

This edition is a reprint of the original, published in 1946. Although later reprintings, reflecting revisions made after the author's passing in 1952 have been widely translated and sold, copies of the original disappeared. Now the original edition is again available with all its inherent power as the great yoga master first presented it, including a final chapter Yoganandaji later wrote about his life and work during his last decade of life.

The Essence of Self-Realization

The Wisdom of Paramhansa Yogananda
Recorded and compiled by his disciple, Swami Kriyananda

This is Kriyanandaji's recollected words of his guru: a priceless guide to spiritual life, filled with lessons, stories, and jewels of wisdom that Yoganandaji shared only with his closest disciples. Many of the three hundred sayings are available nowhere else.

Conversations with Yogananda

Recorded, with reflections, by his disciple Swami Kriyananda

Here are unparalleled intimate glimpses of life with the Master never before shared: nearly five hundred stories, sayings, and insights, plus twenty-five photos nearly all previously unreleased. Swami Kriyananda's TV programme "A Way to Awakening" is based on this book.

The Essence of the Bhagavad Gita

Explained by Paramhansa Yogananda
As remembered by his disciple, Swami Kriyananda

Rarely does a new spiritual classic appear with power to change lives and transform future generations. This is such a book. Paramhansa Yogananda's revelation of India's best-loved scripture brings an entirely fresh perspective, showing its deep allegorical meaning and practicality. Yet it is easy to read and understand. Its themes are universal "how-tos": achieving divine union; preparing for life's "final exam"—death; and triumphing over adversity.

The Bhagavad Gita

According to Paramhansa Yogananda
Edited by his disciple, Swami Kriyananda

This pocket edition of Paramhansa Yogananda's revelation of India's best-loved scripture—a "*Gita* junior"—is limited almost entirely to the verses. Most of the slokas appeared in Swami Kriyananda's larger book *The Essence of the Bhagavad Gita Explained by Paramhansa Yogananda*. Some, however, were intentionally left out: most of Chapter One, which was merely summarised, and the first ten verses of Chapter Two, which form an almost complete dissertation. Though small in size, this edition of the *Gita* is pierced with shafts of light from a towering spiritual figure—Yoganandaji as a modern-day Arjuna.

Revelations of Christ

Proclaimed by Paramhansa Yogananda
Presented by his disciple, Swami Kriyananda

Paramhansa Yogananda's divine mission was to show the oneness of all true religions. He focussed on bringing back original Christianity taught by Jesus Christ with the original yoga teachings of Krishna presented in the Bhagavad Gita. *Revelations* is a resource for those curious about possible Hindu-Christian connections, or desirous of promoting dialogue with friends and furthering religious unity.

After describing two main approaches to Christ's life and teachings—Church authority and historical analysis—Kriyanandaji describes a lesser-known method: studying writings and sayings of saints in direct divine communion (better, living with and studying under them). *Revelations* takes this approach.

Swami Kriyananda: His Life and Work

In Divine Friendship

Letters of Counsel and Reflections
Swami Kriyananda

Here is an extraordinary book of letters written by Swami Kriyananda responding to questions and inquiries from friends, students, and critics over thirty years, addressing almost any concern of spiritual seekers. The friendship expressed in the closings of the letters ("In Divine Friendship") extends to all readers, not merely the original recipient.

Visits to Saints of India

Swami Kriyananda

Chronicling several earlier stays in India, Swami Kriyananda shares inspiration from his visits to many saints, including Anandamayee Ma, Yogi Ramiah (Sri Rama Yogi), Swami Muktananda, Swami Narayan, and Sathya Sai Baba. As a swami steeped in Hindu spiritual heritage but from the West, Kriyanandaji reveals a unique perspective. Like the visits described by his friend Devi Mukherjee in *Shaped by Saints*, Kriyanandaji's story is a spiritual journey, indeed a deeply personal pilgrimage.

Swami Kriyananda As We Have Known Him

Asha Praver

A spiritual teacher's greatness is only partially revealed by the work of his own hands. The rest cannot be told by him but by the influence of his consciousness on those who come in contact with him. This is the story told here in some two hundred vignettes spanning over forty years. Working closely with Kriyanandaji for many years, Asha Praver and her husband have long served as spiritual directors of the Palo Alto Ananda Sangha and Mountain View Community in California. Gifted storyteller and highly respected teacher in her own right, Asha joins her years of closely observing Kriyanandaji with inspiring experiences shared by others.

The New Path

My Life with Paramhansa Yogananda
Swami Kriyananda

This is the fascinating, inspiring tale of one man's search for truth. It is often considered a companion to *Autobiography of a Yogi*, for it continues Paramhansa Yogananda's story past his own account. Many readers, especially those whose own search has been difficult, find in it a parallel to theirs.*The New Path* is largely the disciple's account of life and training with his guru. Over four hundred stories about the great master are included, including rare anecdotes.

Faith Is My Armor

The Life of Swami Kriyananda
Devi Novak

Here is the story of a modern-day hero—a man who has achieved extraordinary victories by demonstrating spiritual courage, determination amid great obstacles, and personal sacrifice. This first published biography of Kriyanandaji will bring its readers inspiration and hope. Devi Novak and her husband Jyotish are Ananda Worldwide's spiritual directors.

Cooperative Spiritual Communities: Yogananda's Model for Mankind

Cities of Light

A New Vision for the Future
Swami Kriyananda

Cities of Light describes the vision and principles of cooperative spiritual living that define Ananda, and how they can help meet the world's need for harmonious groups collaborating toward a better way of life.

Renunciation of home and family has long been considered essential for wholehearted dedication to God. Although formal renunciation will still be the chosen way of many to God, Yoganandaji's ideal of world brotherhood colonies also gives couples and families a way to live a God-centred life with like-minded devotees.

Hope for a Better World!

The Small Communities Solution
Swami Kriyananda

In these turbulent times, a new approach is needed for creation of a truly viable society. Many great Western thinkers have long turned their attention to these issues, but with often flawed results. Swami Kriyananda insightfully analyzes the views of some of these "big guns of Western thought". Even-handedly he describes their conceptions and misconceptions to the individual's relationship to self and society, showing where their influence has proved adverse. He then offers a deeply considered new alternative: *cooperative communities* as a means by which to encourage a common-sense way of life, strengthen human relationships, and inspire people toward their higher potential.

SPACE, LIGHT, AND HARMONY

The Story of Crystal Hermitage
Swami Kriyananda

The story of Crystal Hermitage offers a fascinating look at how personal space can become a sincere expression of consciousness. Describing an adventure in design, building, and living with seventy beautiful colour photos, it shows the evolution of a home—from initial planning to interior decorating—that can serve as a powerful metaphor for personal development and spiritual quest.

Meditation and Spiritual Techniques

MEDITATION FOR STARTERS

Swami Kriyananda

Simple but powerful guidelines for attaining inner peace through meditation are offered in this award-winning book, showing how to prepare body and mind prior to meditation; use special breathing techniques to calm and focus the mind; sharpen will power; and develop intuition.

Spirituality in Daily Life

AWAKEN TO SUPERCONSCIOUSNESS

How to Use Meditation for Inner Peace, Intuitive Guidance, and Greater Awareness
Swami Kriyananda

Many people experience moments of raised consciousness and enlightenment (superconsciousness) but do not know how to purposely enter this exalted state. Yet it is the hidden mechanism behind successful problem-solving, concentration, creativity, spiritual and physical healing, and lasting joy.

The book is for beginning as well as long-time meditators; followers of other spiritual paths who are unaware of the importance of direct spiritual experience; seekers of life's deeper meaning who are not necessarily aware that they do so; and people who simply want greater understanding of consciousness although they are not ready to take up meditation.

INTUITION FOR STARTERS

How to Know and Trust Your Inner Guidance
Swami Kriyananda

Every day we face difficult problems and complicated situations without information for making clear-cut decisions, let alone arriving at answers.Who has not longed for another route to right choices? There *is one*: using intuition, the hidden but most important human faculty for decision-making. Swami Kriyananda describes what it is and where it comes from; practises and attitudes necessary for its development; accessing intuitive guidance at will; and how to cultivate and apply it in all situations.

Sadhu, Beware!

A New Approach to Renunciation

Swami Kriyananda

Here is insight, inspiration, and practical advice for the world's greatest adventure: the inner journey of Self-realisation. Householders and renunciates alike can realise their divine potential by learning how to live rightly, renouncing attachments that bring unhappiness and embracing their true nature of inner freedom and divine joy. Lucid and easy to read, the book encourages every seeker to live up to the heart's and mind's highest aspirations.

Your Sun Sign as a Spiritual Guide

Swami Kriyananda

Hailed as a classic by many astrologers, this book not only maps personal strengths and weaknesses but also reveals astrology's true purpose: guidance toward Self-realisation. Swami Kriyananda's studies embrace both Indian and Western astrology. Fresh, humorous, full of wisdom, *Your Sun Sign* provides much original insight. The specific lessons of each sign are described with clarity and relevance, along with suggested meditation practice.

Higher Consciousness in the Marketplace

Success and Happiness Through Yoga Principles

Swami Kriyananda

This acclaimed programme explains how to use the power of Self-realisation servicefully by manifesting prosperity and success. Adaptable for home, small group, or corporate study, it demonstrates that spirituality and material success are mutually related. Kriyanandaji upholds the ancient aphorism "where there is adherence to right action, there lies victory" as key to India's success in the global market, giving new expression to her ancient teachings through inspired combination of the best of East and West. Many Indian business, government, and educational leaders are applying the tools of this course. It has also proved immensely helpful to those suffering from stressful business rhythms or seeking a more harmonised approach to personal satisfaction through work.

The Art of Supportive Leadership

A Practical Guide for People in Positions of Responsibility

Swami Kriyananda

This is a new approach to leadership, through shared accomplishment rather than personal advancement. Drawn from timeless yogic wisdom, these insights are clear, succinct, and practical, designed for quick results. Widely used in leadership training across the world, it is also invaluable for parents; teachers, and salespeople—indeed anyone wishing to win others to a particular viewpoint.

Money Magnetism

How to Attract What You Need When You Need It

Swami Kriyananda

Filled with new insights, *Money Magnetism* goes far beyond other "money" books. Each principle can be used for both building wealth and attracting whatever is needed in life. The book is changing lives by changing how people think and feel about money. Kriyanandaji vividly shows how and why the principles work, and how to apply them toward greater material and spiritual success.

Education, Philosophy and Religion

Education for Life

Preparing Children to Meet the Challenges

Swami Kriyananda

Education for Life uses the principles of Self-realisation to create an instructional system. It is a constructive, brilliant alternative to contemporary school emphasis on rote learning and technological competence at the expense of spiritual values and personal maturation. Focussing on education at different maturational stages, the system can benefit both teachers and parents in understanding what can be taught when, how, and why.

Based on Paramhansa Yogananda's pioneering educational work in India, this revolutionary system has been tried and proven over three decades at Ananda schools in the USA, with constant accolades from outside evaluators.

Out of the Labyrinth

For Those Who Want to Believe, But Can't

Swami Kriyananda

Praised by scientists and religious leaders alike, this is essential reading for all who struggle for answers to the existential dilemmas of human life today. Through a fresh approach to evolution and directional relativity, Kriyanandaji refutes contemporary scientific and philosophical claims that life is meaningless and merely mechanistic. He shows the genuine compatibility of scientific and religious values and how they actually enrich and reinforce each other.

Art as a Guide to Self-Realization

Swami Kriyananda

Challenging the concept of art for art's sake, Swami Kriyananda—himself a creative genius—insists that art cannot be divorced from meaning but is a powerful influence for shaping meaningful existence and fostering positive attitudes in society. Insightfully commenting on great musicians, artists, and creative thinkers, he offers a blueprint for the future of art.

The Hindu Way of Awakening

Its Revelation, Its Symbols: An Essential View of Religion

Swami Kriyananda

Here Swami Kriyananda brings order

to Hinduism's vast array of symbols and imagery, drawing forth the underlying teachings from which they arise and explaining Hindu iconography's basic purpose as direct inner experience with God. Showing the transcendent unity of all religions, this perspective promotes genuine tolerance and appreciation of religious diversity so needed today.

The Promise of Immortality

The True Teaching of the Bible and the Bhagavad Gita

Swami Kriyananda

Paramhansa Yogananda's guru Sri Yukteswar bridged the scriptures of East and West with his book *The Holy Science*, comparing passages from several Indian scriptures with the Christian Bible. Yoganandaji continued this work with his own commentaries on the Bhagavad Gita and the Bible.

In this tradition, Swami Kriyananda has also selected parallel passages from these scriptures, showing that the original teachings of the avatars Bhagavan Sri Krishna and Jesus Christ come from one timeless underlying truth. Such a view makes unprecedented cooperation and harmony among the world's different religions seem possible.

Gift Books: the Wisdom of Swami Kriyananda

Secrets Books

Swami Kriyananda

Thoughts, said Paramhansa Yogananda, are like seeds, taking root in our consciousness, influencing behavior and moods. The thoughts in the *Secrets* books inspire, uplift, and open the mind to new possibilities for finding joy and meaning each day. Simply and beautifully designed, these small inspirational guides to living are best-selling gifts, available individually or as a "six-pack".

Do It Now!

Swami Kriyananda

This is a collection of suggestions for self-improvement each day of the year: powerful tips for personal transformation. Applied long-term, this little book can serve as a measure of mental and spiritual progress. It can also be a resource to find a special thought to share with someone on a special occasion.

Other Ananda Sangha Publications

Shaped by Saints

Devi Mukherjee with Durga Smallen and Swami Kriyananda

While young, Devi Mukherjee worked with Mahatma Gandhi in the Indian resistance movement and was imprisoned five months. Afterward, Devi began a spiritual quest throughout India, travelling some forty-five years at various times. Upon marrying the daughter of Yoganandaji's childhood friend and later devotee Tulsi Bose, Devi heard many tales of his guru's life. These, many previously unpublished, are among the insights and lessons from the great ones Devi shares, taking readers on a deeply inspiring pilgrimage to meet saints and realised masters of modern India in forest ashrams, mountain caves, holy places, and shrines.

Chakras for Starters

Unlock the Hidden Doors to Peace & Well-BeingBased on the teachings of Swami Kriyananda

Savitri Simpson

This simplified yet deeply meaningful exploration of each chakra offers powerful keys to personal growth and inner peace.

Lessons in Meditation

Jyotish Novak

Small but powerful, this book concisely presents Paramhansa Yogananda's basic spiritual practices, including exercises for relaxation, energisation, concentration, meditation, visualisation, chanting, and prayer with simple, "do-able" suggestions. These lessons offer the initial techniques of Kriya Yoga, including the *Hong-Sau* concentration technique and Yoganandaji's Energisation Exercises for strengthening the body and will power.

Ananda Sangha Contact Information

Ananda Sangha
B–10/8, DLF Phase I, Gurgaon (HR), India 122 002
tel: (0124) 405-9550; +91 98990 14209
fax: (0124) 410-3386
e-mail: ananda@anandaindia.org
web site: www.anandaindia.org

Success and Happiness Through Yoga Princitples
mobile: +91 98734 08784
e-mail: success@anandaindia.org
website: www.materialsuccess.com

Harmony at Work
mobile: +91 98734 08784
e-mail: info@harmonyatwork.in
website: www.harmonyatwork.in

Yogananda's Spirit-in-Nature Essences
mobile: +91 98731 83706; fax: (0124) 410-3386
e-mail: info@yoganandasessences.com
website: www.yoganandasessences.com

Anjali Khadi Clothing
Pvt. Ltd.
mobile: +91 98992 00636
e-mail: anjali@anjalikhadi.com
website: www.anjalikhadi.com

Ananda Solar Technologies
mobile: +91 96577 13074
fax: (0124) 410-3386
e-mail: info@anandasolar.com
website: www.anandasolar.com

The Wishing Tree
Metropolitan Mall, #12,
Gurgaon (HR), India 122 002
tel: (0124) 410-1385, fax: (0124) 410-3386
e-mail: wishingtree@anandaindia.org
website: www.wishingtreeatananda.com

Ananda Sangha Publications

Ananda Sangha Publications
B-10/8 DLF City Phase I
Gurgaon, Haryana 122 002
mobile: +91 98992 67698
tel: (0124) 405-9550
fax: (0124) 410-3386

Mail Order Department
website: www.anandamailorder.com
e-mail: mailorder@anandaindia.org

For the Trade:
website: www.anandapublications.com
e-mail: publications@anandaindia.org